LIBERTY

DICKENSON TITLES OF RELATED INTEREST

Problems of Moral Philosophy: An Introduction, Second Edition
edited by Paul W. Taylor

Reason and Responsibility: Readings in Some Basic Problems of Philosophy, Third Edition
edited by Joel Feinberg

Philosophy of Law
edited by Joel Feinberg and Hyman Gross

The Logic of Grammar
edited by Donald Davidson and Gilbert H. Harman

Philosophical Problems of Causation
edited by Tom L. Beauchamp

Individual Conduct and Social Norms
by Rolf Sartorius

Freedom and Authority: An Introduction to Social and Political Philosophy
edited by Thomas Schwartz

Principles of Ethics: An Introduction
by Paul W. Taylor

Man in Conflict: Traditions in Social and Political Thought
by Louis I. Katzner

Metaphysics: An Introduction
by Keith Campbell

Understanding Moral Philosophy
edited by James Rachels

Morality in the Modern World
edited by Lawrence Habermehl

A Preface to Philosophy
by Mark Woodhouse

A Guide Through the Theory of Knowledge
by Adam Morton

Moral Philosophy: Classic Texts and Contemporary Problems
edited by Joel Feinberg and Henry West

Contemporary Issues in Bioethics
edited by Tom L. Beauchamp and LeRoy Walters

LIBERTY

Selected Readings

edited by
Joel Feinberg
and
Hyman Gross

DICKENSON PUBLISHING COMPANY, INC., ENCINO,
CALIFORNIA AND BELMONT, CALIFORNIA

ISBN–0–8221–0202–1
Library of Congress Catalog Card Number: 76–52729

Printed in the United States of America
Printing (last digit): 9 8 7 6 5 4 3 2 1

Cover by Jill Casty

Parts of this book were originally published as Part 2 of *Philosophy of Law,* edited by Joel Feinberg and Hyman Gross, Dickenson Publishing Company, Inc., © 1975. All rights reserved.

CONTENTS

Foreword   vii

Preface   viii

Introduction   2

Freedom of Expression

JOHN STUART MILL
from *On Liberty*   16

JOEL FEINBERG
"Limits to the Free Expression of Opinion"   28

LOUIS B. SCHWARTZ
"Morals Offenses and the Model Penal Code"   45

COHEN v. CALIFORNIA (United States Supreme Court, 1971)   54

IRVING KRISTOL
"Pornography, Obscenity, and the Case for Censorship"   58

Self-Determination

JOHN F. KENNEDY MEMORIAL HOSPITAL v. HESTON
(Supreme Court of New Jersey, 1971)   65

GERALD DWORKIN
"Paternalism"   67

Privacy

HENRY M. HART, JR., and ALBERT M. SACKS
"The Invitation to Dinner Case"   78

GRISWOLD v. CONNECTICUT (United States Supreme Court, 1965)   79

HYMAN GROSS
"Privacy and Autonomy   84

Sexual Deviance and Civil Liberties

SAMUEL FAHR
"Sexual Psychopath Laws"   90

SPECHT v. PATTERSON (United States Supreme Court, 1967)   109

IN RE LYNCH (Supreme Court of California, 1972)   111

Abortion

ROE v. WADE (United States Supreme Court, 1973)   125

MARY ANNE WARREN
"On the Moral and Legal Status of Abortion"   133

PAUL RAMSEY
"Protecting the Unborn"   143

Euthanasia

ANTONY FLEW
"The Principle of Euthanasia"   151

YALE KAMISAR
"Euthanasia Legislation: Some Non-Religious Objections"   160

NATURAL DEATH ACT (State of California, 1976)   183

Conscientious Disobedience

RONALD M. DWORKIN
"On Not Prosecuting Civil Disobedience"   188

Suggestions for Further Reading   198

THE DICKENSON SERIES IN PHILOSOPHY

Philosophy, said Aristotle, begins in wonder—wonder at the phenomenon of self-awareness, wonder at the infinitude of time, wonder that there should be anything at all. Wonder in turn gives rise to a kind of natural puzzlement: How can mind and body interact? How is it possible that there can be free will in a world governed by natural laws? How can moral judgments be shown to be true?

Philosophical perplexity about such things is a familiar and unavoidable phenomenon. College students who have experienced it and taken it seriously are, in a way, philosophers already, well before they come in contact with the theories and arguments of specialists. The good philosophy teacher, therefore, will not present his subject as some esoteric discipline unrelated to ordinary interests. Instead he will appeal directly to the concerns that already agitate the student, the same concerns that agitated Socrates and his companions and serious thinkers ever since.

It is impossible to be a good teacher of philosophy, however, without being a genuine philosopher oneself. Authors in the Dickenson Series in Philosophy are no exceptions to this rule. In many cases their textbooks are original studies of problems and systems of philosophy, with their own views boldly expressed and defended with argument. Their books are at once contributions to philosophy itself and models of original thinking to emulate and criticize.

That equally competent philosophers often disagree with one another is a fact to be exploited, not concealed. Dickenson anthologies bring together essays by authors of widely differing outlook. This diversity is compounded by juxtaposition, wherever possible, of classical essays with leading contemporary materials. The student who is shopping for a world outlook of his own has a large and representative selection to choose among, and the chronological arrangements, as well as the editor's introduction, can often give him a sense of historical development. Some Dickenson anthologies treat a single group of interconnected problems. Others are broader, dealing with a whole branch of philosophy, or representative problems from various branches of philosophy. In both types of collections, essays with opposed views on precisely the same questions are included to illustrate the argumentative give and take which is the lifeblood of philosophy.

Joel Feinberg
Series Editor

PREFACE

The appearance early in 1975 of our book, *Philosophy of Law,* prompted the suggestion from many quarters that each part be published separately in paperback form for readers with a narrower range of interests. In this volume we act once again on the suggestion, and add to the selections on liberty which appear in that volume further essays and cases dealing with some new and perplexing subjects of current interest to everyone concerned with problems of liberty under law. In this collection we endeavor to explore in a wide range of contexts the dilemmas that arise when the collective interests represented by the state come in conflict with the individual interests of citizens. We believe that these selections provide the opportunity for a comprehensive examination of the principles of liberty that lie at the juncture of law and philosophy.

Joel Feinberg
Hyman Gross

INTRODUCTION

For what purposes can the state rightly interfere with the liberty of individual citizens to do as they please? This central question of political theory becomes a vital question in legal philosophy too in virtue of the fact that in democracies, at least, the legal system is the primary means by which restraints on liberty are imposed. Certain kinds of conduct are directly prohibited by criminal statutes which threaten punishment, typically fines or imprisonment, for noncompliance. Other kinds of undesirable behavior are controlled by regulatory devices which employ the criminal law only indirectly, as a kind of "sanction of last resort." [1] Citizens must be licensed, for example, to drive automobiles or to practice medicine, a requirement that permits the state to regulate these dangerous activities carefully and to withdraw licenses from those who fail to perform to reasonable standards. Withdrawal of license is itself an administrative penalty diminishing the liberty of those subjected to it, but it is not a criminal penalty. The criminal sanction is reserved as a backup threat to prevent persons from driving or practicing medicine without a license. Similarly, "cease and desist" orders and other injunctions restrict the liberty of those to whom they are addressed without any recourse to the criminal law, which comes into play only to prevent or to punish disobedience. Still another form of administrative or noncriminal restriction of liberty is the civil commitment procedure by which mentally disturbed persons judged dangerous to others or incompetent to govern themselves are compelled to reside in hospitals or other nonpenal institutions. For some classes of harmful conduct—for example, defamatory statements, invasions of privacy, and certain kinds of trespass and nuisance—the civil law seems better suited than the criminal law to provide threatened parties with protection. Our liberty to tell damaging lies about our neighbors, to prevent them from enjoying their property, or to tap their telephone lines, is restricted by their legal power to bring a civil suit against us which can culminate in a judgment directing us to pay compensatory or punitive damages to them. Again, the criminal law is not involved except as a backup sanction to enforce court orders.

Most writers agree that restrictions of individual liberty, whether by direct criminal prohibition or by some other legal instrumentality, always need some special justification. That is to say that other things being equal, it is always preferable that individuals be left free to make their own choices and that undesirable conduct be discouraged by such noncoercive measures as education, exhortation, taxation (on undesirable conduct) or provision of positive incentives such as economic subsidies or rewards (for alternatives to undesirable conduct). It is not easy to state the grounds of this presumption in favor of liberty. Various philosophers, in making the presumptive case for liberty, have argued that absence of coercion is a necessary (though certainly not a sufficient) condition for individual self-realization and social progress, and for such specific goods as individual spontaneity, social diversity, and the full flowering of various moral and intellectual virtues. In any case, most of us are fully convinced that our own personal liberty is a precious thing, and consistency inclines us to suppose that it is equally precious, and equally worth respecting, in others.

The value of liberty, however, is easily overstated. Liberty may be precious but it is by no means the only thing of value. Contentment and happiness, while difficult in the absence of freedom, are not impossible. Moreover, one can have perfect political liberty and yet be alienated and discontented, which also shows that no matter how intimately they may be related, freedom and contentment are distinct values not reducible one to the other. Similarly, a given society may enjoy political liberty while yet permitting large-scale social injustice, a possibility which indicates that liberty and justice are distinct social values. Failure to appreciate these distinctions has led hasty thinkers to make certain familiar errors in their discussions of liberty. Some have argued that any liberty that conflicts with contentment or with justice is not "true liberty" but rather some beguiling counterfeit. It is more accurate to say that liberty is but one value among many, that it is vitally important but not sufficient, that it can conflict with other values, and even that in some circumstances it may not be worth its price as measured against other values.

Other writers have argued that political liberty in the absence of certain specific powers and opportunities is not "true liberty" at all, but a sham and a deceit. If an invalid confined to his bed were to scoff at a legal system that grants him freedom of movement, we should no doubt reply to him that our politically guaranteed liberty to move about at will is a genuine liberty and a genuine good, even though it may be worthless to a paralyzed person. What the invalid's plight shows is that health and mobility are also important and independent goods, not that political liberty is a sham. Similarly, the political radical in a capitalist bourgeois society might deny that he has true liberty of speech on the ground that he does not have fair access to the communications media which are dominated by wealthy corporations. Again, this shows that his freedom of expression is not worth as much as a wealthier man's, and that economic power is also an important good, not that he is not "really" at liberty to speak his mind. His complaint shows us that it is possible to praise liberty too much, but if he claims further that he would be no worse off if his political opinions were criminally proscribed, he is either disingenuous or naively under-appreciative of liberty's actual value.

It must be acknowledged, however, that a given person's lack of power or opportunity—his poverty, ignorance, or poor health—may be the *indirect result* of a structure of coercive laws. To take a crude and obvious hypothetical example, racial laws on the South African model might explicitly prohibit blacks from engaging in certain remunerative occupations. As a result blacks would be poorer than other citizens, and perhaps undernourished and undereducated as well. In that case there would be a very real point in describing a given black's lack of power or opportunity to make his views heard and considered as a diminished liberty. Political liberty is best understood as the absence of political coercion (typically, the absence of criminal prohibitions and other coercive legal instrumentalities), and not simply as *de facto* ability or opportunity. But where a law preventing a class of citizens from doing X leads indirectly to an absence of ability or opportunity for members of that class to do Y, there is a clear reason to describe the latter as a negation of the *liberty* to do Y.

FREEDOM OF EXPRESSION

Under what conditions, and for what reasons, can the presumption in favor of political liberty be overridden? This is not merely an abstract question addressed to philosophers, but an unavoidable practical question to be faced by every democratic legislator. In effect, it is a question about the limits beyond which restrictive lawmaking is morally illegitimate. John Stuart Mill, the first essayist presented in this part, gives the classic liberal answer to the question. Restriction of the liberty of one citizen, he argues, can be justified only to prevent harm to others. We can refer to Mill's position as the "harm to others principle," or more succinctly, the "harm principle." Several things should be noted about this principle at the outset. First, Mill means by "harm" not only direct personal injury such as broken bones or the loss of money, but also more diffuse social harms such as air pollution or the impairment of public institutions. Second, the principle does not propose a sufficient condition for the restriction of liberty, because some harms to others are too slight to outbalance the very real harm or danger involved in the restriction of liberty. Thus, in close cases, legislators must balance the value of the interests to be restricted by proposed coercive legislation *and* the collateral costs of enforcing any coercive law on the one hand against the value of the interests to be protected by the proposed legislation on the other. It is only when the probable harms prevented by the statute are greater than those that it will cause that the legislation is justified. Finally, the harm principle should be interpreted as a claim about *reasons:* Only one *kind* of consideration is ever morally relevant to the justification of coercion, namely, that it is necessary to prevent harm to others. It is never a relevant reason that the conduct to be restricted is merely offensive (as opposed to harmful) or even that it is intrinsically immoral, nor is it relevant that coercion is necessary to prevent a person from harming himself (as opposed to others).

No one would disagree that prevention of harm to others is always *a* relevant reason for coercion, but many disagree with Mill's contention that it is the *only* relevant consideration. Thus, no one will seriously suggest that laws against battery, larceny, and homicide are unjustified, but many maintain that the state is also justified, at least in some circumstances, in prohibiting (1) "immoralities" even when they harm no one but their perpetrators (the principle of legal moralism), (2) actions that hurt or endanger the actor himself (the principle of legal paternalism), or (3) conduct that is offensive though not harmful to others (the offense principle). These rival doctrines cannot easily be proved or refuted in the abstract. Rather, they are best judged by how faithfully they reflect, and how systematically they organize, our considered judgments in particular cases; for such principles, after all, purport to be explicit renderings of the axioms to which we are committed by the most confident judgments we make in everyday discourse about problems of liberty. The main areas of controversy in which such problems arise are those concerning unorthodox expressions of opinion, "morals offenses" in the criminal law (especially when committed in private by solitary individuals or among consenting adults), pornography and obscenity (when offered or displayed to the public or to nonconsenting individuals), activities that are harmful or dangerous to those who voluntarily engage in them, voluntary suicide and euthanasia, otherwise harmless invasions of the privacy of others, and conscientious acts of civil disobedience. The cautious theorist will begin with Mill's harm principle as an account of at least one set of reasons that is always relevant in such controversies, and then apply it to the various problem areas to determine the extent, if any, to which it must be supplemented to provide solutions that are both plausible and consistent. In particular, we must decide, in each area, whether we need have recourse to the offense principle, legal moralism, or legal paternalism.

Under most of the problem area headings, there is still another kind of controversy to be settled, namely, whether even the unsupplemented harm principle can justify *too much* coercion, and whether, therefore, doing justice to our considered judgments requires also a doctrine of *natural rights* limiting the applicability of the harm principle (or for that matter of any of the other liberty-limiting principles that might apply at all). This kind of question arises most prominently perhaps in the area of free expression of opinion. There is no doubt that expressions of opinion, in speech or writing, do often cause vast amounts of harm. Politicians sometimes advocate policies that would lead to disastrous consequences if adopted, and scientists sometimes defend theories that are false and detrimental to scientific progress. If we apply the harm principle in a straightforward unqualified way by prohibiting all particular expressions which seem on the best evidence likely to cause more harm than good, we might very well justify widespread invasions of what we should naturally take to be a moral right of free speech. Quite clearly, if he is to avoid this embarrassing consequence, the partisan of the harm principle will have to propose subtle refinements and mediating norms for the application of his principle, weighing such matters as the balancing of rival interests and social costs, and the measurements of probabilities, dangers, and risks.

Mill especially wished to avoid such embarrassment since he placed an extremely high value on free expression. As a utilitarian he wished to forego all benefit in argument from the notion of a natural right, yet he insisted that, short of the usual legal boundaries of libel, slander, incitement, and fraud, *all* restrictions on the expression of opinion are illegitimate, whether in morals, politics, religion, or whatever. His strategy was to establish an extra strong presumption in favor of freedom of expression, even beyond the standing presumption in favor of liberty generally. An individual's own interest in freedom of expression, in the first place, is an especially vital one. Human beings are essentially opinion-forming and communicating animals, and to squelch a person in the in the expression of his opinion is to hurt him "where he lives." Moreover, each individual is in a way wronged by restrictions on the expressions of all the others, for to keep an individual in ignorance of all but officially sanctioned opinions is to violate his autonomy as a rational being who, as another author has said is "sovereign in deciding what to believe and in weighing competing reasons for action." [2] Moreover, it diminishes him as a rational thinker and decider, impairs his dignity, weakens his "moral and intellectual muscles," and so, in a subtle but real way, *harms* him. Mill gives most emphasis, however, to the powerful *social* interest in free expression. Unless all opinions are given a free airing, he argues, we can never be confident that we have the truth about anything, having heard only one side of the case. A political community that deprives itself of important sources of truth is like a ship with a defective rudder, sure to flounder sooner or later on some rocky shore. That legally unhindered open debate of public issues is necessary to the pursuit of truth is a point of lasting importance never made more impressively than by Mill, but to regard the absence of legally enforced orthodoxy as sufficient guarantee of the triumph of truth would be extremely naive. Even Mill, in fact, is subject to some criticism for underemphasizing the importance of equal access to the public media for the effective operation of a "free marketplace of ideas." To tell an impecunious radical who aims to influence public policy that he enjoys political freedom of expression may be very much like congratulating a pauper on his legal right to buy a Cadillac. Free expression does not really fit Mill's description as a means of promoting knowledge and truth unless there are people about, powerful people, to listen.

In the second essay in this section, Joel Feinberg considers further how the harm principle must be qualified if it is to guarantee free expression of opinion in a morally satisfactory way. He examines first the relatively noncontroversial limits on free speech imposed by Anglo-American law: civil liability for defamatory utterances and for nondefamatory statements that reveal information which is properly private, criminal liability for irresponsible statements that cause panics or riots, laws against incitements to crime and (more controversially) sedition. They are considered in part because each raises its own questions of interest for the philosophy of law, and in part because each provides a challenge for the harm principle to provide a rationale for sensible restrictions on liberty that will not at the same time justify restrictions on free speech unacceptable to Mill and other liberals. Feinberg then attempts to provide a philosophical rationale for Justice Holmes's "clear and present danger" test, and then concludes with comments on the inevitable "balancing of interests" so central to the harm principle approach to problems of liberty.

For over a decade beginning in the mid 1950s, a committee of the American Law Institute (an elite group of lawyers, judges, and law professors) worked on a massive rewriting of the criminal law. Their goal was to produce a model penal code that might influence legislatures to rewrite the codes then in effect in most of the fifty states. The main "reporters" for this project, and the authors of the numerous tentative drafts, were Herbert Wechsler of the Columbia University Law School and Louis B. Schwartz of the University of Pennsylvania Law School. In his article included here, Professor Schwartz turns his attention to a class of crimes in our codes that are very difficult to justify by the unsupplemented harm principle. These so-called "offenses against morality" include not only tabooed sexual behavior, but also a somewhat puzzling miscellany of nonsexual conduct including mistreatment of corpses and desecration of the flag. The offense principle provides a rationale for judging some of these as crimes (for example, "open lewdness") even when they cause no one any injury, but other morals offenses (for example, homosexual relations between consenting adults in private) can be defended only by recourse to the principle of legal moralism, which maintains that the law may properly be used to enforce the prevailing morality as such, even in the absence of harm or offense.

The Model Penal Code recommendations about morals offenses are the work of a group of enlightened "would-be lawmakers" who are very much opposed to legal moralism but unwilling, if only on grounds of political realism, to urge extremely radical departures from the past ways of the law. Sexual behavior that is immoral by conventional standards should not be made criminal, according to the code, unless it involves violence or exploitation of children and other incompetents; and the traditional crimes of fornication, adultery, and sodomy are to be wiped from the books. In the absence of harm to others, Schwartz and his colleagues insist, the sexual behavior of individuals is no one else's business. "Open lewdness," on the other hand, like other "flagrant affronts" to the sensibilities of others, is another matter. Not only conventionally "immoral" sexual acts but even perfectly "normal" ones can be criminally proscribed if done in *public,* not because public sex acts harm anyone, but because they cause *offense* (quite another thing) to the unwilling observer. Thus, the Model Penal Code, while rejecting legal moralism, seems to endorse the offense principle.

This combination of principles seems to have rather clear implications in respect to obscenity control. Freely consenting adults, one would think, would be given the unfettered liberty to read or witness anything they choose, provided only that they do not display offensive materials in public or impose them on unsuspecting passersby or on children. The Model Penal Code, however, while approximating this position, prefers a more "oblique approach." The code would ban not only public exhibitions but also advertising and sale of materials "whose predominant appeal is to prurient interest." The target of this restriction, Schwartz assures us, is not "the sin of obscenity" but rather a kind of unfair business practice: "Just as merchants may be prohibited from selling their wares by appeal to the public's weakness for gambling, so they may be restrained from purveying books, movies, or other commercial exhibition by exploiting the well-nigh universal weakness for a look behind the curtain of modesty." This commercial approach to the problem of obscenity apparently influenced the Supreme Court in the famous case that sent Ralph Ginzburg to prison. With the benefit of hindsight, one can wonder whether the Model Penal Code's "oblique approach" is not simply a less direct way of accomplishing what legal moralism would do forthrightly. Is not the legal judgment that prurient interest in sex is a moral "weakness" itself a way of enveloping the conventional morality in the law?

A different aspect of the problem of obscenity was dramatically illustrated in the United States Supreme Court case of *Cohen v. California* in 1971. This case raised issues that connect the themes of the articles by Schwartz and Feinberg. Cohen was convicted by a Los Angeles municipal court for lingering in the corridors of a public building while wearing a jacket emblazoned with the words "Fuck the Draft." In his appeal to the Supreme Court of California and later to the United States Supreme Court, Cohen claimed that his right to free speech guaranteed by the First and Fourteenth Amendments had been violated, whereas the California authorities argued that they had properly applied against him a valid statute forbidding "willfully . . . offensive conduct." Now there are two ways in which a written or spoken statement can be offensive: It can express an opinion that some auditors might find offensive or it can express an opinion in language that is itself offensive independently of the "substantive message it conveys." Neither the United States Constitution nor the libertarian principles of free expression of opinion espoused by Mill and Feinberg would permit legal interference with free speech to prevent the expression of an "offensive opinion." However, restrictions on obscene, scurrilous, and incitive words, quite apart from their role in the expression of unpopular opinions, might well be justified by the offense principle, and indeed by the Constitution itself insofar as it tacitly employs the offense principle to mark out a class of exceptions to the free speech guarantee. Justice Harlan, however, rejected this approach to the case. The free expression of opinion protected by the Constitution, he argued, extends not merely to the proposition declared by a statement, but also to the speaker's (or writer's) emotions, or the intensity of his attitudes—in the case at hand "the depths of his feelings against the Vietnam War and the draft." Harlan's distinction points to an important function of what are ordinarily called obscene words. "Unseemly epithets" can shock and jolt, and in virtue of their very character as socially unacceptable, give expression to intense feelings more accurately than any other words in the language.

Unlike the authors preceding him in this section, Irving Kristol is primarily concerned not with expressions of opinion or attitude, but rather with expression in works of drama and literature and their counterfeits. Moreover, he gives a spirited defense of a kind of censorship which he claims to be quite consistent with a generally liberal attitude toward state coercion. His explicit target is the prevailing liberal view that consenting adults should be permitted to see or read anything they please and that censorship and prior restraint are justified only to protect children and unwilling witnesses. Censorship, he argues, is required for at least two additional kinds of reasons: (1) to protect the general quality of life, indeed our civilized institutions themselves (an appeal to the harm principle); and (2) to exclude practices that "brutalize and debase our citizenry" (an appeal to a kind of "moral paternalism," the need to protect even adults from moral corruption). One of the more difficult challenges Kristol poses for the liberal view he is attacking consists of an embarrassing hypothetical example. Suppose an enterprising promoter sought to stage gladiatorial contests like those of Ancient Rome in Yankee Stadium, in which well-paid gladiators fought to the death to the roars of large crowds. How could he be prevented from doing this on liberal grounds? Presumably the spectacle would be restricted to consenting adults so that interference would not be necessary to protect children and offended witnesses. The gladiators too would be consenting adults, fully prepared to shoulder enormous risks to life and limb, supposedly for the sake of money. (We can imagine that, with closed circuit TV, the promoter could offer the winning gladiator some twenty million dollars.) To interfere with the liberty of the gladiators to make agreements with promoters on the ground that the rewards they seek are not worth the risks they *voluntarily* assume would be to invoke the principle of legal paternalism, which is anathema to liberals who follow Mill. Kristol himself is not so much interested in protecting his hypothetical gladiators from death or physical harm as he is in defending the audience from a kind of moral harm, or harm to character.

SELF-DETERMINATION

The dilemma of paternalism is vividly exemplified in the New Jersey case of *Kennedy Memorial Hospital v. Heston* (1971). In his opinion reprinted here, Chief Justice Weintraub of the New Jersey Supreme Court decided in the affirmative the question whether an adult may be forced to submit against her will and against her religious convictions to a blood transfusion deemed by competent medical authority to be necessary not merely to her health but to her very life. The paternalism issue is not quite as clear in this instance as it might be since the patient was unconscious at the time the decision to proceed with the transfusion had to be made, so that it was her mother whose legal consent was solicited. Like her mother, however, the patient was a member of the Jehovah's Witnesses sect and presumably would have refused to permit the transfusion had she been conscious, and the court therefore addressed itself also to the legal consequences of her hypothetical refusal. There is no legal right to choose to die, the unanimous court concluded, suggesting that a failure to give the transfusion would be, in effect, to aid and abet an act of suicide by omission.

Under the English common law, suicide was a felony, and, unlike the law in most other American states it remains so in New Jersey, where all common law crimes are still punishable "if not otherwise provided for by act of the legislature." [3] Among the other legal consequences of the criminalization of suicide, the following were prominent: Property of the felon was forfeited to the Crown and thus denied to his heirs; life insurance was rendered void; attempted suicide was also a crime, often punished by imprisonment; all citizens had the right and duty to prevent commission of the crime by others when attempted in their presence; successful counseling of suicide, and knowing assistance in another's suicide were both murder; accidental killing of another in an attempt on one's own life was manslaughter (at least). Legal consent to one's own killing by another has always been impossible under Anglo-American law, hence even the merciful extinction of a dying patient's life in order to relieve his suffering *at his request* has been and still is a crime, usually murder. Thus, "under the present law, voluntary euthanasia [mercy killing] would, except in certain narrow circumstances, be regarded as suicide in the patient who consents and murder in the doctor who administers." [4] No doubt, some rationales of these laws are moralistic and others paternalistic, but they all agree that even when no other parties will be harmed, there can be no liberty to extinguish one's own, or another's life, even where death is ardently desired.

In a broader analysis of paternalism, Gerald Dworkin considers in a comprehensive and systematic way the question of whether paternalistic statutes (defined roughly as those interfering with a person's liberty "for his own good") are ever justified. He treats Mill's absolutistic position with respect, but points out how widespread paternalistic restrictions are, and how drastic their total elimination would be. Laws requiring hunters to wear red caps and motorcyclists to wear helmets, and those requiring medical prescriptions for certain therapeutic drugs, for example, seem innocuous to most of us. All the more so do laws actually protecting children and incompetents from their own folly, and laws which persons could regard as "social insurance" against any future decisions of their own that would be not only dangerous but irreversible. Dworkin then attempts to find criteria that can be used to separate unjustified paternalistic restrictions from those he thinks any rational man would welcome.

PRIVACY

The relation of liberty to privacy is often obscured by subtle differences of sense and nuance in various applications of those abstract words. Privacy is often contrasted with liberty, or cited (as in Feinberg's article) as one of the moral limits to free activity. In this sense, one person's privacy is a limit to *another* person's liberty. Privacy so described is what is common to a set of claims citizens have not only against one another but also against policemen and other agents of the state. In other contexts privacy is spoken of as itself a kind of liberty—a liberty to be left alone, to enjoy one's solitude, not to be intruded upon or even known about in certain respects. Expressed in this way, privacy is a negative sort of freedom, a freedom (indeed, a right) *not* to be treated in certain ways. Thus one person's right to privacy characteristically conflicts with more active liberties of movement and surveillance by others. So conceived, privacy is not one of the "liberties" normally ascribed to the state. Some state officials and agencies, to be sure, enjoy immunities and privileges of nondisclosure, but these forms of protected secrecy characteristically have as their rationales the need to enhance efficient functioning, not the need to protect privacy. Only persons have private thoughts, inner lives, and unknown histories that in virtue of their intimate character essentially merit protection from unwanted scrutiny; and the state, as such, is not a genuine person.

The notion of privacy first entered American law in the law of torts where it served to protect a miscellany [5] of personal interests against invasions by private individuals or groups by authorizing law suits for damages. Yet in an implicit way, the idea of a private realm into which the state cannot legitimately penetrate, a domain which is simply not the state's proper business, is both ancient and ubiquitous. In the fictitious "Invitiation to Dinner Case" included in this section, all of the legal requirements for an action for breach of contract appear to have been met, yet it is questionable whether such an action should be entertained. A dinner party, the judge might well be expected to say, is a householder's private affair and no proper concern of the courts. Here in a civil contest is the suggestion, normally made only with regard to criminal prohibitions, that public authority has no business interfering in private affairs.

The idea of privacy made its major entry into American constitutional law through the celebrated case of *Griswold v. Connecticut,* decided by the United States Supreme Court in 1965. The opinions in that case raise a variety of genuinely philosophical issues, and might well have been included with equal relevance in any of the first three sections of this anthology. The decision overturned a Connecticut statute making the use of contraceptives by "any person" a criminal offense. That statute was unconstitutional, Mr. Justice Douglas wrote, because it violated a right of marital privacy, "older than the Bill of Rights," but included in the "penumbra" of the First, Fourth, Fifth, Eighth, Ninth, and Fourteenth Amendments. A "penumbra" of a right is a set of further rights not specifically guaranteed in so many words but properly inferrable from the primary right either as necessary means for its fulfillment or as implied by it in certain factual circumstances not necessarily foreseen by those who formulated it.

Still, the Constitution does not specifically spell out a right of marital privacy, and the dissenters on the Court (Justices Stewart and Black) were suspicious of the technique of finding anything a judge thinks just and reasonable in the penumbra of a specific guarantee. Justice Goldberg in his concurring opinion had rested his case for a constitutional right of marital privacy on the Ninth Amendment's reference to fundamental rights "retained by the people," and Justices Harlan and White in their concurring opinions (not reprinted here) derived the unconstitutionality of the anticontraception statute from its capriciousness, irrationality, and offensiveness to a "sense of fairness and justice." A careful reader of Part One of this book will recognize here the overtones of the natural law tradition, whereas in Justice Black's skeptical stricture on the "catchwords" of "natural justice," in his dissenting opinion, there is the powerful echo of the tradition of legal positivism.

What is this privacy which, in some cultures at least, is held so dear, and which is so easily confused with the privileges of property, the residue of shame, or the essence of personal autonomy, among other things? By sorting out various separable elements, Hyman Gross makes a strong start on a philosophical analysis of the concept. A central theme in his account is that the loss of privacy is a loss of *control* over information about and impressions of oneself. Gross then proceeds to illuminate the connections between this aspect of privacy and self-determination, self-respect, and moral responsibility—connections that help explain the high value put on privacy, both by citizens and (now) by the law.

SEXUAL DEVIANCE AND CIVIL LIBERTIES

Sex offenders who do no violence but who frighten or disgust others have prompted the enactment of legislation that invites abuses of power by the state. In part these laws have roots in the timeless dark recesses of popular imagination where shame and fear lead to a view of deviant sexual behavior as dangerous. In part these laws are fostered by the vision of a brave new world in which all persons who are deemed dangerous are purged of their supposed dangerousness by therapy that eliminates its causes or induces an aversion to the deviant tendencies.

In his article on a typical sexual psychopath statute, Samuel Fahr makes clear the threat to liberty represented by these laws. Disorders that are quite ill-defined are nevertheless supposed to be subject to diagnosis and treatment in order to help those who have engaged in deviant behavior as well as to protect the community. But here diagnosis and treatment are little better than metaphors of medical science, and the hasty procedures by which citizens are subjected to indefinite incarceration serve only to conceal this truth. Since the person who is to be deprived of his liberty is not being put away for a crime, he does not enjoy the many protections the law affords the accused in criminal proceedings, and for all practical purposes a person is deprived of his liberty whenever the judge and the psychiatrists happen to have concurring impressions that make his removal from circulation seem desirable.

In *Specht v. Patterson* the Supreme Court of the United States overturned the decisions of Colorado's highest court and of two lower federal courts. The procedure under Colorado's Sex Offenders Act was found to be a violation of protections constitutionally guaranteed to citizens threatened with the loss of their liberty. The defendant in this case was sentenced under the Sex Offenders Act for an indeterminate term of from one day to life imprisonment, though he had been convicted under a criminal statute which provided a maximum sentence of ten years. The Supreme Court insisted that due process requirements be observed in the proceeding that determined whether the convicted defendant "if at large, constitutes a threat of bodily harm to members of the public, or is an habitual offender and mentally ill." Under *Specht* a person cannot be sentenced to a term other than that provided for his crime without being afforded in further proceedings the Constitutional protections that are required generally when criminal punishment is threatened. This leaves open the question of what protection must be given to a person whose commitment is sought by the state in a noncriminal proceeding authorized under the kind of "dangerous person" law that Professor Fahr discusses. Paradoxically some courts have held that persons only charged with sexual misconduct but not convicted in a criminal proceeding are not entitled in these noncriminal proceedings to the array of protections that now comprise due process in our criminal jurisprudence. The deprivation of liberty may be greater, and often in fact it is; yet because it is for "treatment" rather than "punishment" the state may exercise its power in a far less restrained way. The difficult problem of what in general is due process for civil commitment is presented at this point.

In the recent California case *In re Lynch,* the defendant had been convicted for a second time for the offense of indecent exposure, and he was sentenced to an indeterminate term that might, at the discretion of the authorities, turn out to be life imprisonment. The circumstances of this case make clear once again how fears of deviant sexual behavior present a grave danger to civil liberties when the law acts on those fearful attitudes. Both the crime and the punishment are deeply disturbing. What is it that warrants regarding what the defendant did as a crime at all, much less a serious one? And how can we allow a person's freedom to be disposed of at the whim of an administrative agency once he has been convicted?

ABORTION

In 1973 the United States Supreme Court declared the Texas and Georgia abortion laws to be in violation of the Due Process Clause of the Fourteenth Amendment. In its decision in *Doe v. Bolton,* the court struck down the Georgia statute that permitted abortions only when required by the pregnant woman's health, or to prevent birth of a deformed child, or when the pregnancy was caused by rape. The Texas statute overturned in *Roe v. Wade* was even more narrowly restrictive, confining legal abortions to those considered necessary to save the woman's life. One of the plaintiffs in *Roe v. Wade* had brought suit under the fictitious name of "Jane Roe" in a federal district court seeking an injunction against the enforcement of the Texas statute on the grounds that it violated rights guaranteed by the federal constitution. The Supreme Court in a majority opinion delivered by Justice Blackman, excerpts from which are included in this book, declared the Texas statute, and by implication all statutes similar to it in their sweeping proscription of abortion "without regard to pregnancy stage and without recognition of the other interests involved," to be invalid. At no point before birth, according to Justice Blackman, is the unborn fetus a right-holder or a person "in the whole sense." The fetus therefore has no legal rights that can conflict with the pregnant woman's right to have an abortion if she chooses, a right derived from her constitutionally protected right of privacy or "personal liberty." No state interests in the abortion decision are involved at all during the first trimester of pregnancy when the medical risks in abortion are minimal. But the state may regulate abortion procedures in the second trimester to further its interest in protecting the health and safety of the mother, and in the final trimester (roughly after "the point of viability") it may regulate or "even prohibit abortion outright in promoting its interest in 'the potentiality of human life.' "

In practical terms the court could not avoid or further postpone settling the issues raised in the suit of "Jane Roe." It was equally impossible in theoretical terms for its arguments not to reach philosophical conclusions about the nature of personhood, the status of the fetus, the meaning of privacy, the conflicts of moral claims, and the nature of legitimate "state interests" in pregnancy. In her article "On the Moral and Legal Status of Abortion," Mary Anne Warren reenforces with explicitly philosophical argument the court's position on the nonpersonhood of the fetus. Paul Ramsey, on the other hand, in an article based on his written testimony presented to the subcommittee of the Senate Judiciary Committee holding hearings on various anti-abortion amendments to the constitution, argues that the determination of "the outer limits of the human community" is a task for the people to discharge in public processes in which all citizens have a right to participate, not a question for the courts to decide in dogmatic pronouncements.

EUTHANASIA

Another deeply important question about human liberty concerns the end, rather than the beginning of human life: Should legislatures pass statutes creating a legal right to voluntary euthanasia? Should designated persons be permitted, under carefully specified circumstances to provide a "good death" to those who wish to die but are not capable of taking their own lives? A large number of distinctions must be made before this urgent but vague question can be answered. *Passive euthanasia* or "letting die" by nonaction must be distinguished from *active euthanasia* which is killing by positive action (for example, inserting a fatal substance into the bloodstream with a hypodermic needle) or by discontinuing sustenance (for example, "positively" disconnecting a respirator). In some circumstances killing by omission may seem just as "direct" a form of homicide as killing by action. For that reason, both are sometimes characterized as *direct euthanasia* and distinguished from *indirect euthanasia* (for example, giving a patient as much pain-reliever as possible even when this is likely, as a side-effect, to shorten his life, and not initiating any "extraordinary means" of preserving life). Whether euthanasia is active, passive, or indirect, the person who dies may have been a terminal patient, in any case deprived of only a few hours or days of miserable life, or a person who might have gone on living indefinitely though his life was, for one reason or another, intolerable to him. Perhaps the most important distinction, however, is that between *voluntary* and *nonvoluntary euthanasia.* The former is done at the bidding or with the consent of the person killed; the latter is not. Nonvoluntary euthanasia is sometimes proposed as a fitting and merciful treatment of various sorts of persons who are not competent to grant their consent—newborn infants with painful or incurable deformities; or brain-damaged, senile, or irreversibly comatose adults. When the motive of such killings is to release the person from pain, the comparison with mercy killings of animals (for example, shooting horses with splintered or fractured bones) is striking. One danger in a public policy that permits mercy killings, however, is that they might open the door to *involuntary* (as opposed to merely "nonvoluntary") *euthanasia,* where the consent of the victim is missing not simply because he is legally incapable of giving consent, but rather because he is unwilling to give consent in the first place. Paternalistic killings done for the victim's "own good" (whatever his own view of the matter) and downright malevolent killings of burdensome misfits commonly passed as "euthanasia" in the warped language of the Nazis, though they were in fact simply forms of "legalized murder."

Antony Flew makes a strong moral case for a legal right to voluntary, and only voluntary, euthanasia. Since he does not propose legalizing nonvoluntary euthanasia (and certainly not involuntary euthanasia) it is incumbent on him to rebut the famous "wedge argument" (also called "the foot in the door" and the "slippery slope" argument) that consented-to killings either will lead inevitably to nonconsentaneous killings or that a defense of one logically entails a defense of the other. One of his primary disagreements with Yale Kamisar is over the cogency of such arguments. The positions of Flew and Kamisar make an interesting contraposition in another respect. Flew admits that voluntary euthanasia is not always morally justified. If legislatures make the sorts of laws he advocates then persons will sometimes have a legal right to do what they have no moral right to do. Kamisar, the opponent of legalized euthanasia, on the other hand, concedes that persons are sometimes morally justified in providing euthanasia for others, but insists nevertheless that they ought never to be permitted legally to do so. On his view, then, we sometimes have a moral right to do what we ought never to have a legal right to do.

The advocate of legalized voluntary euthanasia rarely restricts the scope of his proposed legislation to those who are, *at the time their death is desired,* capable of granting their fully voluntary consent. Very often those who appear to "need" or want euthanasia the most are no longer capable of the calm, unemotional deliberation required by fully voluntary consent. How can a person who is beside himself with pain or despair, or else in a stupor induced by pain-relieving drugs, be clear-headed enough to agree *voluntarily* to anything? The most commonly given answer to this question is that adults have had their entire previous lives to give their voluntary consent to euthanasia should certain contingencies arise. They can write testamentary instructions to that effect while they are still of clear mind, and renew them before witnesses at regular intervals. Until very recently no American state had passed a law giving such "living wills" legal effect, though bills permitting their recognition had frequently been introduced in state legislatures. While this book was being prepared, however, California became the first state to adopt such legislation. So that the reader might better understand the Flew-Kamisar debate, we have included the California statute in this section.

CONSCIENTIOUS DISOBEDIENCE

Ronald Dworkin reminds us that dilemmas of liberty and coercion arise also for those charged with administering and enforcing the law. Prosecutors, in particular, have discretion as to whether or not to bring criminal charges against those who have been arrested. How prosecutorial discretion should be exercised then is another question that can lead to an examination of the citizen's moral claim to liberty, its grounds, and its limits. The specific question with which Dworkin is concerned is how the government should deal with those who deliberately disobey laws for reasons of conscience. His article was written in 1968 against a background of increasing numbers of prosecutions for advocating or counseling resistance, through draft evasion or draft refusal, to the then raging Vietnam War. For that reason, it might at first sight seem to be dated. Such an impression, however, would be quite unwarranted.

All of Dworkin's arguments apply equally well to the question of amnesty for conscientious draft evaders, a moral and political question that is still very much with us in this postwar period. More importantly, the problem of how the state should respond to conscientious disobedience to law is a perennial question that has divided writers and statesmen of all political factions in all historical periods. It is not an issue that simply goes away during the brief periods between wars and other crises.

The problem of "civil disobedience" is normally taken to be an ethical problem for the individual citizen who is conscientiously opposed to some law or policy of the state. Put in a general way it has the form: "Under what conditions, if any, would I be justified in disobeying the law?" The philosophy of law, however, is at least equally concerned with the question for political officials: "Given that John Doe has conscientiously refused to obey the requirements of a legal statute, under what conditions, if any, would we be morally, or even legally, justified in permitting him to escape punishment?" For a writer with Dworkin's jurisprudential views questions of law and morality are not easily separated. "In the United States at least," he writes, "almost any law which a significant number of people would be tempted to disobey on moral grounds would be doubtful—if not clearly invalid—on constitutional grounds as well." Typically, then, when conscientious disobedience occurs, the validity of the disobeyed law is itself in doubt,[6] and prosecutors must consider the fairness of prosecuting dissenters for declining to obey a statute they honestly believe to be not only immoral but probably invalid legally as well. Such cases raise a more general and basic problem still for *legislators*, for as Dworkin points out: "So long as the law appears to make acts of dissent criminal, a man of conscience will face danger. What can Congress, which shares the responsibility of leniency, do to lessen this danger?" Dworkin's answer to the question, as we might expect, is subtle and complicated. The legislature must balance numerous conflicting considerations, but by no means the least of these are the social value of respecting an individual's conscience and the unfairness of punishing violations of a doubtful law.

NOTES

1. The phrase is Herbert Packer's. See his *The Limits of the Criminal Sanction* (Stanford, Calif.: Stanford University Press, 1968), pp. 253–56.
2. The quoted phrase is from Thomas Scanlon, "A Theory of Free Expression," *Philosophy and Public Affairs*, Vol. I (1972), p. 215. This essay is somewhat difficult, but very strongly recommended nevertheless.
3. See Glanville Williams, *The Sanctity of Life and the Criminal Law* (New York: Alfred A. Knopf, 1968), p. 289.
4. *Ibid.*, p. 318.
5. Cf. Prosser on *Torts* 2nd ed. (St. Paul, Minn.: West Publishing Co., 1955), Chap. 20.
6. This point does not apply of course to cases of "indirect civil disobedience," where an admittedly valid law is disobeyed in order to protest *another* law or policy held to be unjust or immoral.

JOHN STUART MILL

On Liberty*

The object of this Essay is to assert one very simple principle, as entitled to govern absolutely the dealings of society with the individual in the way of compulsion and control, whether the means used be physical force in the form of legal penalties, or the moral coercion of public opinion. That principle is, that the sole end for which mankind are warranted, individually or collectively, in interfering with the liberty of action of any of their number, is self-protection. That the only purpose for which power can be rightfully exercised over any member of a civilized community, against his will, is to prevent harm to others. His own good, either physical or moral, is not a sufficient warrant. He cannot rightfully be compelled to do or forbear because it will be better for him to do so, because it will make him happier, because, in the opinions of others, to do so would be wise, or even right. There are good reasons for remonstrating with him, or reasoning with him, or persuading him, or entreating him, but not for compelling him, or visiting him with any evil, in case he do otherwise. To justify that, the conduct from which it is desired to deter him must be calculated to produce evil to some one else. The only part of the conduct of any one, for which he is amenable to society, is that which concerns others. In the part which merely concerns himself, his independence is, of right, absolute. Over himself, over his own body and mind, the individual is sovereign.

It is, perhaps, hardly necessary to say that this doctrine is meant to apply only to human beings in the maturity of their faculties. We are not speaking of children, or of young persons below the age which the law may fix as that of manhood or womanhood. Those who are still in a state to require being taken care of by others, must be protected against their own actions as well as against external injury. For the same reason, we may leave out of consideration those backward states of society in which the race itself may be considered as in its nonage. The early difficulties in the way of spontaneous progress are so great, that there is seldom any choice of means for overcoming them; and a ruler full of the spirit of improvement is warranted in the use of any expedients that will attain an end, perhaps otherwise unattainable. Despotism is a legitimate mode of government in dealing with barbarians, provided the end be their improvement, and the means justified by actually effecting that end. Liberty, as a principle, has no application to any state of things anterior to the time when mankind have become capable of being improved by free and equal discussion. Until then, there is nothing for them but implicit obedience to an Akbar or a Charlemagne, if they are so fortunate as to find one. But as soon as mankind have attained the capacity of being guided to their own improvement by conviction or persuasion (a period long since reached in all nations with whom we need here concern ourselves), compulsion, either in the direct form or in that of pains and penalties for non-compliance, is no longer admissible as a means to their own good, and justifiable only for the security of others.

It is proper to state that I forego any advantage which could be derived to my argument from the idea of abstract right, as a thing independent of utility. I regard utility as the ultimate appeal on all ethical questions; but it must be utility in the largest sense, grounded on the permanent interests of man as a progressive being. Those interests, I contend, authorize the subjection of individual spontaneity to external control, only in respect to those actions of each, which concern the interest of other people. If any one does an act

*From *On Liberty.* Excerpts from Chapters I and II, and all of Chapter IV. First published in 1859.

hurtful to others, there is a *primâ facie* case for punishing him, by law, or, where legal penalties are not safely applicable, by general disapprobation. There are also many positive acts for the benefit of others, which he may rightfully be compelled to perform; such as, to give evidence in a court of justice; to bear his fair share in the common defence, or in any other joint work necessary to the interest of the society of which he enjoys the protection; and to perform certain acts of individual beneficence, such as saving a fellow creature's life, or interposing to protect the defenceless against ill-usage, things which whenever it is obviously a man's duty to do, he may rightfully be made responsible to society for not doing. A person may cause evil to others not only by his actions but by his inaction, and in either case he is justly accountable to them for the injury. The latter case, it is true, requires a much more cautious exercise of compulsion than the former. To make any one answerable for doing evil to others, is the rule; to make him answerable for not preventing evil, is, comparatively speaking, the exception. Yet there are many cases clear enough and grave enough to justify that exception. In all things which regard the external relations of the individual, he is *de jure* amenable to those whose interests are concerned, and if need be, to society as their protector. There are often good reasons for not holding him to the responsibility; but these reasons must arise from the special expediencies of the case: either because it is a kind of case in which he is on the whole likely to act better, when left to his own discretion, than when controlled in any way in which society have it in their power to control him; or because the attempt to exercise control would produce other evils, greater than those which it would prevent. When such reasons as these preclude the enforcement of responsibility, the conscience of the agent himself should step into the vacant judgment-seat, and protect those interests of others which have no external protection; judging himself all the more rigidly, because the case does not admit of his being made accountable to the judgment of his fellow-creatures.

But there is a sphere of action in which society, as distinguished from the individual, has, if any, only an indirect interest; comprehending all that portion of a person's life and conduct which affects only himself, or, if it also affects others, only with their free, voluntary, and undeceived consent and participation. When I say only himself, I mean directly, and in the first instance: for whatever affects himself, may affect others *through* himself; and the objection which may be grounded on this contingency, will receive consideration in the sequel. This, then, is the appropriate region of human liberty. It comprises, first, the inward domain of consciousness; demanding liberty of conscience, in the most comprehensive sense; liberty of thought and feeling; absolute freedom of opinion and sentiment on all subjects, practical or speculative, scientific, moral, or theological. The liberty of expressing and publishing opinions may seem to fall under a different principle, since it belongs to that part of the conduct of an individual which concerns other people; but, being almost of as much importance as the liberty of thought itself, and resting in great part on the same reasons, is practically inseparable from it. Secondly, the principle requires liberty of tastes and pursuits; of framing the plan of our life to suit our own character; of doing as we like, subject to such consequences as may follow; without impediment from our fellow-creatures, so long as what we do does not harm them, even though they should think our conduct foolish, perverse, or wrong. Thirdly, from this liberty of each individual, follows the liberty, within the same limits, of combination among individuals; freedom to unite, for any purpose not involving harm to others: the persons combining being supposed to be of full age, and not forced or deceived.

No society in which these liberties are not, on the whole, respected, is free, whatever may be its form of government; and none is completely free in which they do not exist absolute and unqualified. The only freedom which deserves the name, is that of pursuing our own good in our own way, so long as we do not attempt to deprive others of theirs, or impede their efforts to obtain it. Each is the proper guardian of his own health, whether bodily, or mental and spiritual. Mankind are greater gainers by suffering each other to live as seems good to themselves, than by compelling each to live as seems good to the rest ...

We have now recognized the necessity to the mental well-being of mankind (on which all their other well-being depends) of freedom of opinion, and freedom of the expression of opinion, on four distinct grounds; which we will now briefly recapitulate.

First, if any opinion is compelled to silence, that opinion may, for aught we can certainly know, be true. To deny this is to assume our own infallibility.

Secondly, though the silenced opinion be an error, it may, and very commonly does, contain a portion of truth; and since the general or prevailing opinion on any subject is rarely or never the whole truth, it is only by the collision of adverse opinions that the remainder of the truth has any chance of being supplied.

Thirdly, even if the received opinion be not only true, but the whole truth; unless it is suffered to be, and actually is vigorously and earnestly contested, it will, by most of those who receive it, be held in the manner of a prejudice, with little comprehension or feeling of its rational grounds. And not only this, but, fourthly, the meaning of the doctrine itself will be in danger of being lost, or enfeebled, and deprived of its vital effect on the character and conduct: the dogma becoming a mere formal profession, inefficacious for good, but cumbering the ground, and preventing the growth of any real and heartfelt conviction from reason or personal experience . . .

OF THE LIMITS TO THE AUTHORITY OF SOCIETY OVER THE INDIVIDUAL

What, then, is the rightful limit to the sovereignty of the individual over himself? Where does the authority of society begin? How much of human life should be assigned to individuality, and how much to society?

Each will receive its proper share, if each has that which more particularly concerns it. To individuality should belong the part of life in which it is chiefly the individual that is interested; to society, the part which chiefly interests society.

Though society is not founded on a contract, and though no good purpose is answered by inventing a contract in order to deduce social obligations from it, every one who receives the protection of society owes a return for the benefit, and the fact of living in society renders it indispensable that each should be bound to observe a certain line of conduct towards the rest. This conduct consists, first, in not injuring the interests of one another; or rather certain interests, which, either by express legal provision or by tacit

understanding, ought to be considered as rights; and secondly, in each person's bearing his share (to be fixed on some equitable principle) of the labors and sacrifices incurred for defending the society or its members from injury and molestation. These conditions society is justified in enforcing, at all costs to those who endeavor to withhold fulfillment. Nor is this all that society may do. The acts of an individual may be hurtful to others, or wanting in due consideration for their welfare, without going the length of violating any of their constituted rights. The offender may then be justly punished by opinion, though not by law. As soon as any part of a person's conduct affects prejudicially the interests of others, society has jurisdiction over it, and the question whether the general welfare will or will not be promoted by interfering with it, becomes open to discussion. But there is no room for entertaining any such question when a person's conduct affects the interests of no persons besides himself, or needs not affect them unless they like (all the persons concerned being of full age, and the ordinary amount of understanding). In all such cases there should be perfect freedom, legal and social, to do the action and stand the consequences.

It would be a great misunderstanding of this doctrine, to suppose that it is one of selfish indifference, which pretends that human beings have no business with each other's conduct in life, and that they should not concern themselves about the well-doing or well-being of one another, unless their own interest is involved. Instead of any diminution, there is need of a great increase of disinterested exertion to promote the good of others. But disinterested benevolence can find other instruments to persuade people to their good, than whips and scourges, either of the literal or the metaphorical sort. I am the last person to undervalue the self-regarding virtues; they are only second in importance, if even second, to the social. It is equally the business of education to cultivate both. But even education works by conviction and persuasion as well as by compulsion, and it is by the former only that, when the period of education is past, the self-regarding virtues should be inculcated. Human beings owe to each other help to distinguish the better from the worse, and encouragement to choose the former and avoid the latter. They should be forever stimulating each other to increased exercise of their higher faculties, and increased direction of their feelings and aims towards wise instead of foolish, elevating instead of degrading, objects and contemplations. But neither one person, nor any number of persons, is warranted in saying to another human creature of ripe years, that he shall not do with his life for his own benefit what he chooses to do with it. He is the person most interested in his own well-being: the interest which any other person, except in cases of strong personal attachment, can have in it, is trifling, compared with that which he himself has; the interest which society has in him individually (except as to his conduct to others) is fractional, and altogether indirect: while, with respect to his own feelings and circumstances, the most ordinary man or woman has means of knowledge immeasurably surpassing those that can be possessed by anyone else. The interference of society to overrule his judgment and purposes in what only regards himself, must be grounded on general presumptions; which may be altogether wrong, and even if right, are as likely as not to be misapplied to individual cases, by persons no better acquainted with the circumstances of such cases than those are who look at them merely from without. In this department, therefore, of human affairs, Individuality has its proper field of action. In the conduct of human beings towards one another, it is necessary that general rules should for the most part be observed, in order that people may know what they have to expect; but in each person's own concerns, his individual spontaneity is entitled to free exercise. Considerations to aid his judgment, exhortations to strengthen his will, may be offered to him, even obtruded on him, by others; but he, himself, is the final judge. All errors which he is likely to commit against advice and warning, are far outweighed by the evil of allowing others to constrain him to what they deem his good.

I do not mean that the feelings with which a person is regarded by others, ought not to be in any way affected by his self-regarding qualities or deficiencies. This is neither possible nor desirable. If he is eminent in any of the qualities which conduce to his own good, he is, so far, a proper object of admiration. He is so much the nearer to the ideal perfection of human nature. If he is grossly deficient in those qualities, a sentiment the opposite of admiration will follow. There is a

degree of folly, and a degree of what may be called (though the phrase is not unobjectionable) lowness or depravation of taste, which, though it cannot justify doing harm to the person who manifests it, renders him necessarily and properly a subject of distaste, or, in extreme cases, even of contempt: a person would not have the opposite qualities in due strength without entertaining these feelings. Though doing no wrong to anyone, a person may so act as to compel us to judge him, and feel to him, as a fool, or as a being of an inferior order: and since this judgment and feeling are a fact which he would prefer to avoid, it is doing him a service to warn him of it beforehand, as of any other disagreeable consequence to which he exposes himself. It would be well, indeed, if this good office were much more freely rendered than the common notions of politeness at present permit, and if one person could honestly point out to another that he thinks him in fault, without being considered unmannerly or presuming. We have a right, also, in various ways, to act upon our unfavorable opinion of any one, not to the oppression of his individuality, but in the exercise of ours. We are not bound, for example, to seek his society; we have a right to avoid it (though not to parade the avoidance), for we have a right to choose the society most acceptable to us. We have a right, and it may be our duty to caution others against him, if we think his example or conversation likely to have a pernicious effect on those with whom he associates. We may give others a preference over him in optional good offices, except those which tend to his improvement. In these various modes a person may suffer very severe penalties at the hands of others, for faults which directly concern only himself; but he suffers these penalties only in so far as they are the natural, and, as it were, the spontaneous consequences of the faults themselves, not because they are purposely inflicted on him for the sake of punishment. A person who shows rashness, obstinacy, self-conceit—who cannot live within moderate means—who cannot restrain himself from hurtful indulgences—who pursues animal pleasures at the expense of those of feelings and intellect—must expect to be lowered in the opinion of others, and to have a less share of their favorable sentiments, but of this he has no right to complain, unless he has merited their favor by special excellence in his social relations, and has thus established a title to their good offices, which is not affected by his demerits towards himself.

What I contend for is, that the inconveniences which are strictly inseparable from the unfavorable judgment of others, are the only ones to which a person should ever be subjected for that portion of his conduct and character which concerns his own good, but which does not affect the interests of others in their relations with him. Acts injurious to others require a totally different treatment. Encroachment on their rights; infliction on them of any loss or damage not justified by his own rights; falsehood or duplicity in dealing with them; unfair or ungenerous use of advantages over them; even selfish abstinence from defending them against injury—these are fit objects of moral reprobation, and, in grave cases, of moral retribution and punishment. And not only these acts, but the dispositions which lead to them, are properly immoral, and fit subjects of disapprobation which may rise to abhorrence. Cruelty of disposition; malice and ill-nature; that most anti-social and odious of all passions, envy; dissimulation and insincerity; irascibility on insufficient cause, and resentment disproportioned to the provocation; the love of domineering over others; the desire to engross more than one's share of advantages (the πλεονεξία of the Greeks); the pride which derives gratification from the abasement of others; the egotism which thinks self and its concerns more important than everything else, and decides all doubtful questions in his own favor—these are moral vices, and constitute a bad and odious moral character: unlike the self-regarding faults previously mentioned, which are not properly immoralities, and to whatever pitch they may be carried, do not constitute wickedness. They may be proofs of any amount of folly, or want of personal dignity and self-respect; but they are only a subject or moral reprobation when they involve a breach of duty to others, for whose sake the individual is bound to have care for himself. What are called duties to ourselves are not socially obligatory, unless circumstances render them at the same time duties to others. The term duty to oneself, when it means anything more than prudence, means self-respect or self-development; and for none of these is any one accountable to his fellow-creatures, because for none of them is it for the good of mankind that he be held accountable to them.

The distinction between the loss of consideration which a person may rightly incur by defect of prudence or of personal dignity, and the reprobation which is due to him for an offence against the rights of others, is not a merely nominal distinction. It makes a vast difference both in our feelings and in our conduct towards him, whether he displeases us in things in which we think we have a right to control him, or in things in which we know that we have not. If he displeases us, we may express our distaste, and we may stand aloof from a person as well as from a thing that displeases us; but we shall not therefore feel called on to make his life uncomfortable. We shall reflect that he already bears, or will bear, the whole penalty of his error; if he spoils his life by mismanagement, we shall not, for that reason, desire to spoil it still further: instead of wishing to punish him, we shall rather endeavor to alleviate his punishment, by showing him how he may avoid or cure the evils his conduct tends to bring upon him. He may be to us an object of pity, perhaps of dislike, but not of anger or resentment; we shall not treat him like an enemy of society: the worst we shall think ourselves justified in doing is leaving him to himself, if we do not interfere benevolently by showing interest or concern for him. It is far otherwise if he has infringed the rules necessary for the protection of his fellow-creatures, individually or collectively. The evil consequences of his acts do not then fall on himself, but on others; and society, as the protector of all its members, must retaliate on him; must inflict pain on him for the express purpose of punishment, and must take care that it be sufficiently severe. In the one case, he is an offender at our bar, and we are called on not only to sit in judgment on him, but, in one shape or another, to execute our own sentence: in the other case, it is not our part to inflict any suffering on him, except what may incidentally follow from our using the same liberty in the regulation of our own affairs, which we allow to him in his.

The distinction here pointed out between the part of a person's life which concerns only himself, and that which concerns others, many persons will refuse to admit. How (it may be asked) can any part of the conduct of a member of society be a matter of indifference to the other members? No person is an entirely isolated being; it is impossible for a person to do anything seriously or permanently hurtful to himself, without mischief reaching at least to his near connections, and often far beyond them. If he injures his property, he does harm to those who directly or indirectly derived support from it, and usually diminishes, by a greater or less amount, the general resources of the community. If he deteriorates his bodily or mental faculties, he not only brings evil upon all who depended on him for any portion of their happiness, but disqualifies himself for rendering the services which he owes to his fellow-creatures generally; perhaps becomes a burden on their affection or benevolence; and if such conduct were very frequent, hardly any offence that is committed would detract more from the general sum of good. Finally, if by his vices or follies a person does no direct harm to others, he is nevertheless (it may be said) injurious by his example; and ought to be compelled to control himself, for the sake of those whom the sight or knowledge of his conduct might corrupt or mislead.

And even (it will be added) if the consequences of misconduct could be confined to the vicious or thoughtless individual, ought society to abandon to their own guidance those who are manifestly unfit for it? If protection against themselves is confessedly due to children and persons under age, is not society equally bound to afford it to persons of mature years who are equally incapable of self-government? If gambling, or drunkenness, or incontinence, or idleness, or uncleanliness, are as injurious to happiness, and as great a hindrance to improvement, as many or most of the acts prohibited by law, why (it may be asked) should not law, so far as is consistent with practicability and social convenience, endeavor to repress these also? And as a supplement to the unavoidable imperfections of law, ought not opinion at least to organize a powerful police against these vices, and visit rigidly with social penalties those who are known to practise them? There is no question here (it may be said) about restricting individuality, or impeding the trial of new and original experiments in living. The only things it is sought to prevent are things which have been tried and condemned from the beginning of the world until now; things which experience has shown not to be useful or suitable to any person's individuality. There must be some

length of time and amount of experience, after which a moral or prudential truth may be regarded as established: and it is merely desired to prevent generation after generation from falling over the same precipice which has been fatal to their predecessors.

I fully admit that the mischief which a person does to himself, may seriously affect, both through their sympathies and their interests, those nearly connected with him, and in a minor degree, society at large. When, by conduct of this sort, a person is led to violate a distinct and assignable obligation to any other person or persons, the case is taken out of the self-regarding class, and becomes amenable to moral disapprobation in the proper sense of the term. If, for example, a man, through intemperance or extravagance, becomes unable to pay his debts, or, having undertaken the moral responsibility of a family, becomes from the same cause incapable of supporting or educating them, he is deservedly reprobated, and might be justly punished; but it is for the breach of duty to his family or creditors, not for the extravagance. If the resources which ought to have been devoted to them, had been diverted from them for the most prudent investment, the moral culpability would have been the same. George Barnwell murdered his uncle to get money for his mistress, but if he had done it to set himself up in business, he would equally have been hanged. Again, in the frequent case of a man who causes grief to his family by addiction to bad habits, he deserves reproach for his unkindness or ingratitude; but so he may for cultivating habits not in themselves vicious, if they are painful to those with whom he passes his life, or who from personal ties are dependent on him for their comfort. Whoever fails in the consideration generally due to the interests and feelings of others, not being compelled by some more imperative duty, or justified by allowable self-preference, is a subject of moral disapprobation for that failure, but not for the cause of it, nor for the errors, merely personal to himself, which may have remotely led to it. In like manner, when a person disables himself, by conduct purely self-regarding, from the performance of some definite duty incumbent on him to the public, he is guilty of a social offence. No person ought to be punished simply for being drunk; but a soldier or a policeman should be punished for being drunk on duty. Whenever, in short, there is a definite damage, or a definite risk of damage, either to an individual or to the public, the case is taken out of the province of liberty, and placed in that of morality or law.

But with regard to the merely contingent, or, as it may be called, constructive injury which a person causes to society, by conduct which neither violates any specific duty to the public, nor occasions perceptible hurt to any assignable individual except himself; the inconvenience is one which society can afford to bear, for the sake of the greater good of human freedom. If grown persons are to be punished for not taking proper care of themselves, I would rather it were for their own sake, than under pretence of preventing them from impairing their capacity of rendering to society benefits which society does not pretend it has a right to exact. But I cannot consent to argue the point as if society had no means of bringing its weaker members up to its ordinary standard of rational conduct, except waiting till they do something irrational, and then punishing them, legally or morally, for it. Society has had absolute power over them during all the early portion of their existence: it has had the whole period of childhood and nonage in which to try whether it could make them capable of rational conduct in life. The existing generation is master both of the training and the entire circumstances of the generation to come; it cannot indeed make them perfectly wise and good, because it is itself so lamentably deficient in goodness and wisdom; and its best efforts are not always, in individual cases, its most successful ones; but it is perfectly well able to make the rising generation, as a whole, as good as, and a little better than, itself. If society lets any considerable number of its members grow up mere children, incapable of being acted on by rational consideration of distant motives, society has itself to blame for the consequences. Armed not only with all the powers of education, but with the ascendency which the authority of a received opinion always exercises over the minds who are least fitted to judge for themselves; and aided by the *natural* penalties which cannot be prevented from falling on those who incur the distaste or the contempt of those who know them; let not society pretend that it needs, besides all this, the power to issue commands and enforce obedience in the personal concerns of individuals, in which, on all principles of justice and policy, the decision ought to rest with those who are to abide the consequences. Nor is there anything which tends more to discredit and frustrate the better means of influencing conduct, than a resort to the worse. If there be among those whom it is attempted to coerce into prudence or temperance, any of the material of which vigorous and independent characters are made, they will infallibly rebel against the yoke. No such person will ever feel that others have a right to control him in his concerns, such as they have to prevent him from injuring them in theirs; and it easily comes to be considered a mark of spirit and courage to fly in the face of such usurped authority, and do with ostentation the exact opposite of what it enjoins; as in the fashion of grossness which succeeded, in the time of Charles II, to the fanatical moral intolerance of the Puritans. With respect to what is said of the necessity of protecting society from the bad example set to others by the vicious or the self-indulgent; it is true that bad example may have a pernicious effect, especially the example of doing wrong to others with impunity to the wrongdoer. But we are now speaking of conduct which, while it does no wrong to others, is supposed to do great harm to the agent himself: and I do not see how those who believe this, can think otherwise than that the example, on the whole, must be more salutary than hurtful, since, if it displays the misconduct, it displays also the painful or degrading consequences which, if the conduct is justly censured, must be supposed to be in all or most cases attendant on it.

But the strongest of all the arguments against the interference of the public with purely personal conduct, is that when it does interfere, the odds are that it interferes wrongly, and in the wrong place. On questions of social morality, of duty to others, the opinion of the public, that is, of an overruling majority, though often wrong, is likely to be still oftener right; because on such questions they are only required to judge of their own interests; of the manner in which some mode of conduct, if allowed to be practised, would affect themselves. But the opinion of a similar majority, imposed as a law on the minority, on questions of self-regarding conduct, is quite as likely to be wrong as right; for in these cases public opinion means, at the best, some people's opinion of what is good or bad for other people;

while very often it does not even mean that; the public, with the most perfect indifference, passing over the pleasure or convenience of those whose conduct they censure, and considering only their own preference. There are many who consider as an injury to themselves any conduct which they have a distaste for, and resent it as an outrage to their feelings; as a religious bigot, when charged with disregarding the religious feelings of others, has been known to retort that they disregard his feelings, by persisting in their abominable worship or creed. But there is no parity between the feeling of a person for his own opinion, and the feeling of another who is offended at his holding it; no more than between the desire of a thief to take a purse, and the desire of the right owner to keep it. And a person's taste is as much his own peculiar concern as his opinion or his purse. It is easy for any one to imagine an ideal public, which leaves the freedom and choice of individuals in all uncertain matters undisturbed, and only requires them to abstain from modes of conduct which universal experience has condemned. But where has there been seen a public which set any such limit to its censorship? or when does the public trouble itself about universal experience? In its interferences with personal conduct it is seldom thinking of anything but the enormity of acting or feeling differently from itself; and this standard of judgment, thinly disguised, is held up to mankind as the dictate of religion and philosophy, by nine tenths of all moralists and speculative writers. These teach that things are right because they are right; because we feel them to be so. They tell us to search in our own minds and hearts for laws of conduct binding on ourselves and on all others. What can the poor public do but apply these instructions, and make their own personal feelings of good and evil, if they are tolerably unanimous in them, obligatory on all the world?

The evil here pointed out is not one which exists only in theory; and it may perhaps be expected that I should specify the instances in which the public of this age and country improperly invests its own preferences with the character of moral laws. I am not writing an essay on the aberrations of existing moral feeling. That is too weighty a subject to be discussed parenthetically, and by way of illustration. Yet examples are necessary, to show that the principle I maintain is of serious and practical moment, and that I am not

endeavoring to erect a barrier against imaginary evils. And it is not difficult to show, by abundant instances, that to extend the bounds of what may be called moral police, until it encroaches on the most unquestionably legitimate liberty of the individual, is one of the most universal of all human propensities.

As a first instance, consider the antipathies which men cherish on no better grounds than that persons who religious opinions are different from theirs, do not practise their religious observances, especially their religious abstinences. To cite a rather trivial example, nothing in the creed or practice of Christians does more to envenom the hatred of Mahomedans against them, than the fact of their eating pork. There are few acts which Christians and Europeans regard with more unaffected disgust, than Mussulmans regard this particular mode of satisfying hunger. It is, in the first place, an offence against their religion; but this circumstance by no means explains either the degree or the kind of their repugnance; for wine also is forbidden by their religion, and to partake of it is by all Mussulmans accounted wrong, but not disgusting. Their aversion to the flesh of the "unclean beast" is, on the contrary, of that peculiar character, resembling an instinctive antipathy, which the idea of uncleanness, when once it thoroughly sinks into the feelings, seems always to excite even in those whose personal habits are anything but scrupulously cleanly, and of which the sentiment of religious impurity, so intense in the Hindoos, is a remarkable example. Suppose now that in a people, of whom the majority were Mussulmans, that majority should insist upon not permitting pork to be eaten within the limits of the country. This would be nothing new in Mahomedan countries.* Would it be a legitimate exercise of the moral authority of public opinion? and if not, why not?

---

*The case of the Bombay Parsees is a curious instance in point. When this industrious and enterprising tribe, the descendants of the Persian fire-worshippers, flying from their native country before the Caliphs, arrived in Western India, they were admitted to toleration by the Hindoo sovereigns, on condition of not eating beef. When those regions afterwards fell under the dominion of Mahomedan conquerors, the Parsees obtained from them a continuance of indulgence, on condition of refraining from pork. What was at first obedience to authority became a second nature, and the Parsees to this day abstain both from beef and pork. Though not required by their religion, the double abstinence has had time to grow into a custom of their tribe; and custom, in the East, is a religion.

The practice is really revolting to such a public. They also sincerely think that it is forbidden and abhorred by the Deity. Neither could the prohibition be censured as religious persecution. It might be religious in its origin, but it would not be persecution for religion, since nobody's religion makes it a duty to eat pork. The only tenable ground of condemnation would be, that with the personal tastes and self-regarding concerns of individuals the public has no business to interfere.

To come somewhat nearer home: the majority of Spaniards consider it a gross impiety, offensive in the highest degree to the Supreme Being, to worship him in any other manner than the Roman Catholic; and no other public worship is lawful on Spanish soil. The people of all Southern Europe look upon a married clergy as not only irreligious, but unchaste, indecent, gross, disgusting. What do Protestants think of these perfectly sincere feelings, and of the attempt to enforce them against non-Catholics? Yet, if mankind are justified in interfering with each other's liberty in things which do not concern the interests of others, on what principle is it possible consistently to exclude these cases? or who can blame people for desiring to suppress what they regard as a scandal in the sight of God and man? No stronger case can be shown for prohibiting anything which is regarded as a personal immorality, than is made out for suppressing these practices in the eyes of those who regard them as impieties; and unless we are willing to adopt the logic of persecutors, and to say that we may persecute others because we are right, and that they must not persecute us because they are wrong, we must be aware of admitting a principle of which we should resent as a gross injustice the application to ourselves.

The preceding instances may be objected to, although unreasonably, as drawn from contingencies impossible among us: opinion, in this country, not being likely to enforce abstinence from meats, or to interfere with people for worshipping, and for either marrying or not marrying, according to their creed or inclination. The next example, however, shall be taken from an interference with liberty which we have by no means passed all danger of. Wherever the puritans have been sufficiently powerful, as in New England, and in Great Britain at the time of the Commonwealth, they have endeavored, with considerable success, to put down all public, and

nearly all private, amusements: especially music, dancing, public games, or other assemblages for purposes of diversion, and the theatre. There are still in this country large bodies of persons by whose notions of morality and religion these recreations are condemned; and those persons belonging chiefly to the middle class, who are the ascendant power in the present social and political condition of the kingdom, it is by no means impossible that persons of these sentiments may at some time or other command a majority in Parliament. How will the remaining portion of the community like to have the amusements that shall be permitted to them regulated by the religious and moral sentiments of the stricter Calvinists and Methodists? Would they not, with considerable peremptoriness, desire these intrusively pious members of society to mind their own business? This is precisely what should be said to every government and every public, who have the pretension that no person shall enjoy any pleasure which they think wrong. But if the principle of the pretension be admitted, no one can reasonably object to its being acted on in the sense of the majority, or other preponderating power in the country; and all persons must be ready to conform to the idea of a Christian commonwealth, as understood by the early settlers in New England, if a religious profession similar to theirs should ever succeed in regaining its lost ground, as religions supposed to be declining have so often been known to do.

To imagine another contingency, perhaps more likely to be realized than the one last mentioned. There is confessedly a strong tendency in the modern world towards a democratic constitution of society, accompanied or not by popular political institutions. It is affirmed that in the country where this tendency is most completely realized —where both society and the government are most democratic—the United States—the feeling of the majority, to whom any appearance of a more showy or costly style of living than they can hope to rival is disagreeable, operates as a tolerably effectual sumptuary law, and that in many parts of the Union it is really difficult for a person possessing a very large income, to find any mode of spending it, which will not incur popular disapprobation. Though such statements as these are doubtless much exaggerated as a representation of existing facts, the state of things they describe is not only a conceivable and possible, but a probable result of democratic feeling, combined with the notion that the public has a right to a veto on the manner in which individuals shall spend their incomes. We have only further to suppose a considerable diffusion of Socialist opinions, and it may become infamous in the eyes of the majority to possess more property than some very small amount, or any income not earned by manual labor. Opinions similar in principle to these, already prevail widely among the artisan class, and weigh oppressively on those who are amenable to the opinion chiefly of that class, namely, its own members. It is known that the bad workmen who form the majority of the operatives in many branches of industry, are decidedly of opinion that bad workmen ought to receive the same wages as good, and that no one ought to be allowed, through piecework or otherwise, to earn by superior skill or industry more than others can without it. And they employ a moral police, which occasionally becomes a physical one, to deter skilful workmen from receiving, and employers from giving, a larger remuneration for a more useful service. If the public have any jurisdiction over private concerns, I cannot see that these people are in fault, or that any individual's particular public can be blamed for asserting the same authority over his individual conduct, which the general public asserts over people in general.

But, without dwelling upon supposititious cases, there are, in our own day, gross usurpations upon the liberty of private life actually practised, and still greater ones threatened with some expectation of success, and opinions proposed which assert an unlimited right in the public not only to prohibit by law everything which it thinks wrong, but in order to get at what it thinks wrong, to prohibit any number of things which it admits to be innocent.

Under the name of preventing intemperance, the people of one English colony, and of nearly half the United States, have been interdicted by law from making any use whatever of fermented drinks, except for medical purposes: for prohibition of their sale is in fact, as it is intended to be, prohibition of their use. And though the impracticability of executing the law has caused its repeal in several of the States which had adopted it, including the one from which it derives its name,

an attempt has notwithstanding been commenced, and is prosecuted with considerable zeal by many of the professed philanthropists, to agitate for a similar law in this country. The association, or "Alliance" as it terms itself, which has been formed for this purpose, has acquired some notoriety through the publicity given to a correspondence between its Secretary and one of the very few English public men who hold that a politician's opinions ought to be founded on principles. Lord Stanley's share in this correspondence is calculated to strengthen the hopes already built on him, by those who know how rare such qualities as are manifested in some of his public appearances, unhappily are among those who figure in political life. The organ of the Alliance, who would "deeply deplore the recognition of any principle which could be wrested to justify bigotry and persecution," undertakes to point out the "broad and impassable barrier" which divides such principles from those of the association. "All matters relating to thought, opinion, conscience, appear to me," he says, "to be without the sphere of legislation; all pertaining to social act, habit, relation, subject only to a discretionary power vested in the State itself, and not in the individual, to be within it." No mention is made of a third class, different from either of these, viz., acts and habits which are not social, but individual; although it is to this class, surely, that the act of drinking fermented liquors belongs. Selling fermented liquors, however, is trading, and trading is a social act. But the infringement complained of is not on the liberty of the seller, but on that of the buyer and consumer; since the State might just as well forbid him to drink wine, as purposely make it impossible for him to obtain it. The Secretary, however, says, "I claim, as a citizen, a right to legislate whenever my social rights are invaded by the social act of another." And now for the definition of these "social rights." "If anything invades my social rights, certainly the traffic in strong drink does. It destroys my primary right of security, by constantly creating and stimulating social disorder. It invades my right of equality, by deriving a profit from the creation of a misery, I am taxed to support. It impedes my right to free moral and intellectual development, by surrounding my path with dangers, and by weakening and demoralizing society, from which I have a right to claim mutual aid and intercourse." A theory of "social rights," the like of which probably never before found its way into distinct language—being nothing short of this—that it is the absolute social right of every individual, that every other individual shall act in every respect exactly as he ought; that whosoever fails thereof in the smallest particular, violates my social right, and entitles me to demand from the legislature the removal of the grievance. So monstrous a principle is far more dangerous than any single interference with liberty; there is no violation of liberty which it would not justify; it acknowledges no right to any freedom whatever, except perhaps to that of holding opinions in secret, without ever disclosing them: for the moment an opinion which I consider noxious, passes any one's lips, it invades all the "social rights" attributed to me by the Alliance. The doctrine ascribes to all mankind a vested interest in each other's moral, intellectual, and even physical perfection, to be defined by each claimant according to his own standard.

Another important example of illegitimate interference with the rightful liberty of the individual, not simply threatened, but long since carried into triumphant effect, is Sabbatarian legislation. Without doubt, abstinence on one day in the week, so far as the exigencies of life permit, from the usual daily occupation, though in no respect religiously binding on any except Jews, it is a highly beneficial custom. And inasmuch as this custom cannot be observed without a general consent to that effect among the industrious classes, therefore, in so far as some persons by working may impose the same necessity on others, it may be allowable and right that the law should guarantee to each, the observance by others of the custom, by suspending the greater operations of industry on a particular day. But this justification, grounded on the direct interest which others have in each individual's observance of the practice, does not apply to the self-chosen occupations in which a person may think fit to employ his leisure; nor does it hold good, in the smallest degree, for legal restrictions on amusements. It is true that the amusement of some is the day's work of others; but the pleasure, not to say the useful recreation, of many, is worth the labor of a few, provided the occupation is freely chosen, and can be freely resigned. The operatives are perfectly right in thinking that if

all worked on Sunday seven days' work would have to be given for six days' wages: but so long as the great mass of employments are suspended, the small number who for the enjoyment of others must still work, obtain a proportional increase of earnings; and they are not obliged to follow those occupations, if they prefer leisure to emolument. If a further remedy is sought, it might be found in the establishment by custom of a holiday on some other day of the week for those particular classes of persons. The only ground, therefore, on which restrictions on Sunday amusements can be defended, must be that they are religiously wrong; a motive of legislation which never can be too earnestly protested again. "Deorum injuriæ Diis curæ." It remains to be proved that society or any of its officers holds a commission from on high to avenge any supposed offence to Omnipotence, which is not also a wrong to our fellow-creatures. The notion that it is one man's duty that another should be religious, was the foundation of all the religious persecutions ever perpetrated, and if admitted, would fully justify them. Though the feeling which breaks out in the repeated attempts to stop railway travelling on Sunday, in the resistance to the opening of Museums, and the like, has not the cruelty of the old persecutors, the state of mind indicated by it is fundamentally the same. It is a determination not to tolerate others in doing what is permitted by their religion, because it is not permitted by the persecutor's religion. It is a belief that God not only abominates the act of the misbeliever, but will not hold us guiltless if we leave him unmolested.

I cannot refrain from adding to these examples of the little account commonly made of human liberty, the language of downright persecution which breaks out from the press of this country, whenever it feels called on to notice the remarkable phenomenon of Mormonism. Much might be said on the unexpected and instructive fact, that an alleged new revelation, and a religion founded on it, the product of palpable imposture, not even supported by the *prestige* of extraordinary qualities in its founder, is believed by hundreds of thousands, and has been made the foundation of a society, in the age of newspapers, railways, and the electric telegraph. What here concerns us is, that this religion, like other and better religions, has its martyrs; that its prophet and founder was, for his teaching, put to death by a mob; that others of its adherents lost their lives by the same lawless violence; that they were forcibly expelled, in a body, from the country in which they first grew up; while, now that they have been chased into a solitary recess in the midst of a desert, many of this country openly declare that it would be right (only that it is not convenient) to send an expedition against them, and compel them by force to conform to the opinion of other people. The article of the Mormonite doctrine which is the chief provocative to the antipathy which thus breaks through the ordinary restraints of religious tolerance, is its sanction of polygamy; which, though permitted to Mahomedans, and Hindoos, and Chinese, seems to excite unquenchable animosity when practised by persons who speak English, and profess to be a kind of Christians. No one has a deeper disapprobation than I have of this Mormon institution; both for other reasons, and because, far from being in any way countenanced by the principle of liberty, it is a direct infraction of that principle, being a mere riveting of the chains of one half of the community, and an emancipation of the other from reciprocity of obligation towards them. Still, it must be remembered that this relation is as much voluntary on the part of the women concerned in it, and who may be deemed the sufferers by it, as is the case with any other form of the marriage institution; and however surprising this fact may appear, it has its explanation in the common ideas and customs of the world, which teaching women to think marriage the one thing needful, make it intelligible that many a woman should prefer being one of several wives, to not being a wife at all. Other countries are not asked to recognize such unions, or release any portion of their inhabitants from their own laws on the score of Mormonite opinions. But when the dissentients have conceded to the hostile sentiments of others, far more than could justly be demanded; when they have left the countries to which their doctrines were unacceptable, and established themselves in a remote corner of the earth, which they have been the first to render habitable to human beings; it is difficult to see on what principles but those of tyranny they can be prevented from living there under what laws they please, provided they commit no aggression on other nations, and allow perfect freedom of departure to those who are dissatisfied with their ways. A recent writer, in some respects of considerable merit, proposes (to use his own words) not a crusade, but a *civilizade,* against this polygamous community, to put an end to what seems to him a retrograde step in civilization. It also appears so to me, but I am not aware that any community has a right to force another to be civilized. So long as the sufferers by the bad law do not invoke assistance from other communities, I cannot admit that persons entirely unconnected with them ought to step in and require that a condition of things with which all who are directly interested appear to be satisfied, should be put an end to because it is a scandal to persons some thousands of miles distant, who have no part or concern in it. Let them send missionaries, if they please, to preach against it; and let them, by any fair means (of which silencing the teachers is not one), oppose the progress of similar doctrines among their own people. If civilization has got the better of barbarism when barbarism had the world to itself, it is too much to profess to be afraid lest barbarism, after having been fairly got under, should revive and conquer civilization. A civilization that can thus succumb to its vanquished enemy must first have become so degenerate, that neither its appointed priests and teachers, nor anybody else, has the capacity, or will take the trouble, to stand up for it. If this be so, the sooner such a civilization receives notice to quit, the better. It can only go on from bad to worse, until destroyed and regenerated (like the Western Empire) by energetic barbarians.

JOEL FEINBERG

Limits to the Free Expression of Opinion

The purpose of this essay is to determine how the liberal principles that support free expression of opinion generally also define the limits to what the law can permit to be said. The liberal principle in question, put vaguely, is that state coercion is justified only to prevent personal or public harm. That more harm than good can be expected to come from suppression of dissenting opinions in politics and religion has been amply documented by experience and argument, but concentration on this important truth, despite its salutary practical effects, is likely to mislead us into thinking that the liberal "harm principle" is simple in its meaning and easy in its application. For that reason, this essay will only summarize (in Part I) the impressive case for total freedom of expression of opinions of certain kinds in normal contexts, and concentrate instead (in Part II) on the types of expressions *excluded* by the harm principle: defamation and "malicious truth," invasions of privacy, and expressions that cause others to do harm (those that cause panics, provoke retaliatory violence, or incite others to crime or insurrection). Part III will examine the traditional crime of "sedition," and conclude that it is not properly among the categories of expressions excluded by the harm principle. Among the other lessons that will emerge from these exercises, I hope, is that the harm principle is a largely empty formula in urgent need of supplementation by tests for determining the relative importance of conflicting interests and by measures of the degree to which interests are endangered by free expressions.

I THE CASE FOR FREEDOM

The classic case for free expression of opinion was made by John Stuart Mill.[1] Mill's purpose in his famous chapter "Of the Liberty of Thought and Discussion" was to consider, as a beginning, just one class of actions and how his "harm principle" applied to them. The actions in question were instances of expressing orally or in print opinions about matters of fact, and about historical, scientific, theological, philosophical, political, and moral questions. Mill's conclusion was that suppressing such expressions is always more harmful than the expressions themselves would be and therefore is never justified. But don't expressions of opinion *ever* harm others? Of course they do, and it would be silly to ascribe to Mill the absurd contrary view. Expressions of opinion harm others when they are: defamatory (libelous or slanderous), seditious, incitive to violence, malicious publications of damaging or embarrassing truths, or invasions of privacy. In fact, in classifying an expression under one of these headings, we are *ipso facto* declaring that it is harmful. Mill is not radical about this. Putting these obviously harmful expressions to one side (he is best understood as asking) is there any [further] ground for suppressing mere "opinions"? To *this* question Mill's answer is radical and absolutist: If an expression cannot be subsumed under one of these standard headings for harmfulness, then it can never be sufficiently injurious to be justifiably suppressed. Apart from direct harm to assignable persons, no other ground is ever a sufficient reason for overriding the presumption in favor of liberty. One may *never* properly suppress an expression on the grounds, for example, that it is immoral, shocking to sensibilities, annoying, heretical, unorthodox, or "dangerous," and especially not on the ground simply that it is false.

Expressions of opinion thus occupy a very privileged position, in Mill's view. That is because their suppression, he contends, is not only a private injury to the coerced party but also and inevitably a very serious harm to the public in

This essay was previously published in *Philosophy of Law.*
© 1975, Dickenson Publishing Company, Inc.

general. The argument has two distinct branches. The first has us consider the possibility that the suppressed opinion is wholly or partially true. On this assumption, of course, repression will have the harmful social consequence of loss of truth.

The crucial contention in this wing of the argument, however, is much stronger than that. Mill contends that there is *always* a chance, for all we can know, that the suppressed opinion is at least partially true, so that the act of repression itself necessarily involves some risk. Moreover, the risk is always an unreasonable one, never worth taking, since the risk of its alternative—permitting free expression generally—to our interest in acquiring knowledge and avoiding error, is negligible. By letting every opinion, no matter how "certainly true," be challenged, we minimize the risk of permanent commitment to falsehood. In the process, of course, we allow some falsehoods to be expressed, but since the truth is not denied its champions either, there is very little risk that the tolerated falsehood will become permanently enthroned. The balance of favorable risks then is clearly on the side of absolute freedom of expression.

This argument is especially convincing in the world of science, where no hypothesis bears its evidence on its face, and old errors are continually exposed by new and easily duplicable evidence and by more careful and refined experimental techniques. Even totalitarian regimes have learned that it is in their own interest to permit physicists and plant geneticists to go their theoretical ways unencumbered by ideological restrictions. Sometimes, to be sure, the truth of a scientific theory is so apparent that it is well worth acting on even though it strains governmental priorities to do so and requires large investment of funds; but this very confidence, Mill argued, is justified only when every interested party has had an opportunity to refute the theory. In respect at least to scientific theories, the more open to attack an opinion is, the more confident we can eventually be of its truth. That "no one has disproved it yet" is a convincing reason for accepting a theory only when everyone has been free to try.

To deny that it is possible for a given opinion to be true, Mill maintained, is to assume one's own infallibility. This is no doubt an overstatement, but what does seem clear is that to deny that a given proposition can possibly be true is to assume one's own infallibility with respect to *it,* though of course not one's infallibility generally. To say that one cannot possibly be wrong in holding a given belief is to say that one knows that one's knowledge of its truth is authentic. We claim to know infallibly when we claim to know that we know. It is also clear, I think, that we are sometimes justified in making such claims. I know that I know that $2 + 3 = 5$, that I am seated at my desk writing, and that New York is in the United States. In the face of challenges from the relentless epistemological skeptic, I may have to admit that I don't know *how* I know these things, but it doesn't follow from that that I don't know them. It seems then that there is no risk, after all, in suppressing some opinions, namely, the denials of such truisms.

Yet what could ever be the point of forbidding persons from denying that $2 + 3 = 5$ or that New York is in the United States? There is surely no danger that general confidence in these true propositions would be undermined. There is no risk of loss of truth, I suppose, in suppressing their denials, but also no risk in allowing them free circulation. Conceding that we can know truisms infallibly, therefore, can hardly commit us to approve of the suppression of their denials, at least so long as we adhere, with Mill, exclusively to the harm principle. More importantly, there are serious risks involved in granting any mere man or group of men the power to draw the line between those opinions that are known infallibly to be true and those not so known, in order to ban expression of the former. Surely, if there is one thing that is *not* infallibly known, it is how to draw *that* line.

In any case, when we leave tautologies and truisms behind and consider only those larger questions of substance, doctrines about which have in fact been banned by rulers in the past as certainly false (for example, the shape of the earth, the cause of disease, the wisdom of certain wars or economic policies, and the morality of certain kinds of conduct) our own fallibility is amply documented by history. The sad fact is that at every previous stage of history including the recent past there have been questions of the highest importance about which nearly *everyone,* including the wisest and most powerful, has been dead wrong. The more important the doctrines, then, the greater the risk we run in forbidding expressions of disagreement.

Mill's account, in this first wing of his argument, of the public interest in the discovery and effective dissemination of truth has many important practical implications. Mill himself thought that we should seek out our ideological enemies and offer them public forums in which to present and defend their views, or failing that, hire "devil's advocates" to defend unpopular positions in schools and in popular debates. Mill's reasons for these proposals also provide the grounding for the so-called "adversary theory of politics." The argument is (in the words of Zechariah Chafee): "Truth can be sifted out from falsehood only if the government is vigorously and constantly cross-examined . . . Legal proceedings prove that an opponent makes the best cross-examiner."[2] This states the rationale of the two-party system exactly. The role of the out-party is like that of the prosecutor in a criminal trial, or plaintiff in a civil action. It is a vitally important role too. Numerous historical instances suggest that we are in grave danger when both parties agree. Witness, for example, the Vietnam debacle, which was the outcome of a twenty-year "bipartisan foreign policy." Foreign policy decisions are as difficult as they are important; hence the need for constant reexamination, probing for difficulties and soft spots, bringing to light new and relevant facts, and subjecting to doubt hitherto unquestioned first premises. Without these aids, we tend to drift quite complacently into dead ends and quagmires.[3]

The second branch of the argument has us assume that the unorthodox opinion we are tempted to suppress really is false anyway. Even in this case, Mill insists, we will all be the losers, in the end, for banning it. When people are not forced by the stimulus of dissent to rethink the grounds of their convictions, then their beliefs tend to wither and decay. The rationales of the tenets are forgotten, their vital direction and value lost, their very meaning altered, until at last they are held in the manner of dead dogmas rather than living truths.

No part of Mill's argument in *On Liberty* is more impressive than his case for totally free expression of opinion. It is especially ingenious in that it rests entirely on social advantages and foregoes all help that might come from appeals to "the inalienable right to say what one pleases whether it's good for society or not." But that very utilitarian ingenuity may be its Achilles heel; for if liberty of expression is justified only because it is socially useful, then some might think that it is justified only *when* it is socially useful. The possibility of special circumstances in which repression is still *more* useful is real enough to disturb allies of Mill who love liberty fully as much as he and would seek therefore a still more solid foundation for it. But even if the case for absolute liberty of opinion must rest ultimately on some theory of natural rights, Mill has given that case powerful utilitarian reinforcement.

II LIMITS TO FREEDOM

Despite the impressive case for complete liberty of expression, there are obvious instances where permitting a person to speak his mind freely will cause more harm than good all around. These instances have been lumped together in various distinct legal categories whose names have come to stand for torts or crimes and to suggest, by a powerful linguistic convention, unpermitted wrongdoing. Thus, there can be no more right to defame or to incite to riot than there can be a right way, in Aristotle's example,[4] to commit adultery. Underlying these linguistic conventions, however, are a settled residue of interest weightings as well as actual and hypothetical applications of the harm principle, often filled in or mediated in various ways by principles of other kinds. The various categories of excluded expressions are worth examining not only for the light they throw on the harm principle, but also for the conceptual and normative problems each raises on its own for political theory.

1. *Defamation and "Malicious Truth."* Defamatory statements are those that damage a person's reputation by their expression to third parties in a manner that "tends to diminish the esteem in which the plaintiff is held, or to excite adverse feelings or opinions against him."[5] The primary mode of discouraging defamers in countries adhering to the common law has been the threat of civil liability to a court-enforced order to pay cash to the injured party in compensation for the harm done his reputation. In cases of especially malicious defamation, the defendant may be ordered to pay a stiff fine ("punitive damages") to the plaintiff as well. Only in the most

egregious cases (and rarely even then) has criminal liability been imposed for defamation, but nevertheless the threat of civil suit as sufficient to entitle us to say that our law does not leave citizens (generally) free to defame one another. Here then is one clear limit to our freedom of expression.

Not all expressions that harm another's reputation, of course, are legally forbidden. Even when damaging defamation has been proved by the plaintiff, the defendant may yet escape liability by establishing one of two kinds of defense. He may argue that his utterance or publication was "privileged," or simply that it is *true*. The former defense is established by showing either that the defendant, in virtue of his public office or his special relation to the plaintiff, has been granted an absolute immunity from liability for defamation (for example, he spoke in a judicial or legislative proceeding, or he had the prior consent of the plaintiff), or that he had a prior immunity contingent on the reasonableness of his conduct. Examples of this category of privilege are the immunity of a person protecting himself or another by a warning that someone is of poor character, or of a drama, literary, or political critic making "fair comment" of an extremely unfavorable kind about a performance, a book, or a policy. These immunities are still other examples of public policies that protect an interest (in this case, the interest in reputation) just to the point where the protection interferes with interests deemed more important—either to the public in general or to other private individuals. These policies imply that a person's reputation is a precious thing that deserves legal protection just as his life, health, and property do, but on the other hand, a certain amount of rough handling of reputations is to be expected in courtrooms, in the heated spontaneous debates of legislative chambers, in reviews of works presented to the public for critical comment, and in the rough-and-tumble competition among eminent persons for power or public acclaim. To withhold immunities in these special contexts would be to allow nervous inhibitions to keep hard truths out of law courts to the detriment of justice, or out of legislatures to the detriment of the laws themselves; or to make critics overly cautious, to the detriment of those who rely on their judgments; or to make political commentators overly deferential to power and authority, to the detriment of reform.

There is, however, no public interest in keeping those who are not in these special contexts uninhibited when they speak or write about others. Indeed, we should all be nervous when we make unfavorable comments, perhaps not on the ground that feelings and reputations will simply be damaged (there may be both justice and social gain in such damage), but at least on the ground that the unfavorable comment may be *false*. In a way, the rationale for the defamation action at law is the opposite of Mill's case for the free expression of opinion. The great public interest in possessing the truth in science, philosophy, politics, and so on, is best served by keeping everyone uninhibited in the expression of his views; but there are areas where there is a greater interest in avoiding falsehood than in acquiring truth, and here we are best served by keeping people very nervous indeed when they are tempted to speak their minds.

Once the plaintiff has proved that the defendant has published a defamatory statement about him, the defendant may avoid liability in another way, namely, by showing that the statement in question is *true*. "Out of a tender regard for reputations," writes Professor Prosser, "the law presumes in the first instance that all defamation is false, and the defendant has the burden of pleading and proving its truth."[6] In the large majority of American jurisdictions, truth is a "complete defense" which will relieve the defendant of liability even when he published his defamation merely out of spite, in the absence of any reasonable social purpose. One wonders why this should be. Is the public interest in "the truth" so great that it should always override a private person's interest in his own reputation? An affirmative answer, I should think, would require considerable argument.

Most of the historical rationales for the truth defense worked out in the courts and in legal treatises will not stand scrutiny. They all founder, I think, on the following kind of case. A New York girl supports her drug addiction by working as a prostitute in a seedy environment of crime and corruption. After a brief jail sentence, she decides to reform, and travels to the Far West to begin her life anew. She marries a respectable young man, becomes a leader in civic and church affairs, and raises a large and happy family. Then twenty years after her arrival in town, her neurotically jealous neighbor learns of her past, and publishes a lurid but accurate account of it for the eyes of the whole community. As a consequence, her "friends" and associates snub her; she is asked to resign her post as church leader; gossipmongers prattle ceaselessly about her; and obscene inscriptions appear on her property and in her mail. She dare not sue her neighbor for defamation since the defamatory report is wholly true. She has been wronged, but she has no legal remedy.

Applied to this case the leading rationales for the truth defense are altogether unconvincing. One argument claims that the true gravamen of the wrong in defamation is the deception practiced on the public in misrepresenting the truth, so that where there is no misrepresentation there is no injury—as if the injury to the reformed sinner is of no account. A variant of this argument holds the reformed sinner to be deserving of exposure on the ground that he (or she) in covering up his past deceives the public, thereby compounding the earlier delinquency. If this sort of "deception" is morally blameworthy, then so is every form of 'covering up the truth,' from cosmetics to window blinds! Others have argued that a delinquent plaintiff should not be allowed any standing in court because of his established bad character. A related contention is that "a person is in no position to complain of a reputation which is consistent with his actual character and behavior."[7] Both of these rationales apply well enough to the unrepentant sinner, but work nothing but injustice and suffering on the reformed person, on the plaintiff defamed in some way that does not reflect upon his character, or on the person whose "immoralities" have been wholly private and scrupulously kept from the public eye. It does not follow from the fact that a person's reputation is consistent with the truth that it is "deserved."

The most plausible kind of argument for the truth defense is that it serves some kind of overriding public interest. Some have argued that fear of eventual exposure can serve as effectively as the threat of punishment to *deter* wrongdoing. This argument justifies a kind of endless social penalty and is therefore more cruel than a system of criminal law, which usually permits a wrongdoer to wipe his slate clean. Others have claimed that

exposure of character flaws and past sins protects the community by warning it of dangerous or untrustworthy persons. That argument is well put (but without endorsement) by Harper and James when they refer to ". . . the social desirability as a general matter, of leaving individuals free to warn the public of antisocial members of the community, provided only that the person furnishing the information take the risk of its being false."[8] (Blackstone went so far as to assert that the defendant who can show the truth of his defamatory remarks has rendered a public service in exposing the plaintiff and deserves the public's gratitude.)[9] This line of argument is convincing enough when restricted to public-spirited defamers and socially dangerous plaintiffs; but it lacks all plausibility when applied to the malicious and useless exposure of past misdeeds, or to nonmoral failings and "moral" flaws of a wholly private and well-concealed kind.

How precious a thing, after all, is this thing denoted by the glittering abstract noun, the "Truth"? The truth in general is a great and noble cause, a kind of public treasury more important than any particular person's feelings; but the truth about a particular person may be of no great value at all except to that person. When the personal interest in reputation outweighs the dilute public interest in truth (and there is no doubt that this is sometimes the case) then it must be protected even at some cost to our general knowledge of the truth. The truth, like any other commodity, is not so valuable that it is a bargain at *any* cost. A growing number of American states have now modified the truth defense so that it applies only when the defamatory statement has been published with good motives, or is necessary for some reasonable public purpose, or (in some cases) both. The change is welcome.

In summary, the harm principle would permit all harmless statements about others whether true or false (harmless statements by definition are not defamatory), but it would impose liability for all defamatory false statements and all seriously defamatory true statements except those that serve (or seem likely to serve) some beneficial social purpose.

2. *Invasions of Privacy.* Still other expressions are neither defamatory nor false, and yet they can unjustly wound the persons they describe all the same. These do not invade the interest in a good

reputation so much as a special kind of interest in peace of mind, sometimes called a sense of dignity, sometimes the enjoyment of solitude, but most commonly termed the interest in personal privacy. As the legal "right to privacy" is now understood, it embraces a miscellany of things, protecting the right-holder not only from "physical intrusions upon his solitude" and "publicity given to his name or likeness or to private information about him" without his permission, but also from being placed "in a false light [but without defamation] in the public eye" and from the "commercial appropriation of elements of his personality."[10] (Some of these are really invasions of one's property rights through unpermitted commercial exploitation of one's name, image, personality, and so on. For that reason it has been urged that the invaded right in these cases be called "the right to publicity.") What concerns us here are statements conveying true and nondefamatory information about the plaintiff, of a very intimate and properly private kind, gathered and published without his consent, often to his shame and mortification. Business advantage and journalistic profit have become ever stronger motives for such statements, and the invention of tiny, very sensitive snooping devices has made the data easier than ever to come by.

Since the "invasion of privacy" tort has been recognized, plaintiffs have recovered damages from defendants who have shadowed them, looked into their windows, investigated their bank accounts, and tapped their telephone wires. In many of these cases, the court's judgment protected the plaintiff's interest in "being let alone," but in other cases the interest protected was not merely this, or not this at all, but rather the interest in *not being known about.* If there is a right not to be known about in some respects by anyone, then *a fortiori* there is a right not to be known about, in those respects, by nearly everyone. Privacy law has also protected the interests of those who don't want details of their lives called to the public's attention and made the subject of public wonder, amusement, discussion, analysis, or debate. Hence some plaintiffs have recovered from defendants who have published embarrassing details of their illness or physical deformity; their personal letters or unpublished notes, or inventories of their possessions; their photographs in a "good looks" popularity con-

test, or in a "before and after" advertisement for baldness or obesity cures, or on the labels of tomato cans; and from defendants who have published descriptions of the plaintiffs' sexual relations, hygienic habits, and other very personal matters. No life, of course, can be kept wholly private, or immune from public inspection even in some of its most personal aspects. "No one enjoys being stared at," Harper and James remind us, yet if a person "goes out on the street he [can have] no legal objection to people looking at him."[11] On the other hand, life would be hardly tolerable if there were no secrets we could keep (away from "the street"), no preserve of dignity, no guaranteed solitude.

There would probably be very little controversy over the existence of a right to privacy were it not the case that the interest in being let alone is frequently in conflict with other interests that seem at least equally deserving of protection. Even where the right is recognized by law, it is qualified by the recognition of very large classes of privileged expressions. First of all, like most other torts and crimes, the charge of invasion of privacy is completely defeated by proof that the plaintiff gave his consent to the defendant's conduct. Secondly, and more interestingly, the right of privacy can conflict with the constitutionally guaranteed freedom of the press, which, according to Prosser, "justifies the publication of news and all other matters of legitimate public interest and concern."[12] For a court to adjudicate between a paper's right to publish and an individual's right to privacy then, it must employ some standard for determining what is of legitimate public concern or, what amounts to the same thing, which news about a person is "fit to print." Such legal standards are always in the making, never finished, but the standard of "legitimate interest" has begun to take on a definite shape. American courts have decided, first of all, that "the person who intentionally puts himself in the public eye . . . has no right to complain of any publicity which reasonably bears on his activity."[13] The rationale for this judgment invokes the maxim that a person is not wronged by that to which he consents, or by that the risk of which he has freely assumed. The person who steps into the public spotlight ought to know what he is letting himself in for; hence the law presumes that he *does* know, and therefore that he is asking for it. Much the same kind of presumption lies behind the "fair comment" defense in defamation cases: The man who voluntarily publishes his own work is presumed to be inviting criticism and is therefore not entitled to complain when the criticism is adverse or harsh, providing only that it is relevant and not personally abusive. One can put oneself voluntarily into the public eye by running for or occupying public office; by becoming an actor, musician, entertainer, poet, or novelist; by inventing an interesting device or making a geographical or scientific discovery; or even by becoming wealthy. Once a person has become a public figure, he has sacrificed much of his right of privacy to the public's legitimate curiosity. Of course, one never forfeits *all* rights of privacy; even the public figure has a right to the privacy of his very most intimate affairs. (This may, however, be very small consolation to him.)

One cannot always escape the privilege of the press to invade one's privacy simply by avoiding public roles and offices, for the public spotlight can catch up with anyone. "Reluctant public characters" are nonetheless public and therefore, according to the courts, as legitimate objects of public curiosity as the voluntary public figures. Those unfortunates who attract attention unwillingly by becoming involved, even as victims, in accidents, or by being accused of crimes, or even as innocent bystanders to interesting events, have become "news," and therefore subject to the public's right to know. They maintain this unhappy status "until they have reverted to the lawful and unexciting life led by the great bulk of the community," but until then, "they are subject to the privileges which publishers have to satisfy the curiosity of the public as to their leaders, heroes, villains, and victims."[14] Again, the privilege to publish is not unlimited so that "the courts must somehow draw the distinction between conduct which outrages the common decencies and goes beyond what the public mores will tolerate, and that which the plaintiff must be expected in the circumstances to endure."[15]

When interests of quite different kinds head toward collisions, how can one determine which has the right of way? This problem, which lies behind the most puzzling questions about the grounds for liberty and coercion, tends to be concealed by broadly stated principles. The conflict between the personal interest in privacy and the

public curiosity is one of the best illustrations of the problem, but it is hardly unique. In defamation cases, as we have seen, there is often a conflict between the public interest in truth and the plaintiff's interest in his own good name. In nuisance law, there is a conflict between the plaintiff's interest in the peaceful enjoyment of his land and the defendant's interest in keeping a hogpen, or a howling dog, or a small boiler factory. In suburban neighborhoods, the residents' interest in quiet often conflicts with motorcyclists' interest in cheap and speedy transportation. In buses and trains, one passenger's interest in privacy[16] can conflict with another's interest in listening to rock and roll music on a portable radio, or for that matter, with the interests of two nearby passengers in making unavoidably audible, but avoidably inane, conversation. The principle of "the more freedom the better" doesn't tell us whose freedom must give way in these competitive situations.

The invasion of privacy cases are among the very clearest examples of the inevitable clash of interests in populous modern communities. They are, moreover, examples that show that solving the problem is not just a matter of minimizing harm all around. Harm is the invasion of an interest, and invasions do differ in degree, but when interests of radically different kinds are invaded to the same degree, where is the greater harm? Perhaps we should say that some interests are more important than others in the sense that harm to them is likely to lead to greater damage to the whole economy of personal (or as the case may be, community) interests than harm to the lesser interest, just as harm to one's heart or brain will do more damage to one's bodily health than an "equal degree" of harm to less vital organs. Determining which interests are more "vital" in an analogous sense would be no easy task, but even if we could settle this matter, there would remain serious difficulties. In the first place, interests pile up and reinforce one another. My interest in peace and quiet may be more vital in my system than the motorcyclist's interests in speed, excitement, and economy are in his, but there is also the interest of the cyclist's employer in having workers efficiently transported to his factory, and the economic interest of the community in general (including me) in the flourishing of the factory owner's business; the interest of the motorcycle manufacturers in their own profits; the interest of the police and others (perhaps including me) in providing a relatively harmless outlet for adolescent exuberance, and in not having a difficult rule to enforce. There may be nowhere near so great a buildup of reinforcing interests, personal and public, in the quietude of my neighborhood.

There is still another kind of consideration that complicates the delicate task of interest-balancing. Interests differ not only in the extent to which they are thwarted, in their importance or "vitality," and the degree to which they are backed up by other interests, but also in their inherent moral quality. Some interests, simply by reason of their very natures, we might think better worth protecting than others. The interest in knowing the intimate details of Brigitte Bardot's married sex life (the subject of a sensational lawsuit in France) is a morally repugnant peeping tom's interest. The sadist's interest in having others suffer pain is a morbid interest. The interest in divulging a celebrity's private conversations is a busybody's interest. It is probably not conducive to the public good to encourage development of the character flaws from which these interests spring, but even if there were social advantage in the individual vices, there would be a case against protecting their spawned interests, based upon their inherent unworthiness. The interests in understanding, diagnosing, and simply being apprised of newsworthy events might well outbalance a given individual's reluctance to be known about, but photographs and descriptions with no plausible appeal except to the morbid and sensational can have very little weight in the scales.

3. *Causing Panic.* Defamatory statements, "malicious truths," and statements that wrongfully invade privacy do harm to the persons they are about by conveying information or falsehood to third parties. Their publication tends to instill certain beliefs in others, and the very existence of those beliefs constitutes a harm to the person spoken or written about. Other classes of injurious expressions do harm in a rather different way, namely, by causing those who listen to them (or more rarely, those who read them) to act in violent or otherwise harmful ways. In these cases, the expressions need not be about any specifiable persons, or if they are about persons, those individuals are not necessarily the victims of the subsequent harm. When spoken words cause panic, breach the peace, or incite to crime or revolt, a variety of important interests, personal and social, will be seriously harmed. Such expressions, therefore, are typically proscribed by the criminal, and not merely the civil, law.

"The most stringent protection of free speech," wrote Holmes in his most celebrated opinion, "would not protect a man in falsely shouting fire in a theatre and causing a panic."[17] In some circumstances a person can cause even more harm by *truthfully* shouting "Fire!" in a crowded theater, for the flames and smoke might reinforce the tendency of his words to cause panic, and the fire itself might block exits, leading the hysterical crowds to push and trample. But we do not, and cannot fairly, hold the excited alarm sounder criminally responsible for his warning when it was in fact true and shouted with good intentions. We can hardly demand on pain of punishment that persons pick their words carefully in emergencies, when emotions naturally run high and there is no time for judicious deliberation. A person's warning shout in such circumstances is hardly to be treated as a full-fledged voluntary act at all. Perhaps it can be condemned as negligent, but given the mitigating circumstances, such negligence hardly amounts to the gross and wanton kind that can be a basis of criminal liability. The law, then, can only punish harmful words of this class when they are spoken or written with the intention of causing the harm that in fact ensues, or when they are spoken or written in conscious disregard of a high and unreasonable risk that the harm will ensue. The practical joker in a crowded auditorium who whispers to his comrade, "Watch me start a panic," and then shouts "Fire!" could be convicted for using words intentionally to cause a panic. The prankster who is willing to risk a general panic just for the fun of alarming one particular person in the audience could fairly be convicted for the grossly reckless use of dangerous words. Indeed, his recklessness is akin to that of the motorist who drives at an excessive speed just to frighten a timorous passenger.

Suppose, however, that the theater is virtually empty, and as the lights come on at the end of the film, our perverse or dim-witted jokester shouts "Fire! Fire!" just for the sake of confusing the three or four other patrons and alarming the ushers. The ushers quickly see through the ruse and suffer only a few moments of anxiety, and the patrons walk quickly to the exits and depart. No harm to speak of has been done; nor could any have reasonably been anticipated. This example shows how very important are the surrounding circumstances of an utterance to the question of its permissibility. Given the presumptive case for liberty in general, and especially the powerful social interest in leaving persons free to use *words* as they see fit, there can be a countervailing case for suppression on the grounds of the words' dangerous tendency only when the danger in fact is great and the tendency immediate. These matters are determined not only by the particular words used, but by the objective character of the surrounding circumstances—what lawyers call "the time, place, and manner" of utterance.

The question of legal permissibility should not be confused with that of moral blameworthiness or even with civil liability. The practical joker, even in relatively harmless circumstances, is no moral paragon. But then neither are the liar, the vulgarian, the rude man, and the scandalmonger, most of whose faults are not fit subjects for penal legislation. We cannot make every instance of mendacity, rudeness, and malicious gossip criminal, but we can protect people from the serious injury that comes from fraud, battery, or defamation. Similarly, practical jokers should be blamed but not punished, unless their tricks reach the threshold of serious danger to others. On the other hand, almost all lies, bad tales, jokes, and tricks create some risk, and there is no injustice in making the perpetrator compensate (as opposed to being punished) even his unlikely victim. Thus, if a patron in the nearly empty theater described above sprains an ankle in hurrying towards an exit, there is no injustice in requiring the jokester to pay the medical expenses.

It is established in our law that when words did not in fact cause harm the speaker may nevertheless be punished for having uttered them only if there was high danger when they were spoken that serious harm would result. This condition of course could be satisfied even though the harm in fact was averted: Not everything probable becomes actual. Similarly, for a person rightly to be punished even for harm in fact caused by his words, the harm in its resultant magnitude must have been an objectively probable consequence of the spoken words in the circumstances; otherwise the speaker will be punished for an unforeseeable fluke. In either case, then, the clear and present danger that serious harm will follow a speaker's words is necessary if he is rightly to be punished.

As we have seen, punishment for the harm caused by words is proper only if the speaker caused the harm either *intentionally* or *recklessly.* Both of these "mental conditions" of guilt require the satisfaction of the clear and present danger formula, or something like it. Consider recklessness first. For there to be recklessness there must really be a substantial risk consciously and unreasonably run. A speaker is not being reckless if he utters words that have only a remote and speculative tendency to cause panics or riots.

Intentional harm-causing by words raises more complications. Suppose an evil-minded person wishes to cause a panic and believes what is false and wholly unsupported by any real evidence, namely, that his words will have that effect. Imagine that he attends a meeting of the Policemen's Benevolent Association and, at what he takes to be the strategic moment, he stands up and shrieks, "There's a mouse under my chair!" Perhaps these words would cause a panic at a meeting of Girl Scouts but it merely produces a round of contemptuous laughter here. Wanting a panic and sincerely believing that one is causing a panic by one's words, then, are not sufficient. Suppose however we complicate the story so that by some wholly unforeseeable fluke the spoken words do precipitate a panic. The story is hard to invent at this point, but let us imagine that one patrolman laughs so hard that he tips over his chair causing another to drop his pipe, starting a fire, igniting live bullets, et cetera. Now, in addition to evil desire, and conscious belief in causal efficacy, we have a third important element: The words actually do initiate a causal process resulting in the desired panic. But these conditions still are not sufficient to permit us to say that the speaker *intentionally caused* a panic. Without the antecedent objective probability that a panic would follow these words in these circumstances, we have only a bizarre but tragic coincidence.

We would say much the same thing of a superstitious lady who "attempts" to start a riot by magic means. In an inconspicuous corner of a darkened theater, she sticks pins into a doll and mutters under her breath a magic incantation designed to produce a panic. Of course this doesn't work in the way intended, but a near-sighted and neurotic passerby observes her, takes the doll to be a real baby, and screams. The hoped-for panic then really follows. The evil lady cannot be found guilty of intentionally causing a panic, even though she intended to cause one and really did cause (or at least initiate a causal process that resulted in) one. She can be condemned for having very evil motives. But if people are sufficiently ignorant and impotent, the law, applying the harm principle, allows them to be as evil as they wish.

4. *Provoking Retaliatory Violence.* Suppose a person utters words which have as their unhappy effects violence directed *at him* by his angry audience, counterviolence by his friends and protectors, and escalation into a riotous breach of the peace. This is still another way of causing harm by words. Should the speaker be punished? In almost every conceivable case, the answer should be No. There is a sense, of course, in which the speaker did not start the physical violence. He used only words, and while words can sting and infuriate, they are not instruments of violence in the same sense that fists, knives, guns, and clubs are. If the law suppresses public speech, either by withholding permits in advance or punishing afterwards, simply on the ground that the expressed views are so unpopular that some auditors can be expected to start fighting, then the law punishes some for the criminal proclivities of others. "A man does not become a criminal because someone else assaults him . . .," writes Zechariah Chafee. Moreover, he continues, on any such theory, "a small number of intolerant men . . . can prevent *any kind* of meeting . . . A gathering which expressed the sentiment of a majority of law-abiding citizens would become illegal because a small gang of hoodlums threatened to invade the hall."[18] When violent response to speech threatens, the obvious remedy is not suppression, but rather increased police protection.

So much seems evident, but there may be some exceptions. Some words uttered in public places in the presence of many unwilling auditors may be so abusive or otherwise offensive as to be "reasonably considered a direct provocation to violence."[19] The captive auditor, after all, is not looking for trouble as he walks the public streets intent on his private errands. If he is forced to

listen, as he walks past a street meeting, to speakers denouncing and ridiculing his religion, and forced to notice a banner with a large and abusive caricature of the Pope,[20] his blood might reasonably be expected to boil. Antireligious and anti-clerical opinions, of course, no matter how unpopular, are entitled to the full protection of the law. Even abusive, virulent, and mocking expressions of such views are entitled to full protection if uttered to private gatherings, in private or privately reserved places. Such expressions become provocative only when made in public places to captive auditors.

What makes an expression "provocative?" Surely, if words are to be suppressed on the ground that they are provocative of violence, they must be more than merely "provoking," else all unpopular opinions will be suppressed, to the great public loss. As far as I know, the concept of provocation has received thorough legal elaboration only in the law of homicide, where provocation reduces a charge of murder to that of manslaughter, thus functioning as a kind of mitigating consideration rather than as a justification or complete excuse. In the common law, for there to be sufficient provocation to mitigate: (1) The behavior of the victim must have been so aggravating that it would have produced "such excitement and passion as would obscure the reason of an ordinary man and induce him . . . to strike the blow."[21] (2) There must not have elapsed so much time between the provocation and the violence that a reasonable man's blood would have cooled. (3) But for the victim's provocation the violence would not have occurred. In short, provocation mitigates only when it in fact produces a reason-numbing rage in the attacker and is such that it could be expected to produce such a rage in any normal person in his circumstances. Nazi emblems might be expected to have this effect on a former inmate of a Nazi death camp, but the Democratic party line cannot be sufficiently provocative to excuse a violent Republican, and similarly the other way round. Indeed, in the law of homicide, *no mere words alone,* no matter how abusive or scurrilous, can be adequate provocation to justify or totally excuse killing as a response.

There would seem to be equally good reason not to consider mere words either as justifying or totally excusing nonlethal acts of violence. The "reasonable man" in a democracy must be presumed to have enough self-control to refrain from violent responses to odious words and doctrines. If he is followed, insulted, taunted, and challenged, he can get injunctive relief, or bring charges against his tormentor as a nuisance; if there is no time for this and he is backed to the wall he may be justified in using "reasonable force" in self-defense; or if he is followed to his own home, he can use the police to remove the nuisance. But if he is not personally harrassed in these ways, he can turn on his heels and leave the provocation behind, and this is what the law, perhaps, should require of him.

Only when public speech satisfies stringent tests qualifying it as "direct provocation to violence," (if that is possible at all) will the harm principle justify its suppression. But there are many possible modes of suppression, and some are far more restrictive of liberty than others. Orders to cease and desist on pain of arrest are most economical, for they permit the speaker to continue to air his views in a nonprovocative way or else retire with his audience to a less public place. Lawful removal of the provocation (as a public nuisance) may be more satisfactory than permitting violent response to it, and is infinitely preferable to punishing the speaker. Nowhere in the law where provocation is considered as a defense do the rules deem the proven provoker (the victim) a criminal himself! At best his conduct mitigates the crime of his attacker, who is the only criminal.

One final point. While it is conceivable that some public *speech* can satisfy the common law test for provocation by being so aggravating that even a reasonable man could be expected to lose control of his reason when exposed to it, this can never be true of books. One can always escape the provocation of the printed word simply by declining to read it, and where escape from provocation is that easy, no "reasonable man" will succumb to it.

5. *Incitement to Crime or Insurrection.* In the criminal law, anyone who "counsels, commands, or encourages another to commit a crime" is himself guilty of the resultant crime as an "accessory before the fact." Counseling, commanding, and encouraging, however, must consist in more than merely uttering certain words in the presence of others. Surely there must also be serious (as opposed to playful) intent and some possibility at least of the words having their desired effect. It is not possible that these conditions can be satisfied if I tell my secretary that she should overthrow the United States government, or if a speaker tells an audience of bank presidents that they should practice embezzlement whenever they can. These situations are analogous to the efforts to start a panic by magical means or to panic policemen with words about mice.

The problem of interpreting the meaning of a rule making the counseling of crime itself a crime is similar, I should think, to that raised by a statute forbidding the planting of a certain kind of plant. One does not violate such a statute if he scatters the appropriate kind of seeds on asphalt pavement or in barren desert, even with evil intent. (Again, if you are stupid enough, the law—insofar as it derives from the harm principle—can allow you to be as evil as you wish.) To violate the statute, either one would have to dig a little hole in the appropriate sort of soil, deposit the appropriate seeds, cultivate, fertilize, allow for sufficient water, protect against winds, worms, and dogs; *or* one would have to find suitable conditions ready-made, where the soil is already receptive and merely dropping the seeds will create a substantial likelihood that plants will grow and thrive. By analogy, even words of advice, if they are to count as incitements to crime, must fall on reasonably receptive ears. The harm principle provides a ready rationale for this requirement. If we permit coercive repression of nondangerous words we will confer such abundant powers on the repressive organs of the state that they are certain to be abused. Moreover, we will so inhibit persons in their employment of language as to discourage both spontaneity and serious moral discussion, thus doing a great deal of harm and virtually no good at all. (The only "gain," if it is that, to be expected from looser standards of interpretation would be that nondangerous persons with evil motives could be scooped up in the state's tighter nets and punished.)

Counseling others to crime is not the only use of speech that can be described as incitement. We must also come to terms with instigating, egging on, and inflaming others to violence. Even Mill conceded that the opinion that "corn dealers are starvers of the poor," which deserves protection when published in the press, may nevertheless "justly incur punishment when delivered orally to an excited mob assembled before the house of a corn dealer ...".[22] The metaphor of planting seeds in receptive soil is perhaps less apt for this situation than the commonly employed "spark and tinder" analogy. Words which merely express legitimate though unpopular opinion in one context become "incendiary" when addressed to an already inflammable mob. As Chafee put it: "Smoking is all right, but not in a powder magazine."[23] Of course the man who carries a cigar into a powder magazine may not know that the cigar he is carrying is lighted, or he may not know that he has entered a powder magazine. He may plead his lack of intention afterward (if he is still alive) as a defense. Similarly, the man who speaks his opinion to what he takes to be a calm audience, or an excited audience with *different* axes all ground fine, may plead his ignorance in good faith as a defense. But "the law" (as judges are fond of saying) "presumes that a man intends the natural and probable consequences of his actions," so that a defendant who denies that he intended to cause a riot may have the burden of proving his innocent intention to the jury.

In summary, there are two points to emphasize in connection with the punishment of inflammatory incitements. First, the audience must really be tinder, that is to say not merely sullen, but angry to the point of frenzy, and so predisposed to violence. A left-wing radical should be permitted to deliver a revolutionary tirade before the ladies of the D.A.R., even if his final words are "to the barricades!", for that would be to light a match not in a powder magazine but in a Turkish steam bath. Second, no one should be punished for inciting others to violence unless he used words intentionally, or at least recklessly, with respect to that consequence. Otherwise at best a speaker will be punished for his mere negligence, and at worst he will be punished though perfectly innocent.

There is one further problem raised by the concept of incitement as a crime. It might well be asked how one person—the inciter—can be held criminally responsible for the free and deliberate actions of another person—the one who is incited by his words. This problem is common to both kinds of incitement, counseling and inflaming or egging on, but it seems especially puzzling in the case of advising and persuading; for the deliberate, thoughtful, unforced, and undeceived acceptance of the advice of another person is without question itself a voluntary act. Yet there may well be cases which are such that had not the advice been given, the crime would never have been perpetrated, so that the advisor can truly be said to have "got" the advisee to do something he might otherwise never have done. In this case, the initiative was the advisor's, and his advice was the crucial causal factor that led to the criminal act, so that it would be no abuse of usage to call it "the cause." And yet, for all of that, no one *forced* the advisee to act; he could have rejected the advice, but he didn't.

If there is the appearance of paradox in this account, or in the very idea of one person's causing another to act voluntarily, it is no doubt the result of an unduly restrictive conception of what a cause is. There are, of course, a great many ways of causing another person to behave in a given way by the use of words. If we sneak up behind him and shout "boo!" we may startle him so that he jumps and shrieks. In this case our word functioned as a cause not in virtue of its meaning or the mediation of the other person's understanding, but simply as a noise, and the person's startled reaction to this physical stimulus was as involuntary as an eye-twitch or a knee-jerk. Some philosophers would restrict the notion of causing behavior to cases of this kind, but there is no good reason for such a restriction, and a strong case can be built against it based both on its capacity to breed paradox and on common sense and usage. I can "get" an acquaintance to say "Good morning" by putting myself directly in his line of vision, smiling, and saying "Good morning" to him. If I do these things and he predictably responds in the way I intended, I can surely say that my behavior was the cause, in those circumstances, of his behavior; for my conduct is not only a circumstance but for which his action would not have occurred, it is also a circumstance which, when added to those already present, made the difference between his speaking and remaining silent. Yet I did not force him to speak; I did not deceive him; I did not trick him. Rather I exploited those of his known policies and dispositions that made him antecedently "receptive" to my words. To deny that I caused him to act voluntarily, in short, is either to confuse causation with compulsion (a venerable philosophical mistake) or to regard one person's initiative as incompatible with another person's responsibility.[24]

In any case, where one person causes another to act voluntarily either by giving him advice or information or by otherwise capitalizing on his carefully studied dispositions and policies, there is no reason why *both* persons should not be held responsible for the act if it should be criminal. It is just as if the law made it criminal to contribute to a human explosion either by being human dynamite or by being a human spark: either by being predisposed by one's character to crime or by one's passions to violence, or else by providing the words or materials which could fully be anticipated to incite the violent or criminal conduct of others. It is surely no reasonable defense of the spark to say that but for the dynamite there would have been no explosion. Nor is it any more reasonable to defend the dynamite by arguing that but for the spark it should have remained forever quiescent.

There is probably even less reason for excluding from responsibility the speaker haranguing an inflammable mob on the grounds that the individuals in the throng are free adults capable of refraining from violence in the circumstances. A mob might well be understood as a kind of fictitious collective person whose passions are much more easily manipulated and whose actions more easily maneuvered than those of individual persons. If one looks at it this way, the caused behavior of an inflamed mob may be a good deal less than fully voluntary, even though the component individuals in it, being free adults, are all acting voluntarily on their own responsibility.

III SEDITION

Causing panic, provoking violence, and inciting to crime or insurrection are all made punishable by what Chafee calls "the normal criminal law of words."[25] The relevant common law categories are riot, breach of the peace, solicitation, and incitement. All these crimes, as we have seen, require either intentionally harmful or reckless conduct, and all of them require, in addition— and for reasons partly derived from and explicable by the harm principle—that there be some objective likelihood that the relevant sort of harm will be produced by the words uttered in the circumstances. In addition to these traditional common law crimes, many governments have considered it necessary to create statutes making *sedition* a crime. It will be useful to consider the question of sedition against the background of the normal criminal law of words, for this will lead us quickly to two conclusions. The first is that sedition laws are wholly unnecessary to avert the harm they are ostensibly aimed at. The second is that if we must nevertheless put up with sedition laws, they must be applied by the courts in accordance with the same standards of objective likelihood and immediate danger that govern the application of the laws against provoking and inciting violence. Otherwise sedition statutes are likely to do far more social harm than good. Such laws when properly interpreted by enforcers and courts are at best legal redundancies. At worst they are corrosive of the values normally protected by freedom of expression.

The word "sedition," which in its oldest, prelegal sense meant simply divisiveness and strife, has never been the name of a crime in the English common law. Rather the adjective "seditious" forms part of the name of the common law crimes of "seditious words," "seditious libel," and "seditious conspiracy." Apparently the common ingredient in these offenses was so-called "seditious intent." The legal definition of "seditious intent" has changed over the centuries. In the beginning any spoken or written words which in fact had a tendency, however remote, to cause dissension or to weaken the grip of governmental authorities, and were spoken or published intentionally (with or without the further purpose of weakening the government or causing dissension) were held to manifest the requisite intent. In the fifteenth and sixteenth centuries, for example, publicly to call the king a fool, even in jest, was to risk capital punishment. There was to be less danger somewhat later for authors of *printed* words; for all books and printed papers had to be submitted in advance to the censorship (a practice denounced in Milton's eloquent *Areopagitica*), so that authors of politically dangerous words risked not punishment but only prior restraint. There is little evidence, however, that many of them felt more free as a consequence of this development.

The abandonment of the censorship in 1695 was widely hailed as a triumph for freedom of the press, but it was soon replaced by an equally repressive and far more cruel series of criminal trials for "seditious libel." Juries were permitted to decide only narrow factual questions, whereas the matter of "seditious intent" was left up to very conservative judges who knew well where their own personal interests lay. Moreover, truth was not permitted as a defense[26]—a legal restriction which in effect destroyed all right of adverse political criticism. Zechariah Chafee[27] has argued convincingly that the First Amendment to the United States Constitution was proposed and adopted by men who were consciously reacting against the common law of seditious libel, and in particular against the applications of that law in the English trials of the time. "Reform" (of sorts) came in England through Fox's Libel Act of 1792, which allowed juries to decide the question of seditious intent and permitted the truth defense if the opinions were published with good motives. (The ill-advised and short-lived American Sedition Act of 1798 was modeled after this act.) In the hysterical reaction to the French Revolution and the Napoleonic Wars, however, juries proved to be even more savage than judges, and hundreds were punished even for the mildest political unorthodoxy.

Throughout most of the nineteenth century, the prevailing definition of seditious intent in English law derived from a statute passed during the repressive heyday of the Fox Act sedition trials. Men were punished for publishing any words with:

the intention of (1) exciting disaffection, hatred, or contempt against the sovereign, or the government and constitution of the kingdom, or either house of parliament, or the administration of justice, *or* (2) exciting his majesty's subjects to attempt, otherwise than by lawful means, the alteration of any matter in church or state by law established, *or* (3) to promote feelings of ill will and hostility between different classes.[28]

In short, the three possible modes of seditious libel were defamation of the institutions or officers of the government, incitement to unlawful acts, and a use of language that tends toward the breach of the peace "between classes." The normal criminal law of words sufficiently covers the last two modes; and the civil law of defamation would apply to the first. The criminal law, as we have seen, employs a clear and present danger test for incitement and breach of peace, and does

so for good reasons derived from the harm principle and the analysis of "intentional causing." For other good reasons, also derived from the harm principle, the law of defamation privileges fair comment on public officials, and gives no protection at all to institutions. So there would seem to be no further need, at least none demonstrated by the harm principle, for a criminal law of sedition.[29]

Still, many have thought that the harm principle requires sedition laws, and some still do. The issue boils down to the question of whether the normal law of words with its strict standard of immediate danger is too lax to prevent serious harms, and whether, therefore, it needs supplementing by sedition laws employing the looser standards of "bad tendency" and "presumptive intent." By the standard of bad tendency, words can be punished for their dangerous propensity "long before there is any probability that they will break out into unlawful acts";[30] and by the test of presumptive intent, it is necessary only that the defendant intended to publish his words, not that he intended further harm by them. It is clear that most authors of sedition statutes have meant them to be interpreted by the courts in accordance with the tests of bad tendency and presumptive intent (although the United States Supreme Court has in recent decades declared that such interpretations are contrary to the First Amendment of the Constitution). Part of the rationale for the older tests was that if words make a definite contribution to a situation which is on its way to being dangerous, it is folly not to punish them well before that situation reaches the threshold of actual harm. There may seem to be no harm in piling up twigs as such, but if this is done with the purpose (or even the likely outcome) of starting a fire eventually, why not stop it now before it is too late? Those who favor this argument have often employed the harm principle also to defend laws against institutional defamation. The reason why it should be unlawful to bring the Constitution or the courts (or even the *flag*) into disrepute by one's words, they argue, is not simply that such words are offensive, but rather that they tend to undermine respect and loyalty and thereby contribute to more serious harm in the long run.

The focus of the disagreement over sedition laws is the status of *advocacy*. The normal law of words quite clearly outlaws counseling, urging, or demanding (under certain conditions) that others resort to crime or engage in riots, assassinations, or insurrections. But what if a person uses language not directly to counsel or call for violence but rather (where this is different) to *advocate* it? In the wake of the Russian Revolution, many working class parties in America and Europe adopted some variant of an ideology which declared that the propertied classes derived their wealth from the systematic exploitation of the poor; capitalists controlled the major media of news and opinion as well as parliaments and legislators; the grievances of the workers therefore could not be remedied through normal political channels but required instead direct pressure through such means as general strikes, boycotts, and mass demonstrations; and that the working class would inevitably be triumphant in its struggle, expropriate the exploiters, and itself run industry. Spokesmen for this ideology were known for their flamboyant rhetoric, which invariably contained such terms as "arise," "struggle," "victory," and "revolution." Such persons were commonly charged with violations of the Federal Espionage Act during and after World War I, of state sedition laws during the 1920s, and, after World War II, of the Smith Act. Often the key charge in the indictment was "teaching or advocating" riot, assassination, or the violent overthrow of the government.

Trials of Marxists for advocacy of revolution tended to be extremely difficult and problematic partly because it was never clear whether revolution in any usual sense was something taught and approved by them, and partly because it was unclear whether the form of reference to revolution in the Marxist ideology amounted to "advocacy" of it. Marxists disagreed among themselves over the first point. Many thought that forms of group pressure well short of open violence would be sufficient to overturn the capitalists; others thought that "eventually" (when is that?), when conditions were at last ripe, a brief violent seizure of power might be necessary. Does this, in any case, amount to the advocacy of revolution? If it is criminal advocacy to teach that there are conceivable circumstances under which revolution would be justified, then almost everyone, including this author, "advocates" revolution. Suppose one holds further that the "conceivable justifying

conditions" may one day become actual, or that it is even probable that they will be actual at some indeterminate future time. Is this to count as criminal advocacy?

Not according to Justice Holmes in his famous opinion in *U.S. v. Schenk.* Schenk and others had encouraged draft resistance in 1917 by mailing circulars denouncing conscription as unconstitutional and urging in very emotional prose that draft-eligible men "assert their rights." The lower court found this to be advocacy of unlawful conduct, a violation, in particular, of the Espionage Act of 1917. The Supreme Court upheld the conviction but nevertheless laid down in the words of O. W. Holmes the test which was to be applied, in a more generous spirit, in later cases: "The question in every case is whether the words . . . are used in such circumstances and are of such a nature as to create a clear and present danger that they will bring about the substantive evils that Congress has a right to prevent." Since Congress has the right to raise armies, any efforts to interfere by words or action with the exercise of that right are punishable. But the clear and present danger standard brings advocacy under the same kind of test as that used for incitement in the normal law of words. One can "advocate" draft resistance over one's breakfast table to one's daughter (though perhaps not to one's son), but not to a sullen group waiting to be sworn in at the induction center.

There is, on the other hand, never any real danger in this country in permitting the open advocacy of *revolution,* except, perhaps, as Chafee puts it, "in extraordinary times of great tension." He continues:

The chances of success are so infinitesimal that the probability of any serious attempt following the utterances seems too slight to make them punishable. . . . This is especially true if the speaker urges revolution at some future day, so that no immediate check is needed to save the country.[31]

Advocacy of assassination, on the other hand, is less easily tolerated. In the first place, the soil is always more receptive to that seed. It is not that potential assassins are more numerous than potential revolutionaries, although at most times that is true. Potential assassins include among their number persons who are contorted beyond reason by hate, mentally unstable persons, and unpredictable crackpots. Further, a successful assassination requires only one good shot. Since it is more likely to be tried and easier to achieve, its danger is always more "clear and present." There will be many circumstances, therefore, in which Holmes's test would permit advocacy of revolution but punish advocacy of assassination. Still in most contexts of utterance it would punish neither. It should no doubt be criminal for a prominent politician to advocate assassination of the president in a talk over national television, or in a letter to the *New York Times*,[32] but when a patron of a neighborhood tavern heatedly announces to his fellow drinkers that "the bum ought to be shot," the president's life will not be significantly endangered. There are times and places where it doesn't matter in the slightest how carelessly one chooses one's words, and others where one's choice of words can be a matter of life and death.

I shall, in conclusion, sketch a rationale for the clear and present danger test, as a kind of mediating standard for the application of the harm principle in the area of political expression. The natural challenge to the use of that test has been adumbrated above. It is true, one might concede, that the teaching of Communist ideology here and now will not create a clear and present danger of violent revolution. Every one knows that, including the Communists. Every trip, however, begins with some first steps, and that includes trips to forbidden destinations. The beginning steps are meant to increase numbers, add strength, and pick up momentum at later stages. To switch the metaphor to one used previously, the Communists are not just casting seeds on barren ground; their words are also meant to cultivate the ground and irrigate it. If the law prohibits planting a certain kind of shrub and we see people storing the forbidden seeds, garden tools, and fertilizer, and actually digging trenches for irrigation pipes, why wait until they are ready to plant the seed before stopping them? Even at these early stages of preparation, they are clearly attempting to achieve what is forbidden. So the argument goes.

The metaphor employed by the argument, however, is not very favorable to its cause. There is a world of difference between making plans and preparations for a future crime and actually launching an attempt, and this distinction has long been recognized by the ordinary criminal law. Mere preparations without actual steps in the direction of perpetration are not sufficient for the crime of attempt (though if preparation involves talking with collaborators, it may constitute the crime of conspiracy). Not even preliminary "steps" are sufficient; for "the act must reach far enough toward the accomplishment of the desired result to amount to the commencement of the consummation."[33] So the first faltering steps of a surpassingly difficult fifty-year trip toward an illegal goal can hardly qualify as an "attempt" in either the legal or the everyday sense.

If the journey is a collective enterprise, the participants could be charged with *conspiracy* without any violation of usage. The question is whether it would be sound public policy to suppress dissenting voices in this manner so long before they reach the threshold of public danger. The argument to the contrary has been given very clear statement in our time by Zechariah Chafee. Consider what interests are involved when the state employs some coercive technique to prevent a private individual or group from expressing an opinion on some issue of public policy, or from teaching or advocating some political ideology. Chafee would have us put these various interests in the balance to determine their relative weights. In the one pan of the scale, there are the private interests of the suppressed individual or group in having their opinions heard and shared, and in winning support and eventual acceptance for them. These interests will be effectively squelched by state suppression. In the other pan is the public interest in peace and order, and the preservation of democratic institutions. These interests may be endangered to some degree by the advocacy of radical ideologies. Now if these are the only interests involved, there is no question that the public interest (which after all includes all or most private interests) sits heavier in the pan. There is, however, another public interest involved of very considerable weight. That is the public interest in the discovery and dissemination of all information that can have any bearing on public policy, and of all opinions about what public policy should be. The dangers that come from neglecting *that* interest are enormous at all times. (See Part I above.) And the more dangerous the times—the more serious the questions before the country's decision makers (and *especially* when these are questions of war and peace)—the more important it is to keep open all the possible avenues to truth and wisdom.

Only the interest in national safety can outweigh the public interest in open discussion, but *it sits in the scale only to the degree that it is actually imperiled.* From the point of view of the public interest alone, with no consideration whatever of individual rights, it would be folly to sacrifice the social benefits of free speech for the bare possibility that the public safety may be somewhat affected. The greater the certainty and imminence of danger, however, the more the interest in public safety moves on to the scale, until at the point of clear and present danger it is heavy enough to tip the scales its way.

The scales analogy, of course, is only an elaborate metaphor for the sorts of deliberations that must go on among enforcers and interpreters of the law when distinct public interests come into conflict. These clashes of interest are most likely to occur in times of excitement and stress when interest "balancing" calls for a clear eye, a sensitive scale, and a steady hand. At such times the clear and present danger rule is a difficult one to apply, but other guides to decision have invariably gone wrong, while the clear and present danger test has hardly ever been seriously tried. Perhaps that helps account, to some degree, for the sorry human record of cruelty, injustice, and war.

NOTES

1. In Chapter Two of *On Liberty,* not reprinted in this volume.

2. Zechariah Chafee, Jr., *Free Speech in the United States* (1941), p. 33.

3. This point applies especially to discussions of moral, social, political, legal, and economic questions, as well as matters of governmental policy, domestic and foreign. "Cross-examination" in science and philosophy is perhaps less important.

4. Aristotle, *Nicomachean Ethics,* Bk. II, Chap. 6, 1107 ª. "When a man commits adultery, there is no point in asking whether it was with the right woman or at the right time or in the right way, for to do anything like that is simply wrong."

5. William L. Prosser, *Handbook of the Law of Torts,* 2nd ed. (St. Paul: West Publishing Co., 1955), p. 584.

6. *Ibid.,* p. 631.

7. Fowler V. Harper and Fleming James, Jr., *The Law of Torts* (Boston: Little, Brown and Co., 1956), Vol. I, p. 416. The authors do not endorse this view.

8. *Ibid.*

9. William Blackstone, *Commentaries on the Laws of England,* Vol. III, 1765 Reprint (Boston: Beacon Press, 1962), p. 125.

10. Prosser, *op. cit.,* p. 644.

11. Harper and James, *op. cit.,* p. 680.

12. Prosser, *op. cit.,* p. 642.

13. *Loc. cit.*

14. American Law Institute, *Restatement of the Law of Torts* (St. Paul, 1934) § 867, comment c.

15. Prosser, *op. cit.,* p. 644.

16. "There are two aspects of the interest in seclusion. First, the interest in preventing others from seeing and hearing what one does and says. Second, *the interest in avoiding seeing and hearing what other people do and say.* . . . It may be as distasteful to suffer the intrusions of a garrulous and unwelcome guest as to discover an eavesdropper or peeper." Harper and James, *op. cit.,* p. 681. (Emphasis added.)

17. Schenck v. United States, 249 U.S. 47 (1919).

18. Chafee, *op. cit.,* pp. 152, 161, 426. cf. Terminiello v. Chicago 337 U.S. 1, (1949).

19. Chafee, *op. cit.,* p. 426.

20. *Ibid.,* p. 161.

21. Toler v. State, 152 Tenn. 1, 13, 260 S.W. 134 (1923).

22. Mill, *op. cit.,* pp. 67–8.

23. Chafee, *op. cit.,* p. 397.

24. For a more detailed exposition of this view see my "Causing Voluntary Actions" in *Doing and Deserving* (Princeton, N.J.: Princeton University Press, 1970), p. 152.

25. Chafee, *op. cit.,* p. 149.

26. In the words of the great common law judge, William Murray, First Earl of Mansfield, "The Greater the Truth, the Greater the Libel," hence Robert Burns's playful lines in his poem, "The Reproof":
> "Dost not know that old Mansfield
>   Who writes like the Bible,
> Says the more 'tis a truth, sir,
>   The more 'tis a libel?"

27. Chafee, *op. cit.,* pp. 18–22.

28. *Ibid.,* p. 506.

29. Such things, however, as patriotic sensibilities are capable of being highly *offended* by certain kinds of language. The rationale of sedition laws, therefore, may very well derive from the "offense-principle," which warrants prohibition of offensive behavior even when it is (otherwise) harmless.

30. Chafee, *op. cit.,* p. 24.

31. *Ibid.,* p. 175.

32. In which case the newspaper too would be criminally responsible for publishing the letter.

33. Lee v. Commonwealth, 144 Va. 594, 599, 131 S.E. 212, 214 (1926) as quoted in Rollin M. Perkins, *Criminal Law* (Brooklyn Foundation Press, 1957), p. 482.

LOUIS B. SCHWARTZ

Morals Offenses and the Model Penal Code*

What are the "offenses against morals"? One thinks first of the sexual offenses, adultery, fornication, sodomy, incest, and prostitution, and then, by easy extension, of such sex-related offenses as bigamy, abortion, open lewdness, and obscenity. But if one pauses to reflect on what sets these apart from offenses "against the person," or "against property," or "against public administration," it becomes evident that sexual offenses do not involve violation of moral principles in any peculiar sense. Virtually the entire penal code expresses the community's ideas of morality, or at least of the most egregious immoralities. To steal, to kill, to swear falsely in legal proceedings —these are certainly condemned as much by moral and religious as by secular standards. It also becomes evident that not all sexual behavior commonly condemned by prevailing American penal laws can be subsumed under universal moral precepts. This is certainly the case as to laws regulating contraception and abortion. But it is also true of such relatively uncontroversial (in the Western World) "morals" offenses as bigamy and polygamy; plural marriage arrangements approved by great religions of the majority of mankind can hardly be condemned out-of-hand as "immoralities."

What truly distinguishes the offenses commonly thought of as "against morals" is not their relation to morality but the absence of ordinary justification for punishment by a nontheocratic state. The ordinary justification for secular penal controls is preservation of public order. The king's peace must not be disturbed, or, to put the matter in the language of our time, public security must be preserved. Individuals must be able to go about their lawful pursuits without fear of attack, plunder, or other harm. This is an interest

that only organized law enforcement can effectively safeguard. If individuals had to protect themselves by restricting their movements to avoid dangerous persons or neighborhoods, or by restricting their investments for fear of violent dispossession, or by employing personal bodyguards and armed private police, the economy would suffer, the body politic would be rent by conflict of private armies, and men would still walk in fear.

No such results impend from the commission of "morals offenses." One has only to stroll along certain streets in Amsterdam to see that prostitution may be permitted to flourish openly without impairing personal security, economic prosperity, or indeed the general moral tone of a most respected nation of the Western World. Tangible interests are not threatened by a neighbor's rash decision to marry two wives or (to vary the case for readers who may see this as economic suicide) by a lady's decision to be supported by two husbands, assuming that the arrangement is by agreement of all parties directly involved. An obscene show, the predilection of two deviate males for each other, or the marriage of first cousins— all these leave nonparticipants perfectly free to pursue their own goals without fear or obstacle. The same can be said of certain nonsexual offenses, which I shall accordingly treat in this paper as "morals offenses": cruelty to animals, desecration of a flag or other generally venerated symbol, and mistreatment of a human corpse. What the dominant lawmaking groups appear to be seeking by means of morals legislation is not security and freedom in their own affairs but restraint of conduct by others that is regarded as offensive.

Accordingly, Professor Louis Henkin has suggested[1] that morals legislation may contravene constitutional provisions designed to protect lib-

*From *Columbia Law Review,* Vol. 63, p. 669 (1963). Reprinted by permission of the author and the publisher.

erty, especially the liberty to do as one pleases without legal constraints based solely on religious beliefs. There is wisdom in his warning, and it is the purpose of this article to review in the light of that warning some of the Model Penal Code[2] sections that venture into the difficult area of morals legislation. Preliminarily, I offer some general observations on the point of view that necessarily governed the American Law Institute as a group of would-be lawmakers. We were sensitive, I hope, to the supreme value of individual liberty, but aware also that neither legislatures nor courts will soon accept a radical change in the boundary between permissible social controls and constitutionally protected nonconformity.

I. CONSIDERATIONS IN APPRAISING MORALS LEGISLATION

The first proposition I would emphasize is that a statute appearing to express nothing but religious or moral ideas is often defensible on secular grounds.[3] Perhaps an unrestricted flow of obscenity *will* encourage illicit sexuality or violent assaults on women, as some proponents of the ban believe. Perhaps polygamy and polyandry as well as adultery are condemnable on Benthamite grounds. Perhaps tolerance of homosexuality *will* undermine the courage and discipline of our citizen militia, notwithstanding contrary indications drawn from the history of ancient Greece. The evidence is hopelessly inconclusive. Professor Henkin and I may believe that those who legislate morals are minding other people's business, not their own, but the great majority of people believe that morals of "bad" people do, at least in the long run, threaten the security of the "good" people. Thus, *they* believe that it is their own business they are minding. And that belief is not demonstrably false, any more than it is demonstrably true. It is hard to deny people the right to legislate on the basis of their beliefs not demonstrably erroneous, especially if these beliefs are strongly held by a very large majority. The majority cannot be expected to abandon a credo and its associated sensitivities, however irrational, in deference to a minority's skepticism.

The argument of the preceding paragraph does not mean that all laws designed to enforce morality are acceptable or constitutionally valid if enough people entertain a baseless belief in their social utility. The point is rather that recognizing

irrational elements in the controversy over morals legislation, we ought to focus on other elements, about which rational debate and agreement are possible. For example, one can examine side effects of the effort to enforce morality by penal law. One can inquire whether enforcement will be so difficult that the offense will seldom be prosecuted and, therefore, risk of punishment will not in fact operate as a deterrent. One can ask whether the rare prosecutions for sexual derelictions are arbitrarily selected, or facilitate private blackmail or police discriminations more often than general compliance with legal norms. Are police forces, prosecution resources, and court time being wastefully diverted from the central insecurities of our metropolitan life—robbery, burglarly, rape, assault, and governmental corruption?

A second proposition that must be considered in appraising morals legislation is that citizens may legitimately demand of the state protection of their psychological as well as their physical integrity. No one challenges this when the protection takes the form of penal laws guarding against fear caused by threat or menace. This is probably because these are regarded as incipient physical attacks. Criminal libel laws are clearly designed to protect against psychic pain;[4] so also are disorderly conduct laws insofar as they ban loud noises, offensive odors, and tumultuous behavior disturbing the peace. In fact, laws against murder, rape, arson, robbery, burglary, and other violent felonies afford not so much protection against direct attack—that can be done only by self-defense or by having a policeman on hand at the scene of the crime—as psychological security and comfort stemming from the knowledge that the probabilities of attack are lessened by the prospect of punishment and, perhaps, from the knowledge that an attacker will be condignly treated by society.

If, then, penal law frequently or typically protects us from psychic aggression, there is basis for the popular expectation that it will protect us also from blasphemy against a cherished religion, outrage to patriotic sentiments, blatant pornography, open lewdness affronting our sensibilities in the area of sexual mores, or stinging aspersions against race or nationality. Psychiatrists might tell us that the insecurities stirred by these psychic aggressions are deeper and more acute than those involved in crimes of physical violence. Physical violence is, after all, a phenomenon that occurs largely in the domain of the ego; we can rationally measure the danger and its likelihood, and our countermeasures can be proportioned to the threat. But who can measure the dark turbulences of the unconscious when sex, race, religion or patriotism (that extension of father-reverence) is the concern?

If unanimity of strongly held moral views is approached in a community, the rebel puts himself, as it were, outside the society when he arraigns himself against those views. Society owes debt to martyrs, madmen, criminals, and professors who occasionally call into question its fundamental assumptions, but the community cannot be expected to make their first protests respectable or even tolerated by law. It is entirely understandable and in a sense proper that blasphemy should have been criminal in Puritan Massachusetts, and that cow slaughter in a Hindu state, hog-raising in a theocratic Jewish or Moslem state, or abortion in a ninety-nine per cent Catholic state should be criminal. I do not mean to suggest a particular percentage test of substantial unanimity. It is rather a matter of when an ancient and unquestioned tenet has become seriously debatable in a given community. This may happen when it is discovered that a substantial, although inarticulate, segment of the population has drifted away from the old belief. It may happen when smaller numbers of articulate opinion-makers launch an open attack on the old ethic. When this kind of a beach-head has been established in the hostile country of traditional faith, then, and only then, can we expect constitutional principles to restrain the fifty-one per cent majority from suppressing the public flouting of deeply held moral views.

Some may find in all this an encouragement or approval of excessive conservatism. Societies, it seems, are by this argument morally entitled to use force to hold back the development of new ways of thought. I do not mean it so. Rather, I see this tendency to enforce old moralities as an inherent characteristic of organized societies, and I refrain from making moral judgments on group behavior that I regard as inevitable. If I must make a moral judgment, it is in favor of the individual visionaries who are willing to pay the personal cost to challenge the old moral order.

There is a morality in some lawbreaking, even when we cannot condemn the law itself as immoral, for it enables conservative societies to begin the re-examination of even the most cherished principles.

Needless to say, recognizing the legitimacy of the demand for protection against psychic discomfort does not imply indiscriminate approval of laws intended to give such protection. Giving full recognition to that demand, we may still find that other considerations are the controlling ones. Can we satisfy the demand without impairing other vital interests? How can we protect religious feelings without "establishing" religion or impairing the free exercise of proselytizing faiths? How can we protect racial sensibilities without exacerbating race hatreds and erecting a government censorship of discussion?[5] How shall we prevent pain and disgust to many who are deeply offended by portrayal of sensuality without stultifying our artists and writers?

A third aspect of morals legislation that will enter into the calculations of the rational legislator is that some protection against offensive immorality may be achieved as a by-product of legislation that aims directly at something other than immorality. We may be uneasy about attempting to regulate private sexual behavior, but we will not be so hesitant in prohibiting the commercialization of vice. This is a lesser intrusion on freedom of choice in personal relations. It presents a more realistic target for police activity. And conceptually such regulation presents itself as a ban on a form of economic activity rather than a regulation of morals. It is not the least of the advantages of this approach that it preserves to some extent the communal disapproval of illicit sexuality, thus partially satisfying those who would really prefer outright regulation of morality. So also, we may be reluctant to penalize blasphemy or sacrilege, but feel compelled to penalize the mischievous or zealous blasphemer who purposely disrupts a religious meeting or procession with utterances designed to outrage the sensibilities of the group and thus provoke a riot.[6] Reasonable rules for the maintenance of public peace incidentally afford a measure of protection against offensive irreligion. Qualms about public "establishment" of religion must yield to the fact that the alternative would be to permit a kind of violent private interference with freedom to conduct religious ceremonies.

It remains to apply the foregoing analysis to selected provisions of the Model Penal Code.

II. THE MODEL PENAL CODE APPROACH

A. FLAGRANT AFFRONTS AND PENALIZATION OF PRIVATE IMMORALITY

The Model Penal Code does not penalize the sexual sins, fornication, adultery, sodomy or other illicit sexual activity not involving violence or imposition upon children, mental incompetents, wards, or other dependents. This decision to keep penal law out of the area of private sexual relations approaches Professor Henkin's suggestion that private morality be immune from secular regulation. The Comments in Tentative Draft No. 4 declared:

The Code does not attempt to use the power of the state to enforce purely moral or religious standards. We deem it inappropriate for the government to attempt to control behavior that has no substantial significance except as to the morality of the actor. Such matters are best left to religious, educational and other social influences. Apart from the question of constitutionality which might be raised against legislation avowedly commanding adherence to a particular religious or moral tenet, it must be recognized, as a practical matter, that in a heterogeneous community such as ours, different individuals and groups have widely divergent views of the seriousness of various moral derelictions.[7]

Although this passage expresses doubt as to the constitutionality of state regulation of morals, it does so in a context of "widely divergent views of the seriousness of various moral derelictions." Thus, it does not exclude the use of penal sanctions to protect a "moral consensus" against flagrant breach. The Kinsey studies and others are cited to show that sexual derelictions are widespread and that the incidence of sexual dereliction varies among social groups. The Comments proceed to discuss various secular goals that might be served by penalizing illicit sexual relations, such as promoting the stability of marriage, preventing illegitimacy and disease, or forestalling private violence against seducers. The

judgment is made that there is no reliable basis for believing that penal laws substantially contribute to these goals. Punishment of private vice is rejected on this ground as well as on grounds of difficulty of enforcement and the potential for blackmail and other abuse of rarely enforced criminal statutes.[8] The discussion with regard to homosexual offenses follows a similar course.[9]

The Code does, however, penalize "open lewdness"—"any lewd act which [the actor] ... knows is likely to be observed by others who would be affronted or alarmed."[10] The idea that "flagrant affront to commonly held notions of morality" might have to be differentiated from other sorts of immorality appeared in the first discussions of the Institute's policy on sexual offenses, in connection with a draft that would have penalized "open and notorious" illicit relations.[11] Eventually, however, the decision was against establishing a penal offense in which guilt would depend on the level of gossip to which the moral transgression gave rise. Guilt under the open lewdness section turns on the likelihood that the lewd act itself will be observed by others who would be affronted.

Since the Code accepts the propriety of penalizing behavior that affects others only in flagrantly affronting commonly held notions of morality, the question arises whether such repression of offensive immorality need be confined to acts done in public where others may observe and be outraged. People may be deeply offended upon learning of private debauchery. The Code seems ready at times to protect against this type of "psychological assault," at other times not. Section 250.10 penalizes mistreatment of a corpse "in a way that [the actor] ... knows would outrage ordinary family sensibilities," although the actor may have taken every precaution for secrecy. Section 250.11 penalizes cruel treatment of an animal in private as well as in public. On the other hand, desecration of the national flag or other object of public veneration, an offense under section 250.9, is not committed unless others are likely to "observe or discover." And solicitation of deviate sexual relations is penalized only when the actor "loiters in or near any public place" for the purpose of such solicitation.[12] The Comments make it clear that the target of this legislation is not private immorality but a kind of public "nuisance" caused by congregation of homosexuals offensively flaunting their deviance from general norms of behavior.[13]

As I search for the principle of discrimination between the morals offenses made punishable only when committed openly and those punishable even when committed in secrecy, I find nothing but differences in the intensity of the aversion with which the different kinds of behavior are regarded. It was the intuition of the draftsman and his fellow lawmakers in the Institute that disrespectful behavior to a corpse and cruelty to animals were more intolerable affronts to ordinary feelings than disrespectful behavior to a flag. Therefore, in the former cases, but not the latter, we overcame our general reluctance to extend penal controls of immorality to private behavior that disquiets people solely because they learn that things of this sort are going on.

Other possible explanations do not satisfy me. For example, it explains nothing to say that we wish to "protect" the corpse or the mistreated dog, but not the flag itself. The legislation on its face seeks to deter mistreatment of all three. All three cases involve interests beyond, and merely represented by, the thing that is immediately "protected." It is not the mistreated dog who is the ultimate object of concern; his owner is entirely free to kill him (though not "cruelly") without interference from other dog owners. Our concern is for the feelings of other human beings, a large proportion of whom, although accustomed to the slaughter of animals for food, readily identify themselves with a tortured dog or horse and respond with great sensitivity to its sufferings. The desire to protect a corpse from degradation is not a deference to this remnant of a human being—the dead have no legal rights and no legislative lobby—but a protection of the feelings of the living. So also in the case of the flag, our concern is not for the bright bit of cloth but for what it symbolizes, a cluster of patriotic emotions. I submit that legislative tolerance for private flag desecration is explicable by the greater difficulty an ordinary man has in identifying with a country and all else that a flag symbolizes as compared with the ease in identifying with a corpse or a warm-blooded domestic animal. This is only an elaborate way of saying that he does not feel the first desecration as keenly as the others. Perhaps also, in the case of the flag, an element of tolerance is present for the right of political dissent when it goes no further than private disrespect for the symbol of authority.[14]

A penal code's treatment of private homosexual relations presents the crucial test of a legislator's views on whether a state may legimately protect people from "psychological assault" by repressing not merely overt affront to consensus morals but also the most secret violation of that moral code. As is often wise in legislative affairs, the Model Penal Code avoids a clear issue of principle. The decision against penalizing deviate sexuality is rested not merely on the idea of immunity from regulation of private morality, but on a consideration of practical difficulties and evils in attempting to use the penal law in this way.[15] The Comments note that existing laws dealing with homosexual relations are nullified in practice, except in cases of violence, corruption of children, or public solicitation. Capricious selection of a few cases for prosecution, among millions of infractions, is unfair and chiefly benefits extortioners and seekers of private vengeance. The existence of the criminal law prevents some deviates from seeking psychiatric aid. Furthermore, the pursuit of homosexuals involves policemen in degrading entrapment practices, and diverts attention and effort that could be employed more usefully against the crimes of violent aggression, fraud, and government corruption, which are the overriding concerns of our metropolitan civilization.

If state legislators are not persuaded by such arguments to repeal the laws against private deviate sexual relations among adults, the constitutional issue will ultimately have to be faced by the courts. When that time comes, one of the important questions will be whether homosexuality is in fact the subject of a "consensus." If not, that is, if a substantial body of public opinion regards homosexuals' private activity with indifference, or if homosexuals succeed in securing recognition as a considerable minority having otherwise "respectable" status, this issue of private morality may soon be held to be beyond resolution by vote of fifty-one per cent of the legislators.[16] As to the status of homosexuality in this country, it is significant that the Supreme Court has reversed an obscenity conviction involving a magazine that was avowedly published by, for, and about homosexuals and that carried on a ceaseless campaign against the repressive laws.[17] The much smaller group of American polygamists have yet to break out of the class of idiosyncratic heretic-martyrs[18] by bidding for public approval in the same group-conscious way.

B. THE OBSCENITY PROVISIONS

The obscenity provisions of the Model Penal Code best illustrate the Code's preference for an oblique approach to morals offenses, that is, the effort to express the moral impulses of the community in a penal prohibition that is nevertheless pointed at and limited to something else than sin. In this case the target is not the "sin of obscenity," but primarily a disapproved form of economic activity—commercial exploitation of the widespread weakness for titillation by pornography. This is apparent not only from the narrow definition of "obscene" in section 251.4 of the Code, but even more from the narrow definition of the forbidden behavior; only sale, advertising, or public exhibition are forbidden, and noncommercial dissemination within a restricted circle of personal associates is expressly exempt.[19]

Section 251.4 defines obscenity as material whose "predominant appeal is to prurient interest. . . ."[20] The emphasis is on the "appeal" of the material, rather than on its "effect," an emphasis designed explicitly to reject prevailing definitions of obscenity that stress the "effect."[21] This effect is traditionally identified as a tendency to cause "sexually impure and lustful thoughts" or to "corrupt or deprave."[22] The Comments on section 251.4 take the position that repression of sexual thoughts and desires is not a practicable or legitimate legislative goal. Too many instigations to sexual desire exist in a society like ours, which approves much eroticism in literature, movies, and advertising, to suppose that any conceivable repression of pornography would substantially diminish the volume of such impulses. Moreover, "thoughts and desires not manifested in overt antisocial behavior are generally regarded as the exclusive concern of the individual and his spiritual advisors."[23] The Comments, rejecting also the test of tendency to corrupt or deprave, point out that corruption or depravity are attributes of character inappropriate for secular punishment when they do not lead to misconduct, and there is a paucity of evidence linking obscenity to misbehavior.[24]

The meretricious "appeal" of a book or picture is essentially a question of the attractiveness of the merchandise from a certain point of view: what makes it sell. Thus, the prohibition of obscenity takes on an aspect of regulation of unfair business or competitive practices. Just as merchants may be prohibited from selling their wares by appeal to the public's weakness for gambling,[25] so they may be restrained from purveying books, movies, or other commercial exhibition by exploiting the well-nigh universal weakness for a look behind the curtain of modesty. This same philosophy of obscenity control is evidenced by the Code provision outlawing advertising appeals that attempt to sell material "whether or not obscene, by representing or suggesting that it is obscene."[26] Moreover, the requirement under section 251.4 that the material go "substantially beyond customary limits of candor" serves to exclude from criminality the sorts of appeal to eroticism that, being prevalent, can hardly give a particular purveyor a commercial advantage.

It is important to recognize that material may predominantly "appeal" to prurient interest notwithstanding that ordinary adults may actually respond to the material with feelings of aversion or disgust. Section 251.4 explicitly encompasses material dealing with excretory functions as well as sex, which the customer is likely to find *both* repugnant and "shameful" and yet attractive in a morbid, compelling way. Not recognizing that material may be repellent and appealing at the same time, two distinguished commentators on the Code's obscenity provisions have criticized the "appeal" formula, asserting that "hard core pornography," concededly the main category we are trying to repress, has no appeal for "ordinary adults," who instead would be merely repelled by the material.[27] Common experience suggests the contrary. It is well known that policemen, lawyers, and judges involved in obscenity cases not infrequently regale their fellows with viewings of the criminal material. Moreover, a poll conducted by this author among his fellow law professors—"mature" and, for the present purposes, "ordinary" adults—evoked uniformly affirmative answers to the following question: "Would you look inside a book that you had been certainly informed has grossly obscene hard-core pornography if you were absolutely sure that no one else would ever learn that you had looked?"

It is not an answer to this bit of amateur sociological research to say that people would look "out of curiosity." It is precisely such shameful curiosity to which "appeal" is made by the obscene, as the word "appeal" is used in section 251.4.

Lockhart and McClure, the two commentators referred to above, prefer a "variable obscenity" concept over the Institute's "constant obscenity" concept. Under the "constant obscenity" concept, material is normally judged by reference to "ordinary adults."[28] The "variable obscenity" concept always takes account of the nature of the comtemplated audience; material would be obscene if it is "primarily directed to an audience of the sexually immature for the purpose of satisfying their craving for erotic fantasy."[29] The preference for "variable obscenity" rests not only on the mistaken view that hard-core pornography does not appeal to ordinary adults, but also on the ground that this concept facilitates the accomplishment of several ancillary legislative goals, namely, exempting transactions in "obscene" materials by persons with scholarly, scientific, or other legitimate interests in the obscene and prohibiting the advertising of material "not intrinsically pornographic as if it were hard-core pornography."[30] The Code accomplishes these results by explicit exemption for justifiable transactions in the obscene and by specific prohibition of suggestive advertising.[31] This still seems to me the better way to draft a criminal statute.

The Code's exemption for justifiable dealing in obscene material provides a workable criterion of public gain in permitting defined categories of transactions. It requires no analysis of the psyche of customers to see whether they are sexually immature or given to unusual craving for erotic fantasy. It makes no impractical demand on the sophistication of policemen, magistrates, customs officers, or jurymen. The semantics of the variable obscenity concept assumes without basis that the Kinsey researchers were immune to the prurient appeal of the materials with which they worked.[32] Would it not be a safe psychiatric guess that some persons are drawn into research of this sort precisely to satisfy in a socially approved way the craving that Lockhart and McClure deplore? In any event, it seems a confusing distortion of language to say that a pornographic picture is not obscene as respects the blasé [sexually mature?] shopkeeper who stocks it, the policeman who confiscates it, or the Model Penal Code reporter who appraises it.

As for the prohibition against suggestive advertising, this is certainly handled more effectively by explicitly declaring the advertisement criminal without regard to the "obscene" character of the material advertised than by the circumlocution that an advertisement is itself to be regarded as obscene if it appeals to the cravings of the sexually immature. That kind of test will prove more than a little troublesome for the advertising departments of some respectable literary journals.

If the gist of section 251.4 is, as suggested above, commercial exploitation of the weakness for obscenity, the question arises whether the definition of the offense should not be formulated in terms of "pandering to an interest in obscenity," that is, "exploiting such an interest primarily for pecuniary gain. . . ."[33] This proposal, made by Professor Henry Hart, a member of the Criminal Law Advisory Committee, was rejected because of the indefiniteness of "exploiting . . . primarily for pecuniary gain," and because it would clearly authorize a bookseller, for example, to procure any sort of hard-core pornography upon the unsolicited order of a customer. "Exploiting . . . primarily for pecuniary gain" is not a formula apt for guiding either judicial interpretation or merchants' behavior. It is not clear what the prosecution would have to prove beyond sale of the objectionable item. Would advertising or an excessive profit convert sale into "exploitation"? Would the formula leave a bookseller free to enjoy a gradually expanding trade in obscenity so long as he kept his merchandise discreetly under the counter and let word-of-mouth publicize the availability of his tidbits? Despite these difficulties, it may well be that the Code section on obscenity has a constitutional infirmity of the sort that concerned Professor Henkin insofar as the section restricts the freedom of an adult to buy, and thus to read, whatever he pleases. This problem might be met by framing an appropriate exemption for such transactions to be added to those now set forth in subsection (3).

The rejection of the Hart "pandering" formulation highlights another aspect of section 251.4, namely, its applicability to a class of completely noncommercial transactions that could not conceivably be regarded as "pandering." This ban on certain noncommercial disseminations results from the fact that subsection (2) forbids every dissemination except those exempted by subsection (3), and subsection (3) exempts noncommercial dissemination only if it is limited to "personal associates of the actor." Thus, a general distribution or exhibition of obscenity is prohibited even though no one is making money from it: a zealot for sex education may not give away pamphlets at the schoolyard gates containing illustrations of people engaged in erotic practices; a rich homosexual may not use a billboard on Times Square to promulgate to the general populace the techniques and pleasures of sodomy. Plainly, this is not the economic regulation to which I have previously tried to assimilate the Code's anti-obscenity regulations. But equally, it is not merely sin-control of the sort that evoked Professor Henkin's constitutional doubts. Instead, the community is merely saying: "Sin, if you must, in private. Do not flaunt your immoralities where they will grieve and shock others. If we do not impose our morals upon you, neither must you impose yours upon us, undermining the restraints we seek to cultivate through family, church, and school." The interest being protected is not, directly or exclusively, the souls of those who might be depraved or corrupted by the obscenity, but the right of parents to shape the moral notions of their children, and the right of the general public not to be subjected to violent psychological affront.

C. PROSTITUTION

The prostitution provisions of the Model Penal Code, like the obscenity provisions, reflect the policy of penalizing not sin but commercial exploitation of a human weakness, or serious affront to public sensibilities. The salient features of section 251.2 are as follows. Sexual activity is penalized only when carried on as a business or for hire. The section covers any form of sexual gratification. "Promoters" of prostitution—that is, procurers, pimps, keepers of houses of prostitution—are penalized more severely than the prostitutes. The patron of the prostitute is subject to prosecution for a "violation" only, that is, he may be fined but not jailed, and the offense is, by definition, not a "crime." Dependents of a prostitute are not declared to be criminals by virtue of the fact that they live off the proceeds of prostitution, as under many present laws, but the circumstance

of being supported by a prostitute is made presumptive evidence that the person supported is engaged in pimping or some other form of commercial exploitation of prostitution.

The main issues in the evolution of the Institute's position on prostitution were, on the one hand, whether to penalize all "promiscuous" intercourse even if not for hire or, on the other hand, whether even intercourse for hire should be immune from prosecution when it is carried on discreetly out of the public view. Those who favored extending the criminal law to promiscuous noncommercial sexuality did so on secular, not moral, grounds. They pointed to the danger that promiscuous amateurs would be carriers of venereal disease, and they argued that law enforcement against hire-prostitution would be facilitated if the law, proceeding on the basis that most promiscuity is accompanied by hire, dispensed with proof of actual hire. Others doubted the utility or propriety of the law's intervening in private sexual relations on the basis of a vague and moralistic judgment of promiscuity; and these doubts prevailed.

It was more strenuously contended that the Model Penal Code should, following the English pattern, penalize prostitution only when it manifests itself in annoying public solicitation.[34] This position was defeated principally by the argument that "call-houses" were an important cog in the financial machine of the underworld, linked to narcotics peddling and other "rackets." I find more interesting and persuasive the parallel between this problem of the discreet exploitation of sex and the suggestion in the obscenity and context that discreet sale of obscene books to patrons who request them might not constitute "pandering." Both distinctions present the difficulty of drawing an administrable line between aggressive merchandising and passive willingness to make profits by catering to a taste for spicy life or literature.

Other provisions of section 251.2 also demonstrate its basic orientation against undesirable commerce rather than sin. The grading of offenses under the section ranges from the classification of the patron's guilt as a noncriminal "violation," through the "petty misdemeanor" classification (thirty-day maximum imprisonment) for the prostitute herself, and the "misdemeanor" classification (one year maximum) for minor participation in the promotion of prostitution, to the "third degree felony" classification (five year maximum) for owning or managing a prostitution business, bringing about an association between a prostitute and a house of prostitution, or recruiting persons into prostitution. Clearly, from the point of view of the sinfulness of illicit sexual relations, the patron's guilt is equal to that of the prostitute, but it is the seller rather than the sinful customer who is labelled a criminal. And the higher the rank in the selling organization, the graver the penalty—a significant departure from the normal assimilation of accessorial guilt to that of the principal offender. This emphasis on the businessman in sex is underscored by the fact that the higher penalties applicable to him do not depend on whether he is the instigator of the relationship; if a prostitute persuades someone to manage her illicit business or to accept her in a house of prostitution, it is he, not she, who incurs the higher penalty.

In one respect, the Code's provisions against illicit sexual activity depart from the regulation of commerce. Section 251.3 makes it a petty misdemeanor to loiter "in or near any public place for the purpose of soliciting or being solicited to engage in deviate sexual relations." This extension is explained as follows in the accompanying status note:

[T]he main objective is to suppress the open flouting of prevailing moral standards as a sort of nuisance in public thoroughfares and parks. In the case of females, suppression of professionals is likely to accomplish that objective. In the case of males, there is a greater likelihood that non-professional homosexuals will congregate and behave in a manner grossly offensive to other users of public facilities.[35]

The situation is analogous to that of noncommercial dissemination of obscenity by billboard publication or indiscriminate gratuitous distribution of pornography. In a community in which assemblages of "available" women evoke the same degree of violent resentment as assemblages of homosexuals, it would be consistent with this analysis to make public loitering to solicit illicit heterosexual relations an offense regardless of proof of "hire." On the other hand, the legislator may well decide that even in such a community it is not worth risking the possibility of arbitrary

police intrusion into dance halls, taverns, corner drug stores, and similar resorts of unattached adolescents, on suspicion that some of the girls are promiscuous, though not prostitutes in the hire sense . . .

NOTES

1. See Henkin, *Morals and the Constitution: The Sin of Obscenity,* 63 Colum. L. Rev. 391 (1963), to which the present article is a companion piece. Controversy on the role of the state in the enforcement of morals has recently reached a new pitch of intensity. See Hart, *Law, Liberty, and Morality* (1963); Devlin, *The Enforcement of Morals* (1959); Devlin, *Law, Democracy, and Morality,* 110 U. Pa. L. Rev. 635 (1962). I shall not attempt to judge this debate, cf. Rostow, The Sovereign Prerogative 45–80 (1962), and I leave it to others to align the present essay with one or another of the sides. The recent controversy traverses much the same ground as was surveyed in the nineteenth century. See Mill *On Liberty* (1859); Stephen, *Liberty, Equality, Fraternity* (1873).

2. The Model Penal Code is hereinafter cited as MPC. Unless otherwise indicated, all citations are to the 1962 Official Draft.

3. See McGowan v. Maryland, 366 U.S. 420 (1961). The Supreme Court upheld the constitutionality of a law requiring business establishments to close on Sunday, on the ground that such regulation serves the secular goal of providing a common day of rest and recreation, notwithstanding that the statute proscribed profanation of "the Lord's day."

4. The Model Penal Code does not make libel a criminal offense. But this decision rests upon a judgment that the penal law is not a useful or safe instrument for repressing defamation; by no means is it suggested that the hurt experienced by one who is libelled is an inappropriate concern of government. See MPC § 250.7, comment 2 (Tent. Draft No. 13, 1961).

5. See MPC § 250.7 & comments 1–4 (Tent. Draft No. 13, 1961) ("Fomenting Group Hatred"). The section was not included in the Official Draft of 1962.

6. See MPC §§ 250.8, 250.3 & comment (Tent. Draft No. 13, 1961).

7. MPC § 207.1, comment at 207 (Tent. Draft No. 4, 1955).

8. MPC § 207.1, comment at 205–10 (Tent. Draft No. 4, 1955).

9. MPC § 207.5, comment at 278–79 (Tent. Draft NO. 4, 1955). "No harm to the secular interests of the community is involved in atypical sex practice in private between consenting adult partners. This area of private morals is the distinctive concern of spiritual authorities. . . . [T]here is the fundamental question of the protection to which every individual is entitled against state interference in his personal affairs when he is not hurting others." MPC § 207.5, comment at 277–78 (Tent. Draft No. 4, 1955).

10. MPC § 251.1; *cf.* MPC § 213.5, which penalizes exposure of the genitals for the purpose of arousing or gratifying sexual desire in circumstances likely to cause affront or alarm. This later offense carries a heavier penalty than open lewdness, "since the behavior amounts to, or at least is often taken as, threatening sexual aggression." MPC § 213.4 & 251.1, comment at 82 (Tent. Draft No. 13, 1961).

11. MPC § 207.1 & comment at 209 (Tent. Draft No. 4, 1955).

12. MPC § 251.3; see text accompanying note 35 *infra.*

13. MPC § 251.3, status note at 237.

14. Not all legislatures are so restrained. See, e.g., Pa. Stat. Ann. tit. 18, § 4211 (1945) ("publicly or privately muti-

lates, defaces, defiles or tramples upon, or casts contempt either by words or act upon, any such flag"). Query as to the constitutionality of this effort to repress a private expression of political disaffection.

15. MPC § 207.5, comment 278–79 (Tent. Draft No. 4, 1955).

16. *Cf.* Robinson v. California, 371 U.S. 905 (1962) (invalidating statute that penalized addiction to narcotics).

17. One, Inc. v. Oleson, 355 U.S. 371 (1958), *reversing* 241 F.2d 772 (9th Cir. 1957). On the "homosexual community" see Helmer, *New York's "Middle-class" Homosexuals,* Harper's, March 1963, p. 85 (evidencing current nonshocked attitude toward this minority group).

18. See Cleveland v. United States, 329 U.S. 14 (1946); Reynolds v. United States, 98 U.S. 145 (1878).

19. MPC § 251.4(2), (3).

20. (1) *Obscene Defined.* Material is obscene if, considered as a whole, its predominant appeal is to prurient interest, that is, a shameful or morbid interest, in nudity, sex or excretion, and if in addition it goes substantially beyond customary limits of candor in describing or representing such matters. Predominant appeal shall be judged with reference to ordinary adults unless it appears from the character of the material or the circumstances of its dissemination to be designed for children or other specially susceptible audience. . . . MPC § 251.4(1).

21. See MPC § 207.10, comment 6 at 19, 29 (Tent. Draft No. 6, 1957) (§ 207.10 was subsequently renumbered § 251.4).

22. See MPC § 207.10, comment 6 at 19 n.21, 21 (Tent. Draft No. 6, 1957).

23. MPC § 207.10, comment 6 at 20 (Tent. Draft No. 6, 1957).

24. MPC § 207.10, comment 6 at 22–28 (Tent. Draft No. 6, 1957).

25. See FTC v. R. F. Keppel & Brother, 291 U.S. 304 (1934) (sale of penny candy by device of awarding prizes to lucky purchasers of some pieces). The opinion of the Court declares that Section 5 of the Federal Trade Commission Act, proscribing unfair methods of competition, "does not authorize business men," *ibid.,* p. 313, but that the Commission may prevent exploitation of consumers by the enticement of gambling, as well as imposition upon competitors by use of a morally obnoxious selling appeal.

26. MPC § 251.4(2)(e). Equivalent provisions appear in some state laws. E.g., N.Y. Pen. Law § 1141. There is some doubt whether federal obscenity laws reach such advertising. See Manual Enterprises, Inc. v. Day, 370 U.S. 478. 491 (1962). *But see* United States v. Hornick, 229 F.2d 120, 121 (3d Cir. 1956).

27. See Lockhart & McClure, *Censorship of Obscenity: The Developing Constitutional Standards,* 45 Minn. L. Rev. 72–73 (1960).

28. The Model Penal Code employs the "variable obscenity" concept in part, since § 251.4(1) provides that "appeal" shall be judged with reference to the susceptibilities of children or other specially susceptible audience when it appears that the material is designed for or directed to such an audience.

29. Lockhart & McClure, *supra* note 27, at 79.

30. *Ibid.*

31. MPC § 251.4(2)(e), (3)(a).

32. *Cf.* United States v. 31 Photographs, 156 F. Supp. 350 (S.D.N.Y. 1957), in which, absent a statutory exemption, the court was compelled to rely on variable obscenity in order to sanction import of obscene pictures by the [Kinsey] Institute for Sex Research.

33. MPC § 207.10(1) (Tent. Draft No. 6, 1957) (alternative).

34. See Street Offenses Act, 1959, 7 & 8 Eliz. 2, c. 57.

C O H E N   V.   C A L I F O R N I A

United States Supreme Court, 1971*

OPINION OF THE COURT

Mr. Justice Harlan delivered the opinion of the Court.

This case may seem at first blush too inconsequential to find its way into our books, but the issue it presents is of no small constitutional significance.

*408 U.S. 15 (1971). Some footnotes omitted.

Appellant Paul Robert Cohen was convicted in the Los Angeles Municipal Court of violating that part of California Penal Code § 415 which prohibits "maliciously and willfully disturb[ing] the peace or quiet of any neighborhood or person . . . by . . . offensive conduct . . . "[1] He was given 30 days' imprisonment. The facts upon which his conviction rests are detailed in the opinion of the Court of Appeal of California, Second Appellate District, as follows:

"On April 26, 1968, the defendant was observed in the Los Angeles County Courthouse in the corridor outside of division 20 of the municipal court wearing a jacket bearing the words 'Fuck the Draft' which were plainly visible. There were women and children present in the corridor. The defendant was arrested. The defendant testified that he wore the jacket knowing that the words were on the jacket as a means of informing the public of the depth of his feelings against the Vietnam War and the draft.

"The defendant did not engage in, nor threaten to engage in, nor did anyone as the result of his conduct in fact commit or threaten to commit any act of violence. The defendant did not make any loud or unusual noise, nor was there any evidence that he uttered any sound prior to his arrest."*

In affirming the conviction the Court of Appeal held that "offensive conduct" means "behavior which has a tendency to provoke *others* to acts of violence or to in turn disturb the peace," and that the State had proved this element because, on the facts of this case, "[i]t was certainly reasonably foreseeable that such conduct might cause others to rise up to commit a violent act against the person of the defendant or attempt to forceably remove his jacket."* The California Supreme Court declined review by a divided vote. We brought the case here, postponing the consideration of the question of our jurisdiction over this appeal to a hearing of the case on the merits.* We now reverse.

I

In order to lay hands on the precise issue which this case involves, it is useful first to canvass various matters which this record does *not* present.

The conviction quite clearly rests upon the asserted offensiveness of the *words* Cohen used to convey his message to the public. The only "conduct" which the State sought to punish is the fact of communication. Thus, we deal here with a conviction resting solely upon "speech",* not upon any separately identifiable conduct which allegedly was intended by Cohen to be perceived by others as expressive of particular views but which, on its face, does not necessarily convey any message and hence arguably could be regulated without effectively repressing Cohen's ability to express himself.* Further, the State certainly lacks power to punish Cohen for the underlying content of the message the inscription conveyed. At least so long as there is no showing of an intent to incite disobedience to or disruption of the draft, Cohen could not, consistently with the First and Fourteenth Amendments, be punished for asserting the evident position on the inutility or immorality of the draft his jacket reflected.*

Appellant's conviction, then, rests squarely upon his exercise of the "freedom of speech" protected from arbitrary governmental interference by the Constitution and can be justified, if at all, only as a valid regulation of the manner in which he exercised that freedom, not as a permissible prohibition on the substantive message it conveys. This does not end the inquiry, of course, for the First and Fourteenth Amendments have never been thought to give absolute protection to every individual to speak whenever or wherever he pleases, or to use any form of address in any circumstances that he chooses. In this vein, too, however, we think it important to note that several issues typically associated with such problems are not presented here.

In the first place, Cohen was tried under a statute applicable throughout the entire State. Any attempt to support this conviction on the ground that the statute seeks to preserve an appropriately decorous atmosphere in the courthouse where Cohen was arrested must fail in the absence of any language in the statute that would have put appellant on notice that certain kinds of otherwise permissible speech or conduct would nevertheless, under California law, not be tolerated in certain places.* No fair reading of the phrase "offensive conduct" can be said sufficiently to inform the ordinary person that distinctions between certain locations are thereby created.[2]

In the second place, as it comes to us, this case cannot be said to fall within those relatively few categories of instances where prior decisions have established the power of government to deal more comprehensively with certain forms of individual expression simply upon a showing that such a form was employed. This is not, for example, an obscenity case. Whatever else may be necessary to give rise to the States' broader power to prohibit obscene expression, such expression must be, in some significant way, erotic.* It cannot plausibly be maintained that this vulgar allusion to the Selective Service System would conjure up such psychic stimulation in anyone likely to be confronted with Cohen's crudely defaced jacket.

This Court has also held that the States are free to ban the simple use, without a demonstration of additional justifying circumstances, of so-called "fighting words," those personally abusive epithets which, when addressed to the ordinary citizen, are, as a matter of common knowledge, inherently likely to provoke violent reaction.* While the four-letter word displayed by Cohen in relation to the draft is not uncommonly employed in a personally provocative fashion, in this instance it was clearly not "directed to the person of the hearer."* No individual actually or likely to be present could reasonably have regarded the words on appellant's jacket as a direct personal insult. Nor do we have here an instance of the exercise of the State's police power to prevent a speaker from intentionally provok-

*Citation omitted [Eds.]

ing a given group to hostile reaction.* There is, as noted above, no showing that anyone who saw Cohen was in fact violently aroused or that appellant intended such a result.

Finally, in arguments before this Court much has been made of the claim that Cohen's distasteful mode of expression was thrust upon unwilling or unsuspecting viewers, and that the State might therefore legitimately act as it did in order to protect the sensitive from otherwise unavoidable exposure to appellant's crude form of protest. Of course, the mere presumed presence of unwitting listeners or viewers does not serve automatically to justify curtailing all speech capable of giving offense.* While this Court has recognized that government may properly act in many situations to prohibit intrusion into the privacy of the home of unwelcome views and ideas which cannot be totally banned from the public dialogue,* we have at the same time consistently stressed that "we are often 'captives' outside the sanctuary of the home and subject to objectionable speech."* The ability of government, consonant with the Constitution, to shut off discourse solely to protect others from hearing it is, in other words, dependent upon a showing that substantial privacy interests are being invaded in an essentially intolerable manner. Any broader view of this authority would effectively empower a majority to silence dissidents simply as a matter of personal predilections.

In this regard, persons confronted with Cohen's jacket were in a quite different posture than, say, those subjected to the raucous emissions of sound trucks blaring outside their residences. Those in the Los Angeles courthouse could effectively avoid further bombardment of their sensibilities simply by averting their eyes. And, while it may be that one has a more substantial claim to a recognizable privacy interest when walking through a courthouse corridor than, for example, strolling through Central Park, surely it is nothing like the interest in being free from unwanted expression in the confines of one's own home.* Given the subtlety and complexity of the factors involved, if Cohen's "speech" was otherwise entitled to constitutional protection, we do not think the fact that some unwilling "listeners" in a public building may have been briefly exposed to it can serve to justify this breach of the peace conviction where, as here, there was no evidence that persons powerless to avoid appellant's conduct did in fact object to it, and where that portion of the statute upon which Cohen's conviction rests evinces no concern, either on its face or as construed by the California courts, with the special plight of the captive auditor, but, instead, indiscriminately sweeps within its prohibitions all "offensive conduct" that disturbs "any neighborhood or person."*

*Citation omitted [Eds.]

II

Against this background, the issue flushed by this case stands out in bold relief. It is whether California can excise, as "offensive conduct," one particular scurrilous epithet from the public discourse, either upon the theory of the court below that its use is inherently likely to cause violent reaction or upon a more general assertion that the States, acting as guardians of public morality, may properly remove this offensive word from the public vocabulary.

The rationale of the California court is plainly untenable. At most it reflects an "undifferentiated fear or apprehension of disturbance [which] is not enough to overcome the right to freedom of expression."* We have been shown no evidence that substantial numbers of citizens are standing ready to strike out physically at whoever may assault their sensibilities with execrations like that uttered by Cohen. There may be some persons about with such lawless and violent proclivities, but that is an insufficient base upon which to erect, consistently with constitutional values, a governmental power to force persons who wish to ventilate their dissident views into avoiding particular forms of expression. The argument amounts to little more than the self-defeating proposition that to avoid physical censorship of one who has not sought to provoke such a response by a hypothetical coterie of the violent and lawless, the States may more appropriately effectuate that censorship themselves.*

Admittedly, it is not so obvious that the First and Fourteenth Amendments must be taken to disable the States from punishing public utterance of this unseemly expletive in order to maintain what they regard as a suitable level of discourse within the body politic. We think, however, that examination and reflection will reveal the shortcomings of a contrary viewpoint.

At the outset, we cannot overemphasize that, in our judgment, most situations where the State has a justifiable interest in regulating speech will fall within one or more of the various established exceptions, discussed above but not applicable here, to the usual rule that governmental bodies may not prescribe the form or content of individual expression. Equally important to our conclusion is the constitutional backdrop against which our decision must be made. The constitutional right of free expression is powerful medicine in a society as diverse and populous as ours. It is designed and intended to remove governmental restraints from the arena of public discussion, putting the decision as to what views shall be voiced largely into the hands of each of us, in the hope that use of such freedom will ultimately produce a more capable citizenry and more perfect polity and in the belief that no other approach would comport with the premise of individual dignity and choice upon which our political system rests.*

To many, the immediate consequence of this freedom may often appear to be only verbal tumult, discord, and even offensive utterance. These are, however, within established limits, in truth necessary side effects of the broader enduring values which the process of open debate permits us to achieve. That the air may at times seem filled with verbal cacophony is, in this sense not a sign of weakness but of strength. We cannot lose sight of the fact that, in what otherwise might seem a trifling and annoying instance of individual distasteful abuse of a privilege, these fundamental societal values are truly implicated. That is why "[w]holly neutral futilities . . . come under the protection of free speech as fully as do Keats' poems or Donne's sermons," Winters v New York, (1948)* (Frankfurter, J., dissenting), and why "so long as the means are peaceful, the communication need not meet standards of acceptability," Organization for a Better Austin v Keefe, (1971).*

Against this perception of the constitutional policies involved, we discern certain more particularized considerations that peculiarly call for reversal of this conviction. First, the principle contended for by the State seems inherently boundless. How is one to distinguish this from any other offensive word? Surely the State has no right to cleanse public debate to the point where it is grammatically palatable to the most squeamish among us. Yet no readily ascertainable general principle exists for stopping short of that result were we to affirm the judgment below. For, while the particular four-letter word being litigated here is perhaps more distasteful than most others of its genre, it is nevertheless often true that one man's vulgarity is another's lyric. Indeed, we think it is largely because governmental officials cannot make principled distinctions in this area that the Constitution leaves matters of taste and style so largely to the individual.

Additionally, we cannot overlook the fact, because it is well illustrated by the episode involved here, that much linguistic expression serves a dual communicative function: it conveys not only ideas capable of relatively precise, detached explication, but otherwise inexpressible emotions as well. In fact, words are often chosen as much for their emotive as their cognitive force. We cannot sanction the view that the Constitution, while solicitous of the cognitive content of individual speech, has little or no regard for that emotive function which, practically speaking, may often be the more important element of the overall message sought to be communicated. Indeed, as Mr. Justice Frankfurter has said, "[o]ne of the prerogatives of American citizenship is the right to criticize public men and measures—and that means not only informed and responsible criticism but the freedom to speak foolishly and without moderation." Baumgartner v United States, (1944).*

*Citation omitted [Eds.]

Finally, and in the same vein, we cannot indulge the facile assumption that one can forbid particular words without also running a substantial risk of suppressing ideas in the process. Indeed, governments might soon seize upon the censorship of particular words as a convenient guise for banning the expression of unpopular views. We have been able, as noted above, to discern little social benefit that might result from running the risk of opening the door to such grave results.

It is, in sum, our judgment that, absent a more particularized and compelling reason for its actions, the State may not, consistently with the First and Fourteenth Amendments, make the simple public display here involved of this single four-letter expletive a criminal offense. Because that is the only arguably sustainable rationale for the conviction here at issue, the judgment below must be reversed.

SEPARATE OPINION

Mr. Justice **Blackmun,** with whom The **Chief Justice** and Mr. Justice **Black** join.

I dissent, and I do so for two reasons:

1. Cohen's absurd and immature antic, in my view, was mainly conduct and little speech.* The California Court of Appeal appears so to have described it,* and I cannot characterize it otherwise. Further, the case appears to me to be well within the sphere of Chaplinsky v New Hampshire,* where Mr. Justice Murphy, a known champion of First Amendment freedoms, wrote for a unanimous bench. As a consequence, this Court's agonizing First Amendment values seems misplaced and unnecessary.

2. I am not at all certain that the California Court of Appeal's construction of § 415 is now the authoritative California construction . . .

NOTES

1. The statute provides in full:
"Every person who maliciously and willfully disturbs the peace or quiet of any neighborhood or person, by loud or unusual noise, or by tumultuous or offensive conduct, or threatening, traducing, quarreling, challenging to fight, or fighting, or who, on the public streets of any unincorporated town, or upon the public highways in such unincorporated town, run any horse race, either for a wager or for amusement, or fire any gun or pistol in such unincorporated town, or use any vulgar language within the presence or hearing of women or children, in a loud and boisterous manner, is guilty of a misdemeanor, and upon conviction by any Court of competent jurisdiction shall be punished by fine not exceeding two hundred dollars, or by imprisonment in the County Jail for not more than ninety days, or by both fine and imprisonment, or either, at the discretion of the Court."

2. It is illuminating to note what transpired when Cohen entered a courtroom in the building. He removed his jacket and stood with it folded over his arm. Meanwhile, a policeman sent the presiding judge a note suggesting that Cohen be held in contempt of court. The judge declined to do so and Cohen was arrested by the officer only after he emerged from the courtroom.

IRVING KRISTOL

"Pornography, Obscenity, and the Case for Censorship"*

Being frustrated is disagreeable, but the real disasters in life begin when you get what you want. For almost a century now, a great many intelligent, well-meaning, and articulate people—of a kind generally called liberal or intellectual, or both—have argued eloquently against any kind of censorship of art and/or entertainment. And within the past ten years, the courts and the legislatures of most Western nations have found these arguments persuasive—so persuasive that hardly a man is now alive who clearly remembers what the answers to these arguments were. Today, in the United States and other democracies, censorship has to all intents and purposes ceased to exist.

Is there a sense of triumphant exhilaration in the land? Hardly. There is, on the contrary, a rapidly growing unease and disquiet. Somehow, things have not worked out as they were supposed to, and many notable civil libertarians have gone on record as saying this was not what they meant at all. They wanted a world in which "Desire Under the Elms" could be produced, or "Ulysses" published, without interference by philistine busybodies holding public office. They have got that, of course; but they have also got a world in which homosexual rape takes place on the stage, in which the public flocks during lunch hours to witness varieties of professional fornication, in which Times Square has become little more than a hideous market for the sale and distribution of printed filth that panders to all known (and some fanciful) sexual perversions.

But disagreeable as this may be, does it really matter? Might not our unease and disquiet be merely a cultural hangover—a "hangup," as they say? What reason is there to think that anyone was ever corrupted by a book?

* From *The New York Times Magazine,* March 28, 1971. Reprinted by permission of the author. © 1971 by The New York Times Company.

This last question, oddly enough, is asked by the very same people who seem convinced that advertisements in magazines or displays of violence on television do indeed have the power to corrupt. It is also asked, incredibly enough and in all sincerity, by people—for example, university professors and school teachers—whose very lives provide all the answers one could want. After all, if you believe that no one was ever corrupted by a book, you have also to believe that no one was ever improved by a book (or a play or a movie). You have to believe, in other words, that all art is morally trivial and that, consequently, all education is morally irrelevant. No one, not even a university professor, really believes that.

To be sure, it is extremely difficult, as social scientists tell us, to trace the effects of any single book (or play or movie) on an individual reader or any class of readers. But we all know, and social scientists know it too, that the ways in which we use our minds and imaginations do shape our characters and help define us as persons. That those who certainly know this are nevertheless moved to deny it merely indicates how a dogmatic resistance to the idea of censorship can—like most dogmatism—result in a mindless insistence on the absurd.

I have used these harsh terms—"dogmatism" and "mindless"—advisedly. I might also have added "hypocritical." For the plain fact is that none of us is a complete civil libertarian. We all believe that there is some point at which the public authorities ought to step in to limit the "self-expression" of an individual or a group, even where this might be seriously intended as a form of artistic expression, and even where the artistic transaction is between consenting adults. A playwright or theatrical director might, in this crazy world of ours, find someone willing to commit suicide on the stage, as called for by the script.

We would not allow that—any more than we would permit scenes of real physical torture on the stage, even if the victim were a willing masochist. And I know of no one, no matter how free in spirit, who argues that we ought to permit gladiatorial contests in Yankee Stadium, similar to those once performed in the Colosseum at Rome—even if only consenting adults were involved.

The basic point that emerges is one that Prof. Walter Berns has powerfully argued: No society can be utterly indifferent to the ways its citizens publicly entertain themselves.* Bearbaiting and cockfighting are prohibited only in part out of compassion for the suffering animals; the main reason they were abolished was because it was felt that they debased and brutalized the citizenry who flocked to witness such spectacles. And the question we face with regard to pornography and obscenity is whether, now that they have such strong legal protection from the Supreme Court, they can or will brutalize and debase our citizenry. We are, after all, not dealing with one passing incident—one book, or one play, or one movie. We are dealing with a general tendency that is suffusing our entire culture.

I say pornography *and* obscenity because, though they have different dictionary definitions and are frequently distinguishable as "artistic" genres, they are nevertheless in the end identical in effect. Pornography is not objectionable simply because it arouses sexual desire or lust or prurience in the mind of the reader or spectator; this is a silly Victorian notion. A great many nonpornographic works—including some parts of the Bible—excite sexual desire very successfully. What is distinctive about pornography is that, in the words of D. H. Lawrence, it attempts "to do dirt on [sex] . . . [It is an] insult to a vital human relationship."

In other words, pornography differs from erotic art in that its whole purpose is to treat human beings obscenely, to deprive human beings of their specifically human dimension. That is what obscenity is all about. It is light years removed from any kind of carefree sensuality—there is no continuum between Fielding's "Tom Jones" and the Marquis de Sade's "Justine." These works have quite opposite intentions. To quote Susan Sontag: "What pornographic literature does is precisely to drive a wedge between one's existence as a full human being and one's existence as a sexual being—while in ordinary life a healthy person is one who prevents such a gap from opening up." This definition occurs in an essay *defending* pornography—Miss Sontag is a candid as well as gifted critic—so the definition, which I accept, is neither tendentious nor censorious.

Along these same lines, one can point out—as C. S. Lewis pointed out some years back—that it is no accident that in the history of all literatures obscene words—the so-called "four-letter words" —have always been the vocabulary of farce or vituperation. The reason is clear—they reduce men and women to some of their mere bodily functions—they reduce man to his animal component, and such a reduction is an essential purpose of farce or vituperation.

Similarly, Lewis also suggested that it is not an accident that we have no offhand, colloquial, neutral terms—not in any Western European language at any rate—for our most private parts. The words we do use are either (a) nursery terms, (b) archaisms, (c) scientific terms or (d) a term from the gutter (that is, a demeaning term). Here I think the genius of language is telling us something important about man. It is telling us that man is an animal with a difference: he has a unique sense of privacy, and a unique capacity for shame when this privacy is violated. Our "private parts" are indeed private, and not merely because convention prescribes it. This particular convention is indigenous to the human race. In practically all primitive tribes, men and women cover their private parts; and in practically all primitive tribes, men and women do not copulate in public.

It may well be that Western society, in the latter half of the 20th century, is experiencing a drastic change in sexual mores and sexual relationships. We have had many such "sexual revolutions" in the past—and the bourgeois family and bourgeois ideas of sexual propriety were themselves established in the course of a revolution against 18th century "licentiousness"—and we shall doubtless have others in the future. It is, however, highly improbable (to put it mildly) that what we are witnessing is the Final Revolu-

---

*This is as good a place as any to express my profound indebtedness to Walter Berns's superb essay, "Pornography vs. Democracy," in the winter, 1971, issue of The Public Interest.

tion which will make sexual relations utterly un-problematic, permit us to dispense with any kind of ordered relationships between the sexes, and allow us freely to redefine the human condition. And so long as humanity has not reached that utopia, obscenity will remain a problem.

One of the reasons it will remain a problem is that obscenity is not merely about sex, any more than science fiction is about science. Science fiction, as every student of the genre knows, is a peculiar vision of power: what it is really about is politics. And obscenity is a peculiar vision of humanity: what it is really about is ethics and metaphysics.

Imagine a man—a well-known man, much in the public eye—in a hospital ward, dying an agonizing death. He is not in control of his bodily functions, so that his bladder and his bowels empty themselves of their own accord. His consciousness is overwhelmed and extinguished by pain, so that he cannot communicate with us, nor we with him. Now, it would be, technically, the easiest thing in the world to put a television camera in his hospital room and let the whole world witness this spectacle. We don't do it—at least we don't do it as yet—because we regard this as an *obscene* invasion of privacy. And what would make the spectacle obscene is that we would be witnessing the extinguishing of humanity in a human animal.

Incidentally, in the past our humanitarian crusaders against capital punishment understood this point very well. The abolitionist literature goes into great physical detail about what happens to a man when he is hanged or electrocuted or gassed. And their argument was—and is—that what happens is shockingly obscene, and that no civilized society should be responsible for perpetrating such obscenities, particularly since in the nature of the case there must be spectators to ascertain that this horror was indeed being perpetrated in fulfillment of the law.

Sex—like death—is an activity that is both animal and human. There are human sentiments and human ideals involved in this animal activity. But when sex is public, the viewer does not see—cannot see—the sentiments and the ideals. He can only see the animal coupling. And that is why, when men and women make love, as we say,

they prefer to be alone—because it is only when you are alone that you can make love, as distinct from merely copulating in an animal and casual way. And that, too, is why those who are voyeurs, if they are not irredeemably sick, also feel ashamed at what they are witnessing. When sex is a public spectacle, a human relationship has been debased into a mere animal connection.

It is also worth noting that this making of sex into an obscenity is not a mutual and equal transaction, but is rather an act of exploitation by one of the partners—the male partner. I do not wish to get into the complicated question as to what, if any, are the essential differences—as distinct from conventional and cultural differences—between male and female. I do not claim to know the answer to that. But I do know—and I take it as a sign which has meaning—that pornography is, and always has been, a man's work; that women rarely write pornography; and that women tend to be indifferent consumers of pornography.* My own guess, by way of explanation, is that a woman's sexual experience is ordinarily more suffused with human emotion than is man's, that men are more easily satisfied with autoerotic activities, and that men can therefore more easily take a more "technocratic" view of sex and its pleasures. Perhaps this is not correct. But whatever the explanation, there can be no question that pornography is a form of "sexism," as the Women's Liberation Movement calls it, and that the instinct of Women's Lib has been unerring in perceiving that, when pornography is perpetrated, it is perpetrated against them, as part of a conspiracy to deprive them of their full humanity.

But even if all this is granted, it might be said —and doubtless will be said—that I really ought not to be unduly concerned. Free competition in the cultural marketplace—it is argued by people who have never otherwise had a kind word to say for laissez-faire—will automatically dispose of the problem. The present fad for pornography and obscenity, it will be asserted, is just that, a fad. It will spend itself in the course of time; people will

---

*There are, of course, a few exceptions—but of a kind that prove the rule. "L'Histoire d'O," for instance, written by a woman, is unquestionably the most *melancholy* work of pornography ever written. And its theme is precisely the dehumanization accomplished by obscenity.

get bored with it, will be able to take it or leave it alone in a casual way, in a "mature way," and, in sum, I am being unnecessarily distressed about the whole business. The New York Times, in an editorial, concludes hopefully in this vein.

"In the end . . . the insensate pursuit of the urge to shock, carried from one excess to a more abysmal one, is bound to achieve its own antidote in total boredom. When there is no lower depth to descend to, ennui will erase the problem."

I would like to be able to go along with this line of reasoning, but I cannot. I think it is false, and for two reasons, the first psychological, the second political.

The basic psychological fact about pornography and obscenity is that it appeals to and provokes a kind of sexual regression. The sexual pleasure one gets from pornography and obscenity is autoerotic and infantile; put bluntly, it is a masturbatory exercise of the imagination, when it is not masturbation pure and simple. Now, people who masturbate do not get bored with masturbation, just as sadists don't get bored with sadism, and voyeurs don't get bored with voyeurism.

In other words, infantile sexuality is not only a permanent temptation for the adolescent or even the adult—it can quite easily become a permanent, self-reinforcing neurosis. It is because of an awareness of this possibility of regression toward the infantile condition, a regression which is always open to us, that all the codes of sexual conduct ever devised by the human race take such a dim view of autoerotic activities and try to discourage autoerotic fantasies. Masturbation is indeed a perfectly natural autoerotic activity, as so many sexologists blandly assure us today. And it is precisely because it is so perfectly natural that it can be so dangerous to the mature or maturing person, if it is not controlled or sublimated in some way. That is the true meaning of Portnoy's complaint. Portnoy, you will recall, grows up to be a man who is incapable of having an adult sexual relationship with a woman; his sexuality remains fixed in an infantile mode, the prison of his autoerotic fantasies. Inevitably, Portnoy comes to think, in a perfectly *infantile* way, that it was all his mother's fault.

It is true that, in our time, some quite brilliant minds have come to the conclusion that a reversion to infantile sexuality is the ultimate mission and secret destiny of the human race. I am thinking in particular of Norman O. Brown, for whose writings I have the deepest respect. One of the reasons I respect them so deeply is that Mr. Brown is a serious thinker who is unafraid to face up to the radical consequences of his radical theories. Thus, Mr. Brown knows and says that for his kind of salvation to be achieved, humanity must annul the civilization it has created—not merely the civilization we have today, but all civilization—so as to be able to make the long descent backwards into animal innocence.

What is at stake is civilization and humanity, nothing less. The idea that "everything is permitted," as Nietzsche put it, rests on the premise of nihilism and has nihilistic implications. I will not pretend that the case against nihilism and for civilization is an easy one to make. We are here confronting the most fundamental of philosophical questions, on the deepest levels. But that is precisely my point—that the matter of pornography and obscenity is not a trivial one, and that only superficial minds can take a bland and untroubled view of it.

In this connection, I might also point out those who are primarily against censorship on liberal grounds tell us not to take pornography or obscenity seriously, while those who are for pornography and obscenity, on radical grounds, take it very seriously indeed. I believe the radicals—writers like Susan Sontag, Herbert Marcuse, Norman O. Brown, and even Jerry Rubin—are right, and the liberals are wrong. I also believe that those young radicals at Berkeley, some five years ago, who provoked a major confrontation over the public use of obscence words, showed a brilliant political instinct. Once the faculty and administration had capitulated on this issue—saying: "Oh, for God's sake, let's be adult: what difference does it make anyway?"—once they said that, they were bound to lose on every other issue. And once Mark Rudd could publicly ascribe to the president of Columbia a notoriously obscene relationship to his mother, without provoking any kind of reaction, the S.D.S. had already won the day. The occupation of Columbia's buildings merely ratified their victory. Men who show themselves unwilling to defend civilization against nihilism are not going to be either resolute or effective in defending the university against anything.

I am already touching upon a political aspect of pornography when I suggest that it is inherently and purposefully subversive of civilization and its institutions. But there is another and more specifically political aspect,when has to do with the relationship of pornography and/or obscenity to democracy, and especially to the quality of public life on which democratic government ultimately rests.

Though the phrase, "the quality of life," trips easily from so many lips these days, it tends to be one of those clichés with many trivial meanings and no large, serious one. Sometimes it merely refers to such externals as the enjoyment of cleaner air, cleaner water, cleaner streets. At other times it refers to the merely private enjoyment of music, painting or literature. Rarely does it have anything to do with the way the citizen in a democracy views himself—his obligations, his intentions, his ultimate self-definition.

Instead, what I would call the "managerial" conception of democracy is the predominant opinion among political scientists, sociologists and economists, and has, through the untiring efforts of these scholars, become the conventional journalistic opinion as well. The root idea behind this "managerial" conception is that democracy is a "political system" (as they say) which can be adequately defined in terms of—can be fully reduced to—its mechanical arrangements. Democracy is then seen as a set of rules and procedures, and *nothing but* a set of rules and procedures, whereby majority rule and minority rights are reconciled into a state of equilibrium. If everyone follows these rules and procedures, then a democracy is in working order. I think this is a fair description of the democratic idea that currently prevails in academia. One can also fairly say that it is now the liberal idea of democracy par excellence.

I cannot help but feel that there is something ridiculous about being this kind of a democrat, and I must further confess to having a sneaking sympathy for those of our young radicals who also find it ridiculous. The absurdity is the absurdity of idolatry—of taking the symbolic for the real, the means for the end. The purpose of democracy cannot possibly be the endless functioning of its own political machinery. The purpose of any political regime is to achieve some version of the good life and the good society. It is not at all difficult to imagine a perfectly func-

tioning democracy which answers all questions except one—namely, why should anyone of intelligence and spirit care a fig for it?

There is, however, an older idea of democracy —one which was fairly common until about the beginning of this century—for which the conception of the quality of public life is absolutely crucial. This idea starts from the proposition that democracy is a form of self-government, and that if you want it to be a meritorious polity, you have to care about what kind of people govern it. Indeed, it puts the matter more strongly and declares that, if you want self-government, you are only entitled to it if that "self" is worthy of governing. There is no inherent right to self-government if it means that such government is vicious, mean, squalid and debased. Only a dogmatist and a fanatic, an idolater of democratic machinery, could approve of self-government under such conditions.

And because the desirability of self-government depends on the character of the people who govern, the older idea of democracy was very solicitous of the condition of this character. It was solicitous of the individual self, and felt an obligation to educate it into what used to be called "republican virtue." And it was solicitous of that collective self which we call public opinion and which, in a democracy, governs us collectively. Perhaps in some respects it was nervously oversolicitous—that would not be surprising. But the main thing is that it cared, cared not merely about the machinery of democracy but about the quality of life that this machinery might generate.

And because it cared, this older idea of democracy had no problem in principle with pornography and/or obscenity. It censored them—and it did so with a perfect clarity of mind and a perfectly clear conscience. It was not about to permit people capriciously to corrupt themselves. Or, to put it more precisely: in this version of democracy, the people took some care not to let themselves be governed by the more infantile and irrational parts of themselves.

I have, it many be noticed, uttered that dreadful word, "censorship." And I am not about to back away from it. If you think pornography and/or obscenity is a serious problem, you have to be for censorship. I'll go even further and say that if you want to prevent pornography and/or obscenity from becoming a problem, you have to be for censorship. And lest there be any misunderstanding as to what I am saying, I'll put it as bluntly as possible: if you care for the quality of life in our American democracy, then you have to be for censorship.

But can a liberal be for censorship? Unless one assumes that being a liberal *must* mean being indifferent to the quality of American life, then the answer has to be: yes, a liberal can be for censorship—but he ought to favor a liberal form of censorship.

Is that a contradiction in terms? I don't think so. We have no problem in contrasting *repressive* laws governing alcohol and drugs and tobacco with laws *regulating* (that is, discouraging the sale of) alcohol and drugs and tobacco. Laws encouraging temperance are not the same thing as laws that have as their goal prohibition or abolition. We have not made the smoking of cigarettes a criminal offense. We have, however, and with good liberal conscience, prohibited cigarette advertising on television, and may yet, again with good liberal conscience, prohibit it in newspapers and magazines. The idea of restricting individual freedom, in a liberal way, is not at all unfamiliar to us.

I therefore see no reason why we should not be able to distinguish repressive censorship from liberal censorship of the written and spoken word. In Britain, until a few years ago, you could perform almost any play you wished—but certain plays, judged to be obscene, had to be performed in private theatrical clubs which were deemed to have a "serious" interest in theater. In the United States all of us who grew up using public libraries are familiar with the circumstances under which certain books could be circulated only to adults, while still other books had to be read in the library reading room, under the librarian's skeptical eye. In both cases, a small minority that was willing to make a serious effort to see an obscene play or read an obscene book could do so. But the impact of obscenity was circumscribed and the quality of public life was only marginally affected.*

*It is fairly predictable that someone is going to object that this point of veiw is "elitist"—that, under a system of liberal censorship, the rich will have privileged access to pornography and obscenity. Yes, of course they will—just as at present, the rich have privileged access to heroin if they want it. But one would have to be an egalitarian maniac to object to this state of affairs on the grounds of equality.

I am not saying it is easy in practice to sustain a distinction between liberal and repressive censorship, especially in the public realm of a democracy, where popular opinion is so vulnerable to demagoguery. Moreover, an acceptable system of liberal censorship is likely to be exceedingly difficult to devise in the United States today, because our educated classes, upon whose judgment a liberal censorship must rest, are so convinced that there is no such thing as a problem of obscenity, or even that there is no such thing as obscenity at all. But, to counterbalance this, there is the further, fortunate truth that the tolerable margin for error is quite large, and single mistakes or single injustices are not all that important.

This possibility, of course, occasions much distress among artists and academics. It is a fact, one that cannot and should not be denied, that any system of censorship is bound, upon occasion, to treat unjustly a particular work of art—to find pornography where there is only gentle eroticism, to find obscenity where none really exists, or to find both where its existence ought to be tolerated because it serves a larger moral purpose. Though most works of art are not obscene, and though most obscenity has nothing to do with art, there are some few works of art that are, at least in part, pornographic and/or obscene. There are also some few works of art that are in the special category of the comic-ironic "bawdy" (Boccaccio, Rabelais). It is such works of art that are likely to suffer at the hands of the censor. That is the price one has to be prepared to pay for censorship—even liberal censorship.

But just how high is this price? If you believe, as so many artists seem to believe today, that art is the only sacrosanct activity in our profane and vulgar world—that any man who designates himself an artist thereby acquires a sacred office—then obviously censorship is an intolerable form of sacrilege. But for those of us who do not subscribe to this religion of art, the costs of censorship do not seem so high at all.

If you look at the history of American or English literature, there is precious little damage you can point to as a consequence of the censorship that prevailed throughout most of that history. Very few works of literature—of real literary merit, I mean—ever were suppressed; and those that were, were not suppressed for long. Nor have I noticed, now that censorship of the written word has to all intents and purposes ceased in this country, that hitherto suppressed or repressed masterpieces are flooding the market. Yes, we can now read "Fanny Hill" and the Marquis de Sade. Or, to be more exact, we can now openly purchase them, since many people were able to read them even though they were publicly banned, which is as it should be under a liberal censorship. So how much have literature and the arts gained from the fact that we can all now buy them over the counter, that, indeed, we are all now encouraged to buy them over the counter? They have not gained much that I can see.

And one might also ask a question that is almost never raised: how much has literature lost from the fact that everything is now permitted? It has lost quite a bit, I should say. In a free market, Gresham's Law can work for books or theater as efficiently as it does for coinage—driving out the good, establishing the debased. The cultural market in the United States today is being preempted by dirty books, dirty movies, dirty theater. A pornographic novel has a far better chance of being published today than a nonpornographic one, and quite a few pretty good novels are not being published at all simply because they are not pornographic, and are therefore less likely to sell. Our cultural condition has not improved as a result of the new freedom. American cultural life wasn't much to brag about 20 years ago; today one feels ashamed for it.

Just one last point which I dare not leave untouched. If we start censoring pornography or obscenity, shall we not inevitably end up censoring political opinion? A lot of people seem to think this would be the case—which only shows the power of doctrinaire thinking over reality. We had censorship of pornography and obscenity for 150 years, until almost yesterday, and I am not aware that freedom of opinion in this country was in any way diminished as a consequence of this fact. Fortunately for those of us who are liberal, freedom is not indivisible. If it were, the case for liberalism would be indistinguishable from the case for anarchy; and they are two very different things.

But I must repeat and emphasize: What kind of laws we pass governing pornography and obscenity, what kind of censorship—or, since we are still a federal nation—what kinds of censorship we institute in our various localities may indeed be difficult matters to cope with; nevertheless the real issue is one of principle. I myself subscribe to the liberal view of the enforcement problem: I think that pornography should be illegal and available to anyone who wants it so badly as to make a pretty strenuous effort to get it. We have lived with under-the-counter pornography for centuries now, in a fairly comfortable way. But the issue of principle, of whether it should be over or under the counter, has to be settled before we can reflect on the advantages and disadvantages of alternative modes of censorship. I think the settlement we are living under now, in which obscenity and democracy are regarded as equals, is wrong; I believe it is inherently unstable; I think it will, in the long run, be incompatible with any authentic concern for the quality of life in our democracy.

JOHN F. KENNEDY MEMORIAL HOSPITAL v. HESTON

Supreme Court of New Jersey, 1971*

The opinion of the Court was delivered by WEINTRAUB, C.J.

Delores Heston, age 22 and unmarried, was severely injured in an automobile accident. She was taken to the plaintiff hospital where it was determined that she would expire unless operated upon for a ruptured spleen and that if operated upon she would expire unless whole blood was administered. Miss Heston and her parents are Jehovah's Witnesses and a tenet of their faith forbids blood transfusions. Miss Heston insists she expressed her refusal to accept blood, but the evidence indicates she was in shock on admittance to the hospital and in the judgment of the attending physicians and nurses was then or soon became disoriented and incoherent. Her mother remained adamant in her opposition to a transfusion, and signed a release of liability for the hospital and medical personnel. Miss Heston did not execute a release; presumably she could not. Her father could not be located.

Death being imminent, plaintiff on notice to the mother made application at 1:30 A.M. to a judge of the Superior Court for the appointment of a guardian for Miss Heston with directions to consent to transfusions as needed to save her life. At the hearing, the mother and her friends thought a certain doctor would pursue surgery without a transfusion, but the doctor, in response to the judge's telephone call, declined the case. The court appointed a guardian with authority to consent to blood transfusions "for the preservation of the life of Delores Heston." Surgery was performed at 4:00 A.M. the same morning. Blood was administered. Miss Heston survived.

Defendants then moved to vacate the order. Affidavits were submitted by both sides. The trial court declined to vacate the order. This appeal followed. We certified it before argument in the Appellate Division.

The controversy is moot. Miss Heston is well and no longer in plaintiff's hospital. The prospect of her return at some future day in like circumstances is too remote to warrant a declaratory judgment as between the parties. Nonetheless, the public interest warrants a resolution of the cause, and for that reason we accept the issue. (See State v. Perricone, N.J.* 1962).

In *Perricone,* we sustained an order for compulsory blood transfusion for an infant despite the objection of the parents who were Jehovah's Witnesses. In Raleigh Fitkin-Paul Morgan Memorial Hospital v. Anderson, N.J. (1964),* it appeared that both the mother, a Jehovah's Witness, and the child she was bearing would die if blood were not transfused should she hemorrhage. We held that a blood transfusion could be ordered if necessary to save the lives of the mother and the unborn child. We said:

We have no difficulty in so deciding with respect to the infant child. The more difficult question is whether an adult may be compelled to submit to such medical procedures when necessary to save his life. Here we think it is unnecessary to decide that question in broad terms because the welfare of the child and the mother are so intertwined and inseparable that it would be impracticable to attempt to distinguish between them with respect to the sundry factual patterns which may develop. The blood transfusions (including transfusions made necessary by the delivery) may be administered if necessary to save her life or the life of her child, as the physician in charge at the time may determine.

The case at hand presents the question we thus reserved in *Raleigh Fitkin-Paul Morgan Memorial Hospital.*

It seems correct to say there is no constitutional right to choose to die. Attempted suicide was a crime at common law and was held to be a crime under N.J.S.A. 2A:85–1.* It is now denounced as a disorderly persons offense. N.J.S.A. 2A:170–25.6. Ordinarily nothing would be gained by a prosecution, and hence the offense is rarely charged. Nonetheless the Constitution does not deny the State an interest in the subject. It is commonplace for the police and other citizens, often at great risk to themselves, to use force or stratagem to defeat efforts at suicide, and it could hardly be said that thus to save someone from himself violated a right of his under the Constitution subjecting the rescuer to civil or penal consequences.

*58 N.J. 576 (1971).

*Citation omitted [Eds.]

Nor is constitutional right established by adding that one's religious faith ordains his death. Religious beliefs are absolute, but conduct in pursuance of religious beliefs is not wholly immune from governmental restraint. Mountain Lakes Bd. of Educ. v. Maas, N.J.* (1960) (vaccination of children); Bunn v. North Carolina,* (1949) (the use of snakes in a religious ritual); Baer v. City of Bend,* Or. (1956) (fluoridation of drinking water). Of immediate interest is Reynolds v. United States,* (1878), in which it was held that Congress could punish polygamy in a territory notwithstanding that polygamy was permitted or demanded by religious tenet, and in which the Court said:

> * * * Laws are made for the government of actions, and while they cannot interfere with mere religious belief and opinions, they may with practices. Suppose one believed that human sacrifices were a necessary part of religious worship, would it be seriously contended that the civil government under which he lived could not interfere to prevent a sacrifice? Or if a wife religiously believed it was her duty to burn herself upon the funeral pile of her dead husband, would it be beyond the power of the civil government to prevent her carrying her belief into practice?

Complicating the subject of suicide is the difficulty of knowing whether a decision to die is firmly held. Psychiatrists may find that beneath it all a person bent on self-destruction is hoping to be rescued, and most who are rescued do not repeat the attempt, at least not at once. Then, too, there is the question whether in any event the person was and continues to be competent (a difficult concept in this area) to choose to die. And of course there is no opportunity for a trial of these questions in advance of intervention by the State or a citizen.

Appellant suggests there is a difference between passively submitting to death and actively seeking it. The distinction may be merely verbal, as it would be if an adult sought death by starvation instead of a drug. If the State may interrupt one mode of self-destruction, it may with equal authority interfere with the other. It is arguably different when an individual, overtaken by illness, decides to let it run a fatal course. But unless the medical option itself is laden with the risk of death or of serious infirmity, the State's interest in sustaining life in such circumstances is hardly distinguishable from its interest in the case of suicide.

Here we are not dealing with deadly options. The risk of death or permanent injury because of a transfusion is not a serious factor. Indeed, Miss Heston did not resist a transfusion on that basis. Nor did she wish to die. She wanted to live, but her faith demanded that she refuse blood even at the price of her life. The question is not whether the State could punish her for

refusing a transfusion. It may be granted that it would serve no State interest to deal criminally with one who resisted a transfusion on the basis of religious faith. The question is whether the State may authorize force to prevent death or may tolerate the use of force by others to that end. Indeed, the issue is not solely between the State and Miss Heston, for the controversy is also between Miss Heston and a hospital and staff who did not seek her out and upon whom the dictates of her faith will fall as a burden.

Hospitals exist to aid the sick and the injured. The medical and nursing professions are consecrated to preserving life. That is their professional creed. To them, a failure to use a simple, established procedure in the circumstances of this case would be malpractice, however the law may characterize that failure because of the patient's private convictions. A surgeon should not be asked to operate under the strain of knowing that a transfusion may not be administered even though medically required to save his patient. The hospital and its staff should not be required to decide whether the patient is or continues to be competent to make a judgment upon the subject, or whether the release tendered by the patient or a member of his family will protect them from civil responsibility. The hospital could hardly avoid the problem by compelling the removal of a dying patient, and Miss Heston's family made no effort to take her elsewhere.

When the hospital and staff are thus involuntary hosts and their interests are pitted against the belief of the patient, we think it reasonable to resolve the problem by permitting the hospital and its staff to pursue their functions according to their professional standards. The solution sides with life, the conservation of which is, we think, a matter of State interest. A prior application to a court is appropriate if time permits it, although in the nature of the emergency the only question that can be explored satisfactorily is whether death will probably ensue if medical procedures are not followed. If a court finds, as the trial court did, that death will likely follow unless a transfusion is administered, the hospital and the physician should be permitted to follow that medical procedure.

The precedents are few ... With one exception, Erickson v. Dilgard, (Sup.Ct.1962), transfusions for adults were ordered despite their religious tenets.*

Two cases reached an appellate level. In *Georgetown College*, a single judge of the Court of Appeals ordered the transfusion. Thereafter a majority of the court denied a petition for rehearing en banc, without however indicating the precise basis for that denial. One dissenting opinion approached the merits. The sole appellate decision expressly reaching the merits appears to be In re Estate of Brooks.* There a conservator was appointed to authorize the transfusion for a Jehovah's

Witness. After the transfusion, the patient and her husband sought unsuccessfully to have the order expunged. The Supreme Court of Illinois reversed. The court could find no "clear and present danger" warranting interference with the patient's religious proscription. It has been suggested that the "clear and present danger" test, appropriate with respect to free speech, is not the appropriate criterion here, and that the relevant question is whether there is a "compelling State interest" justifying the State's refusal to permit the patient to refuse vital aid.* We think the latter test is the correct one, but it cannot be said with confidence that *Brooks* would have gone the other way if the decision had been made in its light. In fact the court there did mention conceivable interests. Thus it noted that the patient did not have minor children who might become charges of the State. But the court did not expressly consider whether the State had an interest in sustaining life, a consideration which would not be apparent when the focus is upon a "clear and present

*Citation omitted [Eds.]

danger." Nor did the court consider the sufficiency of the interest of a hospital or its staff when the patient is thrust upon them. In fact there the applicant was the patient's regular physician who had long treated her for an ulcer, knew of her religious tenet, and had assured her that he would not administer blood. The court noted, too, a fact of uncertain force in its decision, that the application was made to the trial court without notice to the patient or her husband, although time was adequate to that end.

It is not at all clear that *Brooks* would be applied in Illinois to an emergent factual pattern in which a hospital and its staff are the involuntary custodians of an adult. In any event, for the reasons already given, we find that the interest of the hospital and its staff, as well as the State's interest in life, warranted the transfusion of blood under the circumstances of this case. The judgment is accordingly affirmed. No costs.

For affirmation: Chief Justice WEINTRAUB and Justices JACOBS, FRANCIS, PROCTOR, HALL and SCHETTINO—6.

For reversal: None.

GERALD DWORKIN

Paternalism*

Neither one person, nor any number of persons, is warranted in saying to another human creature of ripe years, that he shall not do with his life for his own benefit what he chooses to do with it. [Mill]

I do not want to go along with a volunteer basis. I think a fellow should be compelled to become better and not let him use his discretion whether he wants to get smarter, more healthy or more honest. [General Hershey]

I take as my starting point the "one very simple principle" proclaimed by Mill *On Liberty* . . .

*From *Morality and the Law* edited by Richard A. Wasserstrom. Copyright © 1971 by Wadsworth Publishing Company, Inc., Belmont, California 94002. Reprinted by permission of the publisher and the author.

That principle is, that the sole end for which mankind are warranted, individually or collectively, in interfering with the liberty of action of any of their number, is self-protection. That the only purpose for which power can be rightfully exercised over any member of a civilized community, against his will, is to prevent harm to others. He cannot rightfully be compelled to do or forbear because it will be better for him to do so, because it will make him happier, because, in the opinion of others, to do so would be wise, or even right.

This principle is neither "one" nor "very simple." It is at least two principles; one asserting that self-protection or the prevention of harm to others is sometimes a sufficient warrant and the other claiming that the individual's own good is *never* a sufficient warrant for the exercise of compulsion either by the society as a whole or by its individual members. I assume that no one, with the possible exception of extreme pacifists or anarchists, questions the correctness of the first half of the principle. This essay is an examination of the negative claim embodied in Mill's principle— the objection to paternalistic interferences with a man's liberty.

I

By paternalism I shall understand roughly the interference with a person's liberty of action justified by reasons referring exclusively to the welfare, good, happiness, needs, interests or values of the person being coerced. One is always well-advised to illustrate one's definitions by examples but it is not easy to find "pure" examples of paternalistic interferences. For almost any piece of legislation is justified by several different kinds of reasons and even if historically a piece of legislation can be shown to have been introduced for purely paternalistic motives, it may be that advocates of the legislation with an antipaternalistic outlook can find sufficient reasons justifying the legislation without appealing to the reasons which were originally adduced to support it. Thus, for example, it may be that the original legislation requiring motorcyclists to wear safety helmets was introduced for purely paternalistic reasons. But the Rhode Island Supreme Court recently upheld such legislation on the grounds that it was "not persuaded that the legislature is powerless to prohibit individuals from pursuing a course of conduct which could conceivably result in their becoming public charges," thus clearly introducing reasons of a quite different kind. Now I regard this decision as being based on reasoning of a very dubious nature but it illustrates the kind of problem one has in finding examples. The following is a list of the kinds of interferences I have in mind as being paternalistic.

II

1. Laws requiring motorcyclists to wear safety helmets when operating their machines.
2. Laws forbidding persons from swimming at a public beach when lifeguards are not on duty.
3. Laws making suicide a criminal offense.
4. Laws making it illegal for women and children to work at certain types of jobs.
5. Laws regulating certain kinds of sexual conduct, for example, homosexuality among consenting adults in private.
6. Laws regulating the use of certain drugs which may have harmful consequences to the user but do not lead to antisocial conduct.
7. Laws requiring a license to engage in certain professions with those not receiving a license subject to fine or jail sentence if they do engage in the practice.
8. Laws compelling people to spend a specified fraction of their income on the purchase of retirement annuities (Social Security).
9. Laws forbidding various forms of gambling (often justified on the grounds that the poor are more likely to throw away their money on such activities than the rich who can afford to).
10. Laws regulating the maximum rates of interest for loans.
11. Laws against duelling.

In addition to laws which attach criminal or civil penalties to certain kinds of action there are laws, rules, regulations, decrees which make it either difficult or impossible for people to carry out their plans and which are also justified on paternalistic grounds. Examples of this are:

1. Laws regulating the types of contracts which will be upheld as valid by the courts, for example, (an example of Mill's to which I shall return) no man may make a valid contract for perpetual involuntary servitude.
2. Not allowing assumption of risk as a defense to an action based on the violation of a safety statute.
3. Not allowing as a defense to a charge of murder or assault the consent of the victim.
4. Requiring members of certain religious sects to have compulsory blood transfusions. This is made possible by not allowing the patient to have recourse to civil suits for assault and battery and by means of injunctions.

5. Civil commitment procedures when these are specifically justified on the basis of preventing the person being committed from harming himself. The D.C. Hospitalization of the Mentally Ill Act provides for involuntary hospitalization of a person who "is mentally ill, and because of that illness, is likely to injure himself or others if allowed to remain at liberty." The term injure in this context applies to unintentional as well as intentional injuries.

All of my examples are of existing restrictions on the liberty of individuals. Obviously one can think of interferences which have not yet been imposed. Thus one might ban the sale of cigarettes, or require that people wear safety belts in automobiles (as opposed to merely having them installed), enforcing this by not allowing motorist to sue for injuries even when caused by other drivers if the motorist was not wearing a seat belt at the time of the accident.

I shall not be concerned with activities which though defended on paternalistic grounds are not interferences with the liberty of persons, for example, the giving of subsidies in kind rather than in cash on the grounds that the recipients would not spend the money on the goods which they really need, or not including a $1,000 deductible provision in a basic protection automobile insurance plan on the ground that the people who would elect it could least afford it. Nor shall I be concerned with measures such as "truth-in-advertising" acts and Pure Food and Drug legislation which are often attacked as paternalistic but which should not be considered so. In these cases all that is provided—it is true by the use of compulsion—is information which it is presumed that rational persons are interested in having in order to make wise decisions. There is no interference with the liberty of the consumer unless one wants to stretch a point beyond good sense and say that his liberty to apply for a loan without knowing the true rate of interest is diminished. It is true that sometimes there is sentiment for going further than providing information, for example when laws against usurious interest are passed preventing those who might wish to contract loans at high rates of interest from doing so, and these measures may correctly be considered paternalistic.

III

Bearing these examples in mind, let me return to a characterization of paternalism. I said earlier that I meant by the term, roughly, interference with a person's liberty for his own good. But, as some of the examples show, the class of persons whose good is involved is not always identical with the class of persons whose freedom is restricted. Thus, in the case of professional licensing it is the practitioner who is directly interfered with but it is the would-be patient whose interests are presumably being served. Not allowing the consent of the victim to be a defense to certain types of crime primarily affects the would-be aggressor but it is the interests of the willing victim that we are trying to protect. Sometimes a person may fall into both classes as would be the case if we banned the manufacture and sale of cigarettes and a given manufacturer happened to be a smoker as well.

Thus we may first divide paternalistic interferences into "pure" and "impure" cases. In "pure" paternalism the class of persons whose freedom is restricted is identical with the class of persons whose benefit is intended to be promoted by such restrictions. Examples: the making of suicide a crime, requiring passengers in automobiles to wear seat belts, requiring a Christian Scientist to receive a blood transfusion. In the case of "impure" paternalism in trying to protect the welfare of a class of persons we find that the only way to do so will involve restricting the freedom of other persons besides those who are benefitted. Now it might be thought that there are no cases of "impure" paternalism since any such case could always be justified on nonpaternalistic grounds, that is, in terms of preventing harm to others. Thus we might ban cigarette manufacturers from continuing to manufacture their product on the grounds that we are preventing them from causing illness to others in the same way that we prevent other manufacturers from releasing pollutants into the atmosphere, thereby causing danger to the members of the community. The difference is, however, that in the former but not the latter case the harm is of such a nature that it could be avoided by those individuals affected if they so chose. The incurring of the harm requires, so to speak, the active cooperation of the victim. It would be mistaken theoretically and hypocritical in practice to assert that our interference in such cases is just like our interference in standard cases of protecting others from harm. At the very least someone interfered with in this way can reply that no one is complaining about his activities. It may be that impure paternalism requires arguments or reasons of a stronger kind in order to be justified, since there are persons who are losing a portion of their liberty and they do not even have the solace of having it be done "in their own interest." Of course in some sense, if paternalistic justifications are ever correct, then we are protecting others, we are preventing some from injuring others, but it is important to see the differences between this and the standard case.

Paternalism then will always involve limitations on the liberty of some individuals in their own interest but it may also extend to interferences with the liberty of parties whose interests are not in question.

IV

Finally, by way of some more preliminary analysis, I want to distinguish paternalistic interference with liberty from a related type with which it is often confused. Consider, for example, legislation which forbids employees to work more than, say, forty hours per week. It is sometimes argued that such legislation is paternalistic for if employees desired such a restriction on their hours of work they could agree among themselves to impose it voluntarily. But because they do not the society imposes its own conception of their best interests upon them by the use of coercion. Hence this is paternalism.

Now it may be that some legislation of this nature is, in fact, paternalistically motivated. I am not denying that. All I want to point out is that there is another possible way of justifying such measures which is not paternalistic in nature. It is not paternalistic because, as Mill puts it in a similar context, such measures are "required not to overrule the judgment of individuals respecting their own interest, but to give effect to that judgment: they being unable to give effect to it except by concert, which concert again cannot be effectual unless it receives validity and sanction from the law." (*Principles of Political Economy*).

The line of reasoning here is a familiar one first found in Hobbes and developed with great sophistication by contemporary economists in the last decade or so. There are restrictions which are in the interests of a class of persons taken collectively but are such that the immediate interest of each individual is furthered by his violating the rule when others adhere to it. In such cases the individuals involved may need the use of compulsion to give effect to their collective judgment of their own interest by guaranteeing each individual compliance by the others. In these cases compulsion is not used to achieve some benefit which is not recognized to be a benefit by those concerned, but rather because it is the only feasible means of achieving some benefit which *is* recognized as such by all concerned. This way of viewing matters provides us with another characterization of paternalism in general. Paternalism might be thought of as the use of coercion to achieve a good which is not recognized as such by those persons for whom the good is intended. Again while this formulation captures the heart of the matter—it is surely what Mill is objecting to in *On Liberty*—the matter is not always quite like that. For example, when we force motorcyclists to wear helmets we are trying to promote a good—the protection of the person from injury—which is surely recognized by most of the individuals concerned. It is not that a cyclist doesn't value his bodily integrity; rather, as a supporter of such legislation would put it, he either places, perhaps irrationally, another value or good (freedom from wearing a helmet) above that of physical well-being or, perhaps, while recognizing the danger in the abstract, he either does not fully appreciate it or he underestimates the likelihood of its occurring. But now we are approaching the question of possible justifications of paternalistic measures and the rest of this essay will be devoted to that question.

V

I shall begin for dialectical purposes by discussing Mill's objections to paternalism and then go on to discuss more positive proposals.

An initial feature that strikes one is the absolute nature of Mill's prohibitions against paternalism. It is so unlike the carefully qualified admonitions of Mill and his fellow utilitarians on other moral issues. He speaks of self-protection as the *sole* end warranting coercion, of the individual's own goals as *never* being a sufficient warrant. Contrast this with his discussion of the prohibition against lying in *Utilitarianism:*

Yet that even this rule, sacred as it is, admits of possible exception, is acknowledged by all moralists, the chief of which is where the with-holding of some fact . . . would save an individual . . . from great and unmerited evil.

The same tentativeness is present when he deals with justice:

It is confessedly unjust to break faith with any one: to violate an engagement, either express or implied, or disappoint expectations raised by our own conduct, at least if we have raised these expectations knowingly and voluntarily. Like all the other obligations of justice already spoken of, this one is not regarded as absolute, but as capable of being overruled by a stronger obligation of justice on the other side.

This anomaly calls for some explanation. The structure of Mill's argument is as follows:

1. Since restraint is an evil the burden of proof is on those who propose such restraint.
2. Since the conduct which is being considered is purely self-regarding, the normal appeal to the protection of the interests of others is not available.
3. Therefore we have to consider whether reasons involving reference to the individual's own good, happiness, welfare, or interests are sufficient to overcome the burden of justification.
4. We either cannot advance the interests of the individual by compulsion, or the attempt to do so involves evils which outweigh the good done.
5. Hence the promotion of the individual's own interests does not provide a sufficient warrant for the use of compulsion.

Clearly the operative premise here is (4), and it is bolstered by claims about the status of the individual as judge and appraiser of his welfare, interests, needs, etcetera:

With respect to his own feelings and circumstances, the most ordinary man or woman has means of knowledge immeasurably surpassing those that can be possessed by any one else.

He is the man most interested in his own well-being: the interest which any other person, except in cases of strong personal attachment, can have in it is trifling, compared to that which he himself has.

These claims are used to support the following generalizations concerning the utility of compulsion for paternalistic purposes.

The interferences of society to overrule his judgment and purposes in what only regards himself must be grounded on general presumptions; which may be altogether wrong, and even if right, are as likely as not to be missapplied to individual cases.

But the strongest of all the arguments against the interference of the public with purely personal conduct is that when it does interfere, the odds are that it interferes wrongly and in the wrong place.

All errors which the individual is likely to commit against advice and warning are far outweighed by the evil of allowing others to constrain him to what they deem his good.

Performing the utilitarian calculation by balancing the advantages and disadvantages, we find that: "Mankind are greater gainers by suffering each other to live as seems good to themselves, than by compelling each other to live as seems good to the rest." Ergo, (4).

This classical case of a utilitarian argument with all the premises spelled out is not the only line of reasoning present in Mill's discussion. There are asides, and more than asides, which look quite different and I shall deal with them later. But this is clearly the main channel of Mill's thought and it is one which has been subjected to vigorous attack from the moment it appeared—most often by fellow utilitarians. The link that they have usually seized on is, as Fitzjames Stephen put it in *Liberty, Equality, Fraternity,* the absence of proof that the "mass of adults are so well acquainted with their own interests and so much disposed to pursue them that no compulsion or restraint put upon them by any others for the purpose of promoting their interest can really promote them." Even so sympathetic a critic as H. L. A. Hart is forced to the conclusion that:

In Chapter 5 of his essay [On Liberty] Mill carried his protests against paternalism to lengths that may now appear to us as fantastic . . . No doubt if we no longer sympathise with this criticism this is due, in part, to a general decline in the belief that individuals know their own interest best.

Mill endows the average individual with "too much of the psychology of a middle-aged man whose desires are relatively fixed, not liable to be artificially stimulated by external influences; who knows what he wants and what gives him satisfaction or happiness; and who pursues these things when he can."

Now it is interesting to note that Mill himself was aware of some of the limitations on the doctrine that the individual is the best judge of his own interests. In his discussion of government intervention in general (even where the intervention does not interfere with liberty but provides alternative institutions to those of the market) after making claims which are parallel to those just discussed, for example, "People understand their own business and their own interests better, and care for them more, than the government does, or can be expected to do," he goes on to an intelligent discussion of the "very large and conspicuous exceptions" to the maxim that:

Most persons take a juster and more intelligent view of their own interest, and of the means of promoting it than can either be prescribed to them by a general enactment of the legislature, or pointed out in the particular case by a public functionary.

Thus there are things

of which the utility does not consist in ministering to inclinations, nor in serving the daily uses of life, and the want of which is least felt where the need is greatest. This is peculiarly true of those things which are chiefly useful as tending to raise the character of human beings. The uncultivated cannot be competent judges of cultivation. Those who most need to be made wiser and better, usually desire it least, and, if they desire it, would be incapable of finding the way to it by their own lights.

. . . A second exception to the doctrine that individuals are the best judges of their own interest, is when an individual attempts to decide irrevocably now what will be best for his interest at some future and distant time. The presumption in favor of individual judgment is only legitimate, where the judgment is grounded on actual, and especially on present, personal experience; not where it is formed antecedently to experience, and not suffered to be reversed even after experience has condemned it.

The upshot of these exceptions is that Mill does not declare that there should never be government interference with the economy but rather that

. . . in every instance, the burden of making out a strong case should be thrown not on those who resist but those who recommend government interference. Letting alone, in short, should be the general practice: every departure from it, unless required by some great good, is a certain evil.

In short, we get a presumption, not an absolute prohibition. The question is why doesn't the argument against paternalism go the same way?

I suggest that the answer lies in seeing that in addition to a purely utilitarian argument Mill uses another as well. As a utilitarian, Mill has to show, in Fitzjames Stephen's words, that: Self-protection apart, no good object can be attained by any compulsion which is not in itself a greater evil than the absence of the object which the compulsion obtains." To show this is impossible, one reason being that it isn't true. Preventing a man from selling himself into slavery (a paternalistic measure which Mill himself accepts as legitimate), or from taking heroin, or from driving a car without wearing seat belts may constitute a lesser evil than allowing him to do any of these things. A consistent utilitarian can only argue against paternalism on the grounds that it (as a matter of fact) does not maximize the good. It is always a contingent question that may be returned by the evidence. But there is also a non-contingent argument which runs through *On Liberty*. When Mill states that "there is a part of the life of every person who has come to years of discretion, within which the individuality of that person ought to reign uncontrolled either by any other person or by the public collectively," he is saying something about what it means to be a person, an autonomous agent. It is because coercing a person for his own good denies this status as an independent entity that Mill objects to it so strongly and in such absolute terms. To be able to choose is a good that is independent of the wisdom of what is chosen. A man's "mode of laying out his existence is the best, not because it is the best in itself, but because it is his own mode." It is the privilege and proper condition of a human being, arrived at the maturity of his faculties, to use and interpret experience in his own way.

As further evidence of this line of reasoning in Mill, consider the one exception to his prohibition against paternalism.

In this and most civilised countries, for example, an engagement by which a person should sell himself, or allow himself to be sold, as a slave, would be null and void; neither enforced by law nor by opinion. The ground for thus limiting his power of voluntarily disposing of his own lot in life, is apparent, and is very clearly seen in this extreme case. The reason for not interfering, unless for the sake of others, with a person's voluntary acts, is consideration for his liberty. His voluntary choice is evidence that what he so chooses is desirable, or at least endurable, to him, and his good is on the whole best provided for by allowing him to take his own means of pursuing it. But by selling himself for a slave, he abdicates his liberty; he foregoes any future use of it beyond that single act. He therefore defeats, in his own case, the very purpose which is the justification of allowing him to dispose of himself. He is no longer free; but is thenceforth in a position which has no longer the presumption in its favour, that would be afforded by his voluntarily remaining in it. The principle of freedom cannot require that he should be free not to be free. It is not freedom to be allowed to alienate his freedom.

Now leaving aside the fudging on the meaning of freedom in the last line, it is clear that part of this argument is incorrect. While it is true that *future* choices of the slave are not reasons for thinking that what he chooses then is desirable for him, what is at issue is limiting his immediate choice; and since this choice is made freely, the individual may be correct in thinking that his interests are best provided for by entering such a contract. But the main consideration for not allowing such a contract is the need to preserve the liberty of the person to make future choices. This gives us a principle—a very narrow one—by which to justify some paternalistic interferences. Paternalism is justified only to preserve a wider range of freedom for the individual in question. How far this principle could be extended, whether it can justify all the cases in which we are inclined upon reflection to think paternalistic measures justified, remains to be discussed. What I have tried to show so far is that there are two strains of argument in Mill—one a straight-forward utilitarian mode of reasoning and one which relies not on the goods which free choice leads to but on the absolute value of the choice itself. The

first cannot establish any absolute prohibition but at most a presumption and indeed a fairly weak one given some fairly plausible assumptions about human psychology; the second, while a stronger line of argument, seems to me to allow on its own grounds a wider range of paternalism than might be suspected. I turn now to a consideration of these matters.

VI

We might begin looking for principles governing the acceptable use of paternalistic power in cases where it is generally agreed that it is legitimate. Even Mill intends his principles to be applicable only to mature individuals, not those in what he calls "non-age." What is it that justifies us in interfering with children? The fact that they lack some of the emotional and cognitive capacities required in order to make fully rational decisions. It is an empirical question to just what extent children have an adequate conception of their own present and future interests but there is not much doubt that there are many deficiencies. For example, it is very difficult for a child to defer gratification for any considerable period of time. Given these deficiencies and given the very real and permanent dangers that may befall the child, it becomes not only permissible but even a duty of the parent to restrict the child's freedom in various ways. There is however an important moral limitation on the exercise of such parental power which is provided by the notion of the child eventually coming to see the correctness of his parent's interventions. Parental paternalism may be thought of as a wager by the parent on the child's subsequent recognition of the wisdom of the restrictions. There is an emphasis on what could be called future-oriented consent—on what the child will come to welcome, rather than on what he does welcome.

The essence of this idea has been incorporated by idealist philosophers into various types of "real-will" theory as applied to fully adult persons. Extensions of paternalism are argued for by claiming that in various respects, chronologically mature individuals share the same deficiencies in knowledge, capacity to think rationally, and the ability to carry out decisions that children possess. Hence in interfering with such people we are in effect doing what they would do if they were fully rational. Hence we are not really opposing their will, hence we are not really interfering with their freedom. The dangers of this move have been sufficiently exposed by Berlin in his *Two Concepts of Freedom*. I see no gain in theoretical clarity nor in practical advantage in trying to pass over the real nature of the interferences with liberty that we impose on others. Still the basic notion of consent is important and seems to me the only acceptable way of trying to delimit an area of justified paternalism.

Let me start by considering a case where the consent is not hypothetical in nature. Under certain conditions it is rational for an individual to agree that others should force him to act in ways which, at the time of action, the individual may not see as desirable. If, for example, a man knows that he is subject to breaking his resolves when temptation is present, he may ask a friend to refuse to entertain his requests at some later stage.

A classical example is given in the Odyssey when Odysseus commands his men to tie him to the mast and refuse all future orders to be set free, because he knows the power of the Sirens to enchant men with their songs. Here we are on relatively sound ground in later refusing Odysseus' request to be set free. He may even claim to have changed his mind but, since it is *just* such changes that he wished to guard against, we are entitled to ignore them.

A process analogous to this may take place on a social rather than individual basis. An electorate may mandate its representatives to pass legislation which when it comes time to "pay the price" may be unpalatable. I may believe that a tax increase is necessary to halt inflation though I may resent the lower pay check each month. However in both this case and that of Odysseus, the measure to be enforced is specifically requested by the party involved and at some point in time there is genuine consent and agreement on the part of those persons whose liberty is infringed. Such is not the case for the paternalistic measures we have been speaking about. What must be involved here is not consent to specific measures but rather consent to a system of government, run by elected representatives, with an understanding that they may act to safeguard our interests in certain limited ways.

I suggest that since we are all aware of our irrational propensities, deficiencies in cognitive and emotional capacities, and avoidable and unavoidable ignorance, it is rational and prudent for us to in effect take out "social insurance policies." We may argue for and against proposed paternalistic measures in terms of what fully rational individuals would accept as forms of protection. Now clearly, since the initial agreement is not about specific measures we are dealing with a more-or-less blank check and therefore there have to be carefully defined limits. What I am looking for are certain kinds of conditions which make it plausible to suppose that rational men could reach agreement to limit their liberty even when other men's interest are not affected.

Of course as in any kind of agreement schema there are great difficulties in deciding what rational individuals would or would not accept. Particularly in sensitive areas of personal liberty, there is always a danger of the dispute over agreement and rationality being a disguised version of evaluative and normative disagreement.

Let me suggest types of situations in which it seems plausible to suppose that fully rational individuals would agree to having paternalistic restrictions imposed upon them. It is reasonable to suppose that there are "goods" such as health which any person would want to have in order to pursue his own good—no matter how that good is conceived. This is an argument used in connection with compulsory education for children but it seems to me that it can be extended to other goods which have this character. Then one could agree that the attainment of such goods should be promoted even when not recognized to be such, at the moment, by the individuals concerned.

An immediate difficulty arises from the fact that men are always faced with competing goods and that there may be reasons why even a value such as health—or indeed life—may be overridden by competing values. Thus the problem with the Christian Scientist and blood transfusions. It may be more important for him to reject "impure substances" than to go on living. The difficult problem that must be faced is whether one can give sense to the notion of a person irrationally attaching weights to competing values.

Consider a person who knows the statistical data on the probability of being injured when not wearing seat belts in an automobile and knows the types and gravity of the various injuries. He also insists that the inconvenience attached to fastening the belt every time he gets in and out of the car outweighs for him the possible risks to himself. I am inclined in this case to think that such a weighing is irrational. Given his life plans, which we are assuming are those of the average person, his interests and commitments already undertaken, I think it is safe to predict that we can find inconsistencies in his calculations at some point. I am assuming that this is not a man who for some conscious or unconscious reasons is trying to injure himself nor is he a man who just likes to "live dangerously." I am assuming that he is like us in all the relevant respects but just puts an enormously high negative value on inconvenience—one which does not seem comprehensible or reasonable.

It is always possible, of course, to assimilate this person to creatures like myself. I, also, neglect to fasten my seat belt and I concede such behavior is not rational but not because I weigh the inconvenience differently from those who fasten the belts. It is just that having made (roughly) the same calculation as everybody else, I ignore it in my actions. [Note: a much better case of weakness of the will than those usually given in ethics tests.] A plausible explanation for this deplorable habit is that although I know in some intellectual sense what the probabilities and risks are I do not fully appreciate them in an emotionally genuine manner.

We have two distinct types of situation in which a man acts in a nonrational fashion. In one case he attaches incorrect weights to some of his values; in the other he neglects to act in accordance with his actual preferences and desires. Clearly there is a stronger and more persuasive argument for paternalism in the latter situation. Here we are really not—by assumption—imposing a good on another person. But why may we not extend out interference to what we might call evaluative delusions? After all, in the case of cognitive delusions we are prepared, often, to act against the expressed will of the person involved. If a man believes that when he jumps out the window he will float upwards—Robert Nozick's example—would not we detain him, forcibly if necessary? The reply will be that this man doesn't wish to be injured and if we could convince him that he is mistaken as to the consequences of his action, he would not wish to perform the action. But part of what is involved in claiming that the

man who doesn't fasten his seat-belts is attaching an incorrect weight to the inconvenience of fastening them is that if he were to be involved in an accident and severely injured he would look back and admit that the inconvenience wasn't as bad as all that. So there is a sense in which, if I could convince him of the consequences of his action, he also would not wish to continue his present course of action. Now the notion of consequences being used here is covering a lot of ground. In one case it's being used to indicate what will or can happen as a result of a course of action and in the other it's making a prediction about the future evaluation of the consequences —in the first sense—of a course of action. And whatever the difference between facts and values —whether it be hard and fast or soft and slow— we are genuinely more reluctant to consent to interferences where evaluative differences are the issue. Let me now consider another factor which comes into play in some of these situations which may make an important difference in our willingness to consent to paternalistic restrictions.

Some of the decisions we make are of such a character that they produce changes which are in one or another way irreversible. Situations are created in which it is difficult or impossible to return to anything like the initial stage at which the decision was made. In particular, some of these changes will make it impossible to continue to make reasoned choices in the future. I am thinking specifically of decisions which involve taking drugs that are physically or psychologically addictive and those which are destructive of one's mental and physical capacities.

I suggest we think of the imposition of paternalistic interferences in situations of this kind as being a kind of insurance policy which we take out against making decisions which are far-reaching, potentially dangerous and irreversible. Each of these factors is important. Clearly there are many decisions we make that are relatively irreversible. In deciding to learn to play chess, I could predict in view of my general interest in games that some portion of my free time was going to be preempted and that it would not be easy to give up the game once I acquired a certain competence. But my whole life style was not going to be jeopardized in an extreme manner. Further it might be argued that even with addictive drugs such as heroin one's normal life plans would not be seriously interfered with if an inexpensive and adequate supply were readily available. So this type of argument might have a much narrower scope than appears to be the case at first.

A second class of cases concerns decisions which are made under extreme psychological and sociological pressures. I am not thinking here of the making of the decision as being something one is pressured into—for example, a good reason for making duelling illegal is that unless this is done many people might have to manifest their courage and integrity in ways in which they would rather not do so—but rather of decisions, such as that to commit suicide, which are usually made at a point where the individual is not thinking clearly and calmly about the nature of his decision. In addition, of course, this comes under the previous heading of all-too-irrevocable decisions. Now there are practical steps which a society could take if it wanted to decrease the possibility of suicide—for example not paying social security benefits to the survivors or, as religious institutions do, not allowing persons to be buried with the same status as natural deaths. I think we may count these as interferences with the liberty of persons to attempt suicide and the question is whether they are justifiable.

Using my argument schema the question is whether rational individuals would consent to such limitations. I see no reason for them to consent to an absolute prohibition but I do think it is reasonable for them to agree to some kind of enforced waiting period. Since we are all aware of the possibility of temporary states, such as great fear of depression, that are inimical to the making of well-informed and rational decisions, it would be prudent for all of us if there were some kind of institutional arrangement whereby we were restrained from making a decision which is so irreversible. What this would be like in practice is difficult to envisage and it may be that if no practical arrangements were feasible we would have to conclude that there should be no restriction at all on this kind of action. But we might have a "cooling off" period, in much the same way that we now require couples who file for divorce to go through a waiting period. Or, more far-fetched, we might imagine a Suicide Board composed of a psychologist and another member picked by the applicant. The Board would be required to meet and talk with the person proposing to take his life, though its approval would not be required.

A third class of decisions—these classes are not supposed to be disjoint—involves dangers which are either not sufficiently understood or appreciated correctly by the persons involved. Let me illustrate, using the example of cigarette smoking, a number of possible cases.

1. A man may not know the facts—for example, smoking between one and two packs a day shortens life expectancy 6.2 years, the costs and pain of the illness caused by smoking, et cetera.
2. A man may know the facts, wish to stop smoking, but not have the requisite willpower.
3. A man may know the facts but not have them play the correct role in his calculation because, say, he discounts the danger psychologically since it is remote in time and/or inflates the attractiveness of other consequences of his decision which he regards as beneficial.

In case 1 what is called for is education, the posting of warnings, etcetera. In case 2 there is no theoretical problem. We are not imposing a good on someone who rejects it. We are simply using coercion to enable people to carry out their own goals. (Note: There obviously is a difficulty in that only a subclass of the individuals affected wish to be prevented from doing what they are doing.) In case 3 there is a sense in which we are imposing a good on someone in that given his current appraisal of the facts he doesn't wish to be restricted. But in another sense we are not imposing a good since what is being claimed—and what must be shown or at least argued for—is that an accurate accounting on his part would lead him to reject his current course of action. Now we all know that such cases exist, that we are prone to disregarding dangers that are only possibilities, that immediate pleasures are often magnified and distorted.

If in addition the dangers are severe and far-reaching, we could agree to allow the state a certain degree of power to intervene in such situations. The difficulty is in specifying in advance, even vaguely, the class of cases in which intervention will be legitimate.

A related difficulty is that of drawing a line so that it is not the case that all ultra-hazardous activities are ruled out, for example, mountain-climbing, bull-fighting, sports-car racing, etcetera. There are some risks—even very great ones—which a person is entitled to take with his life.

A good deal depends on the nature of the deprivation—for example, does it prevent the person from engaging in the activity completely or merely limit his participation—and how important to the nature of the activity is the absence of restriction when this is weighed against the role that the activity plays in the life of the person. In the case of automobile seat belts, for example, the restriction is trivial in nature, interferes not at all with the use or enjoyment of the activity, and does, I am assuming, considerably reduce a high risk of serious injury. Whereas, for example, making mountain-climbing illegal completely prevents a person from engaging in an activity which may play an important role in his life and his conception of the person he is.

In general, the easiest cases to handle are those which can be argued about in the terms which Mill thought to be so important—a concern not just for the happiness or welfare, in some broad sense, of the individual but rather a concern for the autonomy and freedom of the person. I suggest that we would be most likely to consent to paternalism in those instances in which it preserves and enhances for the individual his ability to rationally consider and carry out his own decisions.

I have suggested in this essay a number of types of situations in which it seems plausible that rational men would agree to granting the legislative powers of a society the right to impose restrictions on what Mill calls "self-regarding" conduct. However, rational men knowing something about the resources of ignorance, ill-will and stupidity available to the lawmakers of a society—a good case in point is the history of drug legislation in the United States—will be concerned to limit such intervention to a minimum. I suggest in closing two principles designed to achieve this end.

In all cases of paternalistic legislation there must be a heavy and clear burden of proof placed on the authorities to demonstrate the exact nature of the harmful effects (or beneficial consequences) to be avoided (or achieved) and the probability of their occurrence. The burden of proof here is twofold—what lawyers distinguish as the burden of going forward and the burden of persuasion. That the authorities have the burden of going forward means that it is up to them to raise the question and bring forward evidence of the evils to be avoided. Unlike the case of new drugs, where the manufacturer must produce some evidence that the drug has been tested and found not harmful, no citizen has to show with respect to self-regarding conduct that it is not harmful or promotes his best interest. In addition the nature and cogency of the evidence for the harmfulness of the course of action must be set at a high level. To paraphrase a formulation of the burden of proof for criminal proceedings—better ten men ruin themselves than one man be unjustly deprived of liberty.

Finally, I suggest a principle of the least restrictive alternative. If there is an alternative way of accomplishing the desired end without restricting liberty although it may involve great expense, inconvenience, etcetera, the society must adopt it.

HENRY M. HART, JR. and ALBERT M. SACKS

The Invitation to Dinner Case*

On the way home for lunch on Friday, January 6, 1956, Mr. Patrick met Mr. David an acquaintance of his. Mr. Patrick told Mr. David that he expected Professor Thomas for dinner and would like Mr. David to join them both for dinner and for bridge afterward. Mr. Patrick explained to Mr. David that he must be sure about coming so that there would be enough persons for bridge. Bridge, he said, was a favorite game of Professor Thomas's, and he wanted to humor the professor because he needed his help in getting a job. Mr. David asked what there would be for dinner, and Mr. Patrick promised to have planked steak, which he knew to be a favorite dish of Mr. David's. On hearing this, Mr. David promised firmly to be there at 7 P.M.

At 6:30 P.M., while Mr. David was dressing, the telephone rang. On the line was his friend, Mr. Jack, who asked him to come over for a game of poker. Mr. David agreed at once, and left soon for Jack's house, telling his wife that he was going to Patrick's.

At 9 P.M. the telephone rang in Jack's house, and a voice asked for Mr. David. Mr. David answered, fearful that it was his wife, but it was Mr. Patrick, who could hardly talk from anger. He

said: "So I knew where to find you, you . . . If you do not come over to my place at once, I'll sue you in court." Mr. David hung up the phone without answering, and told the story to Jack and his friends who had a good laugh. All of them kept on playing until the early morning hours.

Mr. Patrick was as good as his word, and his lawyer filed an action against Mr. David. He claimed damages for breach of contract, including the price of a portion of planked steak specially prepared for the defendant; $2,500 compensation for not getting a job (Professor Thomas having left in dudgeon immediately after dinner); and $1,000 for mental suffering.

Mr. Patrick's lawyer claimed that there had been a legally binding contract, supported by consideration, and that the defendant had wilfully and maliciously failed to fulfill his legal and moral obligation. While acknowledging that he could find no case directly in point, he argued that the common law is elastic, and capable of developing a remedy for every wrong, especially in a case such as this where there was reliance on a promise made upon consideration, damage suffered because of malicious default, and warning to the defendant that the matter would be taken to court.

Mr. David appeared without a lawyer, telling the judge that he never thought he could be summoned to court over a social dinner invitation, and asked that the case be dismissed.

How should the judge decide?

*From *The Legal Process* by Henry M. Hart, Jr. and Albert M. Sacks (Cambridge, Mass.: Tentative Edition, 1958), pp. 477–78. Copyright © 1958 by Henry M. Hart, Jr. and Albert M. Sacks. Reprinted by permission of Albert M. Sacks. (This problem was suggested by Mr. Y. Dror, LL.M. Harvard, 1955, and a candidate for the degree of S. J. D. at the Harvard Law School during the academic year 1955–56.)

GRISWOLD v. CONNECTICUT

United States Supreme Court, 1965*

Mr. Justice Douglas delivered the opinion of the Court.

Appellant Griswold is Executive Director of the Planned Parenthood League of Connecticut. Appellant Buxton is a licensed physician and a professor at the Yale Medical School who served as Medical Director for the League at its Center in New Haven—a center open and operating from November 1 to November 10, 1961, when appellants were arrested.

They gave information, instruction, and medical advice to *married persons* as to the means of preventing conception. They examined the wife and prescribed the best contraceptive device or material for her use. Fees were usually charged, although some couples were serviced free.

The statutes whose constitutionality is involved in this appeal are §§ 53–32 and 54–196 of the General Statutes of Connecticut (1958 rev.). The former provides:

"Any person who uses any drug, medicinal article or instrument for the purpose of preventing conception shall be fined not less than fifty dollars or imprisoned not less than sixty days nor more than one year or be both fined and imprisoned."

Section 54–196 provides:

"Any person who assists, abets, counsels, causes, hires or commands another to commit any offense may be prosecuted and punished as if he were the principal offender."

The appellants were found guilty as accessories and fined $100 each, against the claim that the accessory statute as so applied violated the Fourteenth Amendment. The Appellate Division of the Circuit Court affirmed. The Supreme Court of Errors affirmed that judgment.*

We think that appellants have standing to raise the constitutional rights of the married people with whom they had a professional relationship. . . . Certainly the accessory should have standing to assert that the offense which he is charged with assisting is not, or cannot constitutionally be, a crime . . .

*381 U.S. 479 (1965). Excerpts only. Footnotes renumbered.
*Citation omitted (Eds.)

Coming to the merits, we are met with a wide range of questions that implicate the Due Process Clause of the Fourteenth Amendment. Overtones of some arguments suggest that *Lochner* v. *New York,* 198 U.S. 45, should be our guide. But we decline that invitation.* We do not sit as a super-legislature to determine the wisdom, need, and propriety of laws that touch economic problems, business affairs, or social conditions. This law, however, operates directly on an intimate relation of husband and wife and their physician's role in one aspect of that relation.

The association of people is not mentioned in the Constitution nor in the Bill of Rights. The right to educate a child in a school of the parents' choice— whether public or private or parochial—is also not mentioned. Nor is the right to study any particular subject or any foreign language. Yet the First Amendment has been construed to include certain of those rights.

By *Pierce* v. *Society of Sisters,* * the right to educate one's children as one chooses is made applicable to the States by the force of the First and Fourteenth Amendments. By *Meyer* v. *Nebraska,* * the same dignity is given the right to study the German language in a private school. In other words, the State may not, consistently with the spirit of the First Amendment, contract the spectrum of available knowledge. The right of freedom of speech and press includes not only the right to utter or to print, but the right to distribute, the right to receive, the right to read* and freedom of inquiry, freedom of thought, and freedom to teach*—indeed the freedom of the entire university community.* Without those peripheral rights the specific rights would be less secure . . .

In *NAACP* v. *Alabama,* 357 U.S. 449, 462, we protected the "freedom to associate and privacy in one's associations," noting that freedom of association was a peripheral First Amendment right. Disclosure of membership lists of a constitutionally valid association, we held, was invalid "as entailing the likelihood of a substantial restraint upon the exercise by petitioner's members of their right to freedom of association." *Ibid.* In other words, the First Amendment has a penumbra where privacy is protected from governmental intrusion. In like context, we have protected forms of "association" that are not political in the customary sense but pertain to the social, legal, and economic benefit of the members.* In *Schware* v. *Board of Bar Examiners,* 353 U.S. 232, we held it not permissible to bar a lawyer from practice, because he had once been a member of the Communist Party. The man's "association with that Party" was not shown to be "anything more than a political faith in a political party"* and was not action of a kind proving bad moral character.*

Those cases involved more than the "right of assembly"—a right that extends to all irrespective of their race or ideology.* The right of "association," like the right of belief,* is more than the right to attend a meeting; it includes the right to express one's attitudes or philosophies by membership in a group or by affiliation with it or by other lawful means. Association in that context is a form of expression of opinion; and while it is not expressly included in the First Amendment its existence is necessary in making the express guarantees fully meaningful.

The foregoing cases suggest that specific guarantees in the Bill of Rights have penumbras, formed by emanations from those guarantees that help give them life and substance.* Various guarantees create zones of privacy. The right of association contained in the penumbra of the First Amendment is one, as we have seen. The Third Amendment in its prohibition against the quartering of soldiers "in any house" in time of peace without the consent of the owner is another facet of that privacy. The Fourth Amendment explicitly affirms the "right of the people to be secure in their persons, houses, papers, and effects, against unreasonable searches and seizures." The Fifth Amendment in its Self-Incrimination Clause enables the citizen to create a zone of privacy which government may not force him to surrender to his detriment. The Ninth Amendment provides: "The enumeration in the Constitution, of certain rights, shall not be construed to deny or disparage others retained by the people."

The Fourth and Fifth Amendments were described in *Boyd* v. *United States,* 116 U.S. 616, 630, as protection against all governmental invasions "of the sanctity of a man's home and the privacies of life." We recently referred in *Mapp* v. *Ohio,* 367 U.S. 643, 656, to the Fourth Amendment as creating a "right to privacy, no less important than any other right carefully and particularly reserved to the people."* These cases bear witness that the right of privacy which presses for recognition here is a legitimate one.

The present case, then, concerns a relationship lying within the zone of privacy created by several fundamental constitutional guarantees. And it concerns a law which, in forbidding the *use* of contraceptives

rather than regulating their manufacture or sale, seeks to achieve its goals by means having a maximum destructive impact upon that relationship. Such a law cannot stand in light of the familiar principle, so often applied by this Court, that a "governmental purpose to control or prevent activities constitutionally subject to state regulation may not be achieved by means which sweep unnecessarily broadly and thereby invade the area of protected freedoms." *NAACP* v. *Alabama,* 377 U.S. 288, 307. Would we allow the police to search the sacred precincts of marital bedrooms for telltale signs of the use of contraceptives? The very idea is repulsive to the notions of privacy surrounding the marriage relationship.

We deal with a right of privacy older than the Bill of Rights—older than our political parties, older than our school system. Marriage is a coming together for better or for worse, hopefully enduring, and intimate to the degree of being sacred. It is an association that promotes a way of life, not causes; a harmony in living, not political faiths; a bilateral loyalty, not commercial or social projects. Yet it is an association for as noble a purpose as any involved in our prior decisions.

Reversed.

Mr. Justice Goldberg, whom The Chief Justice and Mr. Justice Brennan join, concurring . . . My Brother Stewart dissents on the ground that he "can find no . . . general right of privacy in the Bill of Rights, in any other part of the Constitution, or in any case ever before decided by this Court." He would require a more explicit guarantee than the one which the Court derives from several constitutional amendments. This Court, however, has never held that the Bill of Rights or the Fourteenth Amendment protects only those rights that the Constitution specifically mentions by name . . .

My Brother Stewart, while characterizing the Connecticut birth control law as "an uncommonly silly law," would nevertheless let it stand on the ground that it is not for the courts to " 'substitute their social and economic beliefs for the judgment of legislative bodies, who are elected to pass laws.' " Elsewhere, I have stated that "[w]hile I quite agree with Mr. Justice Brandeis that . . . 'a . . . State may . . . serve as a laboratory; and try novel social and economic experiments,'* I do not believe that this includes the power to experiment with the fundamental liberties of citizens. . . ." The vice of the dissenters' views is that it would permit such experimentation by the States in the area of the fundamental personal rights of its citizens. I cannot agree that the Constitution grants such either to the States or to the Federal Government.

The logic of the dissents would sanction federal or state legislation that seems to me even more plainly

*Citation omitted [Eds.]

unconstitutional than the statute before us. Surely the Government, absent a showing of a compelling subordinating state interest, could not decree that all husbands and wives must be sterilized after two children have been born to them. Yet by their reasoning such an invasion of marital privacy would not be subject to constitutional challenge because, while it might be "silly," no provision of the Constitution specifically prevents the Government from curtailing the marital right to bear children and raise a family. While it may shock some of my Brethren that the Court today holds that the Constitution protects the right of marital privacy in my view it is far more shocking to believe that the personal liberty guaranteed by the Constitution does not include protection against such totalitarian limitation of family size, which is at complete variance with our constitutional concepts. Yet, if upon a showing of a slender basis of rationality, a law outlawing voluntary birth control by married persons is valid, then, by the same reasoning a law requiring compulsory birth control also would seem to be valid. In my view, however, both types of law would unjustifiably intrude upon rights of marital privacy which are constitutionally protected.

In a long series of cases this Court has held that where fundamental personal liberties are involved, they may not be abridged by the States simply on a showing that a regulatory statute has some rational relationship to the effectuation of a proper state purpose. "Where there is a significant encroachment upon personal liberty, the State may prevail only upon showing a subordinating interest which is compelling," *Bates* v. *Little Rock,* 361 U.S. 516, 524. The law must be shown "necessary, and not merely rationally related, to the accomplishment of a permissible state policy." *McLaughlin* v. *Florida,* 379 U.S. 184, 196.*

Although the Connecticut birth-control law obviously encroaches upon a fundamental personal liberty, the State does not show that the law serves any "subordinating [state] interest which is compelling" or that it is "necessary . . . to the accomplishment of a permissible state policy." The State, at most, argues that there is some rational relation between this statute and what is admittedly a legitimate subject of state concern—the discouraging of extra-marital relations. It says that preventing the use of birth-control devices by married persons helps prevent the indulgence by some in such extra-marital relations. The rationality of this justification is dubious, particularly in light of the admitted widespread availability to all persons in the State of Connecticut, unmarried as well as married, of birth-control devices for the prevention of disease, as distin-

guished from the prevention of conception.* But, in any event, it is clear that the state interest in safeguarding marital fidelity can be served by a more discriminately tailored statute, which does not, like the present one, sweep unnecessarily broadly, reaching far beyond the evil sought to be dealt with and intruding upon the privacy of all married couples.* Here, as elsewhere, "[p]recision of regulation must be the touchstone in an area so closely touching our most precious freedoms." *NAACP* v. *Button,* 371 U.S. 415, 438. The State of Connecticut does have statues, the constitutionality of which is beyond doubt, which prohibit adultery and fornication.* These statutes demonstrate that means for achieving the same basic purpose of protecting marital fidelity are available to Connecticut without the need to "invade the area of protected freedoms." *NAACP* v. *Alabama, supra,* at 307.*

Finally, it should be said of the Court's holding today that it in no way interferes with a State's proper regulation of sexual promiscuity or misconduct. As my Brother Harlan so well stated in his dissenting opinion in *Poe* v. *Ullman,*

"Adultery, homosexuality and the like are sexual intimacies which the State forbids . . . but the intimacy of husband and wife is necessarily an essential and accepted feature of the institution of marriage, an institution which the State not only must allow, but which always and in every age it has fostered and protected. It is one thing when the States exerts its power either to forbid extra-marital sexuality . . . or to say who may marry, but it is quite another when, having acknowledged a marriage and the intimacies inherent in it, it undertakes to regulate by means of the criminal law the details of that intimacy."

In sum, I believe that the right of privacy in the marital relation is fundamental and basic—a personal right "retained by the people" within the meaning of the Ninth Amendment. Connecticut cannot constitutionally abridge this fundamental right, which is protected by the Fourteenth Amendment from infringement by the States. I agree with the Court that petitioners' convictions must therefore be reversed . . .

Mr. Justice Black, with whom Mr. Justice Stewart joins, dissenting.

I agree with my Brother Stewart's dissenting opinion. And like him I do not to any extent whatever base my view that this Connecticut law is constitutional on a belief that the law is wise or that its policy is a good one. In order that there may be no room at all to doubt why I vote as I do, I feel constrained to add that the law is every bit as offensive to me as it is to my Brethren of the majority and my Brothers Harlan, White and Goldberg who, reciting reasons why it is offensive to them, hold it unconstitutional. There is no single one of the graphic and eloquent strictures and criticisms fired at the policy of this Connecticut law either by the

*Citation omitted [Eds.]

Court's opinion or by those of my concurring Brethren to which I cannot subscribe—except their conclusion that the evil qualities they see in the law make it unconstitutional . . .

The Court talks about a constitutional "right of privacy" as though there is some constitutional provision or provisions forbidding any law ever to be passed which might abridge the "privacy" of individuals. But there is not. There are, of course, guarantees in certain specific constitutional provisions which are designed in part to protect privacy at certain times and places with respect to certain activities. Such, for example, is the Fourth Amendment's guarantee against "unreasonable searches and seizures." But I think it belittles that Amendment to talk about it as though it protects nothing but "privacy." To treat it that way is to give it a niggardly interpretation, not the kind of liberal reading I think any Bill of Rights provision should be given. The average man would very likely not have his feelings soothed any more by having his property seized openly than by having it seized privately and by stealth. He simply wants his property left alone. And a person can be just as much, if not more, irritated, annoyed and injured by an unceremonious public arrest by a policeman as he is by a seizure in the privacy of his office or home.

One of the most effective ways of diluting or expanding a constitutionally guaranteed right is to substitute for the crucial word or words of a constitutional guarantee another word or words, more or less flexible and more of less restricted in meaning. This fact is well illustrated by the use of the term "right of privacy" as a comprehensive substitute for the Fourth Amendment's guarantee against "unreasonable searches and seizures." "Privacy" is a broad, abstract and ambiguous concept which can easily be shrunken in meaning but which can also, on the other hand, easily be interpreted as a constitutional ban against many things other than searches and seizures. I have expressed the view many times that First Amendment freedoms, for example, have suffered from a failure of the courts to stick to the simple language of the First Amendment in construing it, instead of invoking multitudes of words substituted for those the Framers used.* For these reasons I get nowhere in this case by talk about a constitutional "right of privacy" as an emanation from one or more constitutional provisions. I like my privacy as well as the next one, but I am nevertheless compelled to admit that government has a right to invade it unless prohibited by some specific constitutional provision. For these reasons I cannot agree with the Court's judgment and the reasons it gives for holding this Connecticut law unconstitutional . . .

*Citations omitted [Eds.]

The due process argument which my Brothers Harlan and White adopt here is based, as their opinions indicate, on the premise that this Court is vested with power to invalidate all state laws that it considers to be arbitrary, capricious, unreasonable, or oppressive, or on this Court's belief that a particular state law under scrutiny has no "rational or justifying" purpose, or is offensive to a "sense of fairness and justice." If these formulas based on "natural justice," or others which mean the same thing,[1] are to prevail, they require judges to determine what is or is not constitutional on the basis of their own appraisal of what laws are unwise or unnecessary. The power to make such decisions is of course that of a legislative body. Surely it has to be admitted that no provision of the Constitution specifically gives such blanket power to courts to exercise such a supervisory veto over the wisdom and value of legislative policies and to hold unconstitutional those laws which they believe unwise or dangerous. I readily admit that no legislative body, state or national, should pass laws that can justly be given any of the invidious labels invoked as constitutional excuses to strike down state laws. But perhaps it is not too much to say that no legislative body ever does pass laws without believing that they will accomplish a sane, rational, wise and justifiable purpose. While I completely subscribe to the holding of *Marbury* v. *Madison,* and subsequent cases, that our Court has constitutional power to strike down statutes, state or federal, that violate commands of the Federal Constitution, I do not believe that we are granted power by the Due Process Clause or any other constitutional provision or provisions to measure constitutionality by our belief that legislation is arbitrary, capricious or unreasonable, or accomplishes no justifiable purpose, or is offensive to our own notions of "civilized standards of conduct."[2] Such an appraisal of the wisdom of legislation is an attribute of the power to make laws, not of the power to interpret them. The use by federal courts of such a formula or doctrine or whatnot to veto federal or state laws simply takes away from Congress and States the power to make laws based on their own judgment of fairness and wisdom and transfers that power to this Court for ultimate determination—a power which was specifically denied to federal courts by the convention that framed the Constitution. . . .

My Brother Goldberg has adopted the recent discovery[3] that the Ninth Amendment as well as the Due Process Clause can be used by this Court as authority to strike down all state legislation which this Court thinks violates "fundamental principles of liberty and justice," or is contrary to the "traditions and [collective] conscience of our people." He also states, without proof satisfactory to me, that in making decisions on this basis judges will not consider "their personal and private notions." One may ask how they can avoid considering them. Our Court certainly has no machinery with which to take a Gallup Poll.[4] And the scientific miracles of this age have not yet produced a gadget which the Court can use to determine what traditions are rooted in the "[collective] conscience of our people." Moreover, one would certainly have to look far beyond the language of the Ninth Amendment[5] to find that the Framers vested in this Court any such awesome veto powers over lawmaking, either by the States or by the Congress. Nor does anything in the history of the Amendment offer any support for such a shocking doctrine. The whole history of the adoption of the Constitution and Bill of Rights points the other way, and the very material quoted by my Brother Goldberg shows that the Ninth Amendment was intended to protect against the idea that "by enumerating particular exceptions to the grant of power" to the Federal Government, "those rights which were not singled out, were intended to be assigned into the hands of the General Government [the United States], and were consequently insecure."[6] That Amendment was passed, not to broaden the powers of this Court or any other department of "the General Government," but, as every student of history knows, to assure the people that the Constitution in all its provisions was intended to limit the Federal Government to the powers granted expressly or by necessary implication. If any broad, unlimited power to hold laws unconstitutional because they offend what this Court conceives to be the "[collective] conscience of our people" is vested in this Court by the Ninth Amendment, the Fourteenth Amendment, or any other provision of the Constitution, it was not given by the Framers, but rather has been bestowed on the Court by the Court. This fact is perhaps responsible for the peculiar phenomenon that for a period of a century and a half no serious suggestion was ever made that the Ninth Amendment, enacted to protect state powers against federal invasion, could be used as a weapon of federal power to prevent state legislatures from passing laws they consider appropriate to govern local affairs. Use of any such broad, unbounded judicial authority would make of this Court's members a day-to-day constitutional convention.

NOTES

1. A collection of the catchwords and catch phrases invoked by judges who would strike down under the Fourteenth Amendment laws which offend their notions of natural justice would fill many pages. Thus it has been said that this Court can forbid state action which "shocks the conscience," *Rochin* v. *California*, 342 U.S. 165, 172, sufficiently to "shock itself into the protective arms of the Constitution," *Irvine* v. *Cali-*

fornia, 347 U.S. 128, 138 (concurring opinion). It has been urged that States may not run counter to the "decencies of civilized conduct," *Rochin, supra*, at 173, or "some principle of justice so rooted in the traditions, and conscience of our people as to be ranked as fundamental," *Snyder* v. *Massachusetts*, 291 U.S. 97, 105, or to "those canons of decency and fairness which express the notions of justice of English-speaking peoples," *Malinski* v. *New York*, 324 U.S. 401, 417 (concurring opinion), or to "the community's sense of fair play and decency," *Rochin, supra*, at 173. It has been said that we must decide whether a state law is "fair, reasonable and appropriate," or is rather "an unreasonable, unnecessary and arbitrary interference with the right of the individual to his personal liberty or to enter into . . . contracts," *Lochner* v. *New York*, 198 U.S. 45, 56. States, under this philosophy, cannot act in conflict with "deeply rooted feelings of the community," *Haley* v. *Ohio*, 332 U.S. 596, 604 (separate opinion), or with "fundamental notions of fairness and justice," *id.*, 607. See also, e.g., *Wolf* v. *Colorado*, 338 U.S. 25, 27 ("rights . . . basic to our free society"); *Hebert* v. *Louisiana*, 272 U.S. 312, 316 ("fundamental principles of liberty and justice"); *Adkins* v. *Children's Hospital*, 261 U.S. 525, 561 ("arbitrary restraint of . . . liberties"); *Betts* v. *Brady*, 316 U.S. 455, 462 ("denial of fundamental fairness, shocking to the universal sense of justice"); *Poe* v. *Ullman*, 367 U.S. 497, 539 (dissenting opinion) ("intolerable and unjustifiable"). Perhaps the clearest, frankest and briefest explanation of how this due process approach works is the statement in another case handed down today that this Court is to invoke the Due Process Clause to strike down state procedures or laws which it can "not tolerate." *Linkletter* v. *Walker, post*, p. 618, at 631.

2. See Hand, The Bill of Rights (1958) 70: "[J]udges are seldom content merely to annul the particular solution before them; they do not, indeed they may not, say that taking all things into consideration, the legislators' solution is too strong for the judicial stomach. On the contrary they wrap up their veto in a protective veil of adjectives such as 'arbitrary,' 'artificial,' 'normal,' 'reasonable,' 'inherent.' 'fundamental,' or 'essential,' whose office usually, though quite innocently, is to disguise what they are doing and impute to it a derivation far more impressive than their personal preferences, which are all that in fact lie behind the decision." [Citations omitted—Eds.]

3. See Patterson, The Forgotten Ninth Amendment (1955). Mr. Patterson urges that the Ninth Amendment be used to protect unspecified "natural and inalienable rights." P. 4. The Introduction by Roscoe Pound states that "there is a marked revival of natural law ideas throughout the world. Interest in the Ninth Amendment is a symptom of that revival." P. iii.

4. Of course one cannot be oblivious to the fact that Mr. Gallup has already published the results of a poll which he says show that 46% of the people in this country believe schools should teach about birth control. Washington Post, May 21, 1965, p. 2, col. 1. I can hardly believe, however, that Brother Goldberg would view 46% of the persons polled as so overwhelming a proportion that this Court may now rely on it to declare that the Connecticut law infringes "fundamental" rights, and overrule the long-standing view of the people of Connecticut expressed through their elected representatives.

5. U.S. Const., Amend. IX, provides: "The enumeration in the Constitution, of certain rights, shall not be construed to deny or disparage others retained by the people."

6. Annuals of Congress 439.

HYMAN GROSS

Privacy and Autonomy*

Why is privacy desirable? When is its loss objectionable and when is it not? How much privacy is a person entitled to? These questions challenge at the threshold our concern about protection of privacy. Usually they are pursued by seeking agreement on the boundary between morbid and healthy reticence, and by attempting to determine when unwanted intrusion or notoriety is justified by something more important than privacy. Seldom is privacy considered as the condition under which there is *control* over acquaintance with one's personal affairs by the one enjoying it, and I wish here to show how consideration of privacy in this neglected aspect is helpful in answering the basic questions. First I shall attempt to make clear this part of the idea of privacy, next suggest why privacy in this aspect merits protection, then argue that some important dilemmas are less vexing when we do get clear about these things, and finally offer a cautionary remark regarding the relation of privacy and autonomy.

I

What in general is it that makes certain conduct offensive to privacy? To distinguish obnoxious from innocent interference with privacy we must first see clearly what constitutes loss of privacy at all, and then determine why loss of privacy when it does occur is sometimes objectionable and sometimes not.

Loss of privacy occurs when the limits one has set on acquaintance with his personal affairs are not respected. Almost always we mean not respected by *others,* though in unusual cases we might speak of a person not respecting his own privacy—he is such a passionate gossip, say, that

he gossips even about himself and later regrets it. Limits on acquaintance may be maintained by the physical insulation of a home, office, or other private place within which things that are to be private may be confined. Or such bounds may exist by virtue of exclusionary social conventions, for example those governing a private conversation in a public place; or through restricting conventions which impose an obligation to observe such limits, as when disclosure is made in confidence. Limits operate in two ways. There are restrictions on what is known, and restrictions on who may know it. Thus, a curriculum vitae furnished to or for a prospective employer is not normally an invitation to undertake a detective investigation using the items provided as clues. Nor is there normally license to communicate to others the information submitted. In both instances there would be disregard of limitations implied by considerations of privacy, unless the existence of such limitations is unreasonable under the circumstances (the prospective employer is the CIA, or the information is furnished to an employment agency). But there is no loss of privacy when such limits as do exist are respected, no matter how ample the disclosure or how extensive its circulation. If I submit a detailed account of my life while my friend presents only the barest résumé of his, I am not giving up more of privacy than he. And if I give the information to a hundred employers, I lose no more in privacy than my friend who confides to only ten, provided those informed by each of us are equally restricted. More people know more about me, so my *risk* of losing privacy is greater and the threatened loss more serious. Because I am a less private person than my friend, I am more willing to run that risk. But until there is loss of control over what is known, and by whom, my privacy is uncompromised—though much indeed may be

*From *Nomos XIII, Privacy,* ed. by John Chapman and J. Roland Pennock (New York: Lieber-Atherton, 1971), pp. 169–182. Reprinted by permission of the publisher.

lost in secrecy, mystery, obscurity, and anonymity.

Privacy is lost in either of two ways. It may be given up, or it may be taken away. Abandonment of privacy (though sometimes undesired) is an inoffensive loss, while deprivation by others is an offensive loss.

If one makes a public disclosure of personal matters or exposes himself under circumstances that do not contain elements of restriction on further communication, there is loss of control for which the person whose privacy is lost is himself responsible. Such abandonment may result from indifference, carelessness, or a positive desire to have others become acquainted. There are, however, instances in which privacy is abandoned though this was not intended. Consider indiscrete disclosures while drunk which are rued when sober. If the audience is not under some obligation (perhaps the duty of a confidant) to keep dark what was revealed, there has been a loss of privacy for which the one who suffers it is responsible. But to constitute an abandonment, the loss of privacy must result from voluntary conduct by the one losing it, and the loss must be an expectable result of such conduct. If these two conditions are not met, the person who suffers the loss cannot be said to be responsible for it. Accordingly, a forced revelation, such as an involuntary confession, is not an abandonment of privacy, because the person making it has not given up control but has had it taken from him.

Regarding the requirement of expectability, we may see its significance by contrasting the case of a person whose conversation is overheard in Grand Central Station with the plight of someone made the victim of eavesdropping in his living room. In a public place loss of control is expectable by virtue of the circumstances of communication: part of what we mean when we say a place is public is that there is not present the physical limitation upon which such control depends. But a place may be called private only when there is such limitation, so communication in it is expectably limited and the eavesdropping an offensive violation for which the victim is not himself responsible. And consider the intermediate case of eavesdropping on a conversation in a public place —a distant parabolic microphone focused on a street-corner conversation, or a bugging device planted in an airplane seat. The offensive charac-

ter of such practices derives again from their disregard of expectable limitations, in this instance the force of an exclusionary social convention which applies to all except those whose immediate presence enables them to overhear.

So far there has been consideration of what constitutes loss of privacy, and when it is objectionable. But to assess claims for protection of privacy we must be clear also about *why* in general loss of privacy is objectionable. This becomes especially important when privacy and other things we value are in competition, one needing to be sacrificed to promote the other. It becomes important then to understand what good reasons there are for valuing privacy, and this is our next item of business.

II

There are two sorts of things we keep private, and with respect to each, privacy is desirable for somewhat different reasons. Concern for privacy is sometimes concern about which facts about us can become known, and to whom. This includes acquaintance with all those things which make up the person as he may become known—identity, appearance, traits of personality and character, talents, weaknesses, tastes, desires, habits, interests—in short, things which tell us who a person is and what he's like. The other kind of private matter is about our lives—what we've done, intend to do, are doing now, how we feel, what we have, what we need—and concern about privacy here is to restrict acquaintance with these matters. Together these two classes of personal matters comprise all those things which can be private. Certain items of information do indeed have aspects which fit them for either category. For example, a person's belief is something which pertains to him when viewed as characteristic of him, but pertains to the events of his life when viewed as something he has acquired, acts on, and endeavors to have others adopt.

Why is privacy of the person important? This calls mainly for consideration of what is necessary to maintain an integrated personality in a social setting. Although we are largely unaware of what influences us at the time, we are constantly concerned to control how we appear to others, and act to implement this concern in ways extremely subtle and multifarious. Models of image and behavior are noticed, imitated, adopted, so that nuances in speech, gesture, facial expression, *politesse,* and much more become a person as known on an occasion. The deep motive is to influence the reactions of others, and this is at the heart of human social accommodation. Constraints to imitation and disguise can become a pathological problem of serious proportions when concern with appearances interferes with normal functioning, but normal behavior allows, indeed requires, that we perform critically in presenting and withholding in order to effect certain appearances. If these editorial efforts are not to be wasted, we must have a large measure of control over what of us is seen and heard, when, where, and by whom. For this reason we see as offensive the candid camera which records casual behavior with the intention of later showing it as entertainment to a general audience. The victim is not at the time aware of who will see him and so does not have the opportunity to exercise appropriate critical restraint in what he says and does. Although subsequent approval for the showing eliminates grounds for objection to the publication as an offense to privacy, there remains the lingering objection to the prior disregard of limits of acquaintance which are normal to the situation and so presumably relied on by the victim at the time. The nature of the offense is further illuminated by considering its aggravation when the victim has been deliberately introduced unawares into the situation for the purpose of filming his behavior, or its still greater offensiveness if the setting is a place normally providing privacy and assumed to be private by the victim. What we have here are increasingly serious usurpations of a person's prerogative to determine how he shall appear, to whom, and on what occasion.

The same general objection applies regarding loss of privacy where there is information about our personal affairs which is obtained, accumulated, and transmitted by means beyond our control. It is, however, unlike privacy of personality in its untoward consequences. A data bank of personal information is considered objectionable, but not because it creates appearances over which we have no control. We are willing to concede that acquaintance with our reputation is in general not something we are privileged to control, and that we are not privileged to decide just what our reputation shall be. If the reputation is correct we cannot object because we do not appear

as we would wish. What then are the grounds of objection to a data bank, an objection which indeed persists even if its information is correct and the inferences based on the information are sound? A good reason for objecting is that a data bank is an offense to self-determination. We are subject to being acted on by others because of conclusions about us which we do not know and whose effect we have no opportunity to counteract. There is a loss of control over reputation which is unacceptable because we no longer have the ability to try to change what is believed about us. We feel entitled to know what others believe, and why, so that we may try to change misleading impressions and on occasion show why a decision about us ought not to be based on reputation even if the reputation is justified. If our account in the data bank were made known to us and opportunity given to change its effect, we should drop most (though not all) of our objection to it. We might still fear the danger of abuse by public forces concerned more with the demands of administrative convenience than justice, but because we could make deposits and demand a statement reflecting them, we would at least no longer be in the position of having what is known and surmised about us lie beyond our control.

Two aspects of privacy have been considered separately, though situations in which privacy is violated sometimes involve both. Ordinary surveillance by shadowing, peeping, and bugging commonly consists of observation of personal behavior as well as accumulation of information. Each is objectionable for its own reasons, though in acting against the offensive practice we protect privacy in both aspects. Furthermore, privacy of personality and of personal affairs have some common ground in meriting protection, and this has to do with a person's role as a responsible moral agent.

In general we do not criticize a person for untoward occurrences which are a result of his conduct if (through no fault of his own) he lacked the ability to do otherwise. Such a person is similarly ineligible for applause for admirable things which would not have taken place but for his conduct. In both instances we claim that he is not responsible for what happened, and so should not be blamed or praised. The principle holds true regarding loss of privacy. If a person cannot control how he is made to appear (nor could he have prevented his loss of control), he is not responsible for how he appears or is thought of, and therefore cannot be criticized as displeasing or disreputable (nor extolled as the opposite). He can, of course, be condemned for conduct which is the basis of the belief about him, but that is a different matter from criticism directed solely to the fact that such a belief exists. Personal gossip (even when believed) is not treated by others as something for which the subject need answer, because its existence defies his control. Responsible appraisal of anyone whose image or reputation is a matter of concern requires that certain private items illicitly in the public domain be ignored in the assessment. A political figure may, with impunity, be known as someone who smokes, drinks, flirts, and tells dirty jokes, so long (but only so long) as this is not the public image *he* presents. The contrasting fortunes of recent political leaders remind us that not being responsible for what is believed by others can be most important. If such a man is thought in his private life to engage in discreet though illicit liaisons he is not held accountable for rumors without more. However, once he has allowed himself to be publicly exposed in a situation which is in the slightest compromising, he must answer for mere appearances. And on this same point, we might consider why a woman is never held responsible for the way she appears in the privacy of her toilette.

To appreciate the importance of this sort of disclaimer of responsibility we need only imagine a community in which it is not recognized. Each person would be accountable for himself however he might be known, and regardless of any precautionary seclusion which was undertaken in the interest of shame, good taste, or from other motives of self-regard. In such a world modesty is sacrificed to the embarrassment of unwanted acclaim, and self-criticism is replaced by the condemnation of others. It is part of the vision of Orwell's *1984,* in which observation is so thorough that it forecloses the possibility of a private sector of life under a person's exclusionary control, and so makes him answerable for everything observed without limits of time or place. Because of this we feel such a condition of life far more objectionable than a community which makes the same oppressive social demands of loyalty and conformity but with the opportunity to be free of concern about appearances in private. In a community without privacy, furthermore, there can be no editorial privilege exercised in making oneself known to others. Consider, for example, the plight in which Montaigne would find himself. He observed that "No quality embraces us purely and universally. If it did not seem crazy to talk to oneself, there is not a day when I would not be heard growling at myself: 'Confounded fool!' And yet I do not intend that to be my definition." Respect for privacy is required to safeguard our changes of mood and mind, and to promote growth of the person through self-discovery and criticism. We want to run the risk of making fools of ourselves and be free to call ourselves fools, yet not be fools in the settled opinion of the world, convicted out of our own mouths.

III

Privacy is desirable, but rights to enjoy it are not absolute. In deciding what compromises must be made some deep quandaries recur, and three of them at least seem more manageable in light of what has been said so far.

In the first place, insistence on privacy is often taken as implied admission that there is cause for shame. The assumption is that the only reason for keeping something from others is that one is ashamed of it (although it is conceded that sometimes there is in fact no cause for shame even though the person seeking privacy thinks there is). Those who seek information and wish to disregard interests in privacy often play on this notion by claiming that the decent and the innocent have no cause for shame and so no need for privacy: "Only those who have done or wish to do something shameful demand privacy." But it is unsound to assume that demands for privacy imply such an admission. Pride, or at least wholesome self-regard, is the motive in many situations. The famous Warren and Brandeis article on privacy which appeared in the *Harvard Law Review* in 1890 was impelled in some measure, we are told, by Samuel Warren's chagrin. His daughter's wedding, a very social Boston affair, had been made available to the curious at every newsstand by the local press. Surely he was not ashamed of the wedding even though outraged by the publicity. Or consider Miss Roberson, the lovely lady whose picture was placed on a poster advertising the product of Franklin Mills with the eulogistic slogan "Flour of the family," thereby precipitating a lawsuit whose consequences included the first statutory protection of privacy in the United States. What was exploited was the lady's face, undoubtedly a source of pride.

Both these encroachments on privacy illustrate the same point. Things which people like about themselves are taken by them to belong to them in a particularly exclusive way, and so control over disclosure or publication is especially important to them. The things about himself which a person is most proud of he values most, and thus are things over which he is most interested to exercise exclusive control. It is true that shame is not infrequently the motive for privacy, for often we do seek to maintain conditions necessary to avoid criticism and punishment. But since it is not the only motive, the quest for privacy does not entail tacit confessions. Confusion arises here in part because an assault on privacy always does involve humiliation of the victim. But this is because he has been deprived of control over something personal which is given over to the control of others. In short, unwilling loss of privacy always results in the victim being shamed, not because of what others learn, but because they and not he may then determine who else shall know it and what use shall be made of it.

Defining the privilege to make public what is otherwise private is another source of persistent difficulty. There is a basic social interest in making available information about people, in exploring the personal aspects of human affairs, in stimulating and satisfying curiosity about others. The countervailing interest is in allowing people who have not offered themselves for public scrutiny to remain out of sight and out of mind. In much of the United States the law has strained with the problem of drawing a line of protection which accords respect to both interests. The result, broadly stated, has been recognition of a privilege to compromise privacy for news and other material whose primary purpose is to impart information, but to deny such privileged status to literary and other art, to entertainment, and generally to any appropriation for commercial purposes. Development of the law in New York after Miss Roberson's unsuccessful attempt to restrain public display of her picture serves as a good example. A statute was enacted prohibiting unauthorized use of the name, portrait, or picture of any living person for purposes of trade or advertising, and the legislation has been inter-

preted by the courts along the general lines indicated. But it is still open to speculation why a writer's portrayal of a real person as a character in a novel could qualify as violative, while the same account in biographical or historical work would not. It has not been held that history represents a more important social interest than art and so is more deserving of a privileged position in making known personal matters, or, more generally, that edification is more important than entertainment. Nor is the question ever raised, as one might expect, whether an item of news is sufficiently newsworthy to enjoy a privilege in derogation of privacy. Further, it was not held that the implied statutory criterion of intended economic benefit from the use of a personality would warrant the fundamental distinctions. Indeed, the test of economic benefit would qualify both television's public affairs programs and its dramatic shows as within the statute, and the reportage of *Life* Magazine would be as restricted as the films of De Mille or Fellini. But in each instance the former is in general free of the legal prohibition while the latter is not. What, then, is the basis of distinction? Though not articulated, a sound criterion does exist.

Unauthorized *use* of another person—whether for entertainment, artistic creation, or economic gain—is offensive. So long as we remain in charge of how we are used, we have no cause for complaint. In those cases in which a legal wrong is recognized, there has been use by others in disregard of this authority, but in those cases in which a privilege is found, there is not *use* of personality or personal affairs at all, at least not use in the sense of one person assuming control over another, which is the gist of the offense to autonomy. We do indeed suffer a loss of autonomy whenever the power to place us in free circulation is exercised by others, but we consider such loss offensive only when another person assumes the control of which we are deprived, when we are used and not merely exposed. Failure to make clear this criterion of offensiveness has misled those who wish to define the protectable area, and they conceive the problem as one of striking an optimal balance between two valuable interests, when in fact it is a matter of deciding whether the acts complained of are offensive under a quite definite standard of offensiveness. The difficult cases here have not presented a dilemma of selecting the happy medium, but rather the slippery job of determining whether the defendant had used the plaintiff or whether he had merely caused things about him to become known, albeit to the defendant's profit. The difference is between managing another person as a means to one's own ends, which is offensive, and acting merely as a vehicle of presentation (though not gratuitously) to satisfy established social needs, which is not offensive. Cases dealing with an unauthorized biography that was heavily anecdotal and of questionable accuracy, or with an entertaining article that told the true story of a former child prodigy who became an obscure eccentric, are perplexing ones because they present elements of both offensive and inoffensive publication, and a decision turns on which is predominant.

There remains another balance-striking quandary to be dismantled. It is often said that privacy as an interest must be balanced against security. Each, we think, must sacrifice something of privacy to promote the security of all, though we are willing to risk some insecurity to preserve a measure of privacy. Pressure to reduce restrictions on wiretapping and searches by police seeks to push the balance toward greater security. But the picture we are given is seriously misleading. In the first place we must notice the doubtful assumption on which the argument rests. It may be stated this way: the greater the ability to watch what is going on, or obtain evidence of what has gone on, the greater the ability to prevent crime. It is a notion congenial to those who believe that more efficient law enforcement contributes significantly to a reduction in crime. We must, however, determine if such a proposition is in fact sound, and we must see what crimes are suppressible, even in principle, before any sacrifice of privacy can be justified. There is, at least *in limine,* much to be said for the conflicting proposition that, once a generally efficient system of law enforcement exists, an increase in its efficiency does not result in a corresponding reduction in crime, but only in an increase in punishments. Apart from that point, there is an objection relating more directly to what has been said here about privacy. Security and privacy are both desirable, but measures to promote each are on different moral footing. Men ought to be secure, we say, because only in that condition can they live a good life. Privacy, however, like peace and prosperity, is itself part of what we mean by a good life, a part having to do with self-respect and self-determination. Therefore, the appropriate attitudes when we are asked to sacrifice privacy for security are first a critical one which urges alternatives that minimize or do not at all require the sacrifice, and ultimately regret for loss of a cherished resource if the sacrifice proves necessary.

IV

In speaking of privacy and autonomy, there is some danger that privacy may be conceived as autonomy. Such confusion has been signaled in legal literature by early and repeated use of the phrase "right to be let alone" as a synonym for "right of privacy." The United States Supreme Court succumbed completely in 1965 in its opinion in *Griswold v. Connecticut,* and the ensuing intellectual disorder warrants comment.

In that case legislative prohibition of the use of contraceptives was said to be a violation of a constitutional right of privacy, at least when it affected married people. The court's opinion relied heavily on an elaborate *jeu de mots,* in which different senses of the word "privacy" were punned upon, and the legal concept generally mismanaged in ways too various to recount here. In the *Griswold* situation there had been an attempt by government to regulate personal affairs, not get acquainted with them, and so there was an issue regarding autonomy and not privacy. The opinion was not illuminating on the question of what are proper bounds for the exercise of legislative power, which was the crucial matter before the court. It is precisely the issue of what rights to autonomous determination of his affairs are enjoyed by a citizen. The *Griswold* opinion not only failed to take up that question in a forthright manner, but promoted confusion about privacy in the law by unsettling the intellectual focus on it which had been developed in torts and constitutional law. If the confusion in the court's argument was inadvertent, one may sympathize with the deep conceptual difficulties which produced it, and if it was deliberately contrived, admire its ingenuity. Whatever its origin, its effect is to muddle the separate issues, which must be analyzed and argued along radically different lines when protection is sought either for privacy or for autonomy. Hopefully, further developments will make clear that while an offense to privacy is an offense to autonomy, not every curtailment of autonomy is a compromise of privacy.

S A M U E L M. F A H R

Sexual Psychopath Laws *

On the 14th of April, 1955, a new and potentially very important statute became part of the laws of the State of Iowa. That statute is Chapter 121 of the Laws of the Fifty-sixth General Assembly (H.F. 185), entitled "Criminal Sexual Psychopaths." If unanimity is a witness to virtue, this law was most favored, for it passed both houses without one dissenting vote, the House on February 23 by 100–0 and the Senate on March 28 by 49–0. No extended discussion of this bill was reported by the Des Moines Register; indeed, the only real mention of it at all in "The Newpaper All Iowa Depends Upon" was in an editorial of April 4, generally praising the passage of the law. One may assume, then, that this particular law was regarded on all sides as A Good Thing.

Good or not, it is no new thing, for Iowa was the twenty-fourth American jurisdiction to pass such a law.[1] As long ago as 1937 Michigan passed the first of the so-called "sexual psychopath laws,"[2] and the last fifteen years have seen a flooding tide of this sort of legislation.

MEDICAL BACKGROUND OF THESE STATUTES

The sources of this tide are various. For one thing, there has long been a profound sentiment among many students of the law that criminal punishment, generally justified for its deterrent effect, was not in fact preventing crime nor getting at the heart of the matter, the disturbed personality of the offender. From the sentimental writer for the Sunday supplement ("There is no such thing as a *bad* boy—there are only sick boys and healthy boys") to the more scholarly (and hence duller and less often read) student of human aberrations, the modern emphasis has been on treatment. If only we had enough facilities,

clinical psychologists, psychiatrists and all the rest of the paraphernalia of treatment, perhaps—some would say, certainly—we could "cure" these offenders and send them back into the world, finer, better men. So it is only natural that the sex offender above all should be looked on as sick and hence the proper subject for therapy, not jail. Unquestionably a genuine faith in modern psychology and psychiatry underlies this whole movement to "reform" the law and to bring it up to date with all we have learned of the human being and his works.

The "modern" solution of the type of legislation we are considering is to submit certain persons convicted of, or at least accused of, certain crimes to medical examination, to give them a formal hearing, often with jury trial provided optionally; and then if their personalities fall within the statutory term, "sexual psychopath," to commit them indefinitely to institutions of the sort which can "cure" them. This is a general outline of the statutes; there are many local variations we shall have to consider later. These "sexual psychopath laws" reflect public confidence in the man of science and of near-science, and a desire to be humane, to be in tune with the times.

I am afraid these laws also reflect less worthy motivations. The same popular magazines which regale us with popularizations of psychology furnish us as well sensational articles tending to prove a monstrous tidal wave of crime, much of it sexual in nature. "How Safe Is Your Daughter?" asks J. Edgar Hoover; and well he may, for "depraved human beings, more savage than beasts, are permitted to rove America almost at will."[3] David G. Wittels reported "tens of thousands" of "so-called sex killers" and "degenerates" were "loose in the country today."[4] There is simply no doubt that much of this legislation is *ad hominem* in origin, passed in the fervor stimulated by such sensational writings and often triggered off by some particularly violent or frightful local crime with sexual overtones.[5]

* Samuel M. Fahr, "Iowa's New Sexual Psychopath Law—An Experiment Noble in Propose," *Iowa Law Review,* Vol. 41 (1956), pp. 523–57. Reprinted by permission of the publisher and the author.

So we see in these statutes a blend of progress and enlightenment, as it is thought, tempered to "treat" a dangerous class and yet to pacify those who clamor for sterner measures and harsher punishments. Surely nothing but success could attend a statute which seeks out the sex offender, identifies him, gives him a hearing, and sends him off either to be cured and restored to society or else at least kept out of harm's way if recovery seems impossible. What could be better?

There is no doubt that in all jurisdictions which have adopted "sexual psychopath laws" of one sort or another [6] hope ran high. And yet—these statutes have been almost uniformly criticized in law reviews, in criminological circles, and in medical journals. They have been called "inoperative," "too loosely drawn," "undesirable in principle," "A Star Chamber procedure" and many other things.[7] Two students of the California version, a doctor and a lawyer with extensive experience in the operation of that law, urge outright repeal of it; [8] a Michigan Commission set up to study the operation of all Michigan laws relating to sex deviates urged conditional repeal of the Michigan "sexual psychopath law." [9] Medical journals so abound in writing denigrating this legislation that scarcely one favorable article can be found. Legal journals, too, have had their innings at this popular sport. It would be wrong to give the impression that all reactions to these laws are unfavorable; some have found a good deal to praise.[10] The fact remains, however, that the great bulk of opinion has been highly critical of the sexual psychopath laws. Is it not strange that statutes designed to recognize and take advantage of advances in understanding and treatment of humans are under fire, above all, from the groups which first espoused them and might be expected still to defend them as significant improvements in handling a very difficult problem which concerns us all?

Criticism has not only been verbal, it has been given material expression. In some states, at least, these laws are so rarely used as to have fallen into innocuous desuetude. Judge Jacob M. Braude of the Chicago Municipal Court pointed out in 1950 that in twelve years Illinois had committed only eighteen persons under its law.[11] The District of Columbia, from October 1948, to March 1950, committed twenty-four persons under its statute.[12] In many states this legislation is completely inoperative: Indiana, in 1950, reported one commitment in six years; Wisconsin reported its "law inoperative," as did the State of Washington.[13] In fact, only two states report any real use of these statutes: Michigan, with almost four hundred commitments,[14] and California (no surprise here!) with about eleven hundred in fourteen years.[15] Dr. Paul Tappan, a leading authority in this field and author of the State of New Jersey Report on this problem, sums up opposition to these laws most tellingly when he says: "Aside from offering some temporary quietus to public anxiety, perhaps their greatest saving grace has been the almost uniform lack of enforcement that has followed their enactment." [16]

Strong language, that, when applied to a remedial, socially-conscious, progressive statute; what can have brought about this disillusionment, this desuetude?

Surely much of the dissatisfaction with these laws must stem from the nature of the subject itself. However rational and cool we humans may be when considering securities legislation or revised Sales Acts, when sex rears its head, reasoning and detachment fly off and emotion is likely to fly in. There are enormous differences in attitudes between different social, economic, educational and religious groups.[17] These differences are accentuated by local circumstances. Sexual conduct is an explosive subject; legislation to regulate it, however necessary, is likely to reflect the emotional attitudes of proponents rather than scientific and detached judgment.[18] The fact is, however, that despite arguments to the contrary we do try to regulate sexual conduct by law [19] and it is highly likely that we shall always do so. But it is also highly likely that much of that law will be unsound and some of it will be unpopular. The very fact that sexual psychopath statutes deal with regulation of sex conduct alone is enough to make them unpopular with many.

But more specific charges are made against these laws. One prime mover in the development of this legislation has been a widespread feeling that sex crimes are on the increase. J. Edgar Hoover laid it down that in the 10-year period 1937–47 arrests for rape increased, 62%; for prostitution, 110%; for "other sex offenses," 142%.[20] "All the evidence points to a tremendous increase in the number and seriousness of sex offenses," says a professor of sociology and a judge.[21] But over against this assumption that sexual misconduct is on the increase are set a host of respectable authorities. Guttmacher and Weihofen, whose recent book is a landmark in medico-legal writing, state unequivocally: "All of the careful investigations made recently have failed to demonstrate any persistent trend in that direction" [22]—*i.e.,* toward an "alarming increase of incidence" of sex crimes. The F.B.I.'s own statistics disclose no sweeping trend to an increase in sexual crimes.[23] Karpman, a psychiatrist who probably more than any other man has devoted a lifetime to studying this phase of human behavior, very much doubts the existence of anything like a sex crime wave.[24] Hence, it is entirely possible (I think it probable) that hasty passage of sexual psychopath laws, justified as plugging an imminent deadly breach in the dike, are in fact not justified at all because there is no tidal wave to keep out.

Another common misconception is that all sex offenders tend to be recidivists.[25] This misconception arises in part from a lumping together of all sorts and conditions of sex offenders. The fact is, as Karpman points out,[26] certain types of sex offenders seem to be repetitive and may be subjected to innumerable arrests for the same crime; [27] the exhibitionist and his half-brother, medically speaking, the voyeur ("Peeping Tom") seem to furnish the best examples of recidivism. On the other hand, most sex offenders are no more recidivists than other persons who transgress the law, perhaps less. Doctors Atcheson and Williams found little recidivism among juvenile offenders.[28] In Michigan, sex offenders were found to have a low rate of recidivism and parole violation.[29] A four-year study in California summed it up thus: "Serious sex offenders are popularly believed to be notorious repeaters. Evidence indicates that this belief is untrue. Sex offenders convicted of felonies have comparatively low rates of recidivism either in sex offenses or in other offenses." [30] To multiply examples would be useless; the fact is that the great weight of informed opinion is to the effect that with the possible exceptions of the peeper and exhibitionist (and even then there is doubt), sex offenses are repeated less often than other offenses.

But popular fallacies regarding "sex fiends" are legion. Another common one is to suppose, as a learned judge of this state once put it to me, that the sex offender suffers from a progressive form of disease; that just as folklore believes a cold may grow into the "flu" and thence into pneumonia, so the "Peeping Tom" progresses up—or down—the scale until, unless checked, he is a full-fledged, foaming rapist. Nothing could be further from the truth: "It should be stated explicitly that persons convicted of serious sex crimes do not commonly begin with voyeurism and exhibitionism and work up to crimes of violence." [31] Of course, it may be true that some rapists are really repressed homosexuals,[32] but the medical men are overwhelmingly agreed that sex deviation is not a creeping, progressive disease; here again we owe a debt of misinformation to writers of sensational articles in popular magazines for another misconception underlying the enthusiasm for laws controlling sexual conduct, including the sexual psychopath legislation now being considered.

Another exceedingly common mistake is the widespread belief that sex offenders are a homogeneous group. The average exhibitionist is as much like the average rapist as a confidence man is like a burglar; yet the public and the laws continue to lump all sex offenders together in a kind of legal bed of Procrustes. The prostitute, whose offense is the most common by far,[33] though classed as a sex offender in local laws and F.B.I. statistics, and though indeed she may suffer from a serious personality disorder, feeblemindedness, or worse, is almost certainly not an offender whose trouble is sexual deviation; rather her problem is social and economic; [34] whereas the fetishist has a sexual problem, and generally is harmless, though in some cases his actions are symptoms of deeper causes which may lead to violence.[35] Ordinarily the exhibitionist is not violent and his offense is more annoying or embarrassing than it is dangerous to society; [36] this offense, consisting of exposing the genitals publicly, is a monopoly of white males. And voyeurism or scoptophilia ("peeping" in English!), is very like exhibitionism—annoying but not usually dangerous. Rather more complicated is the case of pedophilia, that is, sex offenses with children. Some of these offenders are young, passive persons afraid of "normal" sex contacts, but also one finds among them, perhaps particularly among certain seniles and psychotics, tendencies to sadism and brutality; and as Bowman says, here we have a particularly dangerous situation because the victim is a young child, with all that implies for the future.[37] Obviously, pedophilia would seem to be a serious offense, quite different from the usual case of fetishism, but it is dangerous even here to generalize. Homosexuality again, generally a crime in the formal sense of the word when it involves sodomy which is detected or reported or cases of adults using minors in homosexual relations or an assault of some sort, is a sexual offense of many gradations, from the "normal" incidence of it among adolescents [38] to all sorts of adult variations and gradations. Some homosexual experiences may be completely isolated in the offenders' total sex life, done for a thrill; in other persons and in widely varying degrees and intensities homosexual experience is of much greater importance.[39] Probably only a few homosexuals are dangerous to others; and the aggressive ones are a small proportion of the whole.[40] Rape, finally, again is diverse; it is clear that statutory rape when the age of consent is 21, as in Kentucky, is not at all the same crime as forced rape, the most serious of all sex offenses. As Guttmacher and Weihofen point out, concerning the rapist who uses force, some rapists are true sex offenders—for example, the latent homosexual, or the sadist—but other rapes are not primarily sexual in origin, as for example the pillaging aggressive young brute who mixes robbery or burglary with his rape, the sum total being a form of plunder.[41] Obviously, to treat all these overt acts as equivalent evidences of sexual deviations would be egregious error, yet that is the unfortunate tendency of the public. To wind up this long paragraph, while it has of course not been possible to give more than a superficial treatment of some of the so-called sex offenses,[42] I hope the reader is at least convinced of the fallacy of treating even all persons whose technical offense is the same as being similar in psychological make-up—how much sillier to lump the peeper with the rapist, the passive homosexual with the sadistic pedophiliac.

The reader ought also to note another thing about what we loosely call "sex crimes"—that they vary a great deal in the danger they present to society. From this, one may fairly conclude that to cram conduct merely annoying into the same legal mold with conduct violent or brutal and pin the same label on the whole will be to ignore the facts, and to make a serious mistake when it comes to controlling these deviations. It seems grossly unfair to treat the peeper like the rapist and it would seem that such unfairness is only justified if the entire class is so dangerous as to justify individual justice.[43] It is doubtful if any legislature has considered this aspect of these statutes.

DIAGNOSIS AND TREATMENT UNDER THESE STATUTES

DIAGNOSIS

This brings us to the two most serious fallacies of all, the twin assumptions on which the sexual psychopath statutes rest: that "sexual psychopaths" can be diagnosed and that they can be treated, as provided by law. Clearly, the success of these laws depends upon recognition of what are "sexual psychopaths" and on treatment which will "cure" them; for if we cannot tell what is a "sexual psychopath," or if we cannot promise him a recovery, the basis of these laws will have turned out to be built upon sand. Unfortunately, we cannot be at all sure that either assumption is more than hopefully correct.

To begin with, what of diagnosis? The doctors, on whose abilities, after all, diagnoses must stand or fall, are not even sure that the *behavior* of most sex offenders is "fundamentally different from that commonplace in the population; such persons are not necessarily to be regarded as suffering with psychiatric disorders or as socially dangerous." [44] The point is sometimes made that what is "peeping" when it takes place on the street, is no crime at all in the marital bedroom. Be that as it may, let us concede that there is conduct of a sexual nature which is deviational and pass on to the problem of diagnosis.

Here we crash head-on into the matter of definition, as raised by statute. We cannot operate under this legislation unless we can determine the class whose mental disorders the statute was intended to include. What it boils down to is that these laws attempt to incorporate, as the basis of their jurisdiction over the person, a medically determined definition, and that if this cannot be done the laws must fail.[45]

Let us examine, then, the definition of the people subject to these laws, or the nature of their disorder, as defined by statutes.[46] Typically, but not universally (because none of these statutes are exactly similar), feebleminded persons (not defined in these statutes) and insane persons (likewise undefined) as excluded from the definition of "sexual psychopath." [47] This at once suggests we know what is meant by "feebleminded" and what is meant by "insane" [48] and that such persons are to receive other special treatment. But, in fact, the gradation between the "insane" person and other persons suffering from "mental disorders" in the language of the statutes, is not sharp but fuzzy, and respected authorities disagree as to where it lies and whether it even should, or can, be drawn. The consequence has been a serious overlap between commitment statutes for the "insane," statutes governing feebleminded persons, and the "sexual psychopath" laws, resulting in "utter confusion" in California.[49] In Massachusetts, too, the situation is serious because of an overlap between the Defective Delinquent Act of 1911 [50] and the sexual psychopath law; [51] consequently, ". . . persons found to be sexual psychopaths who have a lower than normal intelligence may be committed either as defective delinquents *or* as sexual psychopaths. The proceedings, treatment, and methods of release as prescribed by the respective statutes are drastically different." [52] The same overlap is entirely possible in Iowa, under the loose definitions of "feebleminded" used in chapter 222.1 of the Iowa Code of 1954 [53] and "insanity." [54] When one considers the nature of persons committed under these established acts, many of whom have been what now *may* be known as "criminal sexual psychopaths" and treated accordingly, one is not perhaps unduly pessimistic in fearing that Iowa's "confusion" may in time be as "utter" as California's.[55]

But there are still more problems of definition to overcome. Most of these statutes use the term "sexual psychopath," which is, of course, not only found in the Iowa definition but is part of the title of the Iowa Act. This is a good, sound, medical-sounding term—and one abhorred by most medical men! Karpman says the term has "no legitimate place in psychiatric nosology or dynamic classification." [56] Doctors do not even agree on the meaning of the word psychopath; indeed, the latest medical terminology excludes the term "psychopathic personality" entirely and it has become such a portmanteau word, such a wastebasket for all sorts and conditions of mental disorders,[57] that as a statutory definition of a class of persons it is worse than useless. The doctors eschew the term because they cannot agree on what it means; no wonder that under such circumstances they feel hopeless to try to aid the courts in construing the definition.[58] This is made no easier by the fact that physicians themselves do not agree on what is "healthy sex behavior." [59] If the term "sexual psychopath" has any real utility to physicians, it is not as a diagnostic tool but as a label useful in administrative or teaching situations, but the phrase itself, when turned about and made into a part of diagnosis, is simply "a source of confusion and misunderstanding." [60] Where the doctors themselves are in disagreement as to the meaning of a term and where different schools of psychiatric thought reject the concept of "sexual psychopath" with greater or less repugnance, it seems exceedingly strange to incorporate the definition into what is supposed to be a remedial statute. In this state of affairs, how are judge and jury to evaluate the social and cultural bias or the unspecified criteria of judgment and evaluation of examining doctors or reporting superintendents of state hospitals? And bear in mind, that once a term has been entombed in the statutes and construed by the courts, it tends to acquire a rigid fixity, like the M'Naghten rule, which ignores progress and enlightenment. Shall a man's liberty, perhaps for the rest of his life, hang upon a meaningless and discredited phrase and a definition plagued by the "treacherous uncertainties in the present state of psychiatric knowledge?" [61]

Some state statutes in the field of the "sexual psychopath," however, scrupulously avoid these naughty words. Pennsylvania goes as far as any state,[62] its act applying to persons *convicted* of certain "sex offences"; the court is empowered to impose an indeterminate sentence (one day to life!) "if the court is of the opinion that any such person, if at large, constitutes a threat of bodily harm to members of the public, or is an habitual offender and mentally ill." Psychiatric advice is provided the court in this Act. This statute has been described as "unconstitutional" [63] and another commentator has said that "the best thing that can be hoped for from this law is that it will not be utilized at all. . . ." [64] To make matters more interesting for all concerned, Pennsylvania also has the so-called "Greenstein Act" [65] under which the court can get pre-sentence psychiatric examination of a convicted defendant; if the report of the examining physician shows the defendant "though not insane is so mentally ill or mentally deficient as to make it advisable for the welfare of the defendant or the protection of the community that he or she be committed to some institution other than a prison, the court may make such commitment in lieu of sentence." [66] The Group for Advancement of Psychiatry approves this statute as much as it does any.[67] Nonetheless, this language is assuredly vague and misty enough to confuse simple people like myself, and the Act referred to in the first part of this paragraph leaves great discretion in the court with only these vague standards of "threat to bodily harm, habitual offender and mentally ill" to guide him. However, there are those who think this nebulous language a "necessity," because it at least provides a starting point to be improved upon by practice.[68] There is something to be said for this theory, though it is rarely expressed so bluntly; however, in view of the consequences which beset anyone who falls within the possible meaning of these terms it seems a haphazard and unscientific way of experimenting upon human beings.

Illinois adopted a somewhat different definition, classifying as "sexually dangerous persons" "all persons suffering from a mental disorder, which mental disorder has existed for a period of not less than one year, immediately prior to the filing of the petition hereinafter provided for, coupled with criminal propensities to the commission of sex offenses, and who have demonstrated propensities toward acts of sexual assault or acts of sexual molestation of children. . . ." [69] The Missouri statute is much the same, except that it specifically excludes the "insane" and the "feebleminded" and omits direct reference to assaults and molestation.[70] The Iowa definition is clearly copied from the Missouri one, except that it omits the requirement that the "mental disorder" has existed for a year or more. The omission of the one-year requirement may be a real advantage because of the difficulty of proving that the "mental disorder" has lasted that long, which may seriously hamper the proceeding in the case of the first offender (*i.e.,* it is his first time in court) though it may not do so in the case of the defendant who has a record; since this is a civil action,

evidence of prior crimes is admissible to prove the "propensity" and its duration.[71] But what is a "propensity"? Surely it is as vague as the rest of the phrases used in these statutes,[72] and furthermore, it is a "criminal propensity toward the commission of *sex offenses.*"

This raises the further problem of the meaning of the term "sex offenses." So far as I know, no court of record has construed this phrase, so we must speculate as to its meaning. Probably "sex crimes" would be roughly synonymous. At all events, as we have seen, "sex offenders" run the spectrum from the passive "peeper" to the sadistic rapist; no doubt these two extremes are guilty of "sex offenses" and must be lumped together. But what of "lewdness"; is it a "sex offense"? [73] It certainly is in Iowa; under the chapter heading "Obscenity and Indecency" we find sections of the Iowa Code dealing with such diverse matters as "Lewdness-indecent exposure," [74] "Lascivious acts with children," [75] "Immoral plays, exhibitions, and entertainments," [76] and so on. These are offenses *involving* sex, and *may* be included in the specialized term "sex offenses" within the meaning of the act, but it is clear that there is room here for the kind of interpretative argument lawyers like.

When one considers the extraordinary range and scope of laws regulating sexual conduct,[77] from rape and prostitution to nudist camps and advertisements concerning venereal diseases, and when one contrasts some of those laws with the practice of many supposedly reputable citizens,[78] one is entitled at the very least to wonder what kind of standards will be employed in construing this phrase. There is another matter, too; what of the defendant whose crime, in itself nonsexual in nature, is in fact sexually motivated; has he a "propensity toward the commission of sex offenses"? This seems to me a very serious objection to the language of statutes like the Iowa one. Heirens, the Chicago murderer of at least three women, a fetishist, performed numerous burglaries and larcenies to gratify his sexual desires; the murders seem to have been done to prevent discovery and hue and cry.[79] Burglary and larceny are hardly sex offenses, though they and many other crimes may be sexually motivated.[80] Heirens was not "insane" as the criminal law defines the word; yet as the article cited showed, he suffered from a "mental disorder." Is it not a serious loophole in the Iowa law that it fails to cover such as he?

Finally, in construing the term "sex offenses," one must never forget the grave dangers, inherent in all sex offender laws, that unfounded accusations are particularly rife in the sexual field, and very hard to refute; [81] how much more dangerous they can be where, instead of a fine or short prison term, an indeterminate sentence awaits the accused. Unfounded charges were serious enough before; the new law of Iowa, and all like it, multiply the gravity of sex offense charges.[82] Statutory requirements of corroboration are frequently limited to few violent "sex crimes" [83] and in any event very little evidence suffices to corroborate, so that statutes offer little protection against allegations of sexual offenses, which may be the product of malice. Scrupulous care will be needed to prevent the sexual psychopath law from being used as a wastebasket for unwanted family members or as an instrument for blackmail or fantasy.

To sum up, then, much of the success of any sexual psychopath law must depend on the definition of what is a sexual psychopath. That term is in itself vague and largely discredited. In addition, the use of the phrase "propensity toward the commission of sexual offenses" raises acute problems of construction and of the use of medical testimony. Finally, exclusion of the "insane" and "feebleminded" inevitably requires that boundaries be drawn where no doctor cares to draw them. One can only hope for caution, moderation, and largeness of mind on all sides as this definitional lottery runs its course.

TREATMENT

If the first fundamental assumption of these laws is that we can define and recognize the "sexual psychopath," the second such assumption is like unto it: that having found him we can "cure" him. Is this assumption as dubious as the first? Though it may be legal, it would hardly be fair to send a man away for possibly the rest of his life unless there were reasonable assurances that the restraint would do him good.

We assume at the outset that criminal punishment as such neither deters nor cures though, to be sure, there are some who argue that at present prison is preferable to institutional treatment.[84] Successful treatment rests on two legs, one theoretical, one practical: the theoretical leg is the existence of substantial agreement as to the nature of these diseases and therapies to be applied; and the practical leg is that there are facilities available for such treatment.

First, as to theory. Obviously it is to the medical men that we must look: are they agreed on the nature of these disorders and the remedies for them? Dr. Karpman says, "The fact is that as yet very little is known of the subject," [85] though it is his view that most sex deviates suffer from a neurosis. On the other hand, in a symposium on this subject, while a Dr. Musacchio thought Karpman's term "paraphiliac neurosis" a good one, a Dr. Dickel thought the diagnosis of neurosis a poor one in most cases.[86] (And he also was not sure "treatment" was better than confinement.) Sutherland lays it down categorically that psychiatrists "have no diagnostic instruments or criteria by which to arrive at demonstrable conclusions on this question. . . ." [87] Tappan, writing of Danish experience, says their studies indicate simply that there is a "rather distinct group of sex-deviated offenders who are nonpsychotic but disturbed in their emotional and volitional responses. . . ." [88] The Michigan Report says: "In general, recent literature does little more than to make glaringly apparent the present confused state of psychiatric, psychological, and sociological theory in the sex deviation field." [89] On the other hand, Dr. Philip Q. Roche, speaking, I think it fair to say, for many psychiatrists, feels the group sufficiently treatable to make it worthwhile to have such statutes, *but only if facilities, including personnel, are provided.*[90] Abrahamsen, whose study of sex offenders in Sing Sing was intensive rather than extensive, found that only two of 102 offenders studied, were indeed "psychopaths" (a term he believes should be abolished) but that all the offenders studied suffered from mental disorders; in general his analysis of the etiology of these offenders agrees with that of Dr. Roche.[91]

In sum, then, it seems to me that as yet this complex and subtle matter of "normal" and "deviational" sexual habits and urges is little understood by psychiatrists. The origin and development of sex deviation is unclear; there is no "weight of authority" and, I think, no really general agreement among doctors. The problem is hopelessly complex and we are only beginning to get a body of doctrine to help in the eventual goal of unraveling this area of human behavior.[92] This surely does not mean we must throw up our hands in despair; it does mean that easy, ready-made diagnosis and terminology, in the present state of medical understanding, are misleading at the very least. We have a long way to go, and must face up to the fact.

ANY CURE?

Closely allied to the problem of understanding what leads to "sexual psychopathy" is the problem of how to treat or "cure" it. To be fair to the public as well as to persons on whom this statute will operate we must offer reasonable hope for a "cure," or else admit that the enlightened purpose of the law cannot be achieved. There, again, there are many different opinions.

Tappan says treatment success is doubtful.[93] The same author says that in Denmark, where there has been extensive research on the treatment problem, no special treatments have yet been derived which augur well.[94] Davidson says: ". . . cures, if any, must be extremely rare. The demand therefore that these offenders be 'treated' is still a sterile one."[95] In Washington, D.C., experience in therapy has been disheartening, in spite of attempts at a modern hospital by skillful physicians.[96] The Group for Advancement of Psychiatry, though inclined generally to guarded optimism (necessarily so!), is very dubious as to the success of treatment in the case of the homosexual.[97] The Michigan report, digesting many opinions and some rather indigestible, if not inedible, data, finds no treatments currently available really encouraging.[98] In brief, there is a large and respectable body of informed opinion holding that in our present state of ignorance we cannot effectively treat the "sexual psychopath" even when we think we know who he is.

This is not to say, however, that there are not plenty of proponents for the view that, under proper conditions, treatment can "cure" or at least materially improve the mental health of the sex deviate. The general attitude of the Group for the Advancement of Psychiatry is certainly optimistic. (And in any case certainly prefers treatment to punishment.) Slough and Schwinn likewise believe in the efficacy of therapy.[99] Dr. Bromberg reports favorable results in treatment employing psychodrama,[100] and Abrahamsen suggests that about half of his 102 sex offenders responded to psychotherapy.[101] These and other writings studied suggest that, while no responsible person suggests a sure cure for the sex offender, there are indications that success in treatment can be counted on in at least some cases and that in the future, given certain conditions, the recovery rate is almost sure to go up. Consequently, this school of thought argues, it would be a great mistake to conclude that treatment success is so rare as to make it futile.

It is not the purpose of this article to try to make a definitive assessment of the present state of psychiatric knowledge either as to the nature of the mental disorders from which "sex offenders" suffer or as to the prospects for successful treatments of those disorders; I am not competent to do so. But it is my purpose to show that in fact, psychiatrists are in profound disagreement still as to these fundamental matters and that as yet, in lawyers' language, there is no "weight of authority" in any of them. Very much in the way of basic research needs to be done; as yet, we have hardly scratched the surface. Consequently, even in theory we must not expect miracles of recovery as a consequence of any current legislation.

CONFINEMENT

The picture is very much darkened when we turn from the unsettled state of theory to the practicalities of carrying out these statutes. Even if we knew how to identify and cure the sex offender, this knowledge would be useless unless carried out in practice. The brute fact is that while legislatures have rushed to pass these sexual psychopath laws they have generally been unwilling to take the really wrenching step of appropriating money to carry them out. It is not treatment to herd sex deviates into already crowded mental institutions, to throw them in with the usual hodge-podge of seniles, psychotics and the rest. In California, where the state institutions are generally thought excellent, and where they are considered staffed by highly competent men, Hacker and Frym found that treatment was long delayed, inadequate and, in fact, "in all essentials, not different from that practiced in any prison with maximum security regulations."[102] Tappan—whom the reader will by now have noticed is an outstandingly trenchant critic of these laws—says that it is harmful for all concerned, because treatment is almost purely custodial,[103] leaving the sex deviate and all the other inmates, be they psychotic or whatever, to exacerbate each others' illnesses.[104] The same authority points out that we have in this country no large, trained body of therapists available for this sort of work.[105] And the same sorts of complaints came in from every source: the legislature has passed the law creating an added burden on state institutions without in any way adding the money and personnel needed to handle the added burden.[106] Consequently, treatment is cursory, inadequate, and largely a failure, unless you count it a partial success that at least by virtue of this legislation you keep potentially dangerous persons off the streets. But since this legislation was passed to cure persons assumed to be suffering from mental disorder and on the assumption that that was possible, if it does not cure, it must be a failure.

To speak candidly, this is precisely the Iowa situation. As of March 21 of this year, 33 persons, all males, had been committed to the Mount Pleasant Mental Health Institution. They are received there with no dossier as to their offense or previous history.[107] The variety of offense runs the usual gamut. One notes a high incidence of homosexuality or acts connected therewith (including one labeled, "Homosexuality, no overt acts" which leads one to wonder how the patient came within the jurisdiction of H.F. 125). Eight of the patients committed their offense either on the person of or in the presence of a minor, although only two of these offenses involved the use of force (one was attempted rape). One patient was accussed of "Possession of obscene literature and pictures," but whether he possessed them for sale (which might have commercial but not sexual overtones) or for personal gratification appeareth not. (The hospital staff did not consider him a sexual psychopath at all!) The exhibitionists number three. A motley crew, indeed. I think it is significant that so far as we know only eight offenses involved minors, and of these eight, only two involved the use of force. Thus, the sexual conduct most likely to have lasting bad effects either occurs rarely, or goes unreported (a common phenomenon)[108] or is handled at the county level in some other way, for example by criminal prosecution without recourse to the new "sexual psychopath" law.

In any event, there they are, all 33 of them;

what can we do for them? Dr. Brown believes there is "no specific treatment which brings about improvement or cures of such individuals"; this opinion, as we have seen, is hardly heresy. However, the staff feels "obligated to make an effort in their behalf and carry out a therapeutic program to the best of our ability." To this end, occupational therapy and music therapy are employed, "not particularly with therapy in mind but as merely something to occupy their time." The Psychology Department at Mount Pleasant, composed of three employees, one a Ph.D., two having Master's degrees in clinical psychology, has done its best to organize psychotherapy for all sexual psychopaths as offering the best hope for improving their personality disturbances.

In the staff's view, if I may fairly undertake to summarize it, "a certain number of sexual psychopaths can be benefited by a period of hospitalization" although the senior psychologist seems to have reservations even as to this modest ambition.[109] The staff also believes the punitive effect of the new law may be a deterrent or at least make offenders "more cautious about sexual deviations in the future."[110] Hacker and Frym, speaking to this latter point, also say that since defendants committed under these statutes consider them punishments, they tend to condition all they say and do in ways designed to get themselves out as soon as possible rather than take it as a medical treatment dependent on full cooperation and much time.[111] I do not wish it to be thought by anyone that I am critical of the competence or attitude of any of the personnel at Mount Pleasant, for, on the contrary, I respect their aims and sympathize with their efforts, but can these modest ambitions and these generalized treatments be the "cures" of the reformers and apostles of progress? Will the measures now available solve the sex offender problem in Iowa? Is this enlightenment in practice? And is it not obvious that niggardly provisions for treatment will produce niggardly results? If it has no other flaws or questionable aspects, the Iowa "sexual psychopath" law would fail in its purpose for lack of implementation.

JURISDICTION OF THE STATUTE

But there are other matters to consider before we balance the books on this new law. For one thing, there is the question of to whom the law applies. In some states, chief among them Maryland, New York, New Jersey and Pennsylvania, the statutes concerned act only following conviction of specified sex offenses or in the case of certain sex offenses,[112] and in New York the court may award indeterminate sentence to a mental institution in lieu of the prison sentence otherwise provided by law. This is a criminal statute, not a civil one, and the indeterminate sentence may amount to life. Hence, New Jersey has limited commitment to the maximum sentence possible for the crime of which defendant was committed. These statutes have been praised as avoiding the "loose norms" used in the Iowa type of "sexual psychopath" law,[113] and as avoiding any legislative judgments on psychiatric matters. These statutes, being limited to persons convicted of serious crimes, differentiate the "dangerous" sex offender from the merely embarrassing one. They avoid commitment for offenses never proved, or on trumped-up charges, and provide all the procedural safeguards of the criminal law. The chief criticism of this feature of the New York and similar statutes is that, for the very reason that it is confined to persons convicted of serious sex crimes it fails to cover the abnormal person whose crime is sexually motivated but whose offense is nonsexual.

Iowa, in common with most of the states, has brought within the purview of the statute "All persons charged with a public offense." [114] This phrase raises two problems: what is the meaning of "public offense" and secondly, is it good policy to make the statute apply to "all persons *charged*" with such such an offense?

As to the meaning of "public offense" (in some statutes "criminal offense") the question is this: shall "public offense" be limited to a general loose category of "sex crimes," or shall it include all "public offenses," in Iowa both felonies and misdemeanors? Only one court has squarely answered this question; in *People v. Haley* [115] the California District Court of Appeals held "crime" to mean "sex crime"; this decision has stood unquestioned for fifteen years. On the other hand, in dictum, the Supreme Court of Missouri said that the words "when any person is charged with an offense" [116] did not mean "when any person is charged with a *criminal* offense." The dictum is strong dictum and likely to be followed. It is very pertinent to the Iowa law because of the great similarity between the Missouri and Iowa statutes. Illinois has ducked the issue when the question arose; [117] and Wisconsin, under a rather different statute, has held that obscene language may be "disorderly conduct" but is not a "sex crime," which they deduce to be required for operation of their statute.[118] The choice between the California and Missouri constructions is not easy. In favor of California's view, it may be said that as a matter of statutory construction, "crimes" may be in *pari materia* with "sex offenses"; furthermore, it is doubtful whether the legislature thought of crimes sexually motivated in their deliberations, if any; finally, as a practical matter, most states are better off with less "sexual psychopaths" to treat than with more. In favor of the Missouri view, it may be said that if the legislature had wanted to restrict "public offense" to "sex offense" it knew how to do so; and secondly, that we are better off if we are able to treat the sexually motivated offender who commits an assault or some other violent crime which is yet not a sex crime. The Iowa Supreme Court has not yet had to answer this question, but from conversations with Dr. Brown, Superintendent at Mount Pleasant, it has been learned that one of their patients was charged with passing a forged check, so at least one Iowa district court has not restricted "public offense" to "sex offense." [119]

Our second inquiry is as to persons "*charged* with a public offense." This is justifiable as making the law applicable only if defendant has committed a socially dangerous act, but in fact the law may easily be abused, and persons suspected of sex deviation may be charged with some trumped-up "public offense" (after all, breach of the peace will do) and then started on the way to commitment although in fact he has committed no act dangerous to society.[120] That this is no baseless fear may be shown by Iowa experience passage of our Act. At least one inmate at Mount Pleasant had in his home county a reputation for homosexuality. During a wave of public feeling in the area, following two violent "sex crimes," this man was charged with "conspiracy to commit a felony" and though not one step further along those lines was ever taken he was committed as a "sexual psychopath" under the new law. In other words, no act dangerous to society was proved, and the criminal charges were a lever to get rid of a given person for alleged and, indeed, latent homosexual tendencies. A combination of local emotion, a feeling that "something must be done," and the man was committed. In fact, over two-thirds of the Iowa commitments come from the Sioux City area! This statute lends itself as well as any to "railroading" the unpopular or those suspected of evil sexual tendencies.

PROCEDURE UNDER THE STATUTE

The statute does, however, contain certain apparent safeguards. To begin with, it gives discretion to the County Attorney to file the petition "verified upon his information and belief" although "any reputable person" (query as to who is not reputable?) may initiate charges of sexual psychopathy against "any person charged with a public offense," by working through the County Attorney, who alone may act. The Missouri cases make it clear that if he fails to file his petition and is guilty of no abuse of discretion there is no remedy; abuse of discretion is hard to prove, even where the defendant is charged with a sex crime.[121] So there is one very wide-meshed filter to prevent injustice. However, the very fact that County Attorneys have this discretion itself gives them power to use or abuse the law as they like, or at least to employ it as best suits their ends. Sutherland points out that the tendency has been for prosecutors to use the "sexual psychopath laws" only when evidence of a crime is weak and there has been no local outcry for "justice."[122]

There are, however, further safeguards, as the law reads. Upon filing of the "verified petition" the defendant is notified in writing of the charges against him [123] and the court "shall determine whether he shall be medically examined." Apparently the court need not order such examination but may proceed forthwith to the hearing without medical findings. The County Attorney's petition would seem to be sufficient in itself, where it alleges seven prior convictions of sex offenses [124] though the filing of the petition alone does not compel the court to grant a hearing,[125] even though it alleges prior accusations of sex crimes but no prior convictions.[126]

However, it is clear that since the hearing is medical in nature, the court will usually order examination. Whereas some statutes require the medical examination prior to hearing to be by psychiatrists [127] the Iowa law merely mentions "examining physician or physicians." [128] While this may recognize that Iowa has a very short supply of psychiatrists, it entirely fails to recognize the subtle and complex nature of these disorders and by lowering the standards of the medical examination ignores the great weight of informed opinion, which requires that this sort of examination be conducted by psychiatrists.[129]

After studying the allegations of the petition and the medical examination report, the court "shall dismiss the petition" if "sufficient proof" of the aberrant sexual tendencies is not made to the court or if "the fact of a mental disorder to which such propensities are attributable" is not established to the court's satisfaction.[130] If "proof" of the propensities *and* the mental disorder is made, the court *shall* order a final hearing. However, defendant has no absolute right to such a hearing but rather it is granted within the court's discretion.[131] The court is granted rather wide latitude in the exercise of that discretion.[132]

If the court grants a hearing it is in the nature of a "special proceeding" as provided in the Iowa Code.[133] Whereas in some states, such as Indiana, Minnesota, and Ohio, the defendant is not entitled to a jury trial of the issue of sexual psychopathy, in Iowa he is entitled to a jury if he asks for it. Although judges may be loath to take responsibility for indefinite commitments, opinion generally is that a jury is incompetent to decide the question of sexual psychopathy. Sexual disorders and deviations from the accepted (public, at least) usages are not fit subjects for jury trial. A minor offense, though it may signify a serious disorder, may seem small to a jury and cause it to fail to commit indefinitely; on the other hand, in an offense shocking in nature, commitment is liable to be a means of retribution in the jury's eyes.[134] It was unnecessary to provide for a jury trial in the Iowa statute, in view of the fact that these laws are universally held noncriminal in nature [135] and that in Iowa such civil commitments may be made without a jury.[136] So far in Iowa defendants have almost invariably waived jury trail.

As part of the procedural safeguards afforded the defendant, the Iowa law provides he shall have counsel at every stage of the proceedings and that if he has none, the court shall appoint a lawyer for him.[137]

In the conduct of the hearing, the examining

physicians may testify, but their written reports, previously filed with the court, are not admissible in evidence. Although probably unnecessary,[138] the Iowa law in section 10 provides for evidence of past acts of sexual deviation in proof of the defendant's condition and propensities. Cross-examination of witnesses is a plausible natural corollary of these proceedings.[139] The use of hearsay by the examining physicians is not objectionable in such hearings.[140] Adjudications of sexual psychopathy are unlikely to be appealed.[141]

If the defendant is adjudicated a sexual psychopath, he will be committed "to a state hospital for the insane."[142] In Iowa this originally meant Mt. Pleasant, but since that institution is bursting at the seams, they are now committed to hospitals on a regional basis like insane persons. I have commented on treatment available at Mt. Pleasant; the same remarks apply everywhere else.

The hospitals are required to make periodic examinations of the "sexual psychopath" and to report on his progress to the committing court at least once a year.[143] This is designed to prevent an indefinite commitment without hope of release —or "losing" the committed person.

One of the large problems is that of release. If it be conceded that the current state of medical science cannot promise "cures," though it may selectively promise improvement, there is a nice question of when these "sexual psychopaths" may be returned to society. In the District of Columbia, a committed sexual psychopath is released when "sufficiently recovered so as not to be dangerous to other perons . . .;[144] in California he remains till the superintendent of the state hospital certifies that he has recovered to the extent that he is no longer a menace to others or will not benefit further by treatment.[145] In Iowa the new law specifies that a rehearing shall be held, in all respects like the original hearing, in the court of original commitment, when a written application is presented to that court "setting forth facts showing that the criminal psychopath has improved to the extent that his release will not be incompatible with the welfare of society."[146] This is a very loose standard indeed, and far from requiring a "cure," as release of two-thirds of those committed abundantly proves. However, one may only hope it will avoid the really tragic case of Kemmerer, under the

Michigan statute; he committed a misdemeanor, punishable by a fine or one year's imprisonment, and found himself imprisoned for life.[147]

The rehearing is supposed to be in all respects like the original one (though in one case in Iowa none was held, a clear violation of the Code). This would include right to counsel and right of appeal, as these laws have been construed.[148] If discharge is granted, the defendant is on probation for three years; otherwise he is returned to the hospital. At the end of the probationary period he *may* be discharged.[149]

These "sexual psychopath" laws have been attacked as unconstitutional, but they have withstood such assaults sturdily since the original Michigan statute was struck down.[150] They are uniformly held noncriminal, despite the fact the persons they operate on consider them punitive in nature.[151] They have stood up under attacks alleging they deny due process,[152] deny equal protection of the laws,[153] constitute double jeopardy (manifestly false, since they are noncriminal, so they say),[154] or are retroactive or ex post facto laws.[155] (No one seems to have thought of attacking them as violating the Commerce clause.) These results seem justified by the provisions for making the physicians' conclusions advisory rather than conclusive, by provisions for judge or jury to make final determination, preservation of the right of counsel, appeal, and the apparent right to bail.[156] And there is nothing arbitrary about restricting application of the law to one class of person in exercise of the police power.[157]

There is, however, one constitutional, or in Iowa, statutory[158] issue: suppose the accused refuses to talk to physicians on the ground of self-incrimination; may he do so? If he can refuse, no psychiatric examination is possible, and it has been said that this seriously hampered early administration of these laws.[159] The leading Missouri case on the subject, *State ex rel. Sweezer v. Green*,[160] holds that the problem of self-incrimination is not raised in these sexual psychopath laws because they are civil and not criminal in nature. Of course, both the Missouri and Iowa statutes in addition provide that the original written physician's report shall not be admissible in evidence, while providing, as aforesaid, that past acts of the accused are admissible in evidence. Slough and Schwinn believe these acts constitute no violation of the privilege,[161] pointing out the safeguards above and calling attention to the analogy to the insanity hearing. However, in the sexual psychopath laws where the defendant is accused already of a public offense, it cannot be denied he may reveal to psychiatrists facts tending to incriminate him.[162] So long, however, as only the court sees these reports, the privilege would seem preserved; any further use would violate the privilege.[163] The decided cases, few in number, seem to take the view that the privilege is not violated in these statutes.[164]

Thus we see that there is very little likelihood that these sexual psychopath laws will be held unconstitutional, the chief reason being the unanimous opinion that they are not criminal in nature, this view persisting despite evidence that defendants feel them to be criminal in nature because of the arrest, jail confinement, trial, and jail awaiting transfer to the state hospital.[165]

The problem of release raises the question: suppose a patient committed under this act cannot get out, what remedies, if any, has he? It would seem that appeal from any hearing would lie as in any "special action." Also, habeas corpus is available, usually only when other remedies have been exhausted.[166] It is available where appeal from a commitment order is pending[167] and hence, by extension, where a rehearing is unsatisfactory or being appealed. Recovery of sanity is grounds for issuance of the writ in such cases as we are considering.[168] The burden of proof of sanity in this situation is on petitioner,[169] since the condition of mental disorder is presumed to continue until it is proved otherwise. If no treatment is given, habeas corpus may lie,[170] or where a person committed as a sexual psychopath is held in a violent ward.[171] Query whether overcrowding, such as exists in Iowa institutions of mental health, is grounds for the writ?

Release, however obtained, does not end the affair for the sexual psychopath; the new act of Iowa, in contrast to those in other states such as Michigan and New Hampshire, leaves intrenched the question of criminal responsibility. This is too bad, for not only is it a clog upon recovery for the patient, but when he gets out evidence is cold, testimony stale, and witnesses hard to find. For a graphic example of this, consider the unfortunate Mr. Stone of California, who, five years after his original commitment, found himself like Mohammed's tomb, half-way betwixt heaven and earth, unable to get out of the mental hospital (or so he thought) and unable to go to criminal trial because, the court found, "the witnesses desired and necessary have scattered," and the complaining witness, having matured from ten to sixteen years old, had forgotten the circumstances.[172] Thus, unless the "treatment" period (quotes used advisedly) is short, no trial is likely to be held for lack of evidence and enthusiasm. However, the patient may not know this, and in any event he cannot be sure. The reason for this provision in Iowa may be constitutional fears but it would have been better to have provided that commitment disposed of criminal charges.[173]

SUMMARY

In this new statute the Legislature, probably unwittingly, has opened a Pandora's Box. The reform appeal of these laws is great and tempting. However, they are based upon certain assumptions as to the nature of man which are, scientifically speaking, at best half-truths. They seek to crystallize a definition of mental disorder which no doctor will vouch for, and furthermore to subject persons in this medically indefinable class to treatment which is in many instances theoretically impossible and in any event practically unfeasible. In addition, despite sincere statutory attempts to avoid them, there are easy possibilities for injustice and abuse of these laws. The chance of any really significant progress through the "sexual psychopath laws" is small indeed.

It would have been a far better thing to have appropriated money for research on this matter and for development of a staff with proper facilities to carry out such research. This is in fact precisely what every state has done after some experience with such laws as these, and that is the only possible permanent solution, if there is one at all. House File 125 has not solved any problems; it has simply created more of them. It may be that even so poor a law as this is better than punishment alone,[174] but no one should be deceived by the existence of the Iowa "Criminal Sexual Psychopath Law" of 1955: we are still many light years from the "Brave New World."

NOTES

1. The other jurisdictions are: Alabama, California, Florida, Illinois, Indiana, Kansas, Massachusetts, Michigan,

Minnesota, Missouri, Nebraska, New Hampshire, New Jersey, Ohio, Pennsylvania, Utah, Vermont, Virginia, Washington, Wisconsin, Wyoming, and the District of Columbia.

2. This particular statute was declared unconstitutional in People v. Frontezak, 286 Mich. 51, 281 N.W. 534 (1938), but was revised and then held constitutional in a series of cases, beginning with People v. Chapman, 301 Mich. 584, 4 N.W.2d 18 (1942).

3. Am. Mag., July 1947, p. 32.

4. Wittels, *What Can We Do About Sex Crimes?,* Sat. Eve. Post, December 11, 1948, p. 30.

5. Hacker and Frym, *The Sexual Psychopath Act in Practice: A Critical Discussion,* 43 CALIF. L. REV. 766, 767 (1955).

6. From state to state these statutes differ surprisingly as will be seen. The best comparative approach is GROUP FOR THE ADVANCEMENT OF PSYCHIATRY REPORT NO. 9, app. A, THE SEXUAL PSYCHOPATH LAWS (1950) (hereinafter cited as GAP REPORT No. 9). This appendix has all the state laws then available set forth in a chart showing comparative similarities and differences on all main issues in these laws.

7. See GAP REPORT No. 9, app. A, for a collection of epithets applied by administrators of these laws to these laws themselves.

8. Hacker and Frym, *supra* note 5, at 778.

9. REPORT OF THE GOVERNOR'S STUDY COMMISSION ON THE DEVIATED CRIMINAL SEX OFFENDER 14–15 (Michigan 1951) (hereinafter cited as MICHIGAN REPORT). Note how they put it:

> Michigan's criminal sexual psychopath law, the Goodrich Act, should be repealed, provided Recommendations 5 and 23 are carried out. The Commission cautions, however, against the repeal of even so crude and unsatisfactory an instrumentality as the present "Goodrich Act" until there is better legislation, along the lines indicated, capable of doing the job.

The Commission reported most state laws were "either inoperative or ineffective." *Id.* at 128.

10. For example, New Jersey reported "No adverse comment" in reply to a questionnaire sent out by California authorities; FINAL REPORT ON CALIFORNIA SEXUAL DEVIATION RESEARCH (1954) (hereinafter cited as CALIFORNIA REPORT). Reinhardt and Fisher, *The Sexual Psychopath and the Law,* 39 J. CRIM. L. & C. 734 (1949) is generally favorable.

11. Braude, *The Sex Offender and the Court,* Fed. Probation, Sept. 1950, p. 17 (whole issue devoted to the problem). The rate in Illinois may be slowly rising: the California Report lists 80 commitments for Illinois by 1954 (over a 17-year stretch), CALIFORNIA REPORT, at 45.

12. Cruvant, Meltzer, and Tartaglino, *An Institutional Program for Sex Deviants,* 107 AM. JOUR. PSYCH. 190 (1950).

13. GAP REPORT No. 9, app. A.

14. MICHIGAN REPORT, at 35. This covered a period of eleven years of the law; the actual figure was 369 commitments, or about 36 a year, surely not a very high rate, when one considers the population of the state, or when one contrasts it with the Iowa figures which will be given later.

15. CALIFORNIA REPORT, at 45.

16. Tappan, *The Sex Offender Laws and Their Administration,* Fed. Probation, Sept. 1950, pp. 32, 33.

17. Surely the Kinsey Reports, however much one may take issue with recommendations therein (especially Volume II) or doubt the statistical validity of many of the claims made therein, must show the wide divergence between various groups in this country in their attitudes towards sex. On the subject of oral eroticism alone the differences between educational and economic levels is striking; KINSEY, POMEROY, AND MARTIN, SEXUAL BEHAVIOR IN THE HUMAN MALE 369 (1948). In the same work see also chapters 10 and 11. For

a criticism of this stratification theory, however, see Horack, *Sex Offenses and Scientific Investigation,* 44 ILL. L. REV. 149, 155–56 (1949). Whether one agrees with Horack or Kinsey, it's nice to remember that the "hero" of all his statistics was, after all, a lawyer.

18. See generally, GUTTMACHER AND WEIHOFEN, PSYCHIATRY AND THE LAW 110–11 (1952). They point out the emotional impetus behind much regulation of sexual conduct. "And there is doubtless no subject on which one can obtain more definite opinions and less definite knowledge." *Id.* at 110.

19. The number of articles and books on sex and the law is so large as to defy citation in anything less than bibliographical form. For a general survey with many references to writings on all sides of the controversy, the reader is referred to a comprehensive student note, *The Function of Law in the Regulation of Sexual Conduct,* 29 IND. L. REV. 539 (1954). Or he can read the Kinsey Reports and the many reviews of them, which together represent the divergency of views on sex and the law. But it is not my purpose to embroil myself or the reader in any such general controversy. See Bensing, *A Comparative Study of American Sex Statutes,* 42 J. CRIM. L. & C. 57 (1951).

20. Hoover, *How Safe Is Your Daughter,* Am. Mag., July 1947, p. 142.

21. Reinhardt and Fisher, *supra* note 10, at 736. The authors disclaim any need, however, for "fanaticism" in dealing with these "monsters."

22. Guttmacher and Weihofen, *Sex Offenses,* 43 J. CRIM. L. & C. 153, 154 (1952). To the same effect see their book, GUTTMACHER AND WEIHOFEN, *op. cit. supra* note 18, at 111.

23. For instance, in Uniform Crime Reports, July 1955, p. 52, *arrests* were as follows: Rape, 5812; Prostitution, 26,353; Sex offenses (not defined, so not useful), 27,111. There were also 329,394 persons arrested for Disorderly Conduct, a portmanteau phrase covering a multitude of sins, including certain "sex crimes" such as "peeping," exhibitionism, and homosexuality. *Id.* at 53. Considering the population increase, there seems no significant increase in *reported arrests* since 1947.

24. Karpman, *The Sexual Psychopath,* 146 A.M.A.J. 721 (1951). To the same effect, the same author in 42 J. CRIM. L. & C. 184–85 (1951).

25. Reinhardt and Fisher, *supra* note 10, at 737.

26. Karpman, *Considerations Bearing on the Problems of Sex Offenses,* 43 J. CRIM. L. & C. 13, 18 (1952).

27. Karpman, *The Sexual Psychopath,* 146 A.M.A.J. 721, 726 (1951). "There are exhibitionists and voyeurs who have served innumerable and long prison sentences without the slightest effect."

28. Atcheson and Williams, *A Study of Juvenile Sex Offenders,* 111 AM. JOUR. PSYCH. 366, 368–69 (1954). The figure for all these juvenile offenders was only 2.6%.

29. MICHIGAN REPORT, at 4; the rest of the Report bears this out.

30. CALIFORNIA REPORT, at 100. Only homicidal criminals had a lower rate, for rather obvious reasons. Incidentally, the F.B.I.'s own figures in their Uniform Crime Reports show sex crimes as among the least likely to be repeated. Your daughter may be safer (from others) than J. Edgar Hoover thinks—for publication anyway.

31. Bowman, *The Problem of the Sex Offender,* 108 AM. JOUR. PSYCH. 250, 251 (1951). To the same effect, Karpman, *Considerations Bearing on the Problems of Sex Offenses,* 43 J. CRIM. L. & C. 13, 19 (1952); and GUTTMACHER & WEIHOFEN, *op. cit. supra* note 18, at 111.

32. Lowrey, *The Sexual Psychopath,* 43 J. CRIM. L. & C. 592, 608 (1953).

33. Uniform Crime Reports, July 1954, p. 55. The F.B.I. is almost surely wrong in implying in its classification of crimes for statistical purposes that prostitution is a sex offense.

34. GUTTMACHER AND WEIHOFEN, *op. cit. supra* note 18, at 156.

35. Bowman, *supra* note 31, at 253. In this connection, the case of Heirens of Chicago, who murdered at least three women, probably more, is interesting. It is clear that in his case the first overt symptom was the fetishist desire for women's underwear. This developed into a series of burglaries and they in turn led to the murders he committed.

36. GUTTMACHER AND WEIHOFEN, *op. cit. supra* note 18, at 157. In California, where it is said an automobile is necessary really to live, it appears necessary also really to exhibit —at any rate in a study of 471 such cases in Los Angeles more than 50% took place in automobiles. Los Angeles Chamber of Commerce please note this example of gracious living in Sunny California.

37. Bowman, *supra* note 31, at 254. Many of these offenders are impotent senile men. The reader who cares to read case studies of such men, together with suggested diagnosis and therapy, is referred to Hammer and Glueck, *Psycho-dynamic Patterns in the Sex Offender,* in PSYCHIATRY AND THE LAW 157 (Hock and Zubin ed. 1955). When one reads of the brutal and sadistic acts of these offenders it is easy to understand how carnal abuse of a child can arouse community emotions. Some of these offenders were psychotics—most were not.

38. KINSEY, POMEROY, AND MARTIN, *op. cit. supra* note 17, c. 21, generally. They estimate that more than one in three U.S. males have had some homosexual experience involving orgasm. *Id.* at 623. Female homosexual experience seems lower, but significant still (10%); KINSEY, MARTIN, POMEROY, AND GESHARD, SEXUAL BEHAVIOR IN THE HUMAN FEMALE c. 11 (1953).

39. GROUP FOR THE ADVANCEMENT OF PSYCHIATRY REPORT NO. 30, REPORT ON HOMOSEXUALITY 2 (1953) (hereinafter cited as GAP REPORT NO. 30). The authors question which offenders, in this wide and diverse spectrum of homosexuality, should be punished; which of them even need treatment!

40. GAP REPORT NO. 30, at 3. The authors point out, as Kinsey also does, that "perversion" is not homosexuality.

41. GUTTMACHER AND WEIHOFEN, *op. cit. supra* note 18, at 116–17.

42. I refer the lawyer-reader to Guttmacher and Weihofen's excellent book, cited note 18 *supra,* for a full account of "sex crimes" in general. Particularly I urge such readers to study carefully the enormously complex case histories with which the book is seasoned; they should give even a mildly perceptive reader an idea of the extraordinary difficulty of diagnosis and treatment in these cases—as indeed, in many others as well. Just a few of these case histories should convince the twentieth-century mind of what we do *not* know about ourselves and others.

43. Glueck, *Principles of a Rational Penal Code,* 41 HARV. L. REV. 453, 469 (1928).

44. GAP REPORT NO. 9, at 1.

45. Bowman and Rose, *A Criticism of Current Usage of the Term "Sexual Psychopath,"* 109 AM. JOUR. PSYCH. 177 (1952): "The crucial factor in the success or failure of legal proceedings under these statutes is the definition of the mental condition that makes an offender subject to psychiatric commitment rather than penal sentencing."

46. There are two good sources of comparison: The CALIFORNIA REPORT, at 41–58, and GAP REPORT NO. 9, app. A.

47. It is so in Iowa Laws 1955, 56th G.A. c. 121, § 1:

All persons charged with a public offense, who are suffering from a mental disorder and are not a proper subject for the schools for the feeble-minded or for commitment as an insane person, having criminal propensities toward the commission of sex offenses, and who may be considered dangerous to others, are hereby declared to be "criminal sexual psychopaths."
California omits these exclusions and has a longer, fancier definition.

48. "Insanity" is a term doctors use only when dealing with legal matters, where it has a specialized meaning.

49. Note, *Sane Laws for Sexual Psychopaths,* 1 STAN. L. REV. 486, 490 (1949): "The utter confusion of all these provisions can be appreciated only by a reading of the applicable sections and chapters. Unfortunately, the cases do not clear up this confusion." (Citing many cases).

50. MASS. ANN. LAWS, c. 123, § 113 (1949).

51. *Id.* c. 123A.

52. Harris and Gordon, *An Investigation and Critique of the Defective Delinquent Statute in Massachusetts,* 30 B.U.L. REV. 459, 491 (1950).
Regard the Probate Court's definition of a "defective delinquent" in a recent Massachusetts case: "one who displays a permanent mental defect, sometimes in scholastic educability, but always in judgment and moral sense, coupled with strong vicious or criminal propensities on which punishment has little or no deterrent effect, and who requires care, supervision and control for the protection of others." Petition of Commissioner of Correction, 324 Mass. 535, 537, 87 N.E.2d 207, 209 (1949). The object of this definition had displayed brutal sexual tendencies repeatedly, including forcible rape and sodomy. Is it not very clear that under such a definition of "defective" this person might nevertheless perfectly qualify as a "criminal sexual psychopath" within the meaning of the Iowa statute? (See note 47, *supra,* for the Iowa definition.)

53. IOWA CODE, § 222.1 (1954):
"Feeble-minded" defined. The words "feeble-minded person" in this chapter shall be construed to mean any person afflicted with mental defectiveness from birth or from an early age, so pronounced that he is incapable of controlling himself and his affairs and requires supervision, control, and care for his own welfare, or for the welfare of others, or for the welfare of the community, and who is not classifiable as an "insane person" within the meaning of the provisions of the chapters of this title relating to the insane.

54. Especially IOWA CODE § 229.40 (1954), a masterpiece of generality and ambiguity: "The term 'insane' as used in this chapter includes every species of insanity or mental derangement." Section 4.1 (6) has a charming inclusiveness about it: "The words 'insane person' include idiots, lunatics, distracted persons, and persons of unsound mind." MICHIGAN REPORT, at 119, urges that this distinction be omitted.

55. Out of kindness to the reader I forbear to throw into the definitional stew-pot the definition of "Delinquent child":
The term "delinquent child" means any child:
1. Who habitually violates any law of this state, or any town or city ordinance.
2. Who is incorrigible.
3. Who knowingly associates with thieves, or vicious or immoral persons.
4. Who is growing up in idleness or crime.
5. Who knowingly frequents a house of ill fame.
6. Who patronizes any policy shop or place where any gaming device is located.
7. Who habitually wanders about any railroad yards or tracks, gets upon any moving train, or enters any car or engine without lawful authority.

IOWA CODE § 232.3 (1954).

56. Karpman, *The Sexual Psychopath,* 146 A.M.A.J. 721, 722 (1951).

57. See Note, *The Psychopathic Personality,* 10 RUTGERS L. REV. 425 (1955), for a detailed discussion, heavily documented, of the debate raging over the meaning of the term "psychopath."

58. GAP REPORT NO. 9, at 1. Here is what this distinguished group has to say about what has been called one or two inherent defects.

Thus far, all the laws adopted and all those proposed have defined the sex offender as a "psychopath," and have regarded him as mentally ill or as mentally defective. The Committee cautions against the use of this appellation "psychopath," in the law on several grounds. There is still little agreement on the part of psychiatrists as to the precise meaning of the term. Furthermore, the term has no dynamic significance. The Committee believes that in statutes the use of technical psychiatric terms should be avoided whenever possible. Psychiatric knowledge and terminology are in a state of flux. Once having become a part of the public law such a term attains a fixity unresponsive to newer scientific knowledge and application. It is advisable that nosologic labels be avoided and in place the offender's behavior be so described as to come under the purview of mental disorder.

Although the framers of proposed and enacted legislation aimed at the sex offender recognize that sex offense may be a symptom of a kind of mental disorder, they have not succeeded in lifting the recommended procedures of trial and disposition out of the traditional criminal process. In such procedures the psychiatrist continues to be confined to precarious definition (i.e., What is a psychopath?), as he is in most criminal procedures, and it does not seem likely that under such circumstances the psychiatrist can hope to bring a fuller measure of understanding to our courts.

Ibid.

59. Bowman, *supra* note 31, at 250: "It is doubtful if physicians, including psychiatrists and biologists, would all agree as to what is healthy sex behavior."

60. Bowman and Rose, *supra* note 44, at 178.

61. Mr. Justice Frankfurter dissenting in Solesbee v. Balkom, 339 U.S. 9, 25 (1950). To demonstrate the soundness of this dissent, contrast these results of psychiatric examinations and testings: One psychiatrist in the Illinois State Prison diagnosed 98% of the inmates as psychopathic personalities; in similar institutions other psychiatrists have concluded that no more than 5% are in this class. Or consider this: in the Psychiatric Clinic of the Court of General Sessions in New York City, 15.8% of sex offenders were diagnosed as psychopaths, whereas Bellevue Hospital in New York City found 52.9% psychopathic. See Slough and Schwinn, *The Sexual Psychopath,* 19 U. KAN. CITY L. REV. 131, 138, n.24 (1951).

62. PA. STAT. ANN. tit. 19, §§ 1166–74 (Supp. 1954). Minnesota's law, defining "Psychopathic Personality," is as broad as any:

[T]he existence in any person of such conditions of emotional instability, or impulsiveness of behavior, or lack of customary standards of good judgment, or failure to appreciate the consequences of his acts, or a combination of such conditions, as to render such person irresponsible for his conduct with respect to sexual matters and thereby dangerous to other persons.

MINN. STAT. ANN. § 526.09 (1947). This was held constitutional, as construed by one trial court, in State *ex rel.* Pearson v. Probate Ct., 205 Minn. 545, 287 N.W. 297 (1939), *aff'd,*

309 U.S. 270 (1940).

63. 13 U. PITT. L. REV. 739, 740 (1952).

64. 100 U. PA. L. REV. 727, 748 (1952). In fairness to Pennsylvania it should be pointed out that this statute is not, in terms, a "sexual psychopath" law, but represents the "super-modern" or New York type law. N.Y. Sess. Laws 1950, c. 525. As we shall see, one objection to the "sexual psychopath" laws has been that they may deprive the accused of due process; the New York and similar laws act on him only *after* conviction for crimes sexual in nature.

65. PA. STAT. ANN. tit. 19, §§ 1153–54 (1950).

66. *Id.* § 1154.

67. GAP REPORT NO. 9, at 3. The Act is said to be "commendable for both simplicity and comprehensiveness. It is adequate to deal with the sex offender."

68. Schlesinger and Scanlon, *Sex Offender and the Law,* 11 U. PITT. L. REV 636, 646–47 (1950). Compare the court in *In re* Moulton, 96 N.H. 370, 373, 77 A.2d 26, 29 (1951): "This [definition] may mean all things to all men."

69. ILL. REV. STAT. c. 38, § 820.1 (1955). *Id.* § 820.25. This statute and this section were held constitutional in People v. Ross, 344 Ill. App. 407, 101 N.E.2d 112 (1951).

70. MO. ANN. STAT. c. 202, § 700 (Vernon 1952). Held constitutional in State *ex rel.* Sweezer v. Green, 360 Mo. 1249, 232 S.W.2d 897 (1950). See also People v. Chapman, 301 Mich. 584, 4 N.W.2d 18 (1942), holding constitutional the Michigan statute which includes the phrase "coupled with propensities towards the commission of sex offenses."

71. People v. Sims, 382 Ill. App. 472, 47 N.E.2d 703 (1943).

72. WEIHOFEN, MENTAL DISORDER AS A CRIMINAL DEFENSE 198 (1954). He says: "The description of the disorder is as vague as in any other such statute."

73. It is a crime in every state, though not always under that title. See Note, *The Function of Law in the Regulation of Sexual Conduct,* 29 IND. L. REV. 539, 541 (1954), as to what has been held lewdness; note the shocking examples of convictions. *Id.* at 550–53. On the general subject, see PLOSCOWE, SEX AND THE LAW (1953) and SHERWIN, SEX AND THE STATUTORY LAW (1949). Ludwig, *Control of the Sex Criminal,* 25 ST. JOHN'S L. REV. 203, 211 (1951) points out the necessity of unambiguous statutory definition.

74. IOWA CODE § 725.1 (1954). This includes a man and woman (unmarried, at least to each other) who "lewdly and viciously associate and cohabit together" as well as what I take to be the exhibitionist, *i.e.,* any man or woman "guilty of open and gross lewdness" who "designedly makes an open and indecent or obscene exposure of his or her person, or of the person of another." "Lewdness" has been held to mean "the unlawful indulgence of the animal desires," State v. Wilson, 124 Iowa 264, 266, 99 N.W. 1060, 1061 (1904). Is fornication then (not specifically a crime) a "sex offense"? Probably not, because the Iowa Criminal Sexual Psychopath Law requires by definition that defendant suffer from a "mental disorder" and this kind of of lewdness is surely not per se an indication of mental disease if the Kinsey Reports are to be believed!

75. IOWA CODE § 725.2 (1954).

76. *Id.* § 725.3.

77. See Bensing, *A Comparative Study of American Sex Statutes* 42 J. CRIM. L. & C. 57 (1952). He calls these laws "crazy-quilt," both as to scope and as to punishments awarded.

78. See generally, KINSEY, POMEROY, AND MARTIN, *op. cit. supra* note 17; and KINSEY, MARTIN, POMEROY, AND GEBHARD, *op. cit. supra* note 38. Professor Schwartz predicts, very rightly as eight years have shown, that the criminal laws will be little changed by the "revelations" of Kinsey, and that

existing criminal legislation in the field of sex will continue to be enforced as little and as much as ever. Schwartz, Book Review, 96 U. PA. L. REV. 914, 915–16 (1948).

79. See Kennedy, Hoffman and Haines, *Psychiatric Study of William Heirens*, 38 J. CRIM. L. & C. 311 (1947).

80. As, for example, such non-sexual appearing crimes as kleptomania and arson. WEIHOFEN, *op. cit. supra* note 70, at 21. This is one of Karpman's objections to these statutes: *The Sexual Psychopath*, 42 J. CRIM. L. & C. 184, 192 (1951).

81. 107 AM. JOUR. PSYCH. 684 (1951).

82. OVERHOLSER, THE PSYCHIATRIST AND THE LAW 51–55 (1953), gives a telling, though short, summary of the dangers. He makes the suggestion, worth recording here, that in all cases where sex offenses are charged, the complaining witnesses themselves be subjected to psychiatric examination, because of the fantasy and sexual involvement lying at the root of much such testimony.

83. In Iowa, for example, IOWA CODE § 782.4 (1954), requires corroboration only in cases of rape (and included offenses) and seduction.

84. Tappan suggests confinement may be better than treatment as matters stand: *Sentences for Sex Criminals*, 42 J. CRIM. L. 332, 335–36 (Eng. 1951), suggesting also that such treatment as is given can be administered during confinement. He does *not*, however, consider confinement as ideal in these cases. Most authorities, however, agree that, ideally, treatment is the only goal promising any lasting success; see GAP REPORT NO. 9 and Wall and Wylie, *Institutional and Post-Institutional Treatment of the Sex Offender*, 2 VAND. L. REV. 47, 50 (1948).

85. Karpman, *The Sexual Psychopath*, 146 A.M.A.J. 721, 725 (1951).

86. *The Sexual Psychopath, A Symposium*, 43 J. CRIM. L. & C. 592 (1953).

87. Sutherland, *The Sexual Psychopath Laws*, 40 J. CRIM. L. & C. 543, 551 (1950).

88. Tappan, *Treatment of Sex Offenders in Denmark*, 108 AM. JOUR. PSYCH. 241 (1951).

89. MICHIGAN REPORT, at 38.

90. Roche, *Sexual Deviations*, Fed. Probation, Sept. 1950, p. 3. I suppose it is presumptuous for me, a layman, to attempt either to summarize or criticize an expert, but it seems to me that Dr. Roche's view, as expressed in this article, is that the "sex deviant" is essentially immature, a victim of arrested development. This I take to be the view of Freud, also. However valid, does it offer us any solution for the immediate problem which is the administration of this serious piece of legislation?

91. See generally, Abrahamsen, *Study of 103 Sex Offenders at Sing Sing*, Fed. Probation, Sept. 1950, p. 26. In this regard, the CALIFORNIA REPORT, at 20, points out that "Experienced psychiatrists agree neither on exact meaning of the term nor on clinical diagnoses in clinical practice." The same report points out the diverse diagnoses made by psychiatrists in these cases and the sharp differences in opinion they show. *Id.* at 20–22.

92. GUTTMACHER AND WEIHOFEN, *op. cit. supra* note 18, at 122: "Psychiatry is today only beginning to get an insight into the basic makeup of the sexual offender."

93. Tappan, *The Sexual Psychopath—a Civic and Social Responsibility*, 35 SOC. HYGIENE 354, 363 (1949).

94. Tappan, *Treatment of Sex Offenders in Denmark*, 108 AM. JOUR. PSYCH. 241–42 (1951). One hears laymen urge castration as a solution, but in fact it is a failure and a most dangerous remedy for a country like the United States where sex crimes arouse such public emotion. *Id.* at 248, as to the futility of castration. *But cf.* CALIFORNIA REPORT, at 32–33, and articles there cited.

95. Davidson, *Comment on Legislation Dealing With Sex Offenders*, 106 AM. JOUR. PSYCH. 390 (1949). In his treatise, FORENSIC PSYCHIATRY 122 (1952), Dr. Davidson says, "But successful treatment of a sex offender is an exquisitely rare phenomenon . . . ."

96. Cruvant, Meltzer and Tartaglino, *An Institutional Program for Sex Deviants*, 107 AM. JOUR. PSYCH. 190 (1950). Their group of 24 patients included: 8 accused of indecent exposure while drunk; 4 accused of indecent exposure while sober; 7 accused of indecent acts with children; the rest "miscellaneous" (among them two nonaggressive homosexuals and an aggressive sodomist). The conclusion of these authors is that proper therapy is at present not really known. *Id.* at 193. Dr. Georg Stürùp, who directed much of the Danish research, tellingly has outlined the uncertainties of treatment in a recent article, *The Treatment of Criminal Psychopaths in Herstedvester*, 25 BRITISH JOUR. MED. PSYCH. 31 (1952).

97. GAP REPORT NO. 30, at 4. The group suggests psychoanalysis may be promising, but this therapy is simply not available in most institutions. Note—most commitments in Iowa have been for homosexual acts.

98. MICHIGAN REPORT, at 39:
A great deal of experimentation is going on in various places, such as St. Elizabeths and elsewhere, on different techniques of treatment: castration—generally disapproved as not removing the personality defects of offenders; glandular treatment—disappointing or inconclusive; lobotomy—dangerous and uncertain; psychotherapy (sometimes psychoanalysis)—widely utilized but with differing opinions concerning results, depending on age of patient, type and degree of maladjustment, etc., etc.

99. Slough and Schwinn, *supra* note 60, at 151. To the same effect, generally, see Wall and Wylie, *supra* note 82, at 47, and East, *Sexual Offenders—A British View*, 55 YALE L.J. 527 (1944). Curiously enough, lawyers have more faith in doctors than they do themselves. Perhaps not so curious!

100. Bromberg, *The Treatability of the Psychopath*, 110 AM. JOUR. PSYCH. 604 (1954).

101. Abrahamsen, *supra* note 88, at 28–31. He found four different groups:
(a) Violent and untreatable (15%)
(b) Untreatable at present (35%)
(c) Treatable in a mental hospital (40%)
(d) Treatable in a mental hospital as outpatients (10%)
These figures are hardly inspiring and I, for one, seriously doubt that most nonphysicians would have put the percentage of treatable patients anywhere nearly so low. Mind you, Abrahamsen had working with him a highly skilled team and generally favorable conditions. Note that only 10% were treatable as outpatients and that as to the 40% treatable in a "treatment center," the institution referred to was a special one designed for this purpose.

102. Hacker and Frym, *supra* note 5, at 773–74. There was, for example, a long wait even for group psychotherapy, itself a method not very promising for many sex deviates. There seem seem to be no facilities there for individual psychotherapy, which the authors call "in most cases the therapy of choice."

103. Tappan, *The Sex Offender and Their Administration*, Fed. Probation, Sept. 1950, pp. 32, 37.

104. *Id.* at 35.

105. Tappan, *Sentences for Sex Criminals*, 42 J. CRIM. L. 332, 334 (Eng. 1951).

106. The general experience is pretty well summed up in 100 U. PA. L. REV. 727, 738–40 (1952). It is abundantly clear that *no* state has facilities or personnel to do the job. California describes its own facilities as "grossly inadequate" and says the same is true of most states; it could have been less

polite and said *all* states. CALIFORNIA REPORT, at 91. The same reports come in from every source. Michigan reports inadequate facilities and overcrowding which have the double-barreled bad effects of making informed enforcement officers loath to see persons committed as sexual psychopaths, MICHIGAN REPORT, at 79, and of hampering generally the entire mental health program by the crowded conditions created and, what is often forgotten in the enthusiasm of reform, the ill results on all parties of interaction of the sexual psychopaths and the other patients. *Id.* at 93. Michigan reports a further ill effect: the "criminal sexual psychopaths" require double the supervision of the mentally ill. *Id.* at 94. The net effect in Michigan has been overcrowded hospitals jammed with ill-assorted mental cases of all sorts, "treated" (one uses the word for lack of a better) by an over-taxed staff largely untrained for the job. And this is enlightenment, this is progress! It may be that the states like Indiana where these laws are simply neglected are better off, on balance, after all.

107. Letter from Dr. W. B. Brown, Superintendent of the Mental Health Institute, to the author, March 21, 1956. Except where specifically noted, the information in the rest of this discussion of Iowa conditions comes from correspondence between Dr. Brown and the author, which he has very kindly given leave to quote.

108. MICHIGAN REPORT, at 75.

109. Mr. Monroe Fairchild is quoted in the Des Moines Register, March 26, 1956, p. 4, col. 1, as saying, among other things (none of them wildly enthusiastic), that blanket commitment "herds" large numbers into Mt. Pleasant, and that such persons can be helped in private practice just as well. Yes, but is that private practice available, and if it is, will they take advantage of it? Incidentally, the speaker "cautioned that his comments do not mean he condones sex deviations!" Perhaps I should likewise take a strong stand against perversions. Dr. Brown tells me that one problem at Mt. Pleasant is that, owing to shortages of space, homosexuals sometimes are put in the same bedrooms together; the curative effect of this may be said to be doubtful.

110. Would not severer penalties deter those who are deterrable? If they are "sick" can they be deterred? Most authorities think not.

111. Hacker and Frym, *supra* note 5, at 774. Note this—the more limited the staff in experience and training, the thinner it is spread, the easier it is to fool.

112. N.Y. Sess. Laws 1950, c. 525, § 26. See an able student Note, *New York's New Indeterminate Sentence Law for Sex Offenders,* 60 YALE L.J. 346 (1951); this note is generally laudatory in tone, frankly preferring the New York law to those like Iowa's.

113. 60 YALE L.J. 346, 352 (1951). Such crimes may include arson, robbery, mayhem, burglary and others. Karpman tells of a case of a young man who suddenly stabbed a young woman sitting in front of him in a movie theater. He suffered from sexual drives which made him want to murder women by torture, yet statutes like the New York one would not cover him. Would the new Iowa law? See Karpman, *Felonious Assault Revealed as a Symptom of Abnormal Sexuality,* 37 J. CRIM. L. & C. 193 (1946).

114. Iowa Laws 1955, 56 G.A. c. 121, § 1.

115. People v. Haley, 46 Cal. App. 2d 618, 116 P.2d 498 (1941). Defendant was charged with kidnapping, robbery and mayhem. The undisputed evidence disclosed sexual mutilation of the victims. At his trial defendant filed a "verified petition" asking to be declared a "sexual psychopath." This was denied. After a verdict of guilty on the crimes charged defendant moved in arrest of judgment on the ground the court erred in failing to determine the matter of his alleged sexual psychopathy. This movement was denied, and he appealed. The California Court of Appeals held, among other things, that while it was within the trial court's discretion to adjourn criminal proceedings pending a determination of defendant's mental condition, that in this case there was no need to exercise that discretion since "crime" as used in CAL. WELFARE AND INST. CODE § 5501 (1952), referred to "sex offenses" as used in section 5500 of that Code. Hence, "crime" meant "sex crime," in the traditional sense; not, it would seem, "crime sexually motivated."

116. State *ex rel.* Sweezer v. Green, 360 Mo. 1249, 1255, 232 S.W.2d 897, 901 (1950). In this case the defendant had been charged with a "sex crime."

117. People v. Sims, 383 Ill. 472, 47 N.E.2d 703 (1943) (statute much like Iowa's).

118. Wood v. Hanson, Judge, 268 Wis. 165, 66 N.W.2d 722 (1954).

119. This patient, a homosexual, wrote the check as a result of dealings with another homosexual, against whom no charges were filed though there is evidence the latter was the aggressor.

120. See Sutherland, *supra* note 85, at 552–53. On the other hand, Slough and Schwinn are not worried by this possibility—Slough and Schwinn, *supra* note 60, at 140. To require conviction before commitment "sacrifices a measures of social protection in favor of personal liberty." To "apprehend and commit the potential sex offender *before* he commits an offense . . . opens the door to abuse . . . ." GUTTMACHER AND WEIHOFEN, *op. cit. supra* note 18, at 126–27.

121. State *ex rel.* Kirks v. Allen, 255 S.W.2d 144 (Mo. 1953). Defendant was charged with assault with intent to kill and with carnal knowledge. The prosecuting attorney's refusal to file the verified petition was upheld on attack by writ of mandamus; *held,* the word "shall" gives the prosecuting attorney discretion which will be upheld where exercised bona fides.

122. Sutherland, *supra* note 85, at 553. To the same effect see Tappan, *The Sex Offender and Their Administration,* Fed. Probation, Sept. 1950, p. 32, 35.

123. Iowa Laws 1955, 56th G.A. c. 121, § 4.

124. *In re* Faint, 341 MICH. 408, 67 N.W.2d 187 (1954). (There was, however, some medical evidence in the case, too.)

125. State *ex rel.* Sweezer v. Green, 360 Mo. 1249, 232 S.W.2d 897 (1950).

126. *In re* Carter, 337 Mich. 496, 60 N.W.2d 433 (1953). It must be sworn and alleged information and belief: *In re* Craft, 99 N.H. 287, 109 A.2d 853 (1954).

127. In California, for example, "not less than two nor more than three [qualified and certified] psychiatrists. . . ." CAL. WELFARE AND INST. CODE § 5504 (1952).

128. Iowa Laws 1955, 56th G.A. c. 121, §§ 6, 8.

129. GAP REPORT, No. 9, at 3, requires use of psychiatrists of no less than five years' specialist experience. In fact, the Group for the Advancement of Psychiatry provides an elaborate set-up for examination. See the same organization's recommendations. GROUP FOR THE ADVANCEMENT OF PSYCHIATRY REPORT No. 26, CRIMINAL RESPONSIBILITY AND PSYCHIATRIC EXPERT TESTIMONY (1953). Such facilities as they suggest are currently available in only one place in Iowa. MICHIGAN REPORT, at 120, recommends that appointment of examining physicians be mandatory, not discretionary.

130. Iowa Laws 1955, 56 G.A. c. 121, § 8.

131. *In re* Farnsworth, 111 A.2d 825 (N.H. 1955).

132. People v. Hilles, 327 Mich. 124, 41 N.W.2d 343 (1950). An interesting murder case, in which the trial court was upheld in deciding against a hearing as to sexual psychopathy despite allegations in the petition and a request (refused) to appoint two psychiatrists to examine defendant. *But cf.* People v. Barnet, 27 Cal. 2d 649, 166 P.2d 4 (1946)

where the trial court, ignoring the written opinions of three physicians based on personal examinations, was held to have abused its discretion in failing to grant a hearing. Note that in some other statutes (e.g., IND. ANN. STAT. § 9–3404 (Burns, Supp. 1953)), two physicians are required and in order for a hearing to be held must agree that defendant is a sexual psychopath.

133. IOWA CODE c. 611 (1954).

134. GUTTMACHER AND WEIHOFEN, op. cit. supra note 18, at 128. See generally, Weihofen and Overholser, *Commitment of the Mentally Ill,* 24 TEXAS L. REV. 307, 329–30 (1946). Also see GAP REPORT NO. 9—they recommend jury trial only as to guilt of the public offense charged.

135. Annot., 24 A.L.R. 2d 350 (1952); State ex rel. Sweezer v. Green, 360 Mo. 1249, 232 S.W.2d 897 (1950). In Iowa the hearing may be closed to the public but since this is not a criminal proceeding, that raises no constitutional objection, and may be beneficial to defendant. Iowa Laws, 56th G.A. c. 121, § 9.

136. *In re* Brewer, 224 Iowa 773, 276 N.W. 766 (1937). See also comment 25 IOWA L. REV. 156 (1939). The learned student editors there predict that "a 'psychopathic personality' law may receive harsh treatment from the Iowa Court." In the light of recent decisions in other jurisdictions and of the general climate of opinion, I respectfully dissent.

137. Iowa Laws 1955, 56th G.A. c. 121, § 5.

138. See Slough and Knightly, *Other Vices, Other Crimes,* 41 IOWA L. REV. 325, 332–36 (1956); Note, *Admissibility of Other Offense Evidence in Abnormal Sex Crime Cases,* 39 CALIF. L. REV. 584 (1951). It may be that section 10 of the new Iowa Sexual Psychopath Law is needed to clear up an ambiguity in the Iowa law. Slough and Knightly, *supra* at 334, n. 42.

139. People v. Artinian, 320 Mich. 441, 31 N.W.2d 688 (1948).

140. *In re* Mundy, 97 N.H. 239, 85 A.2d 371 (1952) (strong dissent). There was the problem as to examining physicians' reliance on case histories, social histories taken by social workers, and the like.

141. Iowa Laws 1955, 56th G.A. c. 121, § 5. People v. Parrish, 75 Cal. App. 2d 907, 172 P.2d 89 (1946); People v. Clymer, 326 Ill. App. 468, 62 N.E.2d 129 (1945). *But cf.* People v. Artinian, 320 Mich. 441, 31 N.W.2d 688 (1948), where on appeal defendant was released upon showing the adjudication was based solely on one doctor's testimony.

142. Iowa Laws 1955, 56th G.A. c. 121, § 11.

143. *Ibid.*

144. D. C. CODE ANN. § 22–3509 (1951).

145. CAL. WELFARE AND INST. CODE § 5517 (1952).

146. Iowa Laws, 56th G.A. c. 121, § 12.

147. *In re* Kemmerer, 309 Mich. 313, 15 N.W.2d 652 (1944), *cert. denied,* 329 U.S. 767 (1946); Kemmerer v. Benson, 165 F.2d 702 (6th Cir.), *cert. denied,* 334 U.S. 849 (1948). See Note, 100 U. PA. L. REV. 727, 744–45 (1952), for further examples of highly dubious commitments and restraints.

148. Gross v. Superior Court of Los Angeles, 42 Cal. 2d 816, 270 P.2d 1025 (1954).

149. As to the prospects for violation of probation, see MICHIGAN REPORT, at 36–37. Prison and treatment produced about the same results or "cures."

150. People v. Frantezak, 286 Mich. 51, 281 N.W. 534 (1938). Statute amended and held Constitutional in People v. Chapman, 301 Mich. 584, 4 N.W.2d 18 (1942).

151. State ex rel. Sweezer v. Green, 360 Mo. 1249, 232 S.W.2d 897 (1950), and Annot. 24 A.L.R. 2d 350 (1952). *Cf.* Tappan, *The Sex Offender and Their Administration,* Fed. Probation, Sept. 1950, pp. 32, 34: "Here is technicality of the rankest sort, since, in fact, the legal action results in depriva-

tion of liberty no less consequential because the institutional confinement may in some states be under a department of mental health rather than a department of correction." He denies these are like commitment proceedings of the insane, because of the nature of the reason for the defendant's presence before the court and for other reasons.

152. State *ex rel.* Pearson v. Probate Court, 205 Minn. 545, 287 N.W. 297 (1939), *aff'd,* 309 U.S. 270 (1940).

153. *Ibid.*

154. *In re* Keddy, 105 Cal. App. 2d 215, 233 P.2d 159 (1951).

155. State *ex rel.* Sweezer v. Green, 360 Mo. 1249, 232 S.W.2d 897 (1950). Here defendant alleged the statute was retroactive and ex post facto since the crime he was charged with ("public offense" in the Iowa Act) occurred before passage of the statute; the court answered that the statute was nonpenal but in mitigation of offenses and curative in nature.

156. *In re* Keddy, 105 Cal. App. 2d 215, 233, P.2d 159 (1951). Bail, it has been argued, is inadvisable in these cases, as these people are a "menace"; this seems to be the conclusion of Iowa District Courts and County Attorneys—see Note this number entitled, *A Review Procedure for Bail in Iowa.*

157. Skinner v. State, 189 Okla. 235, 115 P.2d 123 (1941); People v. Chapman, 301 Mich. 584, 4 N.W.2d 18 (1942).

158. IOWA CODE § 622.14 (1954).

159. Slough and Schwinn, *supra* note 60, at 142–45.

160. 360 Mo. 1249, 232 S.W.2d 897 (1950).

161. Slough and Schwinn, *supra* note 60, at 142–44.

162. 8 WIGMORE, EVIDENCE §§ 2260–61 (3d ed. 1940).

163. On this point see Note, *Illinois Proposal to Confine Sexually Dangerous Persons,* 40 J. CRIM. L. & C. 186, 192–95 (1949). The author's conclusion is that provisions limiting use of the psychiatric examination results to the court's perusal, as in Iowa, are preferable to a grant of immunity, because in the latter case prosecuting attorneys would tend to by-pass the "sexual psychopath laws" in order not to lose the chance of criminal convictions.

164. People v. Chapman, 301 Mich. 584, 4 N.W.2d 18 (1942) and Annot. 24 A.L.R. 2d 350, 362 (1952). See also People v. Redlich, 402 Ill. 270, 83 N.E.2d 736 (1949); where defendant, having refused to submit to psychiatric examination, was committed to jail for contempt of court; this sentence was reversed in the instant case, on the ground that in the meantime Redlich had been tried (for bestiality) and found guilty; hence the contempt proceedings were moot. But the Illinois Supreme Court assumes throughout that the original contempt proceeding was, of itself, perfectly valid and constitutional.

165. As to the bad and punitive effects of commitment see Flachsuer, *Analysis of Legal and Medical Considerations in Commitment of the Mentally Ill,* 56 YALE L.J. 1178 (1947).

166. Rowan v. People, 147 F.2d 138 (6th Cir. 1945).

167. See generally, Note, *Habeas Corpus as a Method of Release from Mental Institutions,* 38 VA. L. REV. 91 (1952); *In re* Breese, 82 Iowa 573, 48 N.W. 991 (1891). Mandamus against a hospital superintendent is not the remedy. People v. Albin, 111 Cal. App. 2d 800, 245 P.2d 660 (1952).

168. De Marcos v. Overholser, 137 F.2d 698 (D.C. Cir.), *cert. denied,* 302 U.S. 785 (1943). Testimony and argument are necessary: Von Maltke v. Gillies, 332 U.S. 708 (1948).

169. Molesworth v. Banmel, 198 Iowa 1293, 210 N.W. 41 (1924). This is a heavy burden to overcome, as courts tend to give great weight to the hospital superintendent's testimony; see Weihofen, *Eliminating the Battle of the Experts in Criminal Insanity Cases,* 48 MICH. L. REV. 961, 967 (1950).

170. *In re* Kemmerer, 309 Mich. 313, 15 N.W.2d 652 (1944).

171. Miller v. Overholser, 206 F.2d 415 (D.C. Cir. 1953).

Also held: habeas corpus is a proper remedy to use to move a patient, committed under these statutes, to a proper place for treatment.

172. *Ex Parte* Stone, 87 Cal. App. 2d 777, 780, 197 P.2d

847, 848 (1948). P.S.—he went back to the hospital.

173. GUTTMACHER AND WEIHOFEN, *op. cit. supra* note 18, at 129.

174. MICHIGAN REPORT, at 5.

SPECHT v. PATTERSON

United States Supreme Court, 1967 *

MR. JUSTICE DOUGLAS delivered the opinion of the Court.

We held in *Williams* v. *New York,* 337 U.S. 241, that the Due Process Clause of the Fourteenth Amendment did not require a judge to have hearings and to give a convicted person an opportunity to participate in those hearings when he came to determine the sentence to be imposed. We said:

"Under the practice of individualizing punishments, investigational techniques have been given an important role. Probation workers making reports of their investigations have not been trained to prosecute but to aid offenders. Their reports have been given a high value by conscientious judges who want to sentence persons on the best available information rather than on guesswork and inadequate information. To deprive sentencing judges of this kind of information would undermine modern penological procedural policies that have been cautiously adopted throughout the nation after careful consideration and experimentation. We must recognize that most of the information now relied upon by judges to guide them in the intelligent imposition of sentences would be unavailable if information were restricted to that given in open court by witnesses subject to cross-examination. And the modern probation report draws on information concerning every aspect of a defendant's life. The type and extent of this information make totally impractical if not impossible open court testimony with cross-examination. Such a procedure could endlessly delay criminal administration in a retrial of collateral issues." *Id.,* 249–250.

That was a case where at the end of the trial and in the same proceeding the fixing of the penalty for first degree murder was involved—whether life imprisonment or death.

The question is whether the rule of the *Williams* case applies to this Colorado case where petitioner, having been convicted for indecent liberties under one Colorado statute that carries a maximum sentence of 10 years (Colo. Rev. Stat. Ann. § 40-2-32 (1963)) but

not sentenced under it, may be sentenced under the Sex Offenders Act, Colo. Rev. Stat. Ann. §§ 39-19-1 to 10 (1963), for an indeterminate term of from one day to life without notice and full hearing. The Colorado Supreme Court approved the procedure, when it was challenged by habeas corpus (153 Colo. 235, 385 P. 2d 423) and on motion to set aside the judgment. 156 Colo. 12, 396 P. 2d 838. This federal habeas corpus proceeding resulted, the Court of Appeals affirming dismissal of the writ, 357 F. 2d 325. The case is here on a petition for certiorari, 385 U.S. 968.

The Sex Offenders Act may be brought into play if the trial court "is of the opinion that any . . . person [convicted of specified sex offenses], if at large, constitutes a threat of bodily harm to members of the public, or is an habitual offender and mentally ill." § 1. He then becomes punishable for an indeterminate term of from one day to life on the following conditions as specified in §2:

"(2) A complete psychiatric examination shall have been made of him by the psychiatrists of the Colorado psychopathic hospital or by psychiatrists designated by the district court; and

"(3) A complete written report thereof submitted to the district court. Such report shall contain all facts and findings, together with recommendations as to whether or not the person is treatable under the provisions of this article; whether or not the person should be committed to the Colorado state hospital or to the state home and training schools as mentally ill or mentally deficient. Such report shall also contain the psychiatrist's opinion as to whether or not the person could be adequately supervised on probation."

This procedure was followed in petitioner's case; he was examined as required and a psychiatric report prepared and given to the trial judge prior to the sentencing. But there was no hearing in the normal sense, no right of confrontation and so on.

Petitioner insists that this procedure does not satisfy due process because it allows the critical finding to be

* 386 U.S. 605 (1967)

made under §1 of the Sex Offenders Act (1) without a hearing at which the person so convicted may confront and cross-examine adverse witnesses and present evidence of his own by use of compulsory process, if necessary; and (2) on the basis of hearsay evidence to which the person involved is not allowed access.

We adhere to *Williams* v. *New York, supra;* but we decline the invitation to extend it to this radically different situation. These commitment proceedings whether denominated civil or criminal are subject both to the Equal Protection Clause of the Fourteenth Amendment as we held in *Baxstrom* v. *Herold,* 383 U.S. 107, and to the Due Process Clause. We hold that the requirements of due process were not satisfied here.

The Sex Offenders Act does not make the commission of a specified crime the basis for sentencing. It makes one conviction the basis for commencing another proceeding under another Act to determine whether a person constitutes a threat of bodily harm to the public, or is an habitual offender and mentally ill. That is a new finding of fact (*Vanderhoof* v. *People,* 152 Colo. 147, 149, 380 P. 2d 903, 904) that was not an ingredient of the offense charged. The punishment under the second Act is criminal punishment even though it is designed not so much as retribution as it is to keep individuals from inflicting future harm.[1] *United States* v. *Brown,* 381 U.S. 437, 458.

The Court of Appeals for the Third Circuit in speaking of a comparable Pennsylvania statute [2] said:

"It is a separate criminal proceeding which may be invoked after conviction of one of the specified crimes. Petitioner therefore was entitled to a full judicial hearing before the magnified sentence was imposed. At such a hearing the requirements of due process cannot be satisfied by partial or niggardly procedural protections. A defendant in such a proceeding is entitled to the full panoply of the relevant protections which due process guarantees in state criminal proceedings. He must be afforded all those safeguards which are fundamental rights and essential to a fair trial, including the right to confront and cross-examine the witnesses against him." *Gerchman* v. *Maroney,* 355 F. 2d 302, 312.

We agree with that view. Under Colorado's criminal procedure, here challenged, the invocation of the Sex Offenders Act means the making of a new charge leading to criminal punishment. The case is not unlike those under recidivist statutes where an habitual criminal issue is "a distinct issue" (*Graham* v. *West Virginia,* 224 U.S. 616, 625) on which a defendant "must receive reasonable notice and an opportunity to be heard." *Oyler* v. *Boles,* 368 U.S. 448, 452; *Chandler* v. *Fretag,* 348 U.S. 3, 8. Due process, in other words, requires that he be present with counsel, have an opportunity to be heard, be confronted with witnesses against him,

have the right to cross-examine, and to offer evidence of his own. And there must be findings adequate to make meaningful any appeal that is allowed. The case is therefore quite unlike the Minnesota statute [3] we considered in *Minnesota* v. *Probate Court,* 309 U.S. 270, where in a proceeding to have a person adjudged a "psychopathic personality" there was a hearing where he was represented by counsel and could compel the production of witnesses on his behalf. *Id.,* at 275. None of these procedural safeguards we have mentioned is present under Colorado's Sex Offenders Act. We therefore hold that it is deficient in due process as measured by the requirements of the Fourteenth Amendment. *Pointer* v. *Texas,* 380 U.S. 400.

Reversed.

MR. JUSTICE HARLAN agrees with the conclusions reached by the Court, but upon the premises set forth in his opinion concurring in the result in *Pointer* v. *Texas,* 380 U.S. 400, 408.

NOTES

1. Provisions for probation are provided (Colo. Rev. Stat. Ann. § 39–19–5–(3) (1963)); and the Board of Parole has broad powers over the person sentenced. (Colo. Rev. Stat. Ann. §§ 39–19–6 to 10 (1963)).

2. The Pennsylvania statute (Pa. Stat., Tit. 19, §§ 1166–1174 (1964)) provides that if a court is of the opinion that a person convicted before it of certain sex offenses "if at large, constitutes a threat of bodily harm to members of the public, or is an habitual offender and mentally ill," it may, "in lieu of the sentence now provided by law," sentence the person to a state institution for an indeterminate period, from one day to life. Pa. Stat., Tit. 19, § 1166 (1964). The sentence is imposed only after the defendant has undergone a psychiatric examination and the court has received a report containing all the facts necessary to determine whether it shall impose the sentence under the act. Pa. Stat., Tit. 19, § 1167 (1964). If the court, after receiving the report, "shall be of the opinion that it would be to the best interests of justice to sentence such person under the provisions of [the] act, he shall cause such person to be arraigned before him and sentenced to" a state institution designated by the Department of Welfare. Pa. Stat., Tit. 19, § 1170 (1964). After a person is sentenced under the act, the state Board of Parole has exclusive control over him. Pa. Stat., Tit. 19, § 1173 (1964).

3. The Minnesota statute (Chapter 369 of the Laws of Minnesota of 1939) provided that the laws relating to persons found to be insane were to apply to "persons having a psychopathic personality." It defined the term "psychopathic personality" as meaning the existence in a person of certain characteristics which rendered him "irresponsible for his conduct with respect to sexual matters and thereby dangerous to other persons." The statute was not criminal in nature, and was not triggered by a criminal conviction. A person found to have a "psychopathic personality" would be committed, just as a person found to be insane. See Mason's Minn. Stat. c. 74, § 8992–176 (1938 Supp.).

IN RE LYNCH

Supreme Court of California, 1972 *

Mosk, Justice

V

Not only does the punishment here fail to fit the crime, it does not fit the criminal. At the conclusion of the trial in this case the judge was moved to remark, "Mr. Lynch, before you leave, let me say to you in the utmost sincerity, it has been my impression from the very outset of this case that you are a man of great potential. You are a person of unusual appearance, you make a very pleasant appearance, obviously have the capacity to get along well with people, you are obviously a person of superior intellect."

The circumstances of the offense do not undermine this appraisal. This is not a case, for example, in which an exhibitionist forced himself on large numbers of the public by cavorting naked on a busy street at high noon. Instead, a very different picture emerges. The prosecuting witness was a "carhop" or waitress on the night shift at a drive-in restaurant. She testified that between midnight and 1 A.M. petitioner drove into the restaurant area, alone in his car. He first parked in the rear lot, where no car service was provided. Subsequently he moved his vehicle closer and asked the waitress for a cup of coffee. When she returned with a second cup he inquired what time the restaurant would close, and she told him 2:45 A.M. He instructed her to bring him a fresh cup of coffee whenever she thought the previous cup might be cold, explaining that he didn't want to "bother" her. Accordingly, about half an hour later and without being called, the waitress approached petitioner's car with another cup of coffee. A siren happened to be sounding in the street at that moment, and petitioner was looking in its direction, away from the waitress. As she stood by his window she saw the fly of his pants open, his hand on his erect penis and a "pin-up" magazine open on the front seat next to him. When petitioner heard her put the coffee down on his tray he turned, saw her, and said "Oops." The waitress left immediately. Some 15 minutes later, however, she assertedly observed him from a distance through a rearview mirror on his car and saw he was still exposed. The incident was then reported to the police, and petitioner was placed under arrest.

Some idea of the nature of the prosecution's case can be gleaned from the reasoning of the trial court in denying a motion for new trial. The court explained there would be "great merit" in petitioner's position that the exposure was inadvertent "if he had ceased and desisted as soon as the waitress came up to the car and he said 'Oops.' But the evidence was that he didn't cease and desist at that point. He continued for a long period of time thereafter, as evidence by the fact that the waitress again saw it through the mirror. *He may not have known the mirror was in the position that it was in.* But his conduct [in] continuing over in that period of time demonstrates a clear willful and reckless disregard for the consequences of his conduct." (Italics added.)

For this single act petitioner has now spent more than five years in state prison—three and a half of those years in the maximum security confines of Folsom. The Adult Authority has four times denied him release on parole, and has never fixed his sentence at any term less than the life maximum prescribed by section 314.

We recite these facts simply to illustrate the vast disproportion between the conduct of which petitioner was convicted and the punishment he has suffered—and still faces. The fault does not lie in the theory of the indeterminate sentence law, but in the unreasonably high maximum term prescribed for this offense. "If a reasonable maximum sentence were passed, this system could have much to commend it. But when the Court imposes a sentence of 'from one year to life,' . . . the sentence can assume an altogether different character." (Condemned Without Hope in California (1971) 7 The Review (International Commission of Jurists) 17, 18.)

For the reasons stated herein, the recidivist provision of section 314 is void under article I, section 6, of the California Constitution.[26]

One who commits an act of indecent exposure in California is guilty of a simple misdemeanor and can be punished by no more than a brief jail sentence or a small fine.[1] If he commits the identical act a second

* 503 P. 2d 921 (1972) The portion of the opinion which states the facts of the case is presented first. Footnotes are numbered as in the original.

time, however, the law declares him guilty of a felony and inflicts on him a punishment of imprisonment in the state prison for the indeterminate period of one year to life.[2] We adjudicate here the question whether the aggravated penalty for second-offense indecent exposure provided by Penal Code section 314 violates the prohibition of the California Constitution against cruel or unusual punishments. (Cal.Const., art. I, § 6.) We conclude that the penalty offends the Constitution in the respect charged, and petitioner is therefore entitled to relief.

The issue is presented by John Lynch, a state prison inmate. In 1958 he was convicted of misdemeanor indecent exposure in violation of former Penal Code section 311, the predecessor of section 314. For this offense he spent two years on probation. In 1967 he was again convicted of indecent exposure. The court ruled he was not a mentally disordered sex offender, denied probation, and sentenced him to prison for the indeterminate term provided by section 314 in the case of a second offense. The conviction was affirmed on appeal, and petitioner thereafter filed two applications for habeas corpus in this court: in Crim. No. 16232 he levels various constitutional challenges to the power of the Adult Authority to continue holding him under the 1967 conviction, while in Crim. No. 16237 he attacks the validity of the 1958 conviction. We consolidated the applications, issued an order to show cause, and appointed counsel.

I

We inquire, first, whether petitioner's indeterminate sentence under the 1967 conviction constitutes cruel or unusual punishment within the meaning of the California Constitution. We approach this issue with full awareness of and respect for the distinct roles of the Legislature and the courts in such an undertaking. We recognize that in our tripartite system of government it is the function of the legislative branch to define crimes and prescribe punishments, and that such questions are in the first instance for the judgment of the Legislature alone. (People v. Bauer (1969) 1 Cal.3d 368, 375, 82 Cal.Rptr. 357, 461 P.2d 637; People v. Knowles (1950) 35 Cal.2d 175, 181, 217 P.2d 1; People v. Tanner (1935) 3 Cal.2d 279, 298, 44 P.2d 324.)

Yet legislative authority remains ultimately circumscribed by the constitutional provision forbidding the infliction of cruel or unusual punishment, adopted by the people of this state as an integral part of our Declaration of Rights. It is the difficult but imperative task of the judicial branch, as coequal guardian of the Constitution, to condemn any violation of that prohibition. As we concluded in People v. Anderson (1972) 6 Cal.3d 628, 640, 100 Cal. Rptr. 152, 160, 493 P.2d 880, 888, "The Legislature is thus accorded the broadest

discretion possible in enacting penal statutes and in specifying punishment for crime, but the final judgment as to whether the punishment it decrees exceeds constitutional limits is a judicial function." (Accord, Furman v. Georgia (1972) 408 U.S. 238, 269, 92 S.Ct. 2726, 33 L.Ed.2d 346 (opinion of Brennan, J.); Trop v. Dulles (1958) 356 U.S. 86, 103–104, 78 S.Ct. 590, 2 L.Ed.2d 630 (plurality opinion of Warren, C. J.); Weems v. United States (1910) 217 U.S. 349, 378–379, 30 S.Ct. 544, 54 L.Ed. 793.)

We add that the determination of whether a legislatively prescribed punishment is constitutionally excessive is not a duty which the courts eagerly assume or lightly discharge. Here, as in other contexts, " 'mere doubt does not afford sufficient reason for a judicial declaration of invalidity. Statutes must be upheld unless their unconstitutionality clearly, positively and unmistakably appears.' " (In re Dennis M. (1969) 70 Cal.2d 444, 453, 75 Cal.Rptr. 1, 6, 450 P.2d 296, 301, and cases cited.) When such a showing is made, however, we must forthrightly meet our responsibility "to ensure that the promise of the Declaration of Rights is a reality to the individual." (People v. Anderson (1972) supra, 6 Cal.3d 628, 640, 100 Cal.Rptr. 152, 160, 493 P.2d 880, 888.) As our Chief Justice recently explained, "By observing this cautious, often burdensome and sometimes unpopular procedure, the courts can often prevent the will of the majority from unfairly interfering with the rights of individuals who, even when acting as a group, may be unable to protect themselves through the political process. In this way, judicial review assures a government under the laws." (Wright, The Role of the Judiciary: From Marbury to Anderson (1972) 60 Cal.L.Rev. 1262, 1268.)

At the outset we emphasize that petitioner does not contend the indeterminate sentence law is invalid on its face or that an indeterminate sentence of any length whatever constitutes cruel or unusual punishment. Such a contention has already been rejected. (People v. Wade (1968) 266 Cal.App.2d 918, 927–929, 72 Cal. Rptr. 538.) His position, rather, is that the constitutional prohibition is violated by the particular indeterminate sentence imposed on him pursuant to Penal Code section 314. We begin, therefore, by determining what in fact is the "sentence" in this case to be measured against the constitutional yardstick.

The operating features of the California indeterminate sentence law are well known, and need only be summarized here. Under this system[3] the Legislature prescribes both the minimum and the maximum terms for each offense punishable by imprisonment in the state prison. Upon conviction of such an offense, and if neither a new trial nor probation is granted, the trial court does not specify the length of imprisonment but simply sentences the defendant for the term "prescribed by law." (Pen.Code, § 1168.) It is the Adult

Authority, an administrative agency within the Department of Corrections (Pen.Code, §§ 5001, 5075–5082), which thereafter determines within statutory limits the length of the term the defendant will actually be required to serve. (Pen.Code, §§ 3020–3025.)

Three considerations impel us to the conclusion that a defendant under an indeterminate sentence has in effect been sentenced to the maximum term provided by law, and that the constitutional validity of the sentence must be judged by that maximum.

First, the theory of the indeterminate sentence law in California is that it permits the *shortening* of a defendant's sentence upon a showing of rehabilitation. This has not always been the reason invoked elsewhere for indeterminate sentence laws. When they first came into use—in certain countries of continental Europe in the 18th and 19th centuries—their purpose was the contrary, i. e., to permit the *lengthening* of sentences for the preventive detention of dangerous unrehabilitated criminals who had served their original terms. By the middle of the 19th century, however, such laws had generally disappeared. And when the indeterminate sentence system was revived by American prison reformers in the latter part of the century, its purpose was wholly ameliorative. The goal of its proponents was to individualize the rehabilitation process, and to use the power to shorten sentences as an incentive to reformation. (Sellin, Indeterminate Sentence, in 4 Encyc.Soc.Sci. (1937) pp. 650–651.)

California firmly adheres to the latter theory, as this court announced shortly after our first indeterminate sentence law was enacted. (Stat.1917, ch. 527, p. 665.) In the leading case of In re Lee (1918) 177 Cal. 690, 692, 171 p. 958, 959, we undertook "to consider the nature and purposes of the indeterminate sentence law. It is generally recognized by the courts and by modern penologists that the purpose of the indeterminate sentence law, like other modern laws in relation to the administration of the criminal law, is *to mitigate the punishment which would otherwise be imposed upon the offender.* These laws place emphasis upon the reformation of the offender. They seek to make the punishment fit the criminal rather than the crime. They endeavor to put before the prisoner great incentive to well-doing in order that his will to do well should be strengthened and confirmed by the habit of well-doing." (Italics added.) [4]

The relevance of this theory to our present inquiry is clear: if the purpose of the indeterminate sentence law is thus to mitigate a punishment which "would otherwise be imposed," the greater punishment must itself be one which it is within the power of the Legislature to decree. Accordingly, it is the maximum term prescribed by the statute—not a lesser period thereafter fixed as an "incentive to well-doing"—which must survive constitutional scrutiny.

Our second reason for reaching this conclusion is derived from the actual operation of the indeterminate sentence program: Penal Code section 3020 empowers the Adult Authority not only to "determine" the lesser term a defendant will be allowed to serve as an incentive to reformation, but also to "redetermine" that term when appropriate to do so. Pursuant to this power the Adult Authority may, for good cause (In re McLain (1960) 55 Cal.2d 78, 87, 9 Cal.Rptr. 824, 357 P.2d 1080) and at any time prior to a defendant's final discharge, extend a previously fixed lesser term by refixing it at any period up to and including the statutory maximum. Stated otherwise, a defendant under an indeterminate sentence has "no vested right" to have his sentence fixed at the term first prescribed by the Adult Authority "or any other period less than the maximum sentence provided by statute." (In re Cowen (1946) 27 Cal.2d 637, 641, 166 P.2d 279, 281.) [5] Viewed realistically, a defendant's liability is to serve the maximum term, and he is therefore entitled to know that the maximum in his case is lawful.

Our third basis for so concluding is found in the cases upholding the indeterminate sentence law against various constitutional challenges. It was early charged that the indeterminate sentence law violated the separation of powers clause by vesting either a legislative or judicial function—the fixing of terms—in an agency of the executive branch. We rejected this contention in In re Lee (1918) supra, 177 Cal. 690, 693, 71 P. 958, 959, reasoning that "The legislative function is filled by providing the sentence which is to be imposed by the judicial branch upon the determination of the guilt of the offender. This is done by the enactment of the indeterminate sentence law. The judicial branch of the government is intrusted with the function of determining the guilt of the individual and of imposing the sentence provided by law for the offense of which the individual has been found guilty. The actual carrying out of the sentence and the application of the various provisions for ameliorating the same are administrative in character and properly exercised by an administrative body." [6]

Manifestly, if the constitutionality of the indeterminate sentence law is thus upheld by deeming that the "sentence" prescribed by the Legislature and imposed by the court is the term declared by the statute rather than later ameliorated by the administrative agency, that same sentence must also be measured against the constitutional test of cruel or unusual punishment.

In addition, it has often been asserted that an indeterminate sentence violates the due process clause because it is fatally uncertain. The claim has equally often been refuted with the explanation that, as we said in Lee (*id.* 177 Cal. at p. 693, 171 P. at p. 959), "the indeterminate sentence is in legal effect a sentence for the maximum term." [7] But, again, if an indeterminate sentence is thus a sentence for the maximum term "in legal effect," that maximum must in the first instance be constitutionally valid.

The interaction of the foregoing constitutional justifications for the indeterminate sentence law is well illustrated in People v. Sama (1922) 189 Cal. 153, 207 P. 893. There the defendant was convicted of attempted robbery. The punishment for robbery was an indeterminate sentence of five years to life; the punishment for an attempt to commit any crime was imprisonment for up to one-half of the maximum term provided for the completed offense. The judgment purported to sentence the defendant "for the term prescribed by law" under the indeterminate sentence statutes. He appealed, contending that an indeterminate sentence is a sentence for the maximum term, and in fixing a term at less than maximum the prison board is simply exercising clemency; that the sentence in his case must therefore be deemed to be for a term of one-half of his life, a period that obviously cannot be calculated except with hindsight after his death, and hence is void for uncertainty. The Attorney General contended that under the indeterminate sentence law the defendant was first required to serve a definite minimum term of six months; [8] that it thereafter would be the duty of the prison board to fix the remainder of the defendant's term, so that at no time would his sentence be uncertain; and that the statement that an indeterminate sentence is a sentence for the maximum term "is but a theory."

The theory, nevertheless, proved dispositive. Quoting the above language from Lee (177 Cal. at p. 693, 171 p. 958), we reasoned (189 Cal. at pp. 156–157, 207 P. at p. 894): "This being the settled law, it follows that the sentence imposed in the case at bar is one for the maximum term prescribed by law, which, as already indicated, would be for one-half of appellant's life. It also follows from *In re Lee,* supra, that the function which the state board of prison directors would perform in determining what term of years appellant must serve is no part of the actual fixing of the sentence itself; and that if it were so regarded it would be the exercise of a judicial function by an executive board, and void under section 1, article III, of the Constitution. The Legislature has no authority to vest this judicial power in the state board of prison directors, and in so far as section 1168 of the Penal Code purports to do so it is in violation of that section. Hence, *in determining whether or not this sentence is valid, the test is the term of imprisonment called for by the judgment*—one-half of appellant's life—and *not* the term of years which would be fixed by the state board of prison directors at the expiration of the minimum term." (Italics added.) We held that maximum term to be void for uncertainty and remanded the defendant for resentencing.

For each of the above reasons we conclude that when a defendant under an indeterminate sentence challenges that sentence as cruel or unusual punishment in violation of the California Constitution, the test is whether the maximum term of imprisonment permitted by the statute punishing his offense exceeds the constitutional limit, regardless of whether a lesser term may be fixed in his particular case by the Adult Authority.[9]

Applying this test to the proceeding before us, we see that for second-offense indecent exposure section 314 prescribes a punishment of imprisonment in the state prison for "not less than one year." (Fn. 2, *ante.*) In confirmation of the unmistakable meaning of that phrase, Penal Code section 671 provides that "Whenever any person is declared punishable for a crime by imprisonment in the state prison for a term not less than any specified number of years, and no limit to the duration of such imprisonment is declared, punishment, of such offender shall be imprisonment during his natural life," subject to the provisions of the indeterminate sentence law. For present purposes, therefore, we deem this petitioner to be serving a sentence of life imprisonment.[10]

II

The particular constitutional limit said to be exceeded in the case at bar must now be delineated. Petitioner expressly disavows any claim that indecent exposure is a "status" offense which cannot be criminally punished. (Robinson v. California (1962) 370 U.S. 660, 82 S.Ct. 1417, 8 L.Ed. 2d 758.) Nor is there any contention that a sentence of life imprisonment is, in the abstract, a cruel or unusual *method* of punishment. (In re Rosencrantz (1928) 205 Cal. 534, 537, 271 p. 902.) Petitioner urges, rather, that a life sentence *for indecent exposure* is cruel or unusual punishment under the California Constitution because it is grossly disproportionate to the offense.

No California court has yet held a statutory penalty unconstitutional on the ground it is disproportionate to the crime committed. The rule has been recognized, however, in several opinions considering the constitutionality of the death penalty. Thus in In re Finley (1905) 1 Cal.App. 198, 202, 81 P. 1041, 1042, the court stated that a punishment may be denounced as unusual in the constitutional sense only when it "is out of all proportion to the offense, and is beyond question an extraordinary penalty for a crime of ordinary gravity, committed under ordinary circumstances" (italics omitted). In People v. Oppenheimer (1909) 156 Cal. 733, 737, 106 P. 74, 77, the court reasoned that the infliction of the death penalty by ordinary methods is not cruel or unusual punishment "unless perhaps it be so disproportionate to the offense for which it is inflicted as to meet the disapproval and condemnation of the conscience and reason of men generally, 'as to shock the moral sense of the people.' " And in People v. Anderson (1972) supra, 6 Cal.3d 628, 100 Cal.Rptr. 152, 493 P.2d 880, we recognized that "punishments of excessive severity for ordinary offenses" may be both cruel (*id.* at p. 646, 100 Cal.Rptr. at p. 164, 493 P.2d at p. 892) and unusual (*id.* at p. 654, 100 Cal.Rptr. 152, 493 P.2d 880) within the meaning of article I, section 6, of the California Constitution.

A similar rule has evolved at the federal level in the interpretation of the cruel and unusual punishment clause of the Eighth Amendment. In O'Neil v. Vermont (1892) 144 U.S. 323, 12 S.Ct. 693, 36 L.Ed. 450, the defendant was convicted on multiple counts of unauthorized sale of liquor and sentenced to a fine of over $6,000 or, if he could not pay the fine, to hard labor for more than 54 years. A majority of the United States Supreme Court declined on federal-state grounds to consider whether this sentence constituted cruel and unusual punishment. Dissenting, Justice Field would have held the sentence to be "one which, in its severity, considering the offenses of which [the defendant] was convicted, may justly be termed both 'unusual and cruel.' " (*Id.* at p. 339, 12 S.Ct. at p. 699.) He recognized that the cruel and unusual punishment clause was traditionally thought to prohibit physically torturous methods of punishment such as the rack and the screw, but explained: "The inhibition is directed, not only against punishments of the character mentioned, but against all punishments which by their excessive length or severity are greatly disproportioned to the offenses charged. The whole inhibition is against that which is excessive either in the bail required, or fine imposed, or punishment inflicted." (*Id.* at pp. 339–340, 12 S.Ct. at p. 699.)

Less than two decades later Justice Field's view became law in the landmark case of Weems v. United States (1910) supra, 217 U.S. 349, 30 S.Ct. 544, 54 L.Ed. 793. There a disbursing officer in a Philippine government bureau was convicted of making two false entries in his cash books. He was sentenced under a Philippine statute prescribing a minimum of 12 years' imprisonment for this crime, to be served in chains and at "hard and painful" labor, together with a fine, loss of numerous civil rights, and perpetual surveillance. The United States Supreme Court measured the statute against the cruel and unusual punishment clause of the Philippine Bill of Rights, which the court deemed to have the same meaning as the Eighth Amendment. Although undoubtedly influenced by the peculiar penalties imposed in addition to imprisonment, the court did not hold the law unconstitutional merely on the ground of the bizarre method of the punishment. Rather, the court quoted both the foregoing language of Justice Field in *O'Neil* and an early Massachusetts case in which it was acknowledged that " '[imprison-

ment] in the State prison for a long term of years might be so disproportionate to the offense as to constitute a cruel and unusual punishment.' " (*Id.* at pp. 368, 371, 30 S.Ct. at p. 549.)

Reviewing in this light the minimum sentence permissible under the statute, the court observed that "Such penalties for such offenses amaze those who have formed their conception of the relation of a state to even its offending citizens from the practice of the American commonwealth, and believe that it is a precept of justice that punishment for crime should be graduated and proportioned to offense." (*Id.* at pp. 366–367, 30 S.Ct. at p. 549.) The court concluded by invalidating the statute on the twofold ground that "It is cruel in its excess of imprisonment and that which accompanies and follows imprisonment. It is unusual in its character. Its punishments come under the condemnation of the bill of rights, both on account of their degree and kind." (*Id.* at p. 377, 30 S.Ct. at p. 553.) [11]

The principle was recently reaffirmed in Furman v. Georgia (1972) supra, 408 U.S. 238, 92 S.Ct. 2726, 33 L.Ed.2d 346, the United States Supreme Court decision holding the death penalty unconstitutional as applied. In the course of his separate opinion in support of the majority, Justice Brennan gave as his view that "Although the determination that a severe punishment is excessive may be grounded in a judgment that it is disproportionate to the crime, the more significant basis is that the punishment serves no penal purpose more effectively than a less severe punishment." (Fn. omitted; *id.* at p. 280, 92 S.Ct. at p. 2747.) In turn, Justice Marshall recognized that "a penalty may be cruel and unusual because it is excessive and serves no valid legislative purpose. . . . The decisions [of the United States Supreme Court] are replete with assertions that one of the primary functions of the cruel and unusual punishments clause is to prevent excessive or unnecessary penalties [citations]; these punishments are unconstitutional even though popular sentiment may favor them." (*Id.* at p. 331, 92 S.Ct. at p. 2773.)

Although two of the three petitioners in *Furman* were under sentence of death for rape rather than murder, the majority opinions of the high court did not address themselves to the question whether that sentence was unconstitutional because disproportionate to the crime. (Cf. Rudolph v. Alabama (1963) 375 U.S. 889, 84 S.Ct. 155, 11 L.Ed.2d 119 (Goldberg, J., joined by Douglas, J., and Brennan, J., dissenting from denial of certiorari).) The Fourth Circuit Court of Appeals, however, so ruled in Ralph v. Warden (1970) 438 F.2d 786, cert. denied (1972) 408 U.S. 942, 92 S.Ct. 2869, 33 L.Ed.2d 766. There the defendant was sentenced to death under Maryland law for the crime of rape. Relying on the United States Supreme Court cases discussed herein, the federal court held (at p. 793) that a death sentence for the crime of rape without aggravating circumstances is so disproportionate as to offend the Eighth Amendment.

Finally, the highest courts of our sister states have repeatedly invoked the rule of proportionality in applying their equivalents of our cruel or unusual punishment clause.[12] Thus in Workman v. Commonwealth (Ky. 1968) 429 S.W.2d 374, a sentence of life imprisonment without possibility of parole for rape committed by juvenile defendants was held to be unconstitutionally disproportionate to the offense. In Cannon v. Gladden (1955) 203 Or. 629, 281 P.2d 233, a sentence of life imprisonment for assault with intent to commit rape was voided on this ground. In State v. Evans (1952) 73 Idaho 50, 245 P.2d 788, it was held in effect that life imprisonment for lewd and lascivious acts upon a child would be so excessive as to constitute cruel and unusual punishment. In Dembowski v. State (1968) 251 Ind. 250, 240 N.E.2d 815, a 25-year maximum indeterminate sentence for robbery was ruled unconstitutionally disproportionate to a lesser punishment for armed robbery. In State v. Kimbrough (1948) 212 S.C. 348, 46 S.E. 2d 273, a sentence of 30 years at hard labor for burglary was held excessive. In People v. Lorentzen (1972) supra, 387 Mich. 167, 194 N.W.2d 827, a mandatory minimum sentence of 20 years for selling marijuana was held so severe as to violate the cruel or unusual punishment clause.[13]

Whether a particular punishment is disproportionate to the offense is, of course, a question of degree. The choice of fitting and proper penalties is not an exact science, but a legislative skill involving an appraisal of the evils to be corrected, the weighing of practical alternatives, consideration of relevant policy factors, and responsiveness to the public will; in appropriate cases, some leeway for experimentation may also be permissible. The judiciary, accordingly, should not interfere in this process unless a statute prescribes a penalty "out of all proportion to the offense" (Robinson v. California (1962) supra, 370 U.S. 660, 676, 82 S.Ct. 1417, 1425, 8 L.Ed.2d 758 (concurring opinion of Douglas, J.); In re Finley (1905) supra, 1 Cal.App. 198, 202, 81 P. 1041, 1042), i. e., so severe in relation to the crime as to violate the prohibition against cruel or unusual punishment.

The courts have attempted to formulate a general description of that constitutional limit. Workman, for example, would strike down a punishment "so disproportionate to the offense committed as to shock the moral sense of the community." (429 S.W.2d at p. 377.) Cannon invalidates a penalty so disproportionate "as to shock the moral sense of all reasonable men as to what is right and proper." (281 P.2d at p. 235.) Evans would hold unconstitutional a punishment so disproportionate "as to shock the conscience of reasonable men." (245 P.2d at p. 792.) Lorentzen quotes an earlier Michigan case for the rule annulling a punishment so disproportionate "as to shock the moral sense of the public." (194 N.W.2d at p. 831.) And Faulkner would void a penalty so disproportionate "as to be completely arbitrary and shocking to the sense of justice." (445 P.2d at p. 819.)

With slight variation, this is the rhetoric we used in our Oppenheimer opinion, quoted above.[14] However, the precise expression is not significant. It is essential only that in its actual operation the rule ensure that the power to prescribe penalties " 'be exercised within the limits of civilized standards.' " (People v. Anderson (1972) supra, 6 Cal.3d 628, 640, 100 Cal.Rptr. 152, 160, 493 P.2d 880, 888, quoting from Trop v. Dulles (1958) supra, 356 U.S. 86, 100, 78 S.Ct. 590, 2 L.Ed.2d 630 (plurality opinion of Warren, C. J.); Mosk, The Eighth Amendment Rediscovered (1968) 1 Loyola L.A.L.Rev. 4, 22.) "The State, even as it punishes, must treat its members with respect for their intrinsic worth as human beings." (Furman v. Georgia (1972) supra, 408 U.S. 238, 270, 92 S.Ct. 2726, 2742, 33 L.Ed.2d 346 (opinion of Brennan, J.).) Punishment which is so excessive as to transgress those limits and deny that worth cannot be tolerated.

We conclude that in California a punishment may violate article I, section 6, of the Constitution if, although not cruel or unusual in its method, it is so disproportionate to the crime for which it is inflicted that it shocks the conscience and offends fundamental notions of human dignity.[15]

III

To aid in administering this rule, we point to certain techniques used in the decisions discussed herein. First, a number of courts have examined the nature of the offense and/or the offender, with particular regard to the degree of danger both present to society. Thus in Anderson we spoke in this connection of excessive punishment for "ordinary offenses" (6 Cal.3d at p. 646, 100 Cal.Rptr. 152, 493 P.2d 880), and in Finley the court referred to an extraordinary penalty for "a crime of ordinary gravity committed under ordinary circumstances" (italics omitted; 1 Cal.App. at p. 202, 81 P. at p. 1042).

More specifically, in his dissenting opinion in O'Neil Justice Field relied on the facts of the crime in question to demonstrate its triviality: there, a New York liquor dealer was convicted in Vermont of selling liquor to residents of Vermont, a "dry" state. Justice Field stressed that such sales were legal under the law of New York (144 U.S. at p. 337, 12 S.Ct. 693), and that the defendant's sole connection with Vermont was to send individual jugs of liquor, one every three or four days, by common carrier, to persons in Vermont who had ordered them and would pay upon delivery. (Id. at pp. 337–341, 12 S.Ct. 693.) In Weems the court also emphasized the minor nature of the offense before it: the opinion twice notes that the amount of cash which the defendant was convicted of falsely claiming as a government expenditure was only a few hundred pesos (217 U.S. at pp. 358, 366, 30 S.Ct. 544), and twice underscores that an offender may "gain nothing" from this crime and "injure nobody" (*id.* at p. 365, 30 S.Ct. 544).

Also relevant to the question of proportionality is the nonviolent nature of the offense. Thus the court in *Lorentzen* took note of the fact that sale of marijuana is a nonviolent crime and that the defendant was 23 years old, living with his parents, employed at General Motors, and had no prior criminal convictions. (194 N.W.2d at p. 828.) Adding these elements together, the court held (at p. 834) that "A compulsory prison sentence of 20 years for a non-violent crime imposed without consideration for defendant's individual personality and history is so excessive that it 'shocks the conscience.' " (Accord, People v. Sinclair (1972) 387 Mich. 91, 194 N.W.2d 878, 905–906 (concurring opinion of T. G. Kavanagh, J. and Adams, J.).) Likewise, the court in *Ward* (270 A.2d at pp. 4–5) stressed that the charged marijuana possession was for the defendant's own use and that he was both young and a first offender. On the other hand, if the offense is deemed of minimal danger to society the penalty may be disproportionate even though the defendant is neither young nor a first offender; in striking down a 36-year sentence imposed on a 46-year-old man with a prior criminal record for "a single spree of passing bad checks which, according to the indictment, took place in a single day," the *Faulkner* court explained that "the offense is not of sufficient gravity to justify imposing what amounts to a life sentence on appellant." (445 P.2d at pp. 818–819.)

Nor, finally, is nonviolence or absence of a victim a prerequisite to a finding of disproportionality. In appropriate cases the courts have nevertheless held the punishment excessive on the ground that no aggravating circumstances were shown. Thus in *Ralph* it was obviously impossible to contend that the crime committed—forcible rape—was nonviolent or "injured nobody." The court conceded that " 'There is a sense in which life is always endangered by sexual attack' " (438 F.2d at p. 788, quoting from Packer, Making the Punishment Fit the Crime (1964) 77 Harv.L.Rev. 1071, 1077). The court explained, "We use the term, however, in another sense—that there are rational gradations of culpability that can be made on the basis of injury to the victim." The court concluded that imposition of the death penalty on "a rapist whose act is not marked with the great aggravation that often accompanies this crime" is arbitrary, and that the penalty is unconstitutionally disproportionate to the offense in all cases in which "the victim's life is neither

taken nor endangered." (438 F.2d at p. 793.) In another rape case, the *Workman* court emphasized the youth of the defendants in holding that life imprisonment without parole "shocks the general conscience of society today and is intolerable to fundamental fairness." (429 S.W.2d at p. 378.)

The second technique used by the courts is to compare the challenged penalty with the punishments prescribed in the *same jurisdiction* for *different offenses* which, by the same test, must be deemed more serious. The underlying but unstated assumption appears to be that although isolated excessive penalties may occasionally be enacted, e.g., through "honest zeal" (Weems v. United States (1910) supra, 217 U.S. 349, 373, 30 S.Ct. 544, 54 L.Ed. 793) generated in response to transitory public emotion, the Legislature may be depended upon to act with due and deliberate regard for constitutional restraints in prescribing the vast majority of punishments set forth in our statutes. The latter may therefore be deemed illustrative of constitutionally permissible degrees of severity; and if among them are found more serious crimes punished less severely than the offense in question, the challenged penalty is to that extent suspect.

The opinions are replete with examples of this technique. Thus in his dissent in *O'Neil* Justice Field measured the penalty for multiple liquor sales against those inflicted for undeniably more serious crimes under Vermont law: "Had [the defendant] been found guilty of burglary or highway robbery, he would have received less punishment than for the offences of which he was convicted. It was six times as great as any court in Vermont could have imposed for manslaughter, forgery, or perjury." (144 U.S. at p. 339, 12 S.Ct. at p. 699.)

In *Weems* the court illustrated the excessiveness of the penalties for falsifying a public document by listing a variety of more serious federal crimes, including certain degrees of homicide, that were not punished so severely. (217 U.S. at p. 380, 30 S.Ct. 544.) Refining its analysis, the court also examined the punishment for an offense of the same general nature as that charged—forgery or counterfeiting of obligations or securities of the United States or Philippine governments—and found that "the highest punishment possible for a crime which may cause the loss of many thousand of dollars, and to prevent which the duty of the state should be as eager as to prevent the perversion of truth in a public document, is not greater than that which may be imposed for falsifying a single item of a public account." (*Id.* at p. 381, 30 S.Ct. at p. 554.) Great weight was given to these disparities in the holding of unconstitutionality.[16]

Closely related to the foregoing is the third technique used in this inquiry, i. e., a comparison of the challenged penalty with the punishments prescribed for the *same offense* in *other jurisdictions* having an identical or similar constitutional provision. Here the assumption is that the vast majority of those jurisdictions will have prescribed punishments for this offense that are within the constitutional limit of severity; and if the challenged penalty is found to exceed the punishments decreed for the offense in a significant number of those jurisdictions, the disparity is a further measure of its excessiveness.

Again examples abound. In *Weems* the court observed that the punishment prescribed by the Philippine statute "has no fellow in American legislation." (217 U.S. at p. 377, 30 S.Ct. at p. 553.) The court did find a similar offense in the federal criminal code—false and excessive claim of payment of a sum appropriated by Congress—but stressed that the relatively light punishment for that crime "is in great contrast" to the heavy penalties inflicted on Weems. (*Id.* at p. 380, 30 S.Ct. 544.)

In *Trop* the court compared the federal penalty of loss of citizenship for desertion in wartime with the legislation of other countries on this topic, and found that "The civilized nations of the world are in virtual unanimity that statelessness is not to be imposed as punishment for crime." (356 U.S. at p. 102, 78 S.Ct. at p. 599.) More particularly, the court observed that "The United Nations' survey of the nationality laws of 84 nations of the world reveals that only two countries, the Philippines and Turkey, impose denationalization as a penalty for desertion. In this country the Eighth Amendment forbids this to be done." (Fn. omitted; *id.* at p. 103, 78 S.Ct. at p. 599.)

In *Lorentzen* the court explained that "The decency test, of necessity, looks to comparative law for guidelines in determining what penalties are widely regarded as proper for the offense in question." (194 N.W.2d at p. 832.) The court then examined the laws of other states on the topic of sale of marijuana, and found that 26 have no minimum sentence at all for that offense, 22 provide a shorter minimum than Michigan, and only one imposes as severe a minimum term as that state. (*Ibid.*) In *Evans* the court listed the statutory penalties of 27 states for lewd and lascivious acts upon a child and stressed that "Except for California, none allows a greater maximum than twenty years," in contrast to the life term apparently provided by Idaho law. (245 P.2d at pp. 792–793, & fn. 1.)

In *Ralph* the court looked to a variety of sources in assessing the proportionality of the penalty of death for rape. Thus the court observed that "Congressional action in recently repealing the death penalty for rape in the District of Columbia follows a worldwide trend. Presently the United States is one of only four nations in which rape is punishable by death, and in this country 34 states punish rape only by imprisonment.

In none of the 16 remaining states is death mandatory, but it is retained as a sentencing alternate. It appears, therefore, that the overwhelming majority of the nations of the world, legislatures of more than two-thirds of the states of the union, and Congress, as evidenced by its amendment of the District of Columbia Code, now considered the death penalty to be an excessive punishment for the crime of rape." (Fns. omitted; 438 F.2d 786, 791–792.)

The court also gave weight to the views of the draftsmen of respected model legislation, noting that repeal of the death penalty for rape has been recommended in both the proposed Federal Criminal Code of the National Commission on Reform of Federal Criminal Laws and the Model Penal Code of the American Law Institute. (*Id.* at p. 791.)

IV

There is ample authority, then, for applying the foregoing analyses to our inquiry into whether the life sentence prescribed by section 314 inflicts a penalty so disproportionate to the crime as to violate the cruel or unusual punishment clause of the California Constitution. We begin by examining the seriousness of the offense of indecent exposure.

A

At common law indecent exposure was deemed to be no more than a public nuisance, and was punished as a misdemeanor. (Archbold, Criminal Pleading, Evidence and Practice (37th ed. 1969) pp. 1241–1242; 2 Wharton's Criminal Law (12th ed. 1932) pp. 2048–2051; see cases collected in Note, Criminal Offense Predicated Upon Indecent Exposure, 93 A.L.R. 996, 997–1001.) The penalties were generally a fine or a brief jail sentence.

The common law offense was subjected to statutory regulation in the Vagrancy Act of 1824. (5 Geo. 4, ch. 83.) Under section 4 of that act every person guilty of indecent exposure was deemed "a rogue and a vagabond," but could be sentenced to jail for not more than three months. Under sections 5 and 10 of the act a person guilty of indecent exposure with a prior conviction of the same offense was deemed "an incorrigible rogue," but could be sentenced to jail for not more than one year. Subsequently, the offense of indecent exposure in the streets was declared punishable under the Town Police Causes Act of 1847 (10 & 11 Vict., ch. 89, § 28), but the punishment was a fine of not more than 40 shillings or a jail sentence of not more than 14 days.[17]

In California a similar pattern prevailed until the present penalty was added in 1952. (Stats.1953, First Ex.Sess.1952, ch. 23, § 4, p. 381.) Indeed, there was no statute whatever proscribing indecent exposure until the enactment of the Penal Code of 1872. At that time the offense was declared to be a misdemeanor, and there was no increased penalty for subsequent convictions. It was therefore punishable in all cases by a maximum of six months in jail and/or a fine of $500. (Fn. 1, *ante*.) This was the law of our state for 80 years.

The low-key approach of the common law is also that adopted by modern psychiatric science. Clinical studies "support and confirm the traditional legal provisions which have treated this behaviour as a social nuisance, as disorderly conduct rather than an offence causing personal injury." (Gigeroff, Mohr, and Turner, Sex Offenders on Probation: The Exhibitionist (1968) 32 Fed.Prob. (No. 3) 17, 21 [hereinafter referred to as Gigeroff].) This is so because the commission of the offense invariably entails no physical aggression or even contact: "It is generally agreed that the person exposing seeks some reaction from the person exposed to, although exactly what reaction is not clear. The exposure occurs at inappropriate times and places and would seem to be calculated to *surprise* the female. It is doubtful that the reaction sought is one of pleasure and in many cases it seems to be intended to evoke fear and shock. It is generally agreed that the exhibitionist does not seek further contact with the victim; on the contrary, he is afraid of it. There is usually some appreciable distance which separates the exhibitionist and the object and rarely does it occur when the parties are in close proximity." (Gigeroff, at p. 19.)

Turning to the typical offender, we find a similar pattern of nonviolence. "The vast majority of exhibitionists are relatively harmless offenders; mostly they are public nuisances and sources of embarrassments" (Report of Karl M. Bowman, Medical Superintendent of the Langley Porter Clinic, in 2 Assem.J. (1951 Reg. Sess.) p. 2847 [hereinafter referred to as Bowman]).[18] They are characterized as "generally passive, inoffensive people" with low self-esteem.[19] Contrary to common public misconception, "Exhibitionists as a group are young, their age ranging from adolescence to the midthirties with the peak number of charges falling about the age of 25. . . . The onset of symptoms occurs at two peak periods, midpuberty and the early twenties. The first is associated with a period when the person is attempting to establish an identity, to free himself from a mother who has endangered his masculinity. The second occurs at a time of courtship and early marriage when, although he is attracted and bound to a female, he nevertheless experiences this as threatening and frustrating. Personality and background factors consistently show an insecurity in social relations. . . ." (Gigeroff, at pp. 19–20.) Acts of self-exposure, accordingly, are often "triggered by small frustrations" in the home, on the job, or in managing social relationships, particularly "around the time of serious courtship and engagement, marriage and early marital adjustment, the pregnancy of the wife, and the arrival of a child." (*Id.* at pp. 20–21.)

Finally, although indecent exposure is not a "victimless" crime, any harm it may cause appears to be minimal at most. As noted above, the nonviolence of the conduct ensures there is no danger of physical injury to the person who witnesses the exposure. Nor is there any convincing evidence that the person is likely to suffer either long-term or significant psychological damage. (See Mohr, Turner, and Jerry, Pedophilia and Exhibitionism (1964), p. 121.) Indeed, the statute itself defines the offense as exposure in public or in any place where there are persons present who may merely be "offended or annoyed" thereby. (Fn. 2, *ante*.) Such an "annoyance" is not a sufficiently grave danger to society to warrant the heavy punishment of a life-maximum sentence.

B

These considerations make a persuasive case for a finding of unconstitutional disproportionality between the offense and the aggravated penalty prescribed by section 314. The case is further strengthened by a comparison of this penalty with the punishments for other crimes in California which are undeniably of far greater seriousness. For example, is it rational to believe that second-offense indecent exposure is a more dangerous crime than the unlawful *killing* of a human being without malice but in the heat of passion? Yet the punishment for manslaughter (Pen.Code, § 193; up to 15 years) is far less than the life maximum inflicted by section 314. The same is true for such other violent crimes against the person as assault with intent to commit murder (Pen.Code, § 217; 1–14 years), kidnaping (Pen.Code, § 208; 1–25 years), mayhem (Pen.Code, § 204; up to 14 years), assault with intent to commit mayhem or robbery (Pen.Code, § 220; 1–20 years), assault with caustic chemicals, with intent to injure or disfigure (Pen.Code, § 244; 1–14 years), and assault on a peace officer or fireman engaged in the performance of his duties (Pen.Code, § 241; up to 2 years, or up to 1 year in jail; see also Pen.Code, § 243.)

Turning to crimes which, although somewhat more indirect, remain extremely dangerous to life and limb, we note that the penalty for second-offense indecent exposure is also far greater than that imposed for arson (Pen.Code § 447a; 2–20 years), burglary by torch or explosives (Pen.Code, § 464; 10–40 years), wrecking a vehicle of a common carrier, causing bodily harm (Pen.Code, § 219.1; 1–14 years), shooting at an inhabited dwelling (Pen.Code, § 246; 1–5 years, or up to 1 year in jail), poisoning food or drink with the intent to injure a human being (Pen.Code, § 347; 1–10 years), and drunk driving causing bodily injury (Pen.Code, § 367e and Veh.Code, § 23101; up to 5 years, or up to 1 year in jail).

Nor does proportionality appear if we consider only the laws regulating sexual activities. Rather, we observe that the punishment for second-offense indecent exposure is far greater than that prescribed for such antisocial conduct as assault with intent to commit rape or sodomy (Pen.Code, § 220; 1–20 years), forcible abduction for purposes of defilement (Pen.Code, § 265; 2–14 years) or of prostitution (Pen.Code, § 266a; up to 5 years and/or fine up to $1,000), purchasing or selling a woman for prostitution (Pen.Code, §§ 266e and 266f; up to 5 years), and statutory rape (Pen.Code, § 264; up to 50 years, or up to 1 year in jail).

Lastly we may look to the statutes designed to protect children, as section 314 is often defended on that ground. Is it conceivable that indecent exposure twice repeated is a greater danger than the act of one who wilfully inflicts "unjustifiable physical pain" on a child "under circumstances or conditions likely to produce great bodily harm or death"? Or who wilfully inflicts on a child "any cruel or inhuman corporal punishment or injury resulting in a traumatic condition"? Yet the penalty for either of such brutalities (Pen.Code, §§ 273a and 273d; up to 10 years, or up to 1 year in jail) is far less than the life maximum imposed by section 314. And if a major purpose of section 314 is to guard children against assaults upon their sensibilities, what possible justification is there for the great disparity between petitioner's punishment and the simple misdemeanor penalties attached by Penal Code section 273g to the conduct of one who "in the presence of any child indulges in any degrading, lewd, immoral or vicious habits or practices"? [20]

We recognize, of course, that an important additional element must be taken into account: section 314 prescribes a life-maximum sentence for indecent exposure only when the offender has previously been convicted of the same crime or of lewd and lascivious acts upon a child (Pen.Code, § 288). We further recognize that the potential for recidivism is here very real: "exhibitionists are more likely to repeat their offence than other kinds of sex offenders." (Gigeroff, at p. 21; accord, Bowman, at p. 2847.) But this likelihood does not result in a pro tanto repeal of the cruel or unusual punishment clause. Petitioner does not challenge—nor do we consider—the validity of our general habitual criminal law (Pen.Code, § 644) or of any other recidivist statute. He is entitled, however, to question whether in the particular context of indecent exposure the phenomenon of recidivism constitutionally justifies the greatly enhanced punishment of section 314. We hold that it does not.

At the outset we may put aside the Attorney General's suggestion that "in quite a number of such offenders the exhibitionism is only a facet of sexual problems which may manifest themselves in more aggressive acts." This risk appears to be mere fantasy. "Although individual cases have been cited to show that a person convicted of exposing has gone on to commit more serious violent crimes, this is not borne out in our followup studies and these reports are consequently regarded as strongly atypical and rare occurrences. The exhibitionist who commits a further offence is much more likely to repeat the same offence than any other kind. . . ." (Gigeroff, at p. 21). Other well known experts in the field concur: Guttmacher and Weihofen describe as a "widely held misconception" the belief that "sex offenders regularly progress from minor offenses such as exhibitionism to major offenses like forced rape. Such a gradation is almost unknown." (Guttmacher and Weihofen, Sex Offenses (1952) 43 J.Crim.L.C.&P.S. 153, 154.) Bowman is equally forceful: "It should be stated explicitly that persons convicted of serious sex crimes do not commonly begin with voyeurism and exhibitionism and work up to crimes of violence and murder." (Bowman, at p. 2847.)

The Attorney General next contends that the long prison sentence provided by section 314 is "effective" because a substantial proportion of those guilty of indecent exposure "come from a higher socio-economic group than the normal criminal offender" and therefore "are inhibited from further acts because incarceration is more repugnant to those persons." There are two principal flaws in this argument. First, we reject in any event its elitist conclusion. Liberty is not sweeter to the rich than to the poor. Second, there is no compelling evidence of the validity of the premise. Persons from all walks of life are subjected to the pressures and frustrations which can trigger exhibitionism. It is not the private preserve of the successful. Indeed, clinical studies of exhibitionists have shown that "despite an essentially normal intelligence distribution, school achievement is generally lower; in work situations, although generally hard working and conscientious, their low frustration tolerance and sensitivity to criticism leads to difficulties." (Gigeroff, at p. 20.)

The Attorney General also asserts that "the group therapy available in correctional institutions can have a salutary effect on such persons who agree to avail themselves of psychiatric help (see Exhibit F)." But the source to which the Attorney General refers us—an affidavit of T. L. Clanon, M. D., assistant superintendent in charge of psychiatric services at the California Medical Facility—describes the available group therapy as follows: "Such a person is placed in a group whose members suffer from a variety of mental problems. Since some inmates tend to look down on the exhibitionists, if such a person manages to overcome such intimidation and function adequately in such a masculine environment the group therapy will benefit him." We are not told what happens to the individual who does not "manage to overcome" that concerted peer scorn. At best, we suppose, he continues to serve his sentence until a new attempt is made; at worst, we can only presume that the ordeal confirms or even increases his prior feelings of insecurity and inadequacy. In any event, if this is the most optimistic treatment offered for exhibitionism in the most psychiatrically oriented institution in the Department of Corrections, the long prison sentence imposed by section 314 can hardly be justified as an act of benevolence towards the offender.

Finally, we may profitably compare section 314 with other California statutes which prescribe enhanced punishment for recidivism. First, however, we pause to note that in all but three of the above-listed dangerous crimes involving personal violence, sexual assaults, or harm to children, there is no statutory provision increasing the penalty for recidivism. In other words, a man may repeatedly commit manslaughter or mayhem, assault with intent to commit rape or sodomy, child-beating or felony drunk driving, and still be subject each time to a lighter penalty than one who twice exposes his private parts.[21]

Second, of all the statutes which increase the punishment in the case of a second offense, only section 314 and one other compel the enormous single leap from an ordinary misdemeanor to a life-maximum felony.[22] In each of the remaining statutes there is a reasonable relationship between the punishments for the first and subsequent offenses. If the crime is of a minor nature, its enhanced penalty remains proportionately light;[23] if the crime is more serious, its original penalty was proportionately heavy.[24] The theory in each instance is that whatever the response appropriate to the factor of recidivism, the judgment of the Legislature as to the gravity of the act itself should remain relatively constant.

This view is firmly expressed in the recommendation of the American Bar Association Advisory Committee on Sentencing and Review that in structuring habitual offender legislation "Any increased term which can be imposed because of prior criminality should be related in severity to the sentence otherwise provided for the new offense." (A.B.A. Project on Minimum Standards for Criminal Justice, Standards Relating to Sentencing Alternatives and Procedures (1967) p. 22, par. 3.3 (a)(i).) By way of illustration the advisory committee pointed to a minor offense (intentionally damaging property in an amount exceeding $250) which, if repeated, could be punished under New York law by a

life term. The committee explained (*id.* at p. 139) that "A sentence of this magnitude no longer bears any reasonable relationship to the event which triggered its possibility. The major thrust of the proceeding has shifted from the offense to the status of the offender. A proceeding which can result in such a long sentence ought to assume the burden of depending initially and primarily on the criteria which justify it, rather than employ the vehicle of a relatively minor felony to approach the same end indirectly." The committee concluded (*ibid.*) that such an indirect approach "gives rise to all manner of difficulties," including "the moral, if not legal, questions of cruel and unusual punishment."[25] Similar "difficulties" attend any attempt to justify the great disparity between the penalties for first and second offense indecent exposure in California.

Third, the increased punishment provided by section 314 is far more severe than those of other recidivist statutes penalizing conduct that is indisputably more serious. Thus, is it reasonable to suppose that a person who twice exposes himself is more dangerous to society than one who twice commits a felony while armed with a deadly weapon such as a gun, knife, or club? Yet the punishment for such repeated conduct (Pen.Code, § 12022, par. 2; 10–15 years, consecutive) is itself less than the life maximum inflicted by section 314. The same is true of recidivist offenders who threaten public officials with bodily injury (Pen.Code, § 71; up to 5 years), employ minors to print or distribute obscene matter (Pen.Code, § 311.9, subd. (b); up to 5 years), forge prescriptions for narcotic drugs (Health & Saf. Code, § 11715; up to 10 years), and possess heroin or other narcotic (Health & Saf. Code, § 11500; 5–20 years). In each case they can repeat their crime without risking a penalty as severe as that decreed for a second-offense exhibitionist.

C

The last technique to be employed—a comparison of the challenged penalty with the punishments prescribed for the same offense in other jurisdictions—is no less revealing. A study of the indecent exposure statutes of each of our sister states and the District of Columbia reveals only two other states—Michigan and Oklahoma—which permit life-maximum sentences for second-offense exhibitionists. By contrast, 34 states and the District of Columbia do not enhance the punishment for any degree of recidivism; in each, indecent exposure remains a misdemeanor at all times. Of these 35 jurisdictions, the offense is punishable by no more than a fine in 2 states, by 3 years' imprisonment in one state, by a 1-year maximum in 10 states, by a 6-month maximum in 15 states, and by periods of 90 days or less in the remaining states. Seven other states do punish a second-offense indecent exposure more severely than the first; but none among these even approaches the life maximum decreed in California, and in 1 state the punishment for repeated exhibitionism is only 90 days. Three more states enhance the punishment only upon the third offense; of these none exceeds three years' imprisonment, and to reach even this penalty one requires that the three convictions occur within a five-year span. Finally, two states enhance punishment only if the second offense is committed on a minor.

Thus it is the virtually unanimous judgment of our sister states that indecent exposure, no matter how often it may recur, can be adequately and appropriately controlled by the imposition of a short jail sentence and/or a small fine. In this setting the California penalty of a life-maximum sentence in state prison strikes a discordant note indeed.

We end this comparative review by examining two well known model codes and a proposed revision of California's own criminal laws. Section 213.5 of the Model Penal Code of the American Law Institute (Proposed Official Draft 1962) would punish indecent exposure as a misdemeanor, i.e., by a maximum of one year's imprisonment and/or a fine up to $1,000. (§§ 6.03, 6.08.) Similarly, section 1852 of the proposed Federal Criminal Code prepared by the National Commission on Reform of Federal Criminal Laws (Study Draft 1970) would treat indecent exposure as a "class A misdemeanor," deeming it to be "a kind of public nuisance" (comment to § 1853). The commission suggests a one-year maximum term of imprisonment and/or a fine of up to $1,000. (§§ 3204, 3301.)

After lengthy legislative committee studies a proposed Criminal Code has been introduced in the California Legislature, replacing in large part the Penal Code. (Sen. Bill 1506, 1972 Sess.) Section 9312 of the new code would declare indecent exposure to be a "misdemeanor of the second degree," punishable by a county jail sentence not exceeding six months (§ 1303) and/or a fine not exceeding $500 (§ 1304). There is no provision for increasing this punishment upon a second or subsequent conviction of the offense. The proposed legislation, in short, would return the law of California to its posture during the eight decades preceding the 1952 amendment of Penal Code section 314.

Viewing the total disparity between the life-maximum sentence currently inflicted by section 314 for second-offense indecent exposure and the far lighter penalties in force in California and elsewhere, we conclude with Justice McKenna in *Weems* that "this contrast shows more than different exercises of legislative judgment. It is greater than that. It condemns the sentence in this case as cruel and unusual. It exhibits a difference between unrestrained power and that which is exercised under the spirit of constitutional limitations formed to establish justice." (217 U.S. at p. 381, 30 S.Ct. at p. 554.)

VI

The question of relief remains. If petitioner's offense is treated as a misdemeanor, he has long since served his time. If it is treated as a felony, section 314 no longer prescribes a valid punishment; and if no provision is made for punishment in a statute declaring a felony, the offense is "punishable by imprisonment in any of the state prisons, not exceeding five years" (Pen.Code, § 18). Petitioner has now served more than five years, and is therefore entitled to his freedom.

The writ is granted and petitioner is ordered discharged from custody.

WRIGHT, C. J., and PETERS, TOBRINER, BURKE, and SULLIVAN, JJ., concur.

McCOMB, Justice (dissenting).

I dissent. I would deny the writ.

NOTES

1. Under Penal Code section 19 the maximum possible penalty for such an offense is a sentence to county jail not exceeding six months or a fine not exceeding $500, or both.

2. Penal Code section 314 provides: "Every person who willfully and lewdly, . . .

"1. Exposes his person, or the private parts thereof, in any public place, or in any place where there are present other persons to be offended or annoyed thus by; . . . is guilty of a misdemeanor.

"Upon the second and each subsequent conviction under subdivision 1 of this section, or upon a first conviction under sudivision 1 of this section after a previous conviction under Section 288 of this code [lewd or lascivious acts upon a child], every person so convicted is guilty of a felony, and is punishable by imprisonment in state prison for not less than one year."

3. There are, of course, other kinds of indeterminate sentence laws. (See Note, Statutory Structures for Sentencing Felons to Prison (1960) 60 Colum.L.Rev. 1134, 1144–1152; Sentencing Practices of Other States, 22 Assem. Interim Com. Report No. 1, Criminal Procedure (1959–1961) pp. 78–79; Comment, Indeterminate Sentence Laws—The Adolescence of Peno-Correctional Legislation (1937) 50 Harv.L.Rev. 677, 678–683.)

4. That we adhere no less to this theory today is shown by the quotation of this language in our recent decision in In re Minnis (1972) 7 Cal.3d 639, 644, 102 Cal.Rptr. 749, 498 P.2d 997. (See also Briscoe v. Reader's Digest Association, Inc. (1971) 4 Cal.3d 529, 539, fn. 12, 93 Cal.Rptr. 866, 483 P.2d 34; People v. Wade (1968) supra, 266 Cal.App.2d 918, 928, 72 Cal.Rptr. 538.)

5. The rule has been followed in a variety of contexts. (See, e. g., In re Schoengarth (1967) 66 Cal.2d 295, 302, 57 Cal.Rptr. 600, 425 P.2d 200; In re McLain (1960) supra, 55 Cal.2d 78, 87, 9 Cal.Rptr. 824, 357 P.2d 1080; In re Smith (1949) 33 Cal.2d 797, 804, 205 P.2d 662; In re Byrnes (1948) 32 Cal.2d 843, 850, 198 P.2d 685.)

6. This reasoning has met the test of time. (See, e. g., In re Sandel (1966) 64 Cal.2d 412, 415, 50 Cal.Rptr. 462, 412 P.2d 806; In re Larsen (1955) 44 Cal.2d 642, 647, 283 P.2d 1043; People v. Kostal (1958) 159 Cal.App.2d 444, 451–453, 323 P.2d 1020.)

7. This, too, is settled doctrine. (See, e. g., In re Mills (1961) 55 Cal.2d 646, 653, 12 Cal.Rptr. 483, 361 P.2d 15; In

re Larsen (1955) supra, 44 Cal.2d 642, 647, 283 P.2d 1043; People v. Wells (1949) 33 Cal.2d 330, 335–337, 202 P.2d 53; In re Jordan (1923) 190 Cal. 416, 212 P. 913.)

8. A six-month minimum term was part of the indeterminate sentence law until 1963. (Stats. 1963, ch. 1702, p. 3344.)

9. This is the rule to be applied when the *minimum* term prescribed by the statute does not violate the cruel or unusual punishment clause. If an analysis such as we undertake herein demonstrates that the minimum term does violate that clause, the defendant will be entitled to relief without regard to the constitutionality vel non of the maximum. (See, e. g., Weems v. United States (1910) supra, 217 U.S. 349, 30 S.Ct. 544, 54 L.Ed. 793, and People v. Lorentzen (1972) 387 Mich. 167, 194 N.W.2d 827; cf. People v. Clark (1970) 3 Cal.3d 97, 89 Cal.Rptr. 253, 473 P.2d 997.)

10. For certain other purposes, however, an indeterminate sentence with a life maximum should not be treated as the equivalent of a sentence of life imprisonment. (See, e. g., In re Quinn (1945) 25 Cal.2d 799, 154 P.2d 875 (power of trial court to order consecutive sentences); People v. Ralph (1944) 24 Cal.2d 575, 150 P.2d 401 (eligibility for commitment to Youth Authority); People v. Shaw (1965) 237 Cal.App.2d 606, 612–616, 47 Cal.Rptr. 96, and cases cited (right to additional peremptory challenges).)

11. In Trop v. Dulles (1958) supra, 356 U.S. 86, 78 S.Ct. 590, 2 L.Ed.2d 630, the court invalidated the penalty of loss of citizenship for wartime desertion, making it clear that a method of punishment may violate the Eighth Amendment even though it results in no physical torture. (*Id.* at p. 101, 78 S.Ct. 590, plurality opinion of Warren, C. J.) Although excessiveness was not there in issue (*id.* at p. 99, 78 S.Ct. 590), the principle of proportionality was recognized in the statement that "Fines, imprisonment or even execution may be imposed *depending upon the enormity of the crime*" (italics added; *id.* at p. 100, 78 S.Ct. at p. 598).

12. In certain states, it is true, the constitutional provision expressly directs that every penalty be proportioned to the offense. (See People v. Anderson (1972) supra, 6 Cal.3d 628, 636, fns. 15 and 16, 100 Cal.Rptr. 152, 493 P.2d 880; Green v. State (Alaska 1964) 390 P.2d 433, 435, fn. 11.) But the jurisdictions applying the rule are not limited to these few states.

13. Nor is disproportionality confined to long prison sentences: in State v. Ward (1970) 57 N.J. 75, 270 A.2d 1, a punishment of two to three years' imprisonment for possession of marijuana was held excessive when inflicted on youthful first offenders, and in State v. Driver (1878) 78 N.C. 423, a sentence of five years in county jail for wife-beating was ruled unconstitutionally disproportionate. There have also been cases, like *O'Neil,* in which a defendant convicted of multiple identical petty offenses was given a cumulative sentence on all the counts far in excess of the maximum permissible for any one offense, and the total was held invalid. (See, e. g., Faulkner v. State (Alaska 1968) 445 P.2d 815 (sentence of 36 years on 8 bad check counts); Kenimer v. State (1950) 81 Ga.App. 437, 59 S.E.2d 296 (fine of $11,900 or 1,190 days (i. e., over 3 years) for 238 consecutive counts of contempt for violating the child custody provisions of a divorce decree); Kenimer v. State (1950) 83 Ga.App. 264, 63 S.E.2d 280 (sentence for the same offenses of $4,760 or 476 days); State v. Ross (1910) 55 Or. 450, 104 P. 596, 106 P. 1022 (embezzlement of $288,426 punished by a fine of double that amount or imprisonment in county jail for 288,426 days (i. e., 790 years); State ex rel. Garvey v. Whitaker (1896) 48 La.Ann. 527, 19 So. 457, (fine of $720 or 2,160 days (i. e., nearly 6 years) for 72 violations of an ordinance prohibiting destruction of plants in a public square).)

14. ". . . so disproportionate . . . as to meet the disap-

proval and condemnation of the conscience and reason of men generally, 'as to shock the moral sense of the people.' " (156 Cal. at p. 737, 106 P. at p. 77.)

15. A dictum arguably to the contrary in In re Garner (1918) 179 Cal. 409, 415, 177 P. 162, based on an 1860 case, is disapproved.

16. In *Lorentzen* the court compared the penalty for sale of marijuana with the maximum punishments under Michigan law for five crimes similarly involving the "sale of harmful substances to others" (194 N.W.2d at p. 831), and to the maximum punishments for no less than 14 crimes involving "harm to people," including such offenses as manslaughter, aggravated assaults, rape, kidnaping, cruelty to children, and vehicle homicide (*id.* at pp. 831–832); in *Cannon* the court compared the penalty for assault with intent to commit rape to the lesser punishment for rape itself (281 P.2d at p. 235); in *Evans* the court noted that the punishment for lewd and lascivious acts upon a child was much greater than for forcible rape (245 P.2d at p. 793); in *Dembowski* the court measured the sentence for simple robbery against a lesser penalty for armed robbery (240 N.E.2d at pp. 816–818); and in *Driver* the court emphasized that a sentence of five years for wife-beating was cruel and unusual because it was "greater than has ever been prescribed or known or inflicted" (78 N.C. at p. 426).

17. Indecent exposure in England is still punished under these two statutes. (Archbold, op. cit. supra, at p. 1242.)

18. This report was prepared in connection with a sex crimes study authorized by the Legislature in 1949. It was included by the Assembly Interim Committee on Judicial System and Judicial Process in its Progress Report to the Legislature, April 11, 1951. (2 Assem.J. (1951) Reg.Sess., p. 2701.)

19. Affidavit of T. L. Clanon, M.D., assistant superintendent in charge of psychiatric services at the California Medical Facility.

20. We need not emphasize that the life-maximum sentence imposed by section 314 is also greatly in excess of the penalties for such serious crimes against property as grand theft (Pen.Code, § 489; up to 10 years, or up to 1 year in jail), forgery (Pen.Code, § 473; 1–14 years, or up to 1 year in jail), and embezzlement (Pen.Code, § 514; 1–10 years), or such grave offenses against governmental integrity as bribery of an executive officer, a member of the Legislature, a judge, or a juror (Pen.Code, §§ 67, 85, and 92; 1–10 years or 1–14 years).

21. The remaining three crimes (kidnaping, arson, and assault with intent to commit murder) are covered by the habitual criminal provisions of section 644, but even that statute does not come into play until the defendant has been separately convicted at least three times—not twice—of the crimes there specified.

22. The other statute is Penal Code section 647a, which declares that every person who "annoys or molests" any child under the age of 18 is punishable, for a first offense, as a misdemeanant. The 1952 legislation which drastically increased the penalty for second-offense indecent exposure prescribed an identical penalty for a repetition of this crime, i. e., "not less than one year" in state prison. (Stats. 1953, First Ex.Sess.1952, ch. 23, § 5, p. 382.) We do not, of course, adjudicate the constitutionality of the latter penalty in this proceeding.

23. For example, the crime of disturbing the peace on a college campus (Pen.Code, § 415.5) is punishable, if a first offense, by a fine not exceeding $200 or a jail term not exceeding 90 days or both; if a second offense, by a jail term of 10 days to 6 months or by such term and a fine not exceeding $500.

24. For example, the crime of possession of heroin for sale

(Health & Saf.Code, § 11500.5) is punishable, if a first offense, by a term of 5–15 years; if a second offense, by a term of 10 years to life.

25. In particular, the committee "would draw the line at felonies . . . and would not provide for increased punishment on the basis of repeated misdemeanors" (*id.* at p. 169), and as an example stated that "A life sentence for petty larceny reflects a loss of proportion which the Advisory Committee would suggest is intolerable" (*id.* at p. 164). (Compare Pen. Code, §§ 490, 666 and 667.)

26. In Crim. No. 16232 petitioner also contends the Adult Authority has deprived him of due process and equal protection of the law by predicating its repeated denial of parole on (1) alleged additional acts of indecent exposure which petitioner has not been given an opportunity to rebut and (2) his steadfast refusal to confess to committing those acts. In view of the disposition we adopt herein, we need not reach this issue at the present time.

In Crim. No. 16237 petitioner contends his prior conviction of indecent exposure in 1958 was invalid because he was assertedly denied various constitutional rights at that proceeding. This contention, however, has been raised in several prior applications for habeas corpus by petitioner, each of which we have denied. Accordingly, it does not require our reconsideration. (In re Miller (1941) 17 Cal.2d 734, 735, 112 P.2d 10.)

ROE v. WADE

United States Supreme Court, 1973 *

3. *The common law.* It is undisputed that at common law, abortion performed *before* "quickening"—the first recognizable movement of the fetus *in utero,* appearing usually from the 16th to the 18th week of pregnancy [20]—was not an indictable offense.[21] The absence of a common-law crime for pre-quickening abortion appears to have developed from a confluence of earlier philosophical, theological, and civil and canon law concepts of when life begins. These disciplines variously approached the question in terms of the point at which the embryo or fetus became "formed" or recognizably human, or in terms of when a "person" came into being, that is, infused with a "soul" or "animated." A loose consensus evolved in early English law that these events occurred at some point between conception and live birth.[22] This was "mediate animation." Although Christian theology and the canon law came to fix the point of animation at 40 days for a male and 80 days for a female, a view that persisted until the 19th century, there was otherwise little agreement about the precise time of formation or animation. There was agreement, however, that prior to this point the fetus was to be regarded as part of the mother, and its destruction, therefore, was not homicide. Due to continued uncertainty about the precise time when animation occurred, to the lack of any empirical basis for the 40–80-day view, and perhaps to Aquinas' definition of movement as one of the two first principles of life, Bracton focused upon quickening as the critical point. The significance of quickening was echoed by later common-law scholars and found its way into the received common law in this country.

Whether abortion of a *quick* fetus was a felony at common law, or even a lesser crime, is still disputed. Bracton, writing early in the 13th century, thought it homicide.[23] But the later and predominant view, following the great common-law scholars, has been that it was, at most, a lesser offense. In a frequently cited passage, Coke took the position that abortion of a woman "quick with childe" is "a great misprision, and no murder."[24] Blackstone followed, saying that while abortion after quickening had once been considered manslaughter (though not murder), "modern law"

took a less severe view.[25] A recent review of the common-law precedents argues, however, that those precedents contradict Coke and that even post-quickening abortion was never established as a common-law crime.[26] This is of some importance because while most American courts ruled, in holding or dictum, that abortion of an unquickened fetus was not criminal under their received common law,[27] others followed Coke in stating that abortion of a quick fetus was a "misprision," a term they translated to mean "misdemeanor."[28] That their reliance on Coke on this aspect of the law was uncritical and, apparently in all the reported cases, dictum (due probably to the paucity of common-law prosecutions for post-quickening abortion), makes it now appear doubtful that abortion was ever firmly established as a common-law crime even with respect to the destruction of a quick fetus.

5. *The American law.* In this country, the law in effect in all but a few States until mid-19th century was the pre-existing English common law. Connecticut, the first State to enact abortion legislation, adopted in 1821 that part of Lord Ellenborough's Act that related to a woman "quick with child."[29] The death penalty was not imposed. Abortion before quickening was made a crime in that State only in 1860.[30] In 1828, New York enacted legislation[31] that, in two respects, was to serve as a model for early anti-abortion statutes. First, while barring destruction of an unquickened fetus as well as a quick fetus, it made the former only a misdemeanor, but the latter second-degree manslaughter. Second, it incorporated a concept of therapeutic abortion by providing that an abortion was excused if it "shall have been necessary to preserve the life of such mother, or shall have been advised by two physicians to be necessary for such purpose." By 1840, when Texas had received the common law,[32] only eight American States had statutes dealing with abortion.[33] It was not until after the War Between the States that legislation began generally to replace the common law. Most of these initial statutes dealt severely with abortion after quickening but were lenient with it before quickening. Most punished attempts equally with completed abortions. While many statutes included the exception for an abortion thought by one or more physicians to be necessary to save the mother's life, that provision soon disappeared and the typical law required that the procedure actually be necessary for that purpose.

---

* 410 U.S. 113 (1973) Excerpts from the Court's opinion. Footnotes numbered as in the complete opinion.

Gradually, in the middle and late 19th century the quickening distinction disappeared from the statutory law of most States and the degree of the offense and the penalties were increased. By the end of the 1950's, a large majority of the jurisdictions banned abortion, however and whenever performed, unless done to save or preserve the life of the mother.[34] The exceptions, Alabama and the District of Columbia, permitted abortion to preserve the mother's health.[35] Three States permitted abortions that were not "unlawfully" performed or that were not "without lawful justification," leaving interpretation of those standards to the courts.[36] In the past several years, however, a trend toward liberalization of abortion statutes has resulted in adoption, by about one-third of the States, of less stringent laws, most of them patterned after the ALI Model Penal Code, § 230.3,[37] set forth as Appendix B to the opinion in *Doe* v. *Bolton, post,* p. 205.

It is thus apparent that at common law, at the time of the adoption of our Constitution, and throughout the major portion of the 19th century, abortion was viewed with less disfavor than under most American statutes currently in effect. Phrasing it another way, a woman enjoyed a substantially broader right to terminate a pregnancy than she does in most States today. At least with respect to the early stage of pregnancy, and very possibly without such a limitation, the opportunity to make this choice was present in this country well into the 19th century. Even later, the law continued for some time to treat less punitively an abortion procured in early pregnancy.

VII

Three reasons have been advanced to explain historically the enactment of criminal abortion laws in the 19th century and to justify their continued existence.

It has been argued occasionally that these laws were the product of a Victorian social concern to discourage illicit sexual conduct. Texas, however, does not advance this justification in the present case, and it appears that no court or commentator has taken the argument seriously.[42] The appellants and *amici* contend, moreover, that this is not a proper state purpose at all and suggest that, if it were, the Texas statutes are overbroad in protecting it since the law fails to distinguish between married and unwed mothers.

A second reason is concerned with abortion as a medical procedure. When most criminal abortion laws were first enacted, the procedure was a hazardous one for the woman.[43] This was particularly true prior to the development of antisepsis. Antiseptic techniques, of course, were based on discoveries by Lister, Pasteur, and others first announced in 1867, but were not generally accepted and employed until about the turn of the century. Abortion mortality was high. Even after 1900, and perhaps until as late as the development of antibi-

otics in the 1940's, standard modern techniques such as dilation and curettage were not nearly so safe as they are today. Thus, it has been argued that a State's real concern in enacting a criminal abortion law was to protect the pregnant woman, that is, to restrain her from submitting to a procedure that placed her life in serious jeopardy.

Modern medical techniques have altered this situation. Appellants and various *amici* refer to medical data indicating that abortion in early pregnancy, that is, prior to the end of the first trimester, although not without its risk, is now relatively safe. Mortality rates for women undergoing early abortions, where the procedure is legal, appear to be as low as or lower than the rates for normal childbirth.[44] Consequently, any interest of the State in protecting the woman from an inherently hazardous procedure, except when it would be equally dangerous for her to forgo it, has largely disappeared. Of course, important state interests in the areas of health and medical standards do remain. The State has a legitimate interest in seeing to it that abortion, like any other medical procedure, is performed under circumstances that insure maximum safety for the patient. This interest obviously extends at least to the performing physician and his staff, to the facilities involved, to the availability of after-care, and to adequate provision for any complication or emergency that might arise. The prevalence of high mortality rates at illegal "abortion mills" strengthens, rather than weakens, the State's interest in regulating the conditions under which abortions are performed. Moreover, the risk to the woman increases as her pregnancy continues. Thus, the State retains a definite interest in protecting the woman's own health and safety when an abortion is proposed at a late stage of pregnancy.

The third reason is the State's interest—some phrase it in terms of duty—in protecting prenatal life. Some of the argument for this justification rests on the theory that a new human life is present from the moment of conception.[45] The State's interest and general obligation to protect life then extends, it is argued, to prenatal life. Only when the life of the pregnant mother herself is at stake, balanced against the life she carries within her, should the interest of the embryo or fetus not prevail. Logically, of course, a legitimate state interest in this area need not stand or fall on acceptance of the belief that life begins at conception or at some other point prior to live birth. In assessing the State's interest, recognition may be given to the less rigid claim that as long as at least *potential* life is involved, the State may assert interests beyond the protection of the pregnant woman alone.

Parties challenging state abortion laws have sharply disputed in some courts the contention that a purpose of these laws, when enacted, was to protect prenatal life.[46] Pointing to the absence of legislative history to support the contention, they claim that most state laws were designed solely to protect the woman. Because medical advances have lessened this concern, at least with respect to abortion in early pregnancy, they argue that with respect to such abortions the laws can no longer be justified by any state interest. There is some scholarly support for this view of original purpose.[47] The few state courts called upon to interpret their laws in the late 19th and early 20th centuries did focus on the State's interest in protecting the woman's health rather than in preserving the embryo and fetus.[48] Proponents of this view point out that in many States, including Texas,[49] by statute or judicial interpretation, the pregnant woman herself could not be prosecuted for self-abortion or for cooperating in an abortion performed upon her by another.[50] They claim that adoption of the "quickening" distinction through received common law and state statutes tacitly recognizes the greater health hazards inherent in late abortion and impliedly repudiates the theory that life begins at conception.

It is with these interests, and the weight to be attached to them, that this case is concerned.

VIII

The Constitution does not explicitly mention any right of privacy. In a line of decisions, however, going back perhaps as far as *Union Pacific R. Co.* v. *Botsford,* 141 U.S. 250, 251 (1891), the Court has recognized that a right of personal privacy, or a guarantee of certain areas or zones of privacy, does exist under the Constitution. In varying contexts, the Court or individual Justices have, indeed, found at least the roots of that right in the First Amendment, *Stanley* v. *Georgia,* 394 U.S. 557, 564 (1969); in the Fourth and Fifth Amendments, *Terry* v. *Ohio,* 392 U.S. 1, 8–9 (1968), *Katz* v. *United States,* 389 U.S. 347, 350 (1967), *Boyd* v. *United States,* 116 U.S. 616 (1886), see *Olmstead* v. *United States,* 277 U.S. 438, 478 (1928) (Brandeis, J., dissenting); in the penumbras of the Bill of Rights, *Griswold* v. *Connecticut,* 381 U.S., at 484–485; in the Ninth Amendment, *id.,* at 486 (Goldberg, J., concurring); or in the concept of liberty guaranteed by the first section of the Fourteenth Amendment, see *Meyer* v. *Nebraska,* 262 U.S. 390, 399 (1923). These decisions make it clear that only personal rights that can be deemed "fundamental" or "implicit in the concept of ordered liberty," *Palko* v. *Connecticut,* 302 U.S. 319, 325 (1937), are included in this guarantee of personal privacy. They also make it clear that the right has some extension to activities relating to marriage, *Loving* v. *Virginia,* 388 U.S. 1, 12 (1967); procreation, *Skinner* v. *Oklahoma,* 316 U.S. 535, 541–542 (1942); contraception, *Eisenstadt* v. *Baird,* 405 U.S., at 453–454; *id.,* at 460, 463–465 (WHITE, J., concurring in result); family relationships, *Prince* v. *Massachusetts,* 321 U.S. 158, 166 (1944); and child rearing and education, *Pierce* v. *Society of Sisters,* 268 U.S. 510, 535 (1925), *Meyer* v. *Nebraska, supra.*

This right of privacy, whether it be founded in the Fourteenth Amendment's concept of personal liberty and restrictions upon state action, as we feel it is, or, as the District Court determined, in the Ninth Amendment's reservation of rights to the people, is broad enough to encompass a woman's decision whether or not to terminate her pregnancy. The detriment that the State would impose upon the pregnant woman by denying this choice altogether is apparent. Specific and direct harm medically diagnosable even in early pregnancy may be involved. Maternity, or additional offspring, may force upon the woman a distressful life and future. Psychological harm may be imminent. Mental and physical health may be taxed by child care. There is also the distress, for all concerned, associated with the unwanted child, and there is the problem of bringing a child into a family already unable, psychologically and otherwise, to care for it. In other cases, as in this one, the additional difficulties and continuing stigma of unwed motherhood may be involved. All these are factors the woman and her responsible physician necessarily will consider in consultation.

On the basis of elements such as these, appellant and some *amici* argue that the woman's right is absolute and that she is entitled to terminate her pregnancy at whatever time, in whatever way, and for whatever reason she alone chooses. With this we do not agree. Appellant's arguments that Texas either has no valid interest at all in regulating the abortion decision, or no interest strong enough to support any limitation upon the woman's sole determination, are unpersuasive. The Court's decisions recognizing a right of privacy also acknowledge that some state regulation in areas protected by that right is appropriate. As noted above, a State may properly assert important interests in safeguarding health, in maintaining medical standards, and in protecting potential life. At some point in pregnancy, these respective interests become sufficiently compelling to sustain regulation of the factors that govern the abortion decision. The privacy right involved, therefore, cannot be said to be absolute. In fact, it is not clear to us that the claim asserted by some *amici* that one has an unlimited right to do with one's body as one pleases bears a close relationship to the right of privacy previously articulated in the Court's decisions. The Court has refused to recognize an unlimited right of this kind in the past. *Jacobson* v. *Massachusetts,* 197 U.S. 11 (1905) (vaccination); *Buck* v. *Bell,* 274 U.S. 200 (1927) (sterilization).

We, therefore, conclude that the right of personal privacy includes the abortion decision, but that this right is not unqualified and must be considered against important state interests in regulation.

We note that those federal and state courts that have recently considered abortion law challenges have reached the same conclusion. A majority, in addition to the District Court in the present case, have held state laws unconstitutional, at least in part, because of vagueness or because of overbreadth and abridgment of rights.*

Although the results are divided, most of these courts have agreed that the right of privacy, however based, is broad enough to cover the abortion decision; that the right, nonetheless, is not absolute and is subject to some limitations; and that at some point the state interests as to protection of health, medical standards, and prenatal life, become dominant. We agree with this approach.

Where certain "fundamental rights" are involved, the Court has held that regulation limiting these rights may be justified only by a "compelling state interest," *Kramer* v. *Union Free School District,* 395 U.S. 621, 627 (1969); *Shapiro* v. *Thompson,* 394 U.S. 618, 634 (1969), *Sherbert* v. *Verner,* 374 U.S. 398, 406 (1963), and that legislative enactments must be narrowly drawn to express only the legitimate state interests at stake. *Griswold* v. *Connecticut,* 381 U.S., at 485; *Aptheker* v. *Secretary of State,* 378 U.S. 500, 508 (1964); *Cantwell* v. *Connecticut,* 310 U.S. 296, 307–308 (1940); see *Eisenstadt* v. *Baird,* 405 U.S., at 460, 463–464 (WHITE, J., concurring in result).

In the recent abortion cases, cited above, courts have recognized these principles. Those striking down state laws have generally scrutinized the State's interests in protecting health and potential life, and have concluded that neither interest justified broad limitations on the reasons for which a physician and his pregnant patient might decide that she should have an abortion in the early stages of pregnancy. Courts sustaining state laws have held that the State's determinations to protect health or prenatal life are dominant and constitutionally justifiable.

IX

The District Court held that the appellee failed to meet his burden of demonstrating that the Texas statute's infringement upon Roe's rights was necessary to support a compelling state interest, and that, although the appellee presented "several compelling justifications for state presence in the area of abortions," the statutes outstripped these justifications and swept "far beyond any areas of compelling state interest." 314 F. Supp., at 1222–1223. Appellant and appellee both contest that holding. Appellant, as has been indicated, claims an absolute right that bars any state imposition of criminal penalties in the area. Appellee argues that the State's determination to recognize and protect prenatal life from and after conception constitutes a compelling state interest. As noted above, we do not agree fully with either formulation.

A. The appellee and certain *amici* argue that the fetus is a "person" within the language and meaning of the Fourteenth Amendment. In support of this, they outline at length and in detail the well-known facts of fetal development. If this suggestion of personhood is established, the appellant's case, of course, collapses, for the fetus' right to life would then be guaranteed specifically by the Amendment. The appellant conceded as much on reargument.[51] On the other hand, the appellee conceded on reargument [52] that no case could be cited that holds that a fetus is a person within the meaning of the Fourteenth Amendment.

The Constitution does not define "person" in so many words. Section 1 of the Fourteenth Amendment contains three references to "person." The first, in defining "citizens," speaks of "persons born or naturalized in the United States." The word also appears both in the Due Process Clause and in the Equal Protection Clause. "Person" is used in other places in the Constitution: in the listing of qualifications for Representatives and Senators, Art. I, §2, cl. 2, and §3, cl. 3; in the Apportionment Clause, Art. I, §2, cl. 3; [53] in the Migration and Importation provision, Art. I, §9, cl. 1; in the Emolument Clause, Art. I, §9, cl. 8; in the Electors provisions, Art. II, §1, cl. 2, and the superseded cl. 3; in the provision outlining qualifications for the office of President, Art. II, §1, cl. 5; in the Extradition provisions, Art. IV, §2, cl. 2, and the superseded Fugitive Slave Clause 3; and in the Fifth, Twelfth, and Twenty-second Amendments, as well as in §§2 and 3 of the Fourteenth Amendment. But in nearly all these instances, the use of the word is such that it has application only postnatally. None indicates, with any assurance, that it has any possible pre-natal application.[54]

All this, together with our observation, *supra,* that throughout the major portion of the 19th century prevailing legal abortion practices were far freer than they are today, persuades us that the word "person," as used in the Fourteenth Amendment, does not include the unborn.[55] This is in accord with the results reached in those few cases where the issue has been squarely presented.* Ohio St. 2d 65, 275 N.E. 2d 599 (1971). Indeed, our decision in *United States* v. *Vuitch,* 402 U.S. 62 (1971), inferentially is to the same effect, for we there would not have indulged in statutory interpretation favorable to abortion in specified circumstances if the necessary consequence was the termination of life entitled to Fourteenth Amendment protection.

This conclusion, however, does not of itself fully answer the contentions raised by Texas, and we pass on to other considerations.

B. The pregnant woman cannot be isolated in her

privacy. She carries an embryo and, later, a fetus, if one accepts the medical definitions of the developing young in the human uterus. See Dorland's Illustrated Medical Dictionary 478–479, 547 (24th ed. 1965). The situation therefore is inherently different from marital intimacy, or bedroom possession of obscene material, or marriage, or procreation, or education, with which *Eisenstadt* and *Griswold, Stanley, Loving, Skinner,* and *Pierce* and *Meyer* were respectively concerned. As we have intimated above, it is reasonable and appropriate for a State to decide that at some point in time another interest, that of health of the mother or that of potential human life, becomes significantly involved. The woman's privacy is no longer sole and any right of privacy she possesses must be measured accordingly.

Texas urges that, apart from the Fourteenth Amendment, life begins at conception and is present throughout pregnancy, and that, therefore, the State has a compelling interest in protecting that life from and after conception. We need not resolve the difficult question of when life begins. When those trained in the respective disciplines of medicine, philosophy, and theology are unable to arrive at any consensus, the judiciary, at this point in the development of man's knowledge, is not in a position to speculate as to the answer.

It should be sufficient to note briefly the wide divergence of thinking on this most sensitive and difficult question. There has always been strong support for the view that life does not begin until live birth. This was the belief of the Stoics.[56] It appears to be the predominant, though not the unanimous, attitude of the Jewish faith.[57] It may be taken to represent also the position of a large segment of the Protestant community, insofar as that can be ascertained; organized groups that have taken a formal position on the abortion issue have generally regarded abortion as a matter for the conscience of the individual and her family.[58] As we have noted, the common law found greater significance in quickening. Physicians and their scientific colleagues have regarded that event with less interest and have tended to focus either upon conception, upon live birth, or upon the interim point at which the fetus becomes "viable," that is, potentially able to live outside the mother's womb, albeit with artificial aid.[59] Viability is usually placed at about seven months (28 weeks) but may occur earlier, even at 24 weeks.[60] The Aristotelian theory of "mediate animation," that held sway throughout the Middle Ages and the Renaissance in Europe, continued to be official Roman Catholic dogma until the 19th century, despite opposition to this "ensoulment" theory from those in the Church who would recognize the existence of life from the moment of conception.[61] The latter is now, of course, the official belief of the Catholic Church. As one brief *amicus* discloses, this is a view strongly held by many non-Catholics as well, and by many physicians. Substantial problems for precise definition of this view are posed, however, by new embryological data that purport to indicate that conception is a "process" over time, rather than an event, and by new medical techniques such as menstrual extraction, the "morning-after" pill, implantation of embryos, artificial insemination, and even artificial wombs.[62]

In areas other than criminal abortion, the law has been reluctant to endorse any theory that life, as we recognize it, begins before live birth or to accord legal rights to the unborn except in narrowly defined situations and except when the rights are contingent upon live birth. For example, the traditional rule of tort law denied recovery for prenatal injuries even though the child was born alive.[63] That rule has been changed in almost every jurisdiction. In most States, recovery is said to be permitted only if the fetus was viable, or at least quick, when the injuries were sustained, though few courts have squarely so held.[64] In a recent development, generally opposed by the commentators, some States permit the parents of a stillborn child to maintain an action for wrongful death because of prenatal injuries.[65] Such an action, however, would appear to be one to vindicate the parents' interest and is thus consistent with the view that the fetus, at most, represents only the potentiality of life. Similarly, unborn children have been recognized as acquiring rights or interests by way of inheritance or other devolution of property, and have been represented by guardians *ad litem*.[66] Perfection of the interests involved, again, has generally been contingent upon live birth. In short, the unborn have never been recognized in the law as persons in the whole sense.

X

In view of all this, we do not agree that, by adopting one theory of life, Texas may override the rights of the pregnant woman that are at stake. We repeat, however, that the State does have an important and legitimate interest in preserving and protecting the health of the pregnant woman, whether she be a resident of the State or a nonresident who seeks medical consultation and treatment there, and that it has still *another* important and legitimate interest in protecting the potentiality of human life. These interests are separate and distinct. Each grows in substantiality as the woman approaches term and, at a point during pregnancy, each becomes "compelling."

With respect to the State's important and legitimate interest in the health of the mother, the "compelling" point, in the light of present medical knowledge, is at approximately the end of the first trimester. This is so because of the now-established medical fact, referred to above at 149, that until the end of the first trimester mortality in abortion may be less than mortality in normal childbirth. It follows that, from and after this point, a State may regulate the abortion procedure to the extent that the regulation reasonably relates to the preservation and protection of maternal health. Examples of permissible state regulation in this area are requirements as to the qualifications of the person who is to perform the abortion; as to the licensure of that person; as to the facility in which the procedure is to be performed, that is, whether it must be a hospital or may be a clinic or some other place of less-than-hospital status; as to the licensing of the facility; and the like.

This means, on the other hand, that, for the period of pregnancy prior to this "compelling" point, the attending physician, in consultation with his patient, is free to determine, without regulation by the State, that, in his medical judgment, the patient's pregnancy should be terminated. If that decision is reached, the judgment may be effectuated by an abortion free of interference by the State.

With respect to the State's important and legitimate interest in potential life, the "compelling" point is at viability. This is so because the fetus then presumably has the capability of meaningful life outside the mother's womb. State regulation protective of fetal life after viability thus has both logical and biological justifications. If the State is interested in protecting fetal life after viability, it may go so far as to proscribe abortion during that period, except when it is necessary to preserve the life or health of the mother.

Measured against these standards, Art. 1196 of the Texas Penal Code, in restricting legal abortions to those "procured or attempted by medical advice for the purpose of saving the life of the mother," sweeps too broadly. The statute makes no distinction between abortions performed early in pregnancy and those performed later, and it limits to a single reason, "saving" the mother's life, the legal justification for the procedure. The statute, therefore, cannot survive the constitutional attack made upon it here.

This conclusion makes it unnecessary for us to consider the additional challenge to the Texas statute asserted on grounds of vagueness. See *United States* v. *Vuitch*, 402 U.S., at 67–72.

XI

To summarize and to repeat:

1. A state criminal abortion statute of the current Texas type, that excepts from criminality only a *lifesaving* procedure on behalf of the mother, without regard to pregnancy stage and without recognition of the other interests involved, is violative of the Due Process Clause of the Fourteenth Amendment.

(a) For the stage prior to approximately the end of the first trimester, the abortion decision and its effectuation must be left to the medical judgment of the pregnant woman's attending physician.

(b) For the stage subsequent to approximately the end of the first trimester, the State, in promoting its interest in the health of the mother, may, if it chooses, regulate the abortion procedure in ways that are reasonably related to maternal health.

(c) For the stage subsequent to viability, the State in promoting its interest in the potentiality of human life may, if it chooses, regulate, and even proscribe, abortion except where it is necessary, in appropriate medical judgment, for the preservation of the life of health of the mother.

2. The State may define the term "physician," as it has been employed in the preceding paragraphs of this Part XI of this opinion, to mean only a physician currently licensed by the State, and may proscribe any abortion by a person who is not a physician as so defined.

In *Doe* v. *Bolton, post*, p. 179, procedural requirements contained in one of the modern abortion statutes are considered. That opinion and this one, of course, are to be read together.[67]

This holding, we feel, is consistent with the relative weights of the respective interests involved, with the lessons and examples of medical and legal history, with the lenity of the common law, and with the demands of the profound problems of the present day. The decision leaves the State free to place increasing restrictions on abortion as the period of pregnancy lengthens, so long as those restrictions are tailored to the recognized state interests. The decision vindicates the right of the physician to administer medical treatment according to his professional judgment up to the points where important state interests provide compelling justifications for intervention. Up to those points, the abortion decision in all its aspects is inherently, and primarily, a medical decision, and basic responsibility for it must rest with the physician. If an individual practitioner abuses the privilege of exercising proper medical judgment, the usual remedies, judicial and intra-professional, are available.

NOTES

17. *Id.,* at 18; Lader 76.
18. Edelstein 63.
19. *Id.,* at 64.
20. Dorland's Illustrated Medical Dictionary 1261 (24th ed. 1965).
21. E. Coke, Institutes III *50; 1 W. Hawkins, Pleas of the Crown, c. 31, § 16 (4th ed. 1762); 1 W. Blackstone, Commentaries *129–130; M. Hale, Pleas of the Crown 433 (1st Amer. ed. 1847). For discussions of the role of the quickening concept in English common law, see Lader 78; Noonan 223–226; Means, The Law of New York Concerning Abortion and the Status of the Foetus, 1664–1968: A Case of Cessation of Constitutionality (pt. 1), 14 N.Y.L.F. 411, 418–428 (1968) (hereinafter Means I); Stern, Abortion: Reform and the Law, 59 J. Crim. L. C. & P. S. 84 (1968) (hereinafter Stern); Quay 430–432; Williams 152.

22. Early philosophers believed that the embryo or fetus did not become formed and begin to live until at least 40 days after conception for a male, and 80 to 90 days for a female. See, for example, Aristotle, Hist. Anim. 7.3.583b; Gen. Anim. 2.3.736, 2.5.741; Hippocrates, Lib. de Nat. Puer., No. 10. Aristotle's thinking derived from his three-stage theory of life: vegetable, animal, rational. The vegetable stage was reached at conception, the animal at "animation," and the rational soon after live birth. This theory, together with the 40/80 day view, came to be accepted by early Christian thinkers.

The theological debate was reflected in the writings of St. Augustine, who made a distinction between *embryo inanimatus,* not yet endowed with a soul, and *embryo animatus.* He may have drawn upon Exodus 21:22. At one point, however, he expressed the view that human powers cannot determine the point during fetal development at which the critical change occurs. See Augustine, De Origine Animae 4.4 (Pub. Law 44.527). See also W. Reany, The Creation of the Human Soul, c. 2 and 83–86 (1932); Huser, The Crime of Abortion in Canon Law 15 (Catholic Univ. of America, Canon Law Studies No. 162, Washington, D.C., 1942).

Galen, in three treatises related to embryology, accepted the thinking of Aristotle and his followers. Quay 426–427. Later, Augustine on abortion was incorporated by Gratian into the Decretum, published about 1140. Decretum Magistri Gratiani 2.32.2.7 to 2.32.2.10, in 1 Corpus Juris Canonici 1122, 1123 (A. Friedburg, 2d ed. 1879). This Decretal and the Decretals that followed were recognized as the definitive body of canon law until the new Code of 1917.

For discussions of the canon-law treatment, see Means I, pp. 411–412; Noonan 20–26; Quay 426–430; see also J. Noonan, Contraception: A History of Its Treatment by the Catholic Theologians and Canonists 18–29 (1965).

23. Bracton took the position that abortion by blow or poison was homicide "if the foetus be already formed and animated, and particularly if it be animated." 2 H. Bracton, De Legibus et Consuetudinibus Angliae 279 (T. Twiss ed. 1879), or, as a later translation puts it, "if the foetus is already formed or quickened, especially if it is quickened," 2 H. Bracton, On the Laws and Customs of England 341 (S. Thorne ed. 1968). See Quay 431; see also 2 Fleta 60–61 (Book 1, c. 23) (Selden Society ed. 1955).

24. E. Coke, Institutes III *50.

25. 1 W. Blackstone, Commentaries *129–130.

26. Means, The Phoenix of Abortional Freedom: Is a Penumbral or Ninth-Amendment Right About to Arise from the Nineteenth-Century Legislative Ashes of a Fourteenth-Century Common-Law Liberty?, 17 N. Y. L. F. 335 (1971) (herinafter Means II). The author examines the two principal precedents cited marginally by Coke, both contrary to his dictum, and traces the treatment of these and other cases by earlier commentators. He concludes that Coke, who himself participated as an advocate in an abortion case in 1601, may have intentionally misstated the law. The author even suggests a reason: Coke's strong feelings against abortion, coupled with his determination to assert common-law (secular) jurisdiction to assess penalties for an offense that traditionally had been an exclusively ecclesiastical or canon-law crime. See also Lader 78–79, who notes that some scholars doubt that the common law ever was applied to abortion; that the English ecclesiastical courts seem to have lost interest in the problem after 1527; and that the preamble to the English legislation of 1803, 43 Geo. 3, c. 58, § 1, referred to in the text, *infra,* at 136, states that "no adequate means have been hitherto provided for the prevention and punishment of such offenses."

27. *Commonwealth* v. *Bangs,* 9 Mass. 387, 388 (1812); *Commonwealth* v. *Parker,* 50 Mass. (9 Metc.) 263, 265–266 (1845); *State* v. *Cooper,* 22 N. J. L. 52, 58 (1849); *Abrams* v.

Foshee, 3 Iowa 274, 278–280 (1856); *Smith* v. *Gaffard,* 31 Ala. 45, 51 (1857); *Mitchell* v. *Commonwealth,* 78 Ky. 204, 210 (1879); *Eggart* v. *State,* 40 Fla. 527, 532, 25 So. 144, 145 (1898); *State* v. *Alcorn,* 7 Idaho 599, 606, 64 P. 1014, 1016 (1901); *Edwards* v. *State,* 79 Neb. 251, 252, 112 N. W. 611, 612 (1907); *Gray* v. *State,* 77 Tex. Cr. R. 221, 224, 178 S. W. 337, 338 (1915); *Miller* v. *Bennett,* 190 Va. 162, 169, 56 S. E. 2d 217, 221 (1949). Contra, *Mills* v. *Commonwealth,* 13 Pa. 631, 633 (1850); *State* v. *Slagle,* 83 N. C. 630, 632 (1880).

28. See *Smith* v. *State,* 33 Me. 48, 55 (1851); *Evans* v. *People,* 49 N. Y. 86, 88 (1872); *Lamb* v. *State,* 67 Md. 524, 533, 10 A. 208 (1887).

29. Conn. Stat., Tit. 20, § 14 (1821).

30. Conn. Pub. Acts, c. 71, § 1 (1860).

31. N. Y. Rev. Stat., pt. 4, c. 1, Tit. 2, Art. 1, § 9, p. 661, and Tit. 6, § 21, p. 694 (1829).

32. Act of Jan. 20, 1840, § 1, set forth in 2 H. Gammel, Laws of Texas 177–178 (1898); see *Grigsby* v. *Reib,* 105 Tex. 597, 600, 153 S. W. 1124, 1125 (1913).

33. The early statutes are discussed in Quay 435–438. See also Lader 85–88; Stern 85–86; and Means II 375–376.

34. Criminal abortion statutes in effect in the States as of 1961, together with historical statutory development and important judicial interpretations of the state statutes, are cited and quoted in Quay 447–520. See Comment, A Survey of the Present Statutory and Case Law on Abortion: The Contradictions and the Problems, 1972 U. Ill. L. F. 177, 179, classifying the abortion statutes and listing 25 States as permitting abortion only if necessary to save or preserve the mother's life.

35. Ala. Code, Tit. 14, § 9 (1958); D. C. Code Ann. § 22–201 (1967).

36. Mass. Gen. Laws Ann., c. 272, § 19 (1970); N. J. Stat. Ann. § 2A:87–1 (1969); Pa. Stat. Ann., Tit. 18, §§ 4718, 4719 (1963).

37. Fourteen States have adopted some form of the ALI statute. See Ark. Stat. Ann. §§ 41–303 to 41–310 (Supp. 1971); Calif. Health & Safety Code §§ 25950–25955.5 (Supp. 1972); Colo. Rev. Stat. Ann. §§ 40–2–50 to 40–2–53 (Cum. Supp. 1967); Del. Code Ann., Tit. 24, §§ 1790–1793 (Supp. 1972); Florida Law of Apr. 13, 1972, c. 72–196, 1972 Fla. Sess. Law Serv., pp. 380–382; Ga. Code §§ 26–1201 to 26–1203 (1972); Kan. Stat. Ann. § 21–3407 (Supp. 1971); Md. Ann. Code, Art. 43, §§ 137–139 (1971); Miss. Code Ann. § 2223 (Supp. 1972); N. M. Stat. Ann. §§ 40A–5–1 to 40A–5–3 (1972); N. C. Gen Stat. § 14–45.1 (Supp. 1971); Ore. Rev. Stat. §§ 435.405 to 435.495 (1971); S. C. Code Ann. §§ 16–82 to 16–89 (1962 and Supp. 1971); Va. Code Ann. §§ 18.1–62 to 18.1–62.3 (Supp. 1972). Mr. Justice Clark described some of these States as having "led the way." Religion, Morality, and Abortion: A Constitutional Appraisal, 2 Loyola U. (L. A.) L. Rev. 1, 11 (1969).

By the end of 1970, four other States had repealed criminal penalties for abortions performed in early pregnancy by a licensed physician, subject to stated procedural and health requirements. Alaska Stat. § 11.15.060 (1970); Haw. Rev. Stat. § 453–16 (Supp. 1971); N. Y. Penal Code § 125.05, subd. 3 (Supp. 1972–1973); Wash. Rev. Code §§ 9.02.060 to 9.02.080 (Supp. 1972). The precise status of criminal abortion laws in some States is made unclear by recent decisions in state and federal courts striking down existing state laws, in whole or in part.

42. See, for example, *YWCA* v. *Kugler,* 342 F. Supp. 1048, 1074 (N. J. 1972); *Abele* v. *Markle,* 342 F. Supp. 800, 805–806 (Conn. 1972) (Newman, J., concurring in result), appeal docketed, No. 72–56; *Walsingham* v. *State,* 250 So. 2d 857, 863 (Ervin, J., concurring) (Fla. 1971); *State* v. *Gedicke,* 43 N. J. L. 86, 90 (1881); Means II 381–382.

43. See C. Haagensen & W. Lloyd, A Hundred Years of Medicine 19 (1943).

44. Potts, Postconceptive Control of Fertility, 8 Int'l J. of G. & O. 957, 967 (1970) (England and Wales); Abortion Mortality, 20 Morbidity and Mortality 208, 209 (June 12, 1971) (U.S. Dept. of HEW, Public Health Service) (New York City); Tietze, United States: Therapeutic Abortions, 1963–1968, 59 Studies in Family Planning 5, 7 (1970); Tietze, Mortality with Contraception and Induced Abortion, 45 Studies in Family Planning 6 (1969) (Japan, Czechoslovakia, Hungary); Tietze & Lehfeldt, Legal Abortion in Eastern Europe, 175 J. A. M. A. 1149, 1152 (April 1961). Other sources are discussed in Lader 17–23.

45. See Brief of *Amicus* National Right to Life Committee; R. Drinan, The Inviolability of the Right to be Born, in Abortion and the Law 107 (D. Smith ed. 1967); Louisell, Abortion, The Practice of Medicine and the Due Process of Law, 16 U. C. L. A. L. Rev. 233 (1969); Noonan 1.

46. See, *e. g., Abele* v. *Markle,* 342 F. Supp. 800 (Conn. 1972), appeal docketed, No. 72–56.

47. See discussions in Means I and Means II.

48. See, *e.g., State* v. *Murphy,* 27 N.J.L. 112, 114 (1858).

49. *Watson* v. *State,* 9 Tex. App. 237, 244–245 (1880); *Moore* v. *State,* 37 Tex. Cr. R. 552, 561, 40 S. W. 287, 290 (1897); *Shaw* v. *State,* 73 Tex. Cr. R. 337, 339, 165 S. W. 930, 931 (1914); *Fondren* V. *State,* 74 Tex. Cr. R. 552, 557, 169 S. W. 411, 414 (1914); *Gray* v. *State,* 77 Tex. Cr. R. 221, 229, 178 S. W. 337, 341 (1915). There is no immunity in Texas for the father who is not married to the mother. *Hammett* v. *State,* 84 Tex. Cr. R. 635, 209 S. W. 661 (1919); *Thompson* v. *State* (Ct. Crim. App. Tex. 1971), appeal docketed, No. 71–1200.

50. See *Smith* v. *State,* 33 Me., at 55; *In re Vince,* 2 N. J. 443, 450, 67 A. 2d 141, 144 (1949). A short discussion of the modern law on this issue is contained in the Comment to the ALI's Model Penal Code § 207.11, at 158 and nn. 35–37 (Tent. Draft No. 9, 1959)

51. Tr. of Oral Rearg. 20–21.

52. Tr. of Oral Rearg. 24.

53. We are not aware that in the taking of any census under this clause, a fetus has ever been counted.

54. When Texas urges that a fetus is entitled to Fourteenth Amendment protection as a person, it faces a dilemma. Neither in Texas nor in any other State are all abortions prohibited. Despite broad proscription, an exception always exists. The exception contained in Art. 1196, for an abortion procured or attempted by medical advice for the purpose of saving the life of the mother, is typical. But if the fetus is a person who is not to be deprived of life without due process of law, and if the mother's condition is the sole determinant, does not the Texas exception appear to be out of line with the Amendment's command?

There are other inconsistencies between Fourteeth Amendment status and the typical abortion statute. It has already been pointed out, n. 49, *supra,* that in Texas the woman is not a principal or an accomplice with respect to an abortion upon her. If the fetus is a person, why is the woman not a principal or an accomplice? Further, the penalty for criminal abortion specified by Art. 1195 is significantly less than the maximum penalty for murder prescribed by Art. 1257 of the Texas Penal Code. If the fetus is a person, may the penalties by different?

55. Cf. the Wisconsin abortion statute, defining "unborn

child" to mean "a human being from the time of conception until it is born alive," Wis. Stat. § 940.04 (6) (1969), and the new Connecticut statute, Pub. Act No. 1 (May 1972 special session), declaring it to be the public policy of the State and the legislative intent "to protect and preserve human life from the moment of conception."

*Citations omitted [Eds.]

56. Edelstein 16.

57. Lader 97–99; D. Feldman, Birth Control in Jewish Law 251–294 (1968). For a stricter view, see I. Jakobovits, Jewish Views on Abortion, in Abortion and the Law 124 (D. Smith ed. 1967).

58. Amicus Brief for the American Ethical Union et al. For the position of the National Council of Churches and of other denominations, see Lader 99–101.

59. L. Hellman & J. Pritchard, Williams Obstetrics 493 (14th ed. 1971); Dorland's Illustrated Medical Dictionary 1689 (24th ed. 1965).

60. Hellman & Pritchard, *supra,* n. 59, at 493.

61. For discussions of the development of the Roman Catholic position, see D. Callahan, Abortion: Law, Choice, and Morality 409–447 (1970); Noonan 1.

62. See Brodie, The New Biology and the Prenatal Child, 9 J. Family L. 391, 397 (1970); Gorney, The New Biology and the Future of Man, 15 U. C. L. A. L. Rev. 273 (1968); Note, Criminal Law—Abortion—The "Morning-After Pill" and Other Pre-Implantation Birth-Control Methods and the Law, 46 Ore. L. Rev. 211 (1967); G. Taylor, The Biological Time Bomb 32 (1968); A. Rosenfeld, The Second Genesis 138–139 (1969); Smith, Through a Test Tube Darkly: Artificial Insemination and the Law, 67 Mich. L. Rev. 127 (1968); Note, Artificial Insemination and the Law, 1968 U. Ill. L. F. 203.

63. W. Prosser, The Law of Torts 335–338 (4th ed. 1971); 2 F. Harper & F. James, The Law of Torts 1028–1031 (1956); Note, 63 Harv. L. Rev. 173 (1949).

64. See cases cited in Prosser, *supra,* n. 63, at 336–338; Annotation, Action for Death of Unborn Child, 15 A. L. R. 3d 992 (1967).

65. Prosser, *supra,* n. 63, at 338; Note, The Law and the Unborn Child: The Legal and Logical Inconsistencies, 46 Notre Dame Law. 349, 360–354 (1971).

66. Louisell, Abortion, The Practice of Medicine and the Due Process of Law, 16 U. C. L. A. L. Rev. 233, 235–238 (1969); Note, 56 Iowa L. Rev. 994, 999–1000 (1971); Note, The Law and the Unborn Child, 46 Notre Dame Law. 349, 351–354 (1971).

67. Neither in this opinion nor in *Doe* v. *Bolton, post.* p. 179, do we discuss the father's rights, if any exist in the constitutional context, in the abortion decision. No paternal right has been asserted in either of the cases, and the Texas and the Georgia statutes on their face take no cognizance of the father. We are aware that some statutes recognize the father under certain circumstances. North Carolina, for example, N.C. Gen. Stat. § 14–45.1 (Supp. 1971), requires written permission for the abortion from the husband when the woman is a married minor, that is, when she is less than 18 years of age, 41 N. C. A. G. 489 (1971); if the woman is an unmarried minor, written permission from the parents is required. We need not now decide whether provisions of this kind are constitutional.

MARY ANNE WARREN

On the Moral and Legal Status of Abortion *

We will be concerned with both the moral status of abortion, which for our purposes we may define as the act which a woman performs in voluntarily terminating, or allowing another person to terminate, her pregnancy, and the legal status which is appropriate for this act. I will argue that, while it is not possible to produce a satisfactory defense of a woman's right to obtain an abortion without showing that a fetus is not a human being, in the morally relevant sense of that term, we ought not to conclude that the difficulties involved in determining whether or not a fetus is human make it impossible to produce any satisfactory solution to the problem of the moral status of abortion. For it is possible to show that, on the basis of intuitions which we may expect even the opponents of abortion to share, a fetus is not a person, and hence not the sort of entity to which it is proper to ascribe full moral rights.

Of course, while some philosophers would deny the possibility of any such proof,[1] others will deny that there is any need for it, since the moral permissibility of abortion appears to them to be too obvious to require proof. But the inadequacy of this attitude should be evident from the fact that both the friends and the foes of abortion consider their position to be morally self-evident. Because pro-abortionists have never adequately come to grips with the conceptual issues surrounding abortion, most if not all, of the arguments which they advance in opposition to laws restricting access to abortion fail to refute or even weaken the traditional antiabortion argument, i.e., that a fetus is a human being, and therefore abortion is murder.

These arguments are typically of one of two sorts. Either they point to the terrible side effects of the restrictive laws, e.g., the deaths due to illegal abortions, and the fact that it is poor women who suffer the most as a result of these

From *The Monist,* Vol. 57 (1973), pp. 43–61. Reprinted by permission of the publisher and the author.

laws, or else they state that to deny a woman access to abortion is to deprive her of her right to control her own body. Unfortunately, however, the fact that restricting access to abortion has tragic side effects does not, in itself, show that the restrictions are unjustified, since murder is wrong regardless of the consequences of prohibiting it; and the appeal to the right to control one's body, which is generally construed as a property right, is at best a rather feeble argument for the permissibility of abortion. Mere ownership does not give me the right to kill innocent people whom I find on my property, and indeed I am apt to be held responsible if such people injure themselves while on my property. It is equally unclear that I have any moral right to expel an innocent person from my property when I know that doing so will result in his death.

Futhermore, it is probably inappropriate to describe a woman's body as her property, since it seems natural to hold that a person is something distinct from her property, but not from her body. Even those who would object to the identification of a person with his body, or with the conjunction of his body and his mind, must admit that it would be very odd to describe, say, breaking a leg, as damaging one's property, and much more appropriate to describe it as injuring one*self*. Thus it is probably a mistake to argue that the right to obtain an abortion is in any way derived from the right to own and regulate property.

But however we wish to construe the right to abortion, we cannot hope to convince those who consider abortion a form of murder of the existence of any such right unless we are able to produce a clear and convincing refutation of the traditional antiabortion argument, and this has not, to my knowledge, been done. With respect to the two most vital issues which that argument involves, i.e., the humanity of the fetus and its implication for the moral status of abortion, confusion has prevailed on both sides of the dispute.

Thus, both proabortionists and antiabortionists have tended to abstract the question of whether abortion is wrong to that of whether it is wrong to destroy a fetus, just as though the rights of another person were not necessarily involved. This mistaken abstraction has led to the almost universal assumption that if a fetus is a human being, with a right to life, then it follows immediately that abortion is wrong (except perhaps when necessary to save the woman's life), and that it ought to be prohibited. It has also been generally assumed that unless the question about the status of the fetus is answered, the moral status of abortion cannot possibly be determined.

Two recent papers, one by B. A. Brody,[2] and one by Judith Thomson,[3] have attempted to settle the question of whether abortion ought to be prohibited apart from the question of whether or not the fetus is human. Brody examines the possibility that the following two statements are compatible: (1) that abortion is the taking of innocent human life, and therefore wrong; and (2) that nevertheless it ought not to be prohibited by law, at least under the present circumstances.[4] Not surprisingly, Brody finds it impossible to reconcile these two statements, since, as he rightly argues, none of the unfortunate side effects of the prohibition of abortion is bad enough to justify legalizing the *wrongful* taking of human life. He is mistaken, however, in concluding that the incompatibility of (1) and (2), in itself, shows that "the legal problem about abortion cannot be resolved independently of the status of the fetus problem" (p. 369).

What Brody fails to realize is that (1) embodies the questionable assumption that if a fetus is a human being, then of course abortion is morally wrong, and that an attack on *this* assumption is more promising, as a way of reconciling the humanity of the fetus with the claim that laws prohibiting abortion are unjustified, than is an attack on the assumption that if abortion is the wrongful killing of innocent human beings then it ought to be prohibited. He thus overlooks the possibility that a fetus may have a right to life and abortion still be morally permissible, in that the right of a woman to terminate an unwanted pregnancy might override the right of the fetus to be kept alive. The immorality of abortion is no more demonstrated by the humanity of the fetus, in itself, than the immorality of killing in self-defense is demonstrated by the fact that the assailant is a human being. Neither is it demonstrated by the *innocence* of the fetus, since there may be situations in which the killing of innocent human beings is justified.

It is perhaps not surprising that Brody fails to spot this assumption, since it has been accepted with little or no argument by nearly everyone who has written on the morality of abortion. John Noonan is correct in saying that "the fundamental question in the long history of abortion is, How do you determine the humanity of a being?" [5] He summarizes his own antiabortion argument, which is a version of the official position of the Catholic Church, as follows:

. . . it is wrong to kill humans, however poor, weak, defenseless, and lacking in opportunity to develop their potential they may be. It is therefore morally wrong to kill Biafrans. Similarly, it is morally wrong to kill embryos.[6]

Noonan bases his claim that fetuses are human upon what he calls the theologians' criterion of humanity: that whoever is conceived of human beings is human. But although he argues at length for the appropriateness of this criterion, he never questions the assumption that if a fetus is human then abortion is wrong for exactly the same reason that murder is wrong.

Judith Thomson is, in fact, the only writer I am aware of who has seriously questioned this assumption; she has argued that, even if we grant the antiabortionist his claim that a fetus is a human being, with the same right to life as any other human being, we can still demonstrate that, in at least some and perhaps most cases, a woman is under no moral obligation to complete an unwanted pregnancy.[7] Her argument is worth examining, since if it holds up it may enable us to establish the moral permissibility of abortion without becoming involved in problems about what entitles an entity to be considered human, and accorded full moral rights. To be able to do this would be a great gain in the power and simplicity of the proabortion position, since, although I will argue that these problems can be solved at least as decisively as can any other moral problem, we should certainly be pleased to be able to avoid having to solve them as part of the justification of abortion.

On the other hand, even if Thomson's argument does not hold up, her insight, i.e., that it requires *argument* to show that if fetuses are human then abortion is properly classified as murder, is an extremely valuable one. The assumption she attacks is particularly invidious, for it amounts to the decision that it is appropriate, in deciding the moral status of abortion, to leave the rights of the pregnant woman out of consideration entirely, except possibly when her life is threatened. Obviously, this will not do; determining what moral rights, if any, a fetus possesses is only the first step in determining the moral status of abortion. Step two, which is at least equally essential, is finding a just solution to the conflict between whatever rights the fetus may have, and the rights of the woman who is unwillingly pregnant. While the historical error has been to pay far too little attention to the second step, Ms. Thomson's suggestion is that if we look at the second step first we may find that a woman has a right to obtain an abortion *regardless* of what rights the fetus has.

Our own inquiry will also have two stages. In Section I, we will consider whether or not it is possible to establish that abortion is morally permissible even on the assumption that a fetus is an entity with a full-fledged right to life. I will argue that in fact this cannot be established, at least not with the conclusiveness which is essential to our hopes of convincing those who are skeptical about the morality of abortion, and that we therefore cannot avoid dealing with the question of whether or not a fetus really does have the same right to life as a (more fully developed) human being.

In Section II, I will propose an answer to this question, namely, that a fetus cannot be considered a member of the moral community, the set of beings with full and equal moral rights, for the simple reason that it is not a person, and that it is personhood, and not genetic humanity, i.e., humanity as defined by Noonan, which is the basis for membership in this community. I will argue that a fetus, whatever its stage of development, satisfies none of the basic criteria of personhood, and is not even enough *like* a person to be accorded even some of the same rights on the basis of this resemblance. Nor, as we will see, is a fetus's *potential* personhood a threat to the morality of abortion, since, whatever the rights of potential people may be, they are invariably overridden in any conflict with the moral rights of actual people.

I

We turn now to Professor Thomson's case for the claim that even if a fetus has full moral rights, abortion is still morally permissible, at least sometimes, and for some reasons other than to save the woman's life. Her argument is based upon a clever, but I think faulty, analogy. She asks us to picture ourselves waking up one day, in bed with a famous violinist. Imagine that you have been kidnapped, and your bloodstream hooked up to that of the violinist, who happens to have an ailment which will certainly kill him unless he is permitted to share your kidneys for a period of nine months. No one else can save him, since you alone have the right type of blood. He will be unconscious all that time, and you will have to stay in bed with him, but after nine months are over he may be unplugged, completely cured, that is provided that you have cooperated.

Now then, she continues, what are your obligations in this situation? The antiabortionist, if he is consistent, will have to say that you are obligated to stay in bed with the violinist: for all people have a right to life, and violinists are people, and therefore it would be murder for you to disconnect yourself from him and let him die (p. 49). But this is outrageous and so there must be something wrong with the same argument when it is applied to abortion. It would certainly be commendable of you to agree to save the violinist, but it is absurd to suggest that your refusal to do so would be murder. His right to life does not obligate you to do whatever is required to keep him alive; nor does it justify anyone else in forcing you to do so. A law which required you to stay in bed with the violinist would clearly be an unjust law, since it is no proper function of the law to force unwilling people to make huge sacrifices for the sake of other people toward whom they have no such prior obligation.

Thomson concludes that, if this analogy is an apt one, then we can grant the antiabortionist his claim that a fetus is a human being, and still hold that it is at least sometimes the case that a pregnant woman has the right to refuse to be a Good Samaritan towards the fetus, i.e., to obtain an abortion. For there is a great gap between the claim that x has a right to life, and the claim that y is obligated to do whatever is necessary to keep x alive, let alone that he ought to be forced to do so. It is y's duty to keep x alive only if he has somehow contracted a *special* obligation to do so; and a woman who is unwillingly pregnant, e.g., who was raped, has done nothing which obligates her to make the enormous sacrifice which is necessary to preserve the conceptus.

This argument is initially quite plausible, and in the extreme case of pregnancy due to rape it is probably conclusive. Difficulties arise, however, when we try to specify more exactly the range of cases in which abortion is clearly justifiable even on the assumption that the fetus is human. Professor Thomson considers it a virtue of her argument that it does not enable us to conclude that abortion is *always* permissible. It would, she says, be "indecent" for a woman in her seventh month to obtain an abortion just to avoid having to postpone a trip to Europe. On the other hand, her argument enables us to see that "a sick and desperately frightened schoolgirl pregnant due to rape may *of course* choose abortion, and that any law which rules this out is an insane law" (p. 65). So far, so good; but what are we to say about the woman who becomes pregnant not through rape but as a result of her own carelessness, or because of contraceptive failure, or who gets pregnant intentionally and then changes her mind about wanting a child? With respect to such cases, the violinist analogy is of much less use to the defender of the woman's right to obtain an abortion.

Indeed, the choice of a pregnancy due to rape, as an example of a case in which abortion is permissible even if a fetus is considered a human being, is extremely significant; for it is only in the case of pregnancy due to rape that the woman's situation is adequately analogous to the violinist case for our intuitions about the latter to transfer convincingly. The crucial difference between a pregnancy due to rape and the *normal* case of an unwanted pregnancy is that in the normal case we cannot claim that the woman is in no way responsible for her predicament; she could have remained chaste, or taken her pills more faithfully, or abstained on dangerous days, and so on. If, on the other hand, you are kidnapped by strangers, and hooked up to a strange violinist, then

you are free of any shred of responsibility for the situation, on the basis of which it could be argued that you are obligated to keep the violinist alive. Only when her pregnancy is due to rape is a woman clearly just as nonresponsible.[8]

Consequently, there is room for the antiabortionist to argue that in the normal case of unwanted pregnancy a woman has, by her own actions, assumed responsibility for the fetus. For if x behaves in a way which he could have avoided, and which he knows involves, let us say, a 1 percent chance of bringing into existence a human being, with a right to life, and does so knowing that if this should happen then that human being will perish unless x does certain things to keep him alive, then it is by no means clear that when it does happen x is free of any obligation to what he knew in advance would be required to keep that human being alive.

The plausibility of such an argument is enough to show that the Thomson analogy can provide a clear and persuasive defense of a woman's right to obtain an abortion only with respect to those cases in which the woman is in no way responsible for her pregnancy, e.g., where it is due to rape. In all other cases, we would almost certainly conclude that it was necessary to look carefully at the particular circumstances in order to determine the extent of the woman's responsibility, and hence the extent of her obligation. This is an extremely unsatisfactory outcome, from the viewpoint of the opponents of restrictive abortion laws, most of whom are convinced that a woman has a right to obtain an abortion regardless of how and why she got pregnant.

Of course a supporter of the violinist analogy might point out that it is absurd to suggest that forgetting her pill one day might be sufficient to obligate a woman to complete an unwanted pregnancy. And indeed it *is* absurd to suggest this. As we will see, the moral right to obtain an abortion is not in the least dependent upon the extent to which the woman is responsible for her pregnancy. But unfortunately, once we allow the assumption that a fetus has full moral rights, we cannot avoid taking this absurd suggestion seriously. Perhaps we can make this point more clear by altering the violinist story just enough to make it more analogous to a normal unwanted pregnancy and less to a pregnancy due to rape, and then seeing whether it is still obvious that you are obligated to stay in bed with the fellow.

Suppose, then, that violinists are peculiarly prone to the sort of illness the only cure for which is the use of someone else's bloodstream for nine months, and that because of this there has been formed a society of music lovers who agree that whenever a violinist is stricken they will draw lots and the loser will, by some means, be made the one and only person capable of saving him. Now then, would you be obligated to cooperate in curing the violinist if you had voluntarily joined this society, knowing the possible consequences, and then your name had been drawn and you had been kidnapped? Admittedly, you did not promise ahead of time that you would, but you did deliberately place yourself in a position in which it might happen that a human life would be lost if you did not. Surely this is at least a prima facie reason for supposing that you have an obligation to stay in bed with the violinist. Suppose that you had gotten your name drawn deliberately; surely *that* would be quite a strong reason for thinking that you had such an obligation.

It might be suggested that there is one important disanalogy between the modified violinist case and the case of an unwanted pregnancy, which makes the woman's responsibility significantly less, namely, the fact that the fetus *comes into existence* as the result of the woman's actions. This fact might give her a right to refuse to keep it alive, whereas she would not have had this right had it existed previously, independently, and then as a result of her actions become dependent upon her for its survival.

My own intuition, however, is that x has no more right to bring into existence, either deliberately or as a foreseeable result of actions he could have avoided, a being with full moral rights (y), and then refuse to do what he knew beforehand would be required to keep that being alive, than he has to enter into an agreement with an existing person, whereby he may be called upon to save that person's life, and then refuse to do so when so called upon. Thus, x's responsibility for y's existence does not seem to lessen his obligation to keep y alive, if he is also responsible for y's being in a situation in which only he can save him.

Whether or not this intuition is entirely correct, it brings us back once again to the conclusion that once we allow the assumption that a fetus has full moral rights it becomes an extremely complex and difficult question whether and when abortion is justifiable. Thus the Thomson analogy cannot help us produce a clear and persuasive proof of the moral permissibility of abortion. Nor will the opponents of the restrictive laws thank us for anything less; for their conviction (for the most part) is that abortion is obviously *not* a morally serious and extremely unfortunate, even though sometimes justified act, comparable to killing in self-defense or to letting the violinist die, but rather is closer to being a morally neutral act, like cutting one's hair.

The basis of this conviction, I believe, is the realization that a fetus is not a person, and thus does not have a full-fledged right to life. Perhaps the reason why this claim has been so inadequately defended is that it seems self-evident to those who accept it. And so it is, insofar as it follows from what I take to be perfectly obvious claims about the nature of personhood, and about the proper grounds for ascribing moral rights, claims which ought, indeed, to be obvious to both the friends and foes of abortion. Nevertheless, it is worth examining these claims, and showing how they demonstrate the moral innocuousness of abortion, since this apparently has not been adequately done before.

II

The question which we must answer in order to produce a satisfactory solution to the problem of the moral status of abortion is this: How are we to define the moral community, the set of beings with full and equal moral rights, such that we can decide whether a human fetus is a member of this community or not? What sort of entity, exactly, has the inalienable rights to life, liberty, and the pursuit of happiness? Jefferson attributed these rights to all *men,* and it may or may not be fair to suggest that he intended to attribute them *only* to men. Perhaps he ought to have attributed them to all human beings. If so, then we arrive, first, at Noonan's problem of defining what makes a being human, and, second, at the equally vital question which Noonan does not consider, namely, What reason is there for identifying the moral community with the set of all human beings, in whatever way we have chosen to define that term?

1. ON THE DEFINITION OF 'HUMAN'

One reason why this vital second question is so frequently overlooked in the debate over the moral status of abortion is that the term 'human' has two distinct, but not often distinguished, senses. This fact results in a slide of meaning, which serves to conceal the fallaciousness of the traditional argument that since (1) it is wrong to kill innocent human beings, and (2) fetuses are innocent human beings, then (3) it is wrong to kill fetuses. For if 'human' is used in the same sense in both (1) and (2) then, whichever of the two senses is meant, one of these premises is question-begging. And if it is used in two different senses then of course the conclusion doesn't follow.

Thus, (1) is a self-evident moral truth,[9] and avoids begging the question about abortion, only if 'human beings' is used to mean something like 'a full-fledged member of the moral community.' (It may or may not also be meant to refer exclusively to members of the species *Homo sapiens*). We may call this the *moral* sense of 'human.' It is not to be confused with what we call the *genetic* sense, i.e., the sense in which *any* member of the species is a human being, and no member of any other species could be. If (1) is acceptable only if the moral sense is intended, (2) is non-question-begging only if what is intended is the genetic sense.

In "Deciding Who is Human," Noonan argues for the classification of fetuses with human beings by pointing to the presence of the full genetic code, and the potential capacity for rational thought (p. 135). It is clear that what he needs to show, for his version of the traditional argument to be valid, is that fetuses are human in the moral sense, the sense in which it is analytically true that all human beings have full moral rights. But, in the absence of any argument showing that whatever is genetically human is also morally human, and he gives none, nothing more than genetic humanity can be demonstrated by the presence of the human genetic code. And, as we will see, the *potential* capacity for rational thought can at most show that an entity has the potential for *becoming* human in the moral sense.

2. DEFINING THE MORAL COMMUNITY

Can it be established that genetic humanity is sufficient for moral humanity? I think that there are very good reasons for not defining the moral community in this way. I would like to suggest an alternative way of defining the moral community, which I will argue for only to the extent of explaining why it is, or should be, self-evident. The suggestion is simply that the moral community consists of all and only *people,* rather than all and only human beings; [10] and probably the best way of demonstrating its self-evidence is by considering the concept of personhood, to see what sorts of entity are and are not persons, and what the decision that a being is or is not a person implies about its moral rights.

What characteristics entitle an entity to be considered a person? This is obviously not the place to attempt a complete analysis of the concept of personhood, but we do not need such a fully adequate analysis just to determine whether and why a fetus is or isn't a person. All we need is a rough and approximate list of the most basic criteria of personhood, and some idea of which, or how many, of these an entity must satisfy in order to properly be considered a person.

In searching for such criteria, it is useful to look beyond the set of people with whom we are acquainted, and ask how we would decide whether a totally alien being was a person or not. (For we have no right to assume that genetic humanity is necessary for personhood.) Imagine a space traveler who lands on an unknown planet and encounters a race of beings utterly unlike any he has ever seen or heard of. If he wants to be sure of behaving morally toward these beings, he has to somehow decide whether they are people, and hence have full moral rights, or whether they are the sort of thing which he need not feel guilty about treating as, for example, a source of food.

How should he go about making this decision? If he has some anthropological background, he might look for such things as religion, art, and the manufacturing of tools, weapons, or shelters, since these factors have been used to distinguish our human from our prehuman ancestors, in what seems to be closer to the moral than the genetic sense of 'human.' And no doubt he would be right to consider the presence of such factors as good evidence that the alien beings were people, and morally human. It would, however, be overly anthropocentric of him to take the absence of these things as adequate evidence that they were not, since we can imagine people who have progressed beyond, or evolved without ever developing, these cultural characteristics.

I suggest that the traits which are most central to the concept of personhood, or humanity in the moral sense, are, very roughly, the following:

1. consciousness (of objects and events external and/or internal to the being), and in particular the capacity to feel pain;
2. reasoning (the *developed* capacity to solve new and relatively complex problems);
3. self-motivated activity (activity which is relatively independent of either genetic or direct external control);
4. the capacity to communicate, by whatever means, messages of an indefinite variety of types, that is, not just with an indefinite number of possible contents, but on indefinitely many possible topics;
5. the presence of self-concepts, and self-awareness, either individual or racial, or both.

Admittedly, there are apt to be a great many problems involved in formulating precise definitions of these criteria, let alone in developing universally valid behavioral criteria for deciding when they apply. But I will assume that both we and our explorer know approximately what (1)–(5) mean, and that he is also able to determine whether or not they apply. How, then, should he use his findings to decide whether or not the alien beings are people? We needn't suppose that an entity must have *all* of these attributes to be properly considered a person; (1) and (2) alone may well be sufficient for personhood, and quite probably (1)–(3) are sufficient. Neither do we need to insist that any one of these criteria is *necessary* for personhood, although once again (1) and (2) look like fairly good candidates for necessary conditions, as does (3), if 'activity' is construed so as to include the activity of reasoning.

All we need to claim, to demonstrate that a fetus is not a person, is that any being which satisfies *none* of (1)–(5) is certainly not a person. I consider this claim to be so obvious that I think anyone who denied it, and claimed that a being which satisfied none of (1)–(5) was a person all the same, would thereby demonstrate that he had no notion at all of what a person is—perhaps because he had confused the concept of a person with that of genetic humanity. If the opponents of abortion were to deny the appropriateness of these five criteria, I do not know what further arguments would convince them. We would probably have to admit that our conceptual schemes were indeed irreconcilably different, and that our dispute could not be settled objectively.

I do not expect this to happen, however, since I think that the concept of a person is one which is very nearly universal (to people), and that it is common to both proabortionists and antiabortionists, even though neither group has fully realized the relevance of this concept to the resolution of their dispute. Furthermore, I think that on reflection even the antiabortionists ought to agree not only that (1)–(5) are central to the concept of personhood, but also that it is a part of this concept that all and only people have full moral rights. The concept of a person is in part a moral concept; once we have admitted that x is a person we have recognized, even if we have not agreed to respect, x's right to be treated as a member of the moral community. It is true that the claim that x is a *human being* is more commonly voiced as part of an appeal to treat x decently than is the claim that x is a person, but this is either because 'human being' is here used in the sense which implies personhood, or because the genetic and moral senses of 'human' have been confused.

Now if (1)–(5) are indeed the primary criteria of personhood, then it is clear that genetic humanity is neither necessary nor sufficient for establishing that an entity is a person. Some human beings are not people, and there may well be people who are not human beings. A man or woman whose consciousness has been permanently obliterated but who remains alive is a human being which is no longer a person; defective human beings, with no appreciable mental capacity, are not and presumably never will be people; and a fetus is a human being which is not yet a person, and which therefore cannot coherently be said to have full moral rights. Citizens of the next century should be prepared to recognize highly advanced, self-aware robots or computers, should such be developed, and intelligent inhabitants of other worlds, should such be found, as people in the fullest sense, and to respect their moral rights. But to ascribe full moral rights to an entity which is not a person is as absurd as to ascribe moral obligations and responsibilities to such an entity.

3. FETAL DEVELOPMENT AND THE RIGHT TO LIFE

Two problems arise in the application of these suggestions for the definition of the moral community to the determination of the precise moral status of a human fetus. Given that the paradigm example of a person is a normal adult human being, then (1) How like this paradigm, in particular how far advanced since conception, does a human being need to be before it begins to have a right to life by virtue, not of being fully a person as of yet, but of being *like* a person? and (2) To what extent, if any, does the fact that a fetus has the *potential* for becoming a person endow it with some of the same rights? Each of these questions requires some comment.

In answering the first question, we need not attempt a detailed consideration of the moral rights of organisms which are not developed enough, aware enough, intelligent enough, etc., to be considered people, but which resemble people in some respects. It does seem reasonable to suggest that the more like a person, in the relevant respects, a being is, the stronger is the case for regarding it as having a right to life, and indeed the stronger its right to life is. Thus we ought to take seriously the suggestion that, insofar as "the human individual develops biologically in a continuous fashion . . . the rights of a human person might develop in the same way." [11] But we must keep in mind that the attributes which are relevant in determining whether or not an entity is enough like a person to be regarded as having some of the same moral rights are no different from those which are relevant to determining whether or not it is fully a person —i.e., are no different from (1)–(5)—and that being genetically human, or having recognizably human facial and other physical features, or detectable brain activity, or the capacity to survive outside the uterus, are simply not among these relevant attributes.

Thus it is clear that even though a seven- or eight-month fetus has features which make it apt to arouse in us almost the same powerful protective instinct as is commonly aroused by a small infant, nevertheless it is not significantly more personlike than is a very small embryo. It is *somewhat* more personlike; it can apparently feel and respond to pain, and it may even have a rudimentary form of consciousness, insofar as its brain is quite active. Nevertheless, it seems safe to say that it is not fully conscious, in the way that an infant of a few months is, and that it cannot reason, or communicate messages of indefinitely many sorts, does not engage in self-motivated activity, and has no self-awareness. Thus, in the

relevant respects, a fetus, even a fully developed one, is considerably less personlike than is the average mature mammal, indeed the average fish. And I think that a rational person must conclude that if the right to life of a fetus is to be based upon its resemblance to a person, then it cannot be said to have any more right to life than, let us say, a newborn guppy (which also seems to be capable of feeling pain), and that a right of that magnitude could never override a woman's right to obtain an abortion, at any stage of her pregnancy.

There may, of course, be other arguments in favor of placing legal limits upon the stage of pregnancy in which an abortion may be performed. Given the relative safety of the new techniques of artificially inducing labor during the third trimester, the danger to the woman's life or health is no longer such an argument. Neither is the fact that people tend to respond to the thought of abortion in the later stages of pregnancy with emotional repulsion, since mere emotional responses cannot take the place of moral reasoning in determining what ought to be permitted. Nor, finally, is the frequently heard argument that legalizing abortion, especially late in the pregnancy, may erode the level of respect for human life, leading, perhaps, to an increase in unjustified euthanasia and other crimes. For this threat, if it is a threat, can be better met by educating people to the kinds of moral distinctions which we are making here than by limiting access to abortion (which limitation may, in its disregard for the rights of women, be just as damaging to the level of respect for human rights).

Thus, since the fact that even a fully developed fetus is not personlike enough to have any significant right to life on the basis of its personlikeness shows that no legal restrictions upon the stage of pregnancy in which an abortion may be performed can be justified on the grounds that we should protect the rights of the older fetus; and since there is no other apparent justification for such restrictions, we may conclude that they are entirely unjustified. Whether or not it would be *indecent* (whatever that means) for a woman in her seventh month to obtain an abortion just to avoid having to postpone a trip to Europe, it would not, in itself, be *immoral,* and therefore it ought to be permitted.

4. POTENTIAL PERSONHOOD AND THE RIGHT TO LIFE

We have seen that a fetus does not resemble a person in any way which can support the claim that it has even some of the same rights. But what about its *potential,* the fact that if nurtured and allowed to develop naturally it will very probably become a person? Doesn't that alone give it at least some right to life? It is hard to deny that the fact that an entity is a potential person is a strong prima facie reason for not destroying it; but we need not conclude from this that a potential person has a right to life, by virtue of that potential. It may be that our feeling that it is better, other things being equal, not to destroy a potential person is better explained by the fact that potential people are still (felt to be) an invaluable resource, not to be lightly squandered. Surely, if every speck of dust were a potential person, we would be much less apt to conclude that every potential person has a right to become actual.

Still, we do not need to insist that a potential person has no right to life whatever. There may well be something immoral, and not just imprudent, about wantonly destroying potential people, when doing so isn't necessary to protect anyone's rights. But even if a potential person does have some prima facie right to life, such a right could not possibly outweigh the right of a woman to obtain an abortion, since the rights of any actual person invariably outweigh those of any potential person, whenever the two conflict. Since this may not be immediately obvious in the case of a human fetus, let us look at another case.

Suppose that our space explorer falls into the hands of an alien culture, whose scientists decide to create a few hundred thousand or more human beings, by breaking his body into its component cells, and using these to create fully developed human beings, with, of course, his genetic code. We may imagine that each of these newly created men will have all of the original man's abilities, skills, knowledge, and so on, and also have an individual self-concept, in short that each of them will be a bona fide (though hardly unique) person. Imagine that the whole project will take only seconds, and that its chances of success are extremely high, and that our explorer knows all of this, and also knows that these people will be treated fairly. I maintain that in such a situation he would have every right to escape if he could, and thus to deprive all of these potential people of their potential lives; for his right to life outweighs all of theirs together, in spite of the fact that they are all genetically human, all innocent, and all have a very high probability of becoming people very soon, if only he refrains from acting.

Indeed, I think he would have a right to escape even if it were not his life which the alien scientists planned to take, but only a year of his freedom, or, indeed, only a day. Nor would he be obligated to stay if he had gotten captured (thus bringing all these people-potentials into existence) because of his own carelessness, or even if he had done so deliberately, knowing the consequences. Regardless of how he got captured, he is not morally obligated to remain in captivity for *any* period of time for the sake of permitting any number of potential people to come into actuality, so great is the margin by which one actual person's right to liberty outweighs whatever right to life even a hundred thousand potential people have. And it seems reasonable to conclude that the rights of a woman will outweigh by a similar margin whatever right to life a fetus may have by virtue of its potential personhood.

Thus, neither a fetus's resemblance to a person, nor its potential for becoming a person provides any basis whatever for the claim that it has any significant right to life. Consequently, a woman's right to protect her health, happiness, freedom, and even her life,[12] by terminating an unwanted pregnancy, will always override whatever right to life it may be appropriate to ascribe to a fetus, even a fully developed one. And thus, in the absence of any overwhelming social need for every possible child, the laws which restrict the right to obtain an abortion, or limit the period of pregnancy during which an abortion may be performed, are a wholly unjustified violation of a woman's most basic moral and constitutional rights.[13]

POSTSCRIPT ON INFANTICIDE

Since the publication of this article, many people have written to point out that my argument appears to justify not only abortion, but infanticide as well. For a new-born infant is not significantly more person-like than an advanced fetus, and consequently it would seem that if the destruction of the latter is permissible so too must be that of the former. Inasmuch as most people, regardless of how they feel about the morality of abortion, consider infanticide a form of murder, this might appear to represent a serious flaw in my argument.

Now, if I am right in holding that it is only people who have a full-fledged right to life, and who can be murdered, and if the criteria of personhood are as I have described them, then it obviously follows that killing a new-born infant isn't murder. It does *not* follow, however, that infanticide is permissible, for two reasons. In the first place, it would be wrong, at least in this country and in this period of history, and other things being equal, to kill a new-born infant, because even if its parents do not want it and would not suffer from its destruction, there are other people who would like to have it, and would, in all probability, be deprived of a great deal of pleasure by its destruction. Thus, infanticide is wrong for reasons analogous to those which make it wrong to wantonly destroy natural resources, or great works of art.

Secondly, most people, at least in this country, value infants and would much prefer that they be preserved, even if foster parents are not immediately available. Most of us would rather be taxed to support orphanages than allow unwanted infants to be destroyed. So long as there are people who want an infant preserved, and who are willing and able to provide the means of caring for it, under reasonably humane conditions, it is, *ceteris parabis*, wrong to destroy it.

But, it might be replied, if this argument shows that infanticide is wrong, at least at this time and in this country, doesn't it also show that abortion is wrong? After all, many people value fetuses, are disturbed by their destruction, and would much prefer that they be preserved, even at some cost to themselves. Furthermore, as a potential source of pleasure to some foster family, a fetus is just as valuable as an infant. There is, however, a crucial difference between the two cases: so long as the fetus is unborn, its preservation, contrary to the wishes of the pregnant woman, violates her rights to freedom, happiness, and self-determination. Her rights override the rights of those who

would like the fetus preserved, just as if someone's life or limb is threatened by a wild animal, his right to protect himself by destroying the animal overrides the rights of those who would prefer that the animal not be harmed.

The minute the infant is born, however, its preservation no longer violates any of its mother's rights, even if she wants it destroyed, because she is free to put it up for adoption. Consequently, while the moment of birth does not mark any sharp discontinuity in the degree to which an infant possesses the right to life, it does mark the end of its mother's right to determine its fate. Indeed, if abortion could be performed without killing the fetus, she would never possess the right to have the fetus destroyed, for the same reasons that she has no right to have an infant destroyed.

On the other hand, it follows from my argument that when an unwanted or defective infant is born into a society which cannot afford and/or is not willing to care for it, then its destruction is permissible. This conclusion will, no doubt, strike many people as heartless and immoral; but remember that the very existence of people who feel this way, and who are willing and able to provide care for unwanted infants, is reason enough to conclude that they should be preserved.

NOTES

1. For example, Roger Wertheimer, who in "Understanding the Abortion Argument" (*Philosophy and Public Affairs,* 1, No. 1 [Fall, 1971], 67–95), argues that the problem of the moral status of abortion is insoluble, in that the dispute over the status of the fetus is not a question of fact at all, but only a question of how one responds to the facts.

2. B. A. Brody, "Abortion and the Law," *The Journal of Philosophy,* 68, No. 12 (June 17, 1971), 357–69.

3. Judith Thomson, "A Defense of Abortion," *Philosophy and Public Affairs,* 1, No. 1 (Fall, 1971), 47–66.

4. I have abbreviated these statements somewhat, but not in a way which affects the argument.

5. John Noonan, "Abortion and the Catholic Church: A Summary History," *Natural Law Forum,* 12 (1967), 125.

6. John Noonan, "Deciding Who is Human," *Natural Law Forum,* 13 (1968), 134.

7. "A Defense of Abortion."

8. We may safely ignore the fact that she might have avoided getting raped, e.g., by carrying a gun, since by similar means you might likewise have avoided getting kidnapped, and in neither case does the victim's failure to take all possible precautions against a highly unlikely event (as opposed to reasonable precautions against a rather likely event) mean that he is morally responsible for what happens.

9. Of course, the principle that it is (always) wrong to kill innocent human beings is in need of many other modifications, e.g., that it may be permissible to do so to save a greater number of other innocent human beings, but we may safely ignore these complications here.

10. From here on, we will use 'human' to mean genetically human, since the moral sense seems closely connected to, and perhaps derived from, the assumption that genetic humanity is sufficient for membership in the moral community.

11. Thomas L. Hayes, "A Biological View," *Commonweal*, 85 (March 17, 1967), 677–78; quoted by Daniel Callahan, in *Abortion, Law, Choice, and Morality* (London: Macmillan & Co., 1970).

12. That is, insofar as the death rate, for the woman, is higher for childbirth than for early abortion.

13. My thanks to the following people, who were kind enough to read and criticize an earlier version of this paper: Herbert Gold, Gene Glass, Anne Lauterbach, Judith Thomson, Mary Mothersill, and Timothy Binkley.

P A U L   R A M S E Y

Protecting the Unborn *

Generally I am not a social activist. Never before have I knowingly testified before a Congressional committee. I came here today because of what I regard as the deep significance of the issue before you, and the seriousness of this hour in the moral history of this nation—indeed, of mankind.

I am here as a private individual who on January 22, 1973, was robbed of his right as a citizen to participate in the public processes by which we as a people determine the outer limits of human community—the limit at the first of life and soon it may also be the limit at the end of life—within which boundaries an equal justice and equal protectability should prevail for all who bear the agreed "signs of life."

These are judgments about the best factual evidence. Physicians are our deputies in applying the criteria for stating that a man has died; but they alone do not set the criteria. In the unlikely event that physicians began to allow people to die all the way through to the end of cellular life (until hair and nails stopped growing) we would find ways of telling them that is not what we mean by the difference between a still living human being and a corpse. I hope we would do the same

in the (more likely) event that physicians began to declare people dead not on the basis of brain-stem death (the current "up-dating"), but when there is only cessation or destruction of the higher cortical functions of the brain (thus certifying as corpses for burial or for organ donation bodies whose hearts still are beating spontaneously and naturally without any external support-system).

So we have legislation or case-law based on it, wise or unwise, traditional or novel, defining death. This legitimates or deputizes physician declarations of death. Professor Alexander M. Capron of the University of Pennsylvania Law School has recently summarized the need for and the propriety of a societal function in regard to new proposals for updating the criteria for death which physicians apply ("To Decide What Death Means," *The New York Times*, News of the Week, Feb. 24, 1974).

BETWEEN DOCTOR AND PATIENT

Now suppose the Supreme Court were to rule that determining the outer limit of the human community short of which there exists a right to life still resident in the dying is a matter falling strictly within the privacy of the doctor-patient relation, or is even to be decided by physician and family members. On this supposition the State legislatures could limit what physicians do in

* From *Commonweal*, Vol. C, No. 13 (1974), pp. 308–14. Reprinted by permission of the publisher and the author.

making life and death decisions only by licensure. Would the Court decision not be deemed an exercise of "raw judicial power"? Would there not be need for a constitutional amendment to restore the setting of criteria to our public and legislative processes? The deputyship of physicians or of any single individual or group of individuals does not extend to fixing the criteria for determining who shall or shall not be deemed a subject of rights. That surely is the people's business. While saying it did not settle that issue, the Supreme Court did just that—all the while proclaiming that when individual human life begins is a murky theological question. For all practical purposes the Court pronounced that no one enters the human community nor has any rights due him until viability. Questionable as that may be, it at least has the virtue of being based on an implicit claim to possess the best factual evidence in the light of modern knowledge. But behind that is, for me, the monstrous claim that the Court decides such matters.

To restore to political and legislative decision-making processes the power to draw an agreed limit as to the first entrance of a human being into the human community is, of course, to load us the people again with a fearsome responsibility. I see no escaping that, since I know of no revelation of such factual judgments. The only thing more fearful would, however, be for such verdicts to be placed in the hands of private individuals, or to be determined by a 7–2 decision of the Court.

Such have always been among the human, all too human decisions silently taken by mankind in the course of our tortuous history. Christian teachings about abortion, for example, have varied over the centuries. But these have varied according to changing judgments about the evidence for believing there is a new life on the human scene. Fancies about 40 and 80 days of gestational life, reliance on quickening, etc. have been grounds in times past for drawing the line between unprotectable and protectable human life. Only in the nineteenth century after the discovery of the ovum did there come to be a credible rational *basis* for either Catholics or the A.M.A. (see q. in *Wade*) to believe that life begins with conception. Before that no one could conceive of "conception."

What has generally been invariant in Western civilization has been the rights and dignity and protection to be accorded to the individual life deemed to be human. Our religious faiths, our philosophies of life, our humanistic visions have to do with justifying and upholding the worth we recognize in or impute to human life. "Subsuming cases" under the value of life—to say, *this* is a human life that has now put in his claim upon the human community to be accorded equal justice and protection—that is a different sort of judgment, and one to be made with fear and trembling. Yet we collectively must decide such matters, and shall continue to do so as long as we have the courage to accept the necessity for together setting the criteria for finding a life to be human life at either end of the scale. It is only the pretense that we can remain civilized after such decisions are left up to the vagaries of private judgment that has to be denied.

I candidly state to you that I am not very hopeful over what people generally through their representatives will decide about these life-and-death issues—in a technologically medical era when "quality of life" is judged to override being alive, and "Choose" has replaced "Choose life" as our moral maxim.

Some comfort may be taken from the fact that over ten years ago the demographer Judith Blake took a look at the anti-permissive abortion sentiment in this country and advised that the only way to accomplish an arbitrary liberty to choose between one life and another in its early stages was to go to the Supreme Court to see whether it would take from the legislatures their power to determine and represent the social compact. I take it, however, that any so-called "pro-lifer" had rather be out-voted than overruled and deprived of voice concerning the limits and the life-and-death terms of our social compact. This, not winning, is what is at stake in the profound alienation of millions and millions and millions of people brought about by the Court's decision in January 1973. I am very sorry that (as reported in the press) Justice Blackmun has received a good deal of "hate mail" since the decision he wrote for the Court. But I pray that he can fathom even in that the moral outrage over being deprived as a people of one of the most important aspects of our together being a people over the course of time. Everyone knows along the pulses that for whomever the bell tolls in these arbitrary life-and-death decisions, now surfaced to consciousness and made "safe" by modern medicine, it could have tolled for him long ago and may yet toll for him at the end of life's span.

With power restored to the people to determine agreed criteria for including anyone in or excluding anyone from the human community, we still may go on our way toward some technological version of the definitional solution practiced by the Nuer tribe in Africa who treat infants born with grave deformities or suffering from genetic anomalies as baby hippopotamuses, accidentally born to humans and, with this labeling, the appropriate action is clear: they gently lay them in the river where they belong. (Mary Douglas, *Purity and Danger: An Analysis of Concepts of Pollution and Taboo.* London: Rutledge and Kegan Paul, 1966, p. 39; E. E. Evans-Pritchard, *Nuer Religion.* Oxford University Press, 1956, p. 84.) A shudder along the spine of every American is surely a fitting reaction to the Court's account of why Western medicine has always been concerned to protect unborn lives. This is to be accounted for, we are told, because Christianity happened to take up the views of the Pythagoreans, a small sect in the Graeco-Roman world, with its Hippocratic oath pledging physicians never to give abortificants. In now overcoming that limitation, we are asked to recall that pagan outlooks in general and medicine in particular in pre-Christian ages opposed neither abortion nor suicide. Passed over in silence is the fact that approval of abortion was also associated with approval of infanticide.

In this there is retrospective prophecy well on the way toward fulfillment today! A doctor at Yale-New Haven Hospital, explaining on television the newly announced policy of benign neglect of defective infants in that medical center, says that to have a life worth living a baby must be "lovable." (Allowing to die is quite different from killing; but there too there should be private decisions privately made only in accord with established and uniform public standards.) Millard S. Everett in his book *Ideals of Life* writes that "no child should be admitted into the society of the living" who suffers "any physical or mental defect that would prevent marriage or would make others tolerate his company only from a sense of mercy . . ." Who is there among us who need not reply to that, "Mercy, me!"? Michael Tooley, professor of philosophy at Stanford University, concludes that while it would be reprehensible to *torture* kittens, infants or other sentient creatures for an hour, it would not be wrong and *no denial of rights* to *kill* babies in the hospital nursery during the first two weeks after medically checking their acceptability, since human babies are no more than kittens and cannot be bearers of rights until they have *self-consciousness* of themselves as persons ("Abortion and Infanticide," *Philosophy and Public Affairs,* Vol. 2, No. 1, Fall 1972). A physician at the University of Virginia writes that he believes a woman's decision to allow a defective baby to die is "her second chance to have an abortion." A fellow theologian, I regret to say, always replies when I use the term "infanticide": I prefer to call it "neo-naticide"! I myself am surprised by none of these views, nor for that matter do I consider them illogical extensions of what we are doing in the matter of abortion, nor are they without some backing. The legal and moral chaos they bespeak stems rather from letting decisions about the criteria for acceptable life and rightful death decisions fall under the arbitration of private individuals.

To say the least, the Court started these retrogressions into technological medical barbarism from which we shall not soon recover, when it exercised no judicial restraint, when it refused to trust the people's moral sensibility and legislative deliberation to achieve rough agreement about who belongs with us in the community of equal-rights bearers. That decision must somehow be reversed and life-and-death standard-setting must again be deprivatized. In doing this, the Court itself rolled back by one stroke of the pen steadily increasing respect for the unborn child in the law itself—propelled onward and upward for decades by our increased knowledge of the humanity of unborn life in the modern period. That knowledge had all but opened a "new age of human childhood." Yet the Court declared that "the unborn have never been recognized in the law *as persons in the whole sense*" (italics added). That, I believe, is demonstrably erroneous. Perhaps the Court meant to say that *the whole law* has never recognized the unborn as legal persons. That I think is true, e.g., "perfection" of standing and of the right to sue for prenatal injury only comes with birth. But "entitlement" to property conveyed to someone *in utero* is *as to right* perfect at that time; further "perfection" here can only mean collecting the cash to which right was fully established at the time of conveyal.

Then there is the N.J. case *Raleigh Fitkin-Paul Morgan Memorial Hospital v. Anderson,* 201 A2d 537, 42 N.J. 421 (1964), perhaps the crest of legal acknowledgment of the unborn as full legal persons in one part of our law. Here in the case of a Jehovah's Witness mother who refused a blood transfusion *and who was pregnant,* the court confronted the alternative of whether to bring this case under (1) the line of cases of *adult* Witnesses which generally respects their First Amendment right of religious liberty and does not compel transfusions even to save physical life, or under (2) the line of cases dealing with infants or minors of Jehovah's Witnesses whose parents refuse to authorize blood transfusions: here generally the courts have taken jurisdiction of the children and authorized the recommended or necessary medical treatment even against the religious conscience of the parents.

Which sort of case was *Fitkin?* Both child and mother would die unless the State intervened. Chief Justice Weintraub wrote for a unanimous court: "We are satisfied that the unborn child is entitled to the law's protection and that an appropriate order should be made to insure blood transfusions to the mother. . . . We have no difficulty in so deciding with respect to the infant child. . . . It is unnecessary to decide the question [of compelling the adult against her conscience] because the welfare of the child and the mother are so intertwined and inseparable that it would be impractical to distinguish between them . . ." Notably in this case the humanity and rights of the unborn child prevailed over the First Amendment rights of the mother, which is a near-absolute in American law, when these were inseparably intertwined. There can scarcely be stronger evidence for the recognition in our law of the unborn as a person in the whole sense, granting that this does not hold for the whole of our law.

In this instance the issues in the case were decided after Mrs. Anderson had left the hospital. Following *Wade,* we can imagine another escape: she could request an elective abortion, thereby prevent our law from successfully treating her child as a legally protectable person, and from her point of view deliver both him and herself intact of soul ("the blood is the life") until the day of the general resurrection! Such is by comparison the measure of the far more trivial reasons conscious persons may now use to disregard the rightful claims of the unborn, if indeed these exist any longer at all following *Wade.* The privatization of abortion decisions means that no one need reach for a First Amendment right to consider overriding the right of the unborn to his or her life. No parity or balancing judgment need now be made, not even one favoring the mother's conscience. Instead, States are now expressly forbidden to bring the rights of the unborn *as such* into consideration. The minimum of regulations that are allowed indirectly expressive of some interest in "the potentiality of life" must every one be reasonably related directly only to the life and health of the mother. She is the one life to be treated as a person in the whole sense; or, I should say, even partially so in the face of the law.

The fetus is not *fully* protectable (not fully a legal person), even after viability! Even *after* viability, the unborn child's right to *life* is not treated as needing to be in parity with the mother's life before being killed. Her health also may outweigh the child's life. The Court said hypothetically: *"If the State is interested* in protecting fetal life after viability, it *may go so far* as to proscribe abortion during that period except when it is necessary to preserve the life *or health* of the mother" (italics added). I suppose most procedures directed toward trying to save a viable baby may have *some* adverse effect on the "health" of the mother, especially as that term is now too broadly interpreted by the medical profession. In an article generally favorable to permissive abortion and the Court's decision, Sissela Bok, lecturer in Medical Ethics at Radcliffe College (the President of Harvard is her consort) pleads: "Every effort must be made by physicians and others to construe the Supreme Court's statement [the foregoing statement] to concern, in effect, *only the life* or *threat to life* of the mother" ("Ethical Problems of Abortion," *Hastings Center Studies,* Vol. 2, No. 1, January 1974, p. 44, n. 18, italics added). In a civilized society, why would Sissela Bok have so to plead? Why should the decision to what extent a *viable* baby should be valued be privatized? Why should physicians be endowed with such arbitrary power over young life that they need to be enjoined not to use it? In this, as well as in its reference to the unborn's capacity for "meaningful" life outside the uterus, the Court steps across the line into "neo-naticide" of *viable* babies.

Still the rightful claims of the unborn are manifest in the ambiguity that remains. There are taxpayers' or orhter sorts of suits going forward in the courts asking that, following *Wade,* jurisdictions that interpreted the Aid to Dependent Children Act to include *pregnant* welfare women be prohibited from doing so—on the ground, I suppose, that these women are not yet "with child" in the law's meaning. Other lower court decisions have held to the contrary that these women cannot constitutionally be refused listing as welfare *mothers.* These latter cases raise the question, How can the state make payments in support of a person who does not exist? to her on account of no human being within? They raise the even more crucial moral question: If ADC payments are made to a woman for one or two months after her pregnancy is affirmed, and she then decides to elect an abortion under other laws that now treat her as the only person involved in that issue, has she not to say the least frustrated the purpose of the ADC payments to her? Surely there now is an intolerable contradiction between the legal personhood and the legal no-personhood ascribed to the unborn.

Such are the perplexities that flow from violating ordinary language in speaking of the unborn, especially in an era in which this usage has the backing of our modern knowledge of the independent, individual humanity of unborn life. We do not ordinarily say a woman is "with embryo" or that she is "carrying a fetus." The attempt to say "fetus" rather than "child" is always an effort at first. We can become habituated to it, of course, just as we now customarily say "interrupt a pregnancy" when we mean abortion, although that expression was once the way doctors spoke of Caesarian sections to save an unborn life that could not be brought to natural birth!

So too my own church has schooled itself to speak in its statement of Social Principles (adopted by General Conference in Atlanta, 1972) of "the sanctity of unborn human life," of "the sacredness of the life and well-being of the mother (sic)" and in the same breath to call for "the removal of abortion from the criminal code, placing it instead under laws relating to other procedures of standard medical practice." If there is unborn human life and if there indeed is a "mother," then abortion is not like any other "standard medical practice." Not until euthanasia or "neo-naticide" becomes "standard." And life-and-death decisions involving lives possessing sanctity have never before in the history of our civil community been believed to be a proper subject for purely privatized choices.[1]

I urge this Committee and the U.S. Senate as a body to move an amendment to the Constitution that would return to the States their legislative power to protect the unborn child from privatized physician-patient decisions about its life or death. Such an amendment would in no way bind in advance the decisions subsequently to be taken by the States. Liberalization of abortion, perhaps its entire decriminalization would still be options open to the States. This would be a minimum remedy, and the Senate may view it as optimal. The thrust of my testimony, however, is to leave the content of an amendment up to the wisdom of the Senate; and for my own part simply to say that almost any remedy at this point in time would be better than no remedy at all. For the thrust of my testimony has been to the point of reversing the privatization *by the Court* of decisions concerning protectable humanity, and toward the right of the people to decide matters of such crucial importance to our social compact through ongoing public debate and the political and legislative processes of this nation. I am willing to have my own views on abortion, and those who agree with them, kept within the public forum; and not enshrine them in the Constitution or in Court-made law—a restraint the pro-permissive abortion advocates were not willing to exercise.

It may be that we have passed the point of no return to that remedy; and that this Committee and the U.S. Senate will judge it wiser to frame an amendment in some fashion substantively protecting the unborn from arbitrary choices. Here there may be an analogy with what followed in the wake of the Dred Scott decision. That decision took from the free States and territories the right and the power to recognize the humanity and protect rights of black people and escaped slaves. We all know the sequel: a tragic civil war, a more perfect union wrought out through carnage and sacrifice, the Fourteenth Amendment imposed on the former slave states. Perhaps that direct approach and substantive constitutional protection of the rights and liberties of black ex-slaves was the better way—instead of trusting the far slower process of political and legislative deliberation in the free states and the gradual erosion of slavery where it existed. Perhaps, then, some form of substantive constitutional protection of unborn human life is needed to overturn the "substantive due process" of a judicial decision that has the effect of turning every question both as to the wisdom and as to the morality of abortion over to private decision-makers.

One must at the least insist on the strong analogy between these two constitutional crises. This nation is in a state of civil and moral strife. Not because "prolife" people are generally speaking unwilling to be outvoted; but because they now have no vote to cast about the extent of the human community in which we are to live. The right to life is so basic to our civil compact that one can imagine the divisions among us leading to open conflict, but for two differences: (1) Because of the more perfect union wrought by the Civil War there now exist no States claiming or actually exercising the sovereignty they once did: another loss of rights and powers formerly reserved to the States cannot now be resisted, and of course ought not to be. (2) In our present case no one has a "property" self-interest to assert or to deny in the case of the unborn child as in the case of slaves. (The claim that a woman has a right to do what she will "with her own body" comes close to a property-claim over the fetus; but perhaps that language ought not to be taken seriously.) For these reasons, our present constitutional crisis is apt to expend itself in moral passion; and, unless there is remedy, further steps privatizing life-and-death decisions and massive alienation from the body politic that has given over to private choices the determination of who belongs with us as a people each counting for one and no one for more than one.

There will be others testifying before you who will object to my placing confidence in the people through their representatives to judge who counts as a human life. This confidence may seem like the Court's touching faith in physicians to make independent medical decisions and not to perform abortions on request, or its privatizing of these decisions and regulating the wisdom and

justice of such decisions only by licensure as if they are matters of standard medical practice and not *also political or societal decisions* about the boundary of the human community of an equal justice to all. My point is simply that physicians are society's deputies in applying the criteria for stating that a new human being has put in his appearance or has passed from among us. My point thereafter is simply that decisions as to the criteria are necessarily human decisions, too; that such decisions as to *the extent* of our social compact must rest with the people and our deliberative processes; that "the buck stops here" and cannot be appealed to anyone's private "revelation" nor ought it to be taken from us and then handed over to a pair of other human beings to decide or to any group less than the total body politic.

Perhaps my confidence that returning the abortion issue to the States may be a sufficient remedy rests back upon my belief that the factual evidence (that is all it can be: a set of factual "good reasons") for the individuated humanity of the unborn child is now quite as clear as the evidence for the human countenance of any black, or of any Senator or of anyone who testifies before you. Before we were so rudely interrupted on January 22, 1973, the weight of the evidence had opened a new era of human childhood, as I have said, and this weight was making its imprint on our law itself. The Court might have taken judicial notice of that evidence, instead of facing away from it. It is certainly the business of State legislatures and now of the Congress to take notice of facts concerning the unborn. There is *reason* enough in our modern knowledge for a constitutional amendment substantively protecting the unborn in some fashion and from some stage in their achievement of individuated humanity.

That would be a maximal remedy; my tentative proposal is a minimal one; Congress should say which is optimal and/or feasible. Taken alone, Senator Mondale's "family impact" test would, I suspect, have led us long ago in the direction of federal marriage and divorce legislation, as now maybe that test should lead us to see the need for some substantive decision-making at the constitutional level or at the federal legislative level on the matter of abortion. But our system is built upon the 50 State jurisdictions; and, because of this, and in spite of some clear disadvantages that has, I incline toward a constitutional solution limited to returning to the States and the people within each of those jurisdictions the question of what we mean by the social compact of life with life.

Professor Paul Freund, the distinguished authority on constitutional law at Harvard University, has said that our system of division of powers—executive, legislative, and judicial —ultimately must rest upon the exercise of what he calls "constitutional morality." The staff of the House Judiciary Committee must have had "constitutional morality" in mind when in its memorandum on the meaning of an impeachable offense it said that a President has the duty "not to abuse his powers or transgress their limits— . . . not to act in derogation of powers vested elsewhere by the Constitution"; and again in its reference to "adverse impact on the system of government" (*N.Y. Times,* February 22, 1974). If that is correct, then impeachment of a President is a remedy for any derogation of powers vested elsewhere by the Constitution; it is a way to insure "constitutional morality."

The fact is, however, that impeachment is no remedy for an exercise of judicial power in derogation of powers vested elsewhere or for decisions of the Court that have an adverse effect on our system of government. It is no remedy for decisions "beyond the call of constitutional duty." That remedy is constitutional amendment; that is the way to insure that "constitutional morality" shall continue constantly to be a restraint upon judicial activism. To our founding Fathers in Constitutional Convention, Professor Edward Corwin has pointed out in his book *The President, Office and Powers,* "the executive magistracy was the natural enemy, the legislative assembly the natural friend, of liberty." The members of the Constitutional Convention, of course, knew nothing of the judicial review that was later to become established. They could not have imagined that the judicial magistracy might become the natural enemy of liberty or of the legislative power in its direction of an ordered liberty. It would be ironical if the natural friend of liberty, our national legislature, should now be aroused to institute impeachment procedures against an "imperial Presidency" for acts in derogation of powers vested elsewhere by the Constitution or for acts having adverse impact on our

system of government, and if then the Congress does not bestir itself to use the remedy of constitutional amendment to correct a decision of an imperial Court that likewise has effects in derogation of powers vested elsewhere by the Constitution and adverse impact on the division between the judicial and the legislative power.

It would be undefendable if impeachment may be used to chasten the executive magistracy and not an amendment to chasten the judicial magistracy; if against the one but not the other "constitutional morality" can be sustained. In this regard, the extent to which a Supreme Court decision is popularly and automatically believed to be the last word on *what the law is* is also a measure of how legislative and amendatory authority has slipped from "the legislative assembly." The Court, of course, in *Bolton* (issued, I suppose, one minute after *Wade*) ceremonially refers to *Wade* in the matter of *what the law is.* There can be no objection to that manner of speaking when the Court does it. But if the people, the State legislatures and the Congress join the chant, that is a certain sign that we wish to crown the judicial magistracy and legitimate its word as our final law. The amendatory procedure is more legitimate still; and it is our chief recourse for insuring that what Freund called "constitutional morality" shall be a force in the interplay of the separate powers in our government.

In any case, anyone who believes that there was need to submit to the States an "equal rights" amendment, going beyond the Fourteenth in guaranteeing equal rights for women, cannot with any consistency object to an amendment going beyond the Fourteenth, and correcting the Court's interpretation of it in *Wade* and *Bolton,* now being submitted to the States for possible adoption into our fundamental law. Object they surely will, with inconsistency and distrust of the people and of their right to amend in this instance. Unhesitatingly, the call should go forth for the Congress to move an amendment that at the least restores to the States legislative power to decide whether and how human life-and-death questions shall be dealt with in the criminal law and in regulation of the fateful actions of physicians.

The opponents of a Life Amendment may finally be correct. The issue is the right of choice or decision. But that must be rightly understood.

The issue is the right of a people through the legislative process to set the "credentials," the criteria, the signs of humanity to be used in making life-and-death decisions. Setting the outer limits of the human community should not be allowed to pass into the hands of private individuals, one, two, or many.

NOTES

1. The stark contradiction in the Methodist statement on the subject—calling for further inquiry—was pointed out by another Methodist Theologian, J. Robert Nelson, Dean of the Boston University School of Theology in "Abortion: What Was Said and Unsaid in Atlanta," (*Response,* July-Aug. 1972, pp. 23–5). The "legislative history" of that statement was that the call for removing abortion from the criminal code was an amendment hurriedly introduced in too brief debate in Atlanta. Hence the contradiction of moral outlooks between that call and the meaning of the language according human life to the unborn, with all that implies. I suggest—if church statements are admitted here—that it would be reasonable for any Senator to find no legislative direction to be discernible in the Methodist statement, unless and until the *Christian* and the *contemporary* modes of thought at war in it are resolved one way or the other. Bishop James Armstrong, in his oral testimony on March 8, entirely resolved the ambiguity, however, and departed from the official statement of his church, when he said that the question of the human rights of the unborn is a question that need not be raised.

ANTONY FLEW

The Principle of Euthanasia *

1

My particular concern here is to deploy a general moral case for the establishment of a legal right to voluntary euthanasia. The first point to emphasize is that the argument is about *voluntary* euthanasia. Neither I nor any other contributor to the present volume advocates the euthanasia of either the incurably sick or the miserably senile except in so far as this is the strong, constant, and unequivocally expressed wish of the afflicted candidates themselves. Anyone, therefore, who dismisses what is in fact being contended on the gratuitously irrelevant grounds that he could not tolerate compulsory euthanasia, may very reasonably be construed as thereby tacitly admitting inability to meet and to overcome the case actually presented.

Second, my argument is an argument for the establishment of a legal right. What I am urging is that any patient whose condition is hopeless and painful, who secures that it is duly and professionally certified as such, and who himself clearly and continuously desires to die should be enabled to do so: and that he should be enabled to do so without his incurring, or his family incurring, or those who provide or administer the means of death incurring, any legal penalty or stigma whatsoever. To advocate the establishment of such a legal right is not thereby to be committed even to saying that it would always be morally justifiable, much less that it would always be morally obligatory, for any patient to exercise this right if he found himself in a position so to do. For a legal right is not as such necessarily and always a moral right; and hence, *a fortiori*, it is not necessarily and always a moral duty to exercise whatever legal rights you may happen to possess.

This is a vital point. It was—to refer first to an issue now at last happily resolved—crucial to the question of the relegalization in Great Britain of homosexual relations between consenting male

adults. Only when it was at last widely grasped, and grasped in its relation to this particular question, could we find the large majorities in both Houses of Parliament by which a liberalizing bill was passed into law. For presumably most members of those majorities not only found the idea of homosexual relations repugnant—as most of us do—but also believed such relations to be morally wrong—as I for one do not. Yet they brought themselves to recognize that neither the repugnance generally felt towards some practice, nor even its actual wrongness if it actually is wrong, by itself constitutes sufficient reason for making or keeping that practice illegal. By the same token it can in the present instance be entirely consistent to urge, both that there ought to be a legal right to voluntary euthanasia, and that it would sometimes or always be morally wrong to exercise that legal right.

Third, the case presented here is offered as a moral one. In developing and defending such a case I shall, of course, have to consider certain peculiarly religious claims. Such claims, however, become relevant here only in so far as they either consitute, or may be thought to constitute, or in so far as they warrant, or may be thought to warrant, conclusions incompatible with those which it is my primary and positive purpose to urge.

Fourth, and finally, this essay is concerned primarily with general principles, not with particular practicalities. I shall not here discuss or —except perhaps quite incidentally—touch upon any questions of comparative detail: questions, for instance, of how a Euthanasia Act ought to be drafted; [1] of what safeguards would need to be incorporated to prevent abuse of the new legal possibilities by those with disreputable reasons for wanting someone else dead; of exactly what and how much should be taken as constituting an unequivocal expression of a clear and constant wish; of the circumstances, if any, in which we ought to take earlier calculated expressions of a patient's desires as constituting still adequate

* From *Euthanasia and the Right to Death,* edited by A. B. Downing. Published by Peter Owen Ltd., London. Reprinted by permission.

grounds for action when at some later time the patient has become himself unable any longer to provide sufficiently sober, balanced, constant and unequivocal expressions of his wishes; and so on.

I propose here as a matter of policy largely to ignore such particular and practical questions. This is not because I foolishly regard them as unimportant, or irresponsibly dismiss them as dull. Obviously they could become of the most urgent interest. Nor yet is it because I believe that my philosophical cloth disqualifies me from contributing helpfully to any down-to-earth discussions. On the contrary, I happen to be one of those numerous academics who are convinced, some of them correctly, that they are practical and businesslike men! The decisive reason for neglecting these vital questions of detail here in, and in favour of, a consideration of the general principle of the legalization of voluntary euthanasia is that they are all secondary to that primary issue. For no such subordinate question can properly arise as relevantly practical until and unless the general principle is conceded. Some of these practical considerations are in any event dealt with by other contributors to this volume.

2

So what can be said in favour of the principle? There are two main, and to my mind decisive, moral reasons. But before deploying these it is worth pausing for a moment to indicate why the onus of proof does not properly rest upon us. It may seem as if it does, because we are proposing a change in the present order of things; and it is up to the man who wants a change to produce the reasons for making whatever change he is proposing. This most rational principle of conservatism is in general sound. But here it comes into conflict with the overriding and fundamental liberal principle. It is up to any person and any institution wanting to prevent anyone from doing anything he wishes to do, or to compel anyone to do anything he does not wish to do, to provide positive good reason to justify interference. The question should therefore be: *not* 'Why should people be given this new legal right?'; *but* 'Why should people in this matter be restrained by law from doing what they want?'

Yet even if this liberal perspective is accepted, as it too often is not, and even if we are able to

dispose of any reasons offered in defence of the present legal prohibitions, still the question would arise, whether the present state of the law represents a merely tiresome departure from sound liberal principles of legislation, or whether it constitutes a really substantial evil. It is here that we have to offer our two main positive arguments.

(1) First, there are, and for the foreseeable future will be, people afflicted with incurable and painful diseases who urgently and fixedly want to die quickly. The first argument is that a law which tries to prevent such sufferers from achieving this quick death, and usually thereby forces other people who care for them to watch their pointless pain helplessly, is a very cruel law. It is because of this legal cruelty that advocates of euthanasia sometimes speak of euthanasia as 'mercy-killing.' In such cases the sufferer may be reduced to an obscene parody of a human being, a lump of suffering flesh eased only by intervals of drugged stupor. This, as things now stand, must persist until at last every device of medical skill fails to prolong the horror.

(2) Second, a law which insists that there must be no end to this process—terminated only by the overdue relief of 'death by natural causes'—is a very degrading law. In the present context the full force of this second reason may not be appreciated immediately, if at all. We are so used to meeting appeals to 'the absolute value of human personality,' offered as the would-be knockdown objection to any proposal to legalize voluntary euthanasia, that it has become hard to realize that, in so far as we can attach some tolerably precise meaning to the key phrase, this consideration would seem to bear in the direction precisely opposite to that in which it is usually mistaken to point. For the agonies of prolonged terminal illness can be so terrible and so demoralizing that the person is blotted out in ungovernable nerve reactions. In such cases as this, to meet the patient's longing for death is a means of showing for human personality that respect which cannot tolerate any ghastly travesty of it. So our second main positive argument, attacking the present state of the law as degrading, derives from a respect for the wishes of the individual person, a concern for human dignity, an unwillingness to let the animal pain disintegrate the man.

Our first main positive argument opposes the present state of the law, and of the public opinion which tolerates it, as cruel. Often and appositely this argument is supported by contrasting the tenderness which rightly insists that on occasion dogs and horses must be put out of their misery, with the stubborn refusal in any circumstances to permit one person to assist another in cutting short his suffering. The cry is raised, 'But people are not animals!' Indeed they are not. Yet this is precisely not a ground for treating people worse than brute animals. Animals are like people, in that they too can suffer. It is for this reason that both can have a claim on our pity and our mercy.[2]

But people are also more than brute animals. They can talk and think and wish and plan. It is this that makes it possible to insist, as we do, that there must be no euthanasia unless it is the firm considered wish of the person concerned. People also can, and should, have dignity as human beings. That is precisely why we are urging that they should be helped and not hindered when they wish to avoid or cut short the often degrading miseries of incurable disease or, I would myself add, of advanced senile decay.

3

In the first section I explained the scope and limitations of the present chapter. In the second I offered—although only after suggesting that the onus of proof in this case does not really rest on the proposition—my two main positive reasons in favour of euthanasia. It is time now to begin to face, and to try to dispose of, objections. This is the most important phase in the whole exercise. For to anyone with any width of experience and any capacity for compassion the positive reasons must be both perfectly obvious and strongly felt. The crucial issue is whether or not there are decisive, overriding objections to these most pressing reasons of the heart.

(1) Many of the objections commonly advanced, which are often mistaken to be fundamental, are really objections only to a possible specific manner of implementing the principle of voluntary euthanasia. Thus it is suggested that if the law permitted doctors on occasion to provide their patients with means of death, or where necessary to do the actual killing, and they did so, then the doctors who did either of these things would be violating the Hippocratic Oath, and the prestige of and public confidence in the medical profession would be undermined.

As to the Hippocratic Oath, this makes two demands which in the special circumstances we have in mind may become mutually contradictory. They then cannot both be met at the same time. The relevant section reads: 'I will use treatments to help the sick according to my ability and judgment, but never with a view to injury and wrong-doing. I will not give anyone a lethal dose if asked to do so, nor will I suggest such a course.'[3] The fundamental undertaking 'to help the sick according to my ability and judgment' may flatly conflict with the further promise not to 'give anyone a lethal dose if asked to do so.' To observe the basic undertaking a doctor may have to break the further promise. The moral would, therefore, appear to be: not that the Hippocratic Oath categorically and unambiguously demands that doctors must have no dealings with voluntary euthanasia; but rather that the possible incompatibility in such cases of the different directives generated by two of its logically independent clauses constitutes a reason for revising that Oath.

As to the supposed threat to the prestige of and to our confidence in the medical profession, I am myself inclined to think that the fears expressed are—in more than one dimension—disproportionate to the realities. But whatever the truth about this the whole objection would bear only against proposals which permitted or required doctors to do, or directly to assist in, the actual killing. This is not something which is essential to the whole idea of voluntary euthanasia, and the British Euthanasia Society's present draft bill is so formulated as altogether to avoid this objection. It is precisely such inessential objections as this which I have undertaken to eschew in this essay, in order to consider simply the general principle.

(2) The first two objections which do really bear on this form a pair. One consists in the contention that there is no need to be concerned about the issue, since in fact there are not any, or not many, patients who when it comes to the point want to die quickly. The other bases the same complacent conclusion on the claim that in fact, in the appropriate cases, doctors already mercifully take the law into their own hands. These two comfortable doctrines are, like many other similarly reassuring bromides, both entirely wrong and rather shabby.

(a) To the first the full reply would probably

have to be made by a doctor, for a medical layman can scarcely be in a position to make an estimate of the number of patients who would apply and could qualify for euthanasia.[4] But it is quite sufficient for our immediate purposes to say two things. First, there can be few who have reached middle life, and who have not chosen to shield their sensibilities with some impenetrable carapace of dogma, who cannot recall at least one case of an eager candidate for euthanasia from their own experience—even from their own peacetime experience only. If this statement is correct, as my own inquiries suggest that it is, then the total number of such eager candidates must be substantial. Second, though the need for enabling legalization becomes progressively more urgent the greater the numbers of people personally concerned, I wish for myself to insist that it still matters very much indeed if but one person who would have decided for a quick death is forced to undergo a protracted one.

(b) To the second objection, which admits that there are many cases where euthanasia is indicated, but is content to leave it to the doctors to defy the law, the answer is equally simple. First, it is manifestly not true that all doctors are willing on the appropriate occasions either to provide the means of death or to do the killing. Many, as they are Roman Catholics, are on religious grounds absolutely opposed to doing so. Many others are similarly opposed for other reasons, or by force of training and habit. And there is no reason to believe that among the rest the proportion of potential martyrs is greater than it is in any other secular occupational group. Second, it is entirely wrong to expect the members of one profession as a regular matter of course to jeopardize their whole careers by breaking the criminal law in order to save the rest of us the labour and embarrassment of changing that law.

Here I repeat two points made to me more than once by doctor friends. First, if a doctor were convinced he ought to provide euthanasia in spite of the law, it would often be far harder for him to do so undetected than many laymen think, especially in our hospitals. Second, the present attitude of the medical establishment is such that if a doctor did take the chance, was caught and brought to trial, and even if the jury, as they well might, refused to convict, still he must expect to face complete professional disaster.

(3) The next two objections, which in effect bear on the principle, again form a pair. The first pair had in common the claim that the facts were such that the question of legislative action need not arise. The second pair are alike in that whereas both might appear to be making contentions of fact, in reality we may have in each a piece of exhortation or of metaphysics masquerading as an empirical proposition.

(a) Of this second relevant pair the first suggests that there is no such thing as an incurable disease. This implausible thesis becomes more intelligible, though no more true, when we recall how medical ideologues sometimes make proclamations: 'Modern medicine cannot recognize any such thing as a disease which is incurable'; and the like. Such pronouncements may sound like reports on the present state of the art. It is from this resemblance that they derive their peculiar idiomatic point. But the advance of medicine has not reached a stage where all diseases are curable. And no one seriously thinks that it has. At most this continuing advance has suggested that we need never despair of finding cures *some day*. But this is not at all the same thing as saying, what is simply not true, that *even now* there is no condition which is at any stage incurable. This medical ideologue's slogan has to be construed as a piece of exhortation disguised for greater effect as a paradoxical statement of purported fact. It may as such be instructively compared with certain favourite educationalists' paradoxes: 'We do not teach subjects, we teach children!'; or 'There are no bad children, only bad teachers!'

(b) The second objection of this pair is that no one can ever be certain that the condition of any particular patient is indeed hopeless. This is more tricky. For an objection of this form might be given two radically different sorts of content. Yet it would be easy and is common to slide from one interpretation to the other, and back again, entirely unwittingly.

Simply and straightforwardly, such an objection might be made by someone whose point was that judgments of incurability are, as a matter of purely contingent fact, so unreliable that no one has any business to be certain, or to claim to know, that anyone is suffering from an incurable affliction. This contention would relevantly be backed by appealing to the alleged fact that judgments that 'this case is hopeless, *period*' are far more frequently proven to have been mistaken than judgments that, for instance, 'this patient will recover fully, *provided that* he undergoes the appropriate operation.' This naive objector's point could be made out, or decisively refuted, only by reference to quantitative studies of the actual relative reliabilities and unreliabilities of different sorts of medical judgments. So unless and until such quantitative empirical studies are actually made, and unless and until their results are shown to bear upon the question of euthanasia in the way suggested, there is no grounded and categorical objection here to be met.

But besides this first and straightforwardly empirical interpretation there is a second interpretation of another quite different sort. Suppose someone points to an instance, as they certainly could and well might, where some patient whom all the doctors had pronounced to be beyond hope nevertheless recovers, either as the result of the application of new treatment derived from some swift and unforeseen advance in medical science, or just through nature taking its unexpected course. This happy but chastening outcome would certainly demonstrate that the doctors concerned had on this occasion been mistaken; and hence that, though they had sincerely claimed to know the patient's condition to have been incurable, they had not really known this. The temptation is to mistake it that such errors show that no one ever really knows. It is this perfectly general contention, applied to the particular present case of judgments of incurability, which constitutes the second objection in its second interpretation. The objector seizes upon the point that even the best medical opinion turns out sometimes to have been wrong (as here). He then urges, simply because doctors thus prove occasionally to have been mistaken (as here) and because it is always—theoretically if not practically—possible that they may be mistaken again the next time, that therefore none of them ever really knows (at least in such cases). Hence, he concludes, there is after all no purchase for the idea of voluntary euthanasia. For this notion presupposes that there are patients recognizably suffering from conditions known to be incurable.

The crux to grasp about this contention is that, notwithstanding that it may be presented and pressed as if it were somehow especially relevant to one particular class of judgments, in truth it applies—if it applies at all—absolutely generally. The issue is thus revealed as not medical but metaphysical. If it follows that if someone is ever mistaken then he never really knows, and still more if it follows that if it is even logically possible that he may be mistaken then he never really knows, then, surely, the consequence must be that none of us ever does know—not *really*. (When a metaphysician says that something is never really such and such, what he really means is that it very often is, *really*.) For it is of the very essence of our cognitive predicament that we do all sometimes make mistakes; while always it is at least theoretically possible that we may. Hence the argument, if it holds at all, must show that knowledge, *real* knowledge, is for all us mortal men for ever unattainable.

What makes the second of the present pair of objections tricky to handle is that it is so easy to pass unwittingly from an empirical to a metaphysical interpretation. We may fail to notice, or noticing may fail convincingly to explain, how an empirical thesis has degenerated into metaphysics, or how metaphysical misconceptions have corrupted the medical judgment. Yet, once these utterly different interpretations have been adequately distinguished, two summary comments should be sufficient.

First, in so far as the objection is purely metaphysical, to the idea that *real* knowledge is possible, it applies absolutely generally; or not at all. It is arbitrary and irrational to restrict it to the examination of the principle of voluntary euthanasia. If doctors never really know, we presumably have no business to rely much upon any of their judgments. And if, for the same metaphysical reasons, there is no knowledge to be had anywhere, then we are all of us in the same case about everything. This may be as it may be, but it is nothing in particular to the practical business in hand.

Second, when the objection takes the form of a pretended refusal to take any decision in matters of life and death on the basis of a judgment which theoretically might turn out to have been mistaken, it is equally unrealistic and arbitrary. It is one thing to claim that judgments of incurability are peculiarly fallible: if that suggestion were to be proved to be correct. It is quite another to claim that it is improper to take vital decisions on the basis of sorts of judgment which either are in principle fallible, or even prove occasionally in fact to have been wrong. It is an inescapable feature of the human condition that no one is infallible about anything, and there is no sphere of life in which mistakes do not occur. Nevertheless we cannot as agents avoid, even in matters of life and death and more than life and death, making decisions to act or to abstain. It is only necessary and it is only possible to insist on ordinarily strict standards of warranted assertability, and on ordinarily exacting rather than obsessional criteria of what is beyond reasonable doubt.

Of course this means that mistakes will sometimes be made. This is in practice a corollary of the uncontested fact that infallibility is not an option. To try to ignore our fallibility is unrealistic, while to insist on remembering it only in the context of the question of voluntary euthanasia is arbitrary. Nor is it either realistic or honourable to attempt to offload the inescapable burdens of practical responsibility, by first claiming that we never really *know,* and then pretending that a decision not to act is somehow a decision which relieves us of all proper responsibility for the outcome.

(4) The two pairs of relevant objections so far considered have both been attempts in different ways to show that the issue does not, or at any rate need not, arise as a practical question. The next concedes that the question does arise and is important, but attempts to dispose of it with the argument that what we propose amounts to the legalization, in certain circumstances, of murder, or suicide, or both; and that this cannot be right because murder and suicide are both gravely wrong always. Now even if we were to concede all the rest it would still not follow, because something is gravely wrong in morals, that there ought to be a law against it; and that we are wrong to try to change the law as it now subsists. We have already urged that the onus of proof must always rest on the defenders of any restriction.

(a) In fact the rest will not do. In the first place, if the law were to be changed as we want, the present legal definition of 'murder' would at the same time have to be so changed that it no longer covered the provision of euthanasia for a patient who had established that it was his legal right. 'Does this mean,' someone may indignantly protest, 'that right and wrong are created by Acts of Parliament?' Emphatically, yes: and equally emphatically, no. Yes indeed, if what is intended is *legal* right and *legal* offence. What is meant by the qualification 'legal' if it is not that these rights are the rights established and sanctioned by the law? Certainly not, if what is intended is *moral* right and *moral* wrong. Some moral rights happen to be at the same time legal rights, and some moral wrongs similarly also constitute offences against the law. But, notoriously, legislatures may persist in denying moral rights; while, as I insisted earlier, not every moral wrong either is or ought to be forbidden and penalized by law.

Well then, if the legal definition of 'murder' can be changed by Act of Parliament, would euthanasia nevertheless be murder, morally speaking? This amounts to asking whether administering euthanasia legally to someone who is incurably ill, and who has continually wanted it, is in all relevant respects similar to, so to speak, a standard case of murder; and whether therefore it is to be regarded morally as murder. Once the structure of the question is in this way clearly displayed it becomes obvious that the cases are different in at least three important respects. First, whereas the murder victim is (typically) killed against his will, a patient would be given or assisted in obtaining euthanasia only if he steadily and strongly desired to die. Second, whereas the murderer kills his victim, treating him usually as a mere object for disposal, in euthanasia the object of the exercise would be to save someone, at his own request, from needless suffering, to prevent the degradation of a human person. Third, whereas the murderer by his action defies the law, the man performing euthanasia would be acting according to law, helping another man to secure what the law allowed him.

It may sound as if that third clause goes back on the earlier repudiation of the idea that moral right and wrong are created by Act of Parliament. That is not so. For we are not saying that this action would now be justifiable, or at least not murder morally, simply because it was now permitted by the law; but rather that the change in the law would remove one of possible reasons for moral objection. The point is this: that although the fact that something is enjoined, permitted, or forbidden by law does not necessarily make it right, justifiable, or wrong morally, nevertheless the fact that something is enjoined or forbidden by a law laid down by established authority does constitute one moral reason for obedience. So a doctor who is convinced that the objects of the Euthanasia Society are absolutely right should at least hesitate to take the law into his own hands, not only for prudential but also for moral reasons. For to defy the law is, as it were, to cast your vote against constitutional procedures and the rule of law, and these are the foundations and framework of any tolerable civilized society. (Consider here the injunction posted by some enlightened municipal authorities upon their public litter bins: 'Cast your vote here for a tidy New York!'—or wherever it may be.)

Returning to the main point, the three differences which we have just noticed are surely sufficient to require us to refuse to assimilate legalized voluntary euthanasia to the immoral category of murder. But to insist on making a distinction between legalized voluntary euthanasia and murder is not the same thing as, nor does it by itself warrant, a refusal to accept that both are equally immoral. What an appreciation of these three differences, but crucially of the first, should do is to suggest that we ought to think of such euthanasia as a special case not of murder but of suicide. Let us therefore examine the second member of our third pair of relevant objections. (b) This objection was that to legalize voluntary euthanasia would be to legalize, in certain conditions, the act of assisting suicide. The question therefore arises: 'Is suicide always morally wrong?'

The purely secular considerations usually advanced and accepted are not very impressive. First, it is still sometimes urged that suicide is unnatural, in conflict with instinct, a breach of the putative law of self-preservation. All arguments of this sort, which attempt directly to deduce conclusions about what *ought* to be from premises stating, or mis-stating, only what *is* are—surely—unsound: they involve what philosophers label, appropriately, the 'Naturalistic Fallacy.' There is also a peculiar viciousness about appealing to what is supposed to be a descriptive law of nature to provide some justification for the prescription to obey that supposed law. For if the law really obtained as a description of what always and unavoidably happens, then there would be no point in prescribing that it should; whereas if the descriptive law does not

in fact hold, then the basis of the supposed justification does not exist.[5] Furthermore, even if an argument of this first sort could show that suicide is always immoral, it could scarcely provide a reason for insisting that it ought also to be illegal.

Second, it is urged that the suicide by his act deprives other people of the services which he might have rendered them had he lived longer. This can be a strong argument, especially where the suicide has clear, positive family or public obligations. It is also an argument which, even in a liberal perspective, can provide a basis for legislation. But it is irrelevant to the circumstances which advocates of the legalization of voluntary euthanasia have in mind. In such circumstances as these, there is no longer any chance of being any use to anyone, and if there is any family or social obligation it must be all the other way—to end your life when it has become a hopeless burden both to yourself and to others.

Third, it is still sometimes maintained that suicide is in effect murder—'self-murder.' To this, offered in a purely secular context, the appropriate and apparently decisive reply would seem to be that by parity of reasoning marriage is really adultery—'own-wife-adultery.' For, surely, the gravamen of both distinctions lies in the differences which such paradoxical assimilations override. It is precisely because suicide is the destruction of oneself (by one's own choice), while murder is the destruction of somebody else (against his wishes), that the former can be, and is, distinguished from the latter.

Yet there is a counter to this own-wife-adultery-move. It begins by insisting, rightly, that sexual relations—which are what is common to both marriage and adultery—are not in themselves wrong: the crucial question is, 'Who with?' It then proceeds to claim that what is common to both murder and suicide is the killing of a human being; and here the questions of 'Which one?' or 'By whom?' are not, morally, similarly decisive. Finally appeal may be made, if the spokesman is a little old-fashioned, to the Sixth Commandment, or if he is in the contemporary swim, to the Principle of the Absolute Sanctity of Human Life.

The fundamental difficulty which confronts anyone making this counter move is that of finding a formulation for his chosen principle about

the wrongness of all killing, which is both sufficiently general not to appear merely question-
begging in its application to the cases in dispute,
and which yet carries no consequences that the
spokesman himself is not prepared to accept.
Thus, suppose he tries to read the Sixth Commandment as constituting a veto on any killing
of human beings. Let us waive here the immediate scholarly objections: that such a reading involves accepting the mistranslation 'Thou shalt
not kill' rather than the more faithful 'Thou shalt
do no murder'; and that neither the children of
Israel nor even their religious leaders construed
this as a law forbidding all war and all capital
punishment.[6] The question remains whether our
spokesman himself is really prepared to say that
all killing, without any exception, is morally
wrong.

It is a question which has to be pressed, and
which can only be answered by each man for
himself. Since I cannot give your answer, I can
only say that I know few if any people who would
sincerely say 'Yes.' But as soon as any exceptions
or qualifications are admitted, it becomes exces-
sively difficult to find any presentable principle
upon which these can be admitted while still excluding suicide and assistance to suicide in a case
of euthanasia. This is not just because, generally,
once any exceptions or qualifications have been
admitted to any rule it becomes hard or impossible not to allow others. It is because, particularly,
the case for excluding suicide and assisting suicide from the scope of any embargo on killing
people is so strong that only some absolutely universal rule admitting no exceptions of any sort
whatever could have the force convincingly to
override it.

Much the same applies to the appeal to the
Principle of the Absolute Sanctity of Human
Life. Such appeals were continually made by conservatives—many of them politically not Conservative but Socialist—in opposition to the recent efforts to liberalize the British abortion laws.
Such conservatives should be, and repeatedly
were, asked whether they are also opponents of
all capital punishment and whether they think
that it is always wrong to kill in a 'just war.' (In
fact none of those in Parliament could honestly
have answered 'Yes' to both questions.) In the
case of abortion their position could still be saved
by inserting the qualification 'innocent,' a qualifi-

cation traditionally made by cautious moralists
who intend to rest on this sort of principle. But
any such qualification, however necessary, must
make it almost impossible to employ the principle
thus duly qualified to proscribe all suicide. It
would be extraordinarily awkward and far-
fetched to condemn suicide or assisting suicide as
'taking an innocent life.'

Earlier in the present subsection I described
the three arguments I have been examining as
secular. This was perhaps misleading. For all
three are regularly used by religious people: indeed versions of all three are to be found in St
Thomas Aquinas's *Summa Theologica,* the third
being there explicitly linked with St Augustine's
laboured interpretation of the Sixth Commandment to cover suicide.[7] And perhaps the incon-
gruity of trying to make the amended Principle
of the Absolute Sanctity of Innocent Human Life
yield a ban on suicide is partly to be understood
as a result of attempting to derive from secular-
ized premises conclusions which really depend
upon a religious foundation. But the next two
arguments are frankly and distinctively religious.

The first insists that human beings are God's
property: 'It is our duty to take care of God's
property entrusted to our charge—our souls and
bodies. They belong not to us but to God'; [8]
'Whoever takes his own life sins against God,
even as he who kills another's slave sins against
that slave's master'; [9] and 'Suicide is the destruction of the temple of God and a violation of the
property rights of Jesus Christ.' [10]

About this I restrict myself to three comments
here. First, as it stands, unsupplemented by appeal to some other principle or principles, it must
apply, if it applies at all, equally to *all* artificial
and intentional shortening *or* lengthening of any
human life, one's own *or* that of anyone else.
Alone and unsupplemented it would commit one
to complete quietism in all matters of life and
death; for all interference would be interference
with someone else's property. Otherwise one
must find further particular moral revelations by
which to justify capital punishment, war, medicine, and many other such at first flush impious
practices. Second, it seems to presuppose that a
correct model of the relation between man and
God is that of slave and slave-master, and that
respect for God's property ought to be the fundamental principle of morals. It is perhaps signifi-

cant that it is to this image that St Thomas and the pagan Plato, in attacking suicide, both appeal. This attempt to derive not only theological but all obligations from the putative theological fact of Creation is a commonplace of at least one tradition of moral theology. In this derivation the implicit moral premise is usually that unconditional obedience to a Creator, often considered as a very special sort of owner, is the primary elemental obligation.[11] Once this is made explicit it does not appear to be self-evidently true; nor is it easy to see how a creature in absolute ontological dependence could be the genuinely responsible subject of obligations to his infinite Creator.[12] Third, this objection calls to mind one of the sounder sayings of the sinister Tiberius: 'If the gods are insulted let them see to it themselves.' This remark is obviously relevant only to the question of legalization, not to that of the morality or the prudence of the action itself.

The second distinctively religious argument springs from the conviction that God does indeed see to it Himself, with a penalty of infinite severity. If you help someone to secure euthanasia, 'You are sending him from the temporary and comparatively light suffering of this world to the eternal suffering of hell.' Now if this appalling suggestion could be shown to be true it would provide the most powerful moral reason against helping euthanasia in any way, and for using any legislative means which might save people from suffering a penalty so inconceivably cruel. It would also be the strongest possible prudential reason against 'suiciding oneself.' [13] (Though surely anyone who knowingly incurred such a penalty would by that very action prove himself to be genuinely of unsound mind; and hence not *justly* punishable at all. Not that a Being contemplating such unspeakable horrors could be expected to be concerned with justice!)

About this second, peculiarly religious, argument there is, it would seem, little to be done except: either simply to concede that for anyone holding this belief it indeed is reasonable to oppose euthanasia, and to leave it at that; or, still surely conceding this, to attempt to mount a general offensive against the whole system of which it forms a part.

(5) The final objection is one raised, with appropriate modifications, by the opponents of every reform everywhere. It is that even granting that the principle of the reform is excellent it would, if adopted, lead inevitably to something worse; and so we had much better not make any change at all. Thus G. K. Chesterton pronounced that the proponents of euthanasia now seek only the death of those who are a nuisance to themselves, but soon it will be broadened to include those who are a nuisance to others.[14] Such cosy arguments depend on two assumptions: that the supposedly inevitable consequences are indeed evil and substantially worse than the evils the reform would remove; and that the supposedly inevitable consequences really are inevitable consequences.

In the present case we certainly can grant the first assumption, if the consequence supposed is taken to be large-scale legalized homicide in the Nazi manner. But whatever reason is there for saying that this would, much less inevitably must, follow? For there are the best of reasons for insisting that there is a world of difference between legalized voluntary euthanasia and such legalized mass-murder. Only if public opinion comes to appreciate their force will there be any chance of getting the reform we want. Then we should have no difficulty, in alliance doubtless with all our present opponents, in blocking any move to legalize murder which might conceivably arise from a misunderstanding of the case for voluntary euthanasia. Furthermore, it is to the point to remind such objectors that the Nazi atrocities they probably have in mind were in fact not the result of any such reform, but were the work of people who consciously repudiated the whole approach to ethics represented in the argument of the present essay. For this approach is at once human and humanitarian. It is concerned above all with the reduction of suffering; but concerned at the same time with other values too, such as human dignity and respect for the wishes of the individual person. And always it is insistent that morality should not be 'left in the dominion of vague feeling or inexplicable internal conviction, but should be . . . made a matter of reason and calculation.' [15]

NOTES

1. See Appendix.
2. Thus Jeremy Bentham, urging that the legislator must not neglect animal sufferings, insists that the 'question is not "Can they *reason?*" nor "Can they *talk?*" but "Can they *suffer?*" ' (*Principles of Morals and Legislation*, Chap. XVII, n.)

3. The Greek text is most easily found in *Hippocrates and the Fragments of Heracleitus,* ed. W. H. S. Jones and E. T. Withington for the Loeb series (Harvard Univ. Pr. and Heinemann), Vol. I, p. 298. The translation in the present essay is mine.

4. See Downing, pp. 20–1; also pp. 23–4 for his reference to Professor Hinton's work, *Dying* (Pelican, 1967).

5. I have argued this kind of point more fully in *Evolutionary Ethics* (London: Macmillan, 1967). See Chap. IV, 'From *Is* to *Ought.*'

6. See, f.i., Joseph Fletcher, *Morals and Medicine* (1954; Gollancz, 1955), pp. 195–6. I recommend this excellent treatment by a liberal Protestant of a range of questions in moral theology too often left too far from liberal Roman Catholics.

7. Part II: Q. 64, A5. The Augustine reference is to *The City of God,* I, 20. It is worth comparing, for ancient Judaic attitudes, E. Westermarck's *Origin and Development of the Moral Ideas,* Vol. I, pp. 246–7.

8. See the Rev. G. J. MacGillivray, 'Suicide and Euthanasia,' p. 10; a widely distributed Catholic Truth Society pamphlet.

9. Aquinas, loc. cit.

10. Koch-Preuss, *Handbook of Moral Theology,* Vol. II, p. 76. This quotation has been taken from Fletcher, op. cit., p. 192.

11. Cf., for convenience, MacGillivray, loc. cit.; and for a Protestant analogue the Bishop of Exeter quoted by P. Nowell-Smith in *Ethics* (Penguin, 1954), pp. 37–8 *n.*

12. I have developed this contention in *God and Philosophy* (Hutchinson, 1966), §§ 2.34 ff.

13. This rather affected-sounding gallicism is adopted deliberately: if you believe, as I do, that suicide is not always and as such wrong, it is inappropriate to speak of 'committing suicide'; just as correspondingly if you believe, as I do not, that (private) profit is wrong, it becomes apt to talk of those who 'commit a profit.'

14. I take this quotation, too, from Fletcher, op. cit., p. 201: it originally appeared in *The Digest* (Dec. 23, 1937). Another, much more recent specimen of this sort of obscurantist flim-flam may be found in Lord Longford's speech to the House of Lords against Mr David Steel's Abortion Bill as originally passed by the Commons. Lord Longford (formerly Pakenham) urged that if that bill were passed, we might see the day when senile members of their lordships' House were put down willy-nilly.

15. J. S. Mill's essay on Bentham quoted in F. R. Leavis, *Mill on Bentham and Coleridge* (Chatto & Windus, 1950), p. 92.

YALE KAMISAR

Euthanasia Legislation: Some Non-Religious Objections *

A book by Glanville Williams, *The Sanctity of Life and the Criminal Law,*[1] once again brought to the fore the controversial topic of euthanasia, more popularly known as 'mercy-killing.' In keeping with the trend of the euthanasia movement over the past generation, Williams concentrates his efforts for reform on the *voluntary* type of euthanasia, for example the cancer victim begging for death, as opposed to the *involuntary* variety—that is, the case of the congenital idiot, the permanently insane or the senile.

When a legal scholar of Williams's stature joins the ranks of such formidable law thinkers as America's Herbert Wechsler and the late

Jerome Michael, and England's Hermann Mannheim in approving voluntary euthanasia at least in certain circumstances, a major exploration of the bases for the euthanasia prohibition seems in order. This need is underscored by the fact that Williams's book arrived on the scene soon after the stir caused by the plea for voluntary euthanasia contained in a book by a brilliant American Anglican clergyman.[2]

The Law on the Books condemns all mercy-killings.[3] That this has a substantial deterrent effect, even its harshest critics admit. Of course, it does not stamp out all mercy-killings, just as murder and rape provisions do not stamp out all murder and rape, but presumably it does impose a substantially greater responsibility on physicians and relatives in a euthanasia situation and

* From *Minnesota Law Review.* Vol. 4 (1958). Reprinted by permission of the publisher and the author.

turns them away from significantly more doubtful cases than would otherwise be the practice under any proposed euthanasia legislation to date. When a mercy-killing occurs, however, The Law in Action is as malleable as The Law on the Books is uncompromising. The high incidence of failures to indict, acquittals, suspended sentences and reprieves lends considerable support to the view that:

If the circumstances are so compelling that the defendant ought to violate the law, then they are compelling enough for the jury to violate their oaths. The law does well to declare these homicides unlawful. It does equally well to put no more than the sanction of an oath in the way of an acquittal.

The complaint has been registered that 'the prospect of a sentimental acquittal cannot be reckoned as a certainty.' [4] Of course not. The defendant is not always *entitled* to a sentimental acquittal. The few American convictions cited for the proposition that the present state of affairs breeds 'inequality' in application may be cited as well for the proposition that it is characterized by elasticity and flexibility. In any event, if inequality of application suffices to damn a particular provision of the criminal law, we might as well tear up all our codes—beginning with the section on chicken stealing.

The existing law on euthanasia is hardly perfect. But if it is not too good, neither, as I have suggested, is it much worse than the rest of the criminal law. At any rate, the imperfections of existing law are not cured by Williams's proposal. Indeed, I believe adoption of his views would add more difficulties than it would remove.

Williams strongly suggests that 'euthanasia can be condemned only according to a religious opinion.' [5] He tends to view the opposing camps as Roman Catholics versus Liberals. Although this has a certain initial appeal to me, a non-Catholic and self-styled liberal, I deny that this is the only way the battle lines can, or should, be drawn. I leave the religious arguments to the theologians. I share the view that 'those who hold the faith may follow its precepts without requiring those who do not hold it to act as if they did.' [6] But I do find substantial utilitarian obstacles on the high road to euthanasia. I am not enamoured of the *status quo* on mercy-killing. But while I am not prepared to defend it against all comers, I am prepared to defend it against the proposals for change which have come forth to date.

As an ultimate philosophical proposition, the case for voluntary euthanasia is strong. Whatever may be said for and against suicide generally, the appeal of death is immeasurably greater when it is sought not for a poor reason or just any reason, but for 'good cause,' so to speak; when it is invoked not on behalf of a 'socially useful' person, but on behalf of, for example, the pain-racked 'hopelessly incurable' cancer victim. If a person is *in fact* (1) presently incurable, (2) beyond the aid of any respite which may come along in his life expectancy, suffering (3) intolerable and (4) unmitigable pain and of a (5) fixed and (6) rational desire to die, I would hate to have to argue that the hand of death should be stayed. But abstract propositions and carefully formed hypotheticals are one thing; specific proposals designed to cover everyday situations are something else again.

In essence, Williams's specific proposal is that death be authorized for a person in the above situation "by giving the medical practitioner a wide discretion and trusting to his good sense.' [7] This, I submit, raises too great a risk of abuse and mistake to warrant a change in the existing law. That a proposal entails risk of mistake is hardly a conclusive reason against it. But neither is it irrelevant. Under any euthanasia programme the consequences of mistake, of course, are always fatal. As I shall endeavour to show, the incidence of mistake of one kind or another is likely to be quite appreciable. If this indeed be the case, unless the need for the authorized conduct is compelling enough to override it, I take it the risk of mistake *is* a conclusive reason against such authorization. I submit, too, that the possible radiations from the proposed legislation—for example, involuntary euthanasia of idiots and imbeciles (the typical 'mercy-killings' reported by the press)—and the emergence of the legal precedent that there are lives not 'worth living,' give additional cause for reflection.

I see the issue, then, as the need for voluntary euthanasia versus (1) the incidence of mistake and abuse; and (2) the danger that legal machinery initially designed to kill those who are a nuisance to themselves may some day engulf those who are a nuisance to others. [8]

The 'freedom to choose a merciful death by euthanasia' may well be regarded as a special area of civil liberties. This is definitely a part of Professor Williams's approach:

If the law were to remove its ban on euthanasia, the effect would merely be to leave this subject to the individual conscience. This proposal would . . . be easy to defend, as restoring personal liberty in a field in which men differ on the question of conscience. . . . On a question like this there is surely everything to be said for the liberty of the individual.[9]

I am perfectly willing to accept civil liberties as the battlefield, but issues of 'liberty' and 'freedom' mean little until we begin to pin down *whose* 'liberty' and 'freedom' and for *what* need and at *what* price. Williams champions the 'personal liberty' of the dying to die painlessly. I am more concerned about the life and liberty of those who would needlessly be killed in the process or who would irrationally choose to partake of the process. Williams's price on behalf of those who are *in fact* 'hopeless incurables' and *in fact* of a fixed and rational desire to die is the sacrifice of (1) some few, who, though they know it not, because their physicians know it not, need not and should not die; (2) others, probably not so few, who, though they go through the motions of 'volunteering,' are casualties of strain, pain or narcotics to such an extent that they really know not what they do. My price on behalf of those who, despite appearances to the contrary, have some relatively normal and reasonably useful life left in them, or who are incapable of making the choice, is the lingering on for awhile of those who, if you will, *in fact* have no desire and no reason to linger on.

I. A CLOSE-UP VIEW OF VOLUNTARY EUTHANASIA

A. THE EUTHANASIAST'S DILEMMA AND WILLIAMS'S PROPOSED SOLUTION

As if the general principle they advocate did not raise enough difficulties in itself, euthanasiasts have learned only too bitterly that specific plans of enforcement are often much less palatable than the abstract notions they are designed to effectuate. In the case of voluntary euthanasia, the means of implementation vary from (1) the simple proposal that mercy-killings by anyone, typically relatives, be immunized from the criminal law; to (2) the elaborate legal machinery contained in the bills of the Euthanasia Society (England) and the Euthanasia Society of America for carrying out euthanasia.

The British Society, in the Bill it originally proposed, would require the eligible patient—that is, a person over twenty-one who is 'suffering from a disease involving severe pain and of an incurable and fatal character,'[10] to forward a specially prescribed application, along with two medical certificates, one signed by the attending physician, and the other by a specially qualified physician, to a specially appointed Euthanasia Referee 'who shall satisfy himself by means of a personal interview with the patient and otherwise that the said conditions shall have been fulfilled and that the patient fully understands the nature and purpose of the application'; and, if so satisfied, shall then send a euthanasia permit to the patient; which permit shall, seven days after receipt, become 'operative' in the presence of an official witness; unless the nearest relative manages to cancel the permit by persuading a court of appropriate jurisdiction that the requisite conditions have not been met.

The American Society would have the eligible patient—that is, one over twenty-one 'suffering from severe physical pain caused by a disease for which no remedy affording lasting relief or recovery is at the time known to medical science,'[11] petition for euthanasia in the presence of two witnesses and file same, along with the certificate of an attending physician, in a court of appropriate jurisdiction; said court then to appoint a committee of three, of whom at least two must be physicians, 'who shall forthwith examine the patient and such other persons as they deem advisable or as the court may direct and within five days after their appointment, shall report to the court whether or not the patient understands the nature and purpose of the petition and comes within the [act's] provisions'; whereupon, if the report is in the affirmative, the court shall—'unless there is some reason to believe that the report is erroneous or untrue'—grant the petition; in which event euthanasia is to be administered in the presence of the committee, or any two members thereof.

As will be seen, and as might be expected, the simple negative proposal to remove 'mercy-killings' from the ban of the criminal law is strenuously resisted on the ground that it offers the patient far too little protection from not-so-necessary or not-so-merciful killings. On the other hand, the elaborate affirmative proposals of the Euthanasia Societies meet much pronounced eye-blinking, not a few guffaws, and sharp criticism that the legal machinery is so drawn-out, so complex, so formal and so tedious as to offer the patient far too little solace.

The naked suggestion that mercy-killing be made a good defence against a charge of criminal homicide appears to have no prospect of success in the foreseeable future. Only recently, the Royal Commission on Capital Punishment 'reluctantly' concluded that such homicides could not feasibly be taken out of the category of murder, let alone completely immunized:

[Witnesses] thought it would be most dangerous to provide that 'mercy-killings' should not be murder, because it would be impossible to define a category which could not be seriously abused. Such a definition could only be in terms of the motive of the offender . . . which is notoriously difficult to establish and cannot, like intent, be inferred from a person's overt actions. Moreover, it was agreed by almost all witnesses, including those who thought that there would be no real difficulty in discriminating between genuine and spurious suicide pacts, that, even if such a definition could be devised, it would in practice often prove extremely difficult to distinguish killings where the motive was merciful from those where it was not. How, for example, were the jury to decide whether a daughter had killed her invalid father from compassion, from a desire for material gain, from a natural wish to bring to an end a trying period of her life, or from a combination of motives? [12]

While the appeal in simply taking 'mercy-killings' off the books is dulled by the likelihood of abuse, the force of the idea is likewise substantially diminished by the encumbering protective features proposed by the American and British Societies. Thus, Lord Dawson, an eminent medical member of the House of Lords and one of the great leaders of the British medical profession, protested that the British Bill 'would turn the sick-room into a bureau,' that he was revolted by 'the very idea of the sick-chamber being visited by officials and the patient, who is struggling with this dire malady, being treated as if it was a case of insanity.' [13] Dr A. Leslie Banks, then Principal Medical Officer of the Ministry of Health, reflected that the proposed machinery would 'produce an atmosphere quite foreign to all accepted notions of dying in peace.' [14] Dr I. Phillips Frohman has similarly objected to the American Bill as one whose 'whole procedure is so lengthy that it does not seem consonant either with the "mercy" motive on which presumably it is based, or with the "bearableness" of the pain.' [15]

The extensive procedural concern of the euthanasia bills has repelled many, but perhaps the best evidence of its psychological misconception is that it has distressed sympathizers with the movement as well. The very year the British Society was organized and a proposed bill drafted, Dr Harry Roberts observed:

We all realize the intensified horror attached to the death-penalty by its accompanying formalities—from the phraseology of the judge's sentence, and his black cap, to the weight-gauging visit of the hangman to the cell, and the correct attendance at the final scene of the surpliced chaplain, the doctor and the prison governor. This is not irrelevant to the problem of legalized euthanasia. [16]

After discussing the many procedural steps of the British Bill Dr Roberts observed, 'I can almost hear the cheerful announcement: "Please, ma'am, the euthanizer's come." '

At a meeting of the Medico-Legal Society, Dr Kenneth McFadyean, after reminding the group that 'some time ago I stated from a public platform that I had practised euthanasia for twenty years and I do not believe I am running risks because I have helped a hopeless sufferer out of this life,' commented on the British Bill that

There was no comparison between being in a position to make a will and making a patient choose his own death at any stated moment. The patient had to discuss it—not once with his own doctor, but two, three, or even four times with strangers, which was no solace or comfort to people suffering intolerable pain. [17]

Nothing rouses Professor Glanville Williams's ire more than the fact that opponents of the euthanasia movement argue that euthanasia proposals offer either inadequate protection or over-elaborate safeguards. Williams appears to meet this dilemma with the insinuation that because arguments are made in the antithesis *they must each be invalid, each be obstructionist, and each be made in bad faith*. [18]

It just may be, however, that each alternative argument is quite valid, that the trouble lies with the euthanasiasts themselves in seeking a goal which is *inherently inconsistent:* a procedure for death which *both* (1) provides ample safeguards against abuse and mistake, and (2) is 'quick' and 'easy' in operation. Professor Williams meets the problem with more than bitter comments about the tactics of the opposition. He makes a brave try to break through the dilemma:

[T]he reformers might be well advised, in their next proposal, to abandon all their cumbrous safeguards and to do as their opponents wish, giving the medical practitioner a wide discretion and trusting to his good sense.

[T]he essence of the bill would then be simple. It would provide that no medical practitioner should be guilty of an offence in respect of an act done intentionally to accelerate the death of a patient who is seriously ill, unless it is proved that the act was not done in good faith with the consent of the patient and for the purpose of saving him from severe pain in an illness believed to be of an incurable and fatal character. Under this formula it would be for the physician, if charged, to show that the patient was seriously ill, but for the prosecution to prove that the physician acted from some motive other than the humanitarian one allowed to him by law.[19]

Evidently, the presumption is that the general practitioner is a sufficient buffer between the patient and the restless spouse, or overwrought or overreaching relative, as well as a depository of enough general scientific know-how and enough information about current research developments and trends, to assure a minimum of error in diagnosis and anticipation of new measures of relief. Whether or not the general practitioner will accept the responsibility Williams would confer on him is itself a problem of major proportions.[20] Putting that question aside, the soundness of the underlying premises of Williams's 'legislative suggestion' will be examined in the course of the discussion of various aspects of the euthanasia problem.

B. THE 'CHOICE'

Under current proposals to establish legal machinery, elaborate or otherwise, for the administration of a quick and easy death, it is not enough that those authorized to pass on the question decide that the patient, in effect, is 'better off dead.' The patient must concur in this opinion. Much of the appeal in the current proposal lies in this so-called 'voluntary' attribute.

But is the adult patient really in a position to concur?[21] Is he truly able to make euthanasia a 'voluntary' act? There is a good deal to be said, is there not, for Dr Frohman's pithy comment that the 'voluntary' plan is supposed to be carried out 'only if the victim is both sane and crazed by pain.'[22]

By hypothesis, voluntary euthanasia is not to be resorted to until narcotics have long since been administered and the patient has developed a tolerance to them. *When,* then, does the patient make the choice? While heavily drugged?[23] Or is narcotic relief to be withdrawn for the time of decision? But if heavy dosage no longer deadens pain, indeed, no longer makes it bearable, how overwhelming is it when whatever relief narcotics offer is taken away too?

'Hypersensitivity to pain after analgesia has worn off is nearly always noted.'[24] Moreover, 'the mental side-effects of narcotics, unfortunately for anyone wishing to suspend them temporarily without unduly tormenting the patient, appear to outlast the analgesic effect' and 'by many hours.'[25] The situation is further complicated by the fact that 'a person in terminal stages of cancer who had been given morphine steadily for a matter of weeks would certainly be dependent upon it physically and would probably be addicted to it and react with the addict's response.'[26]

The narcotics problem aside, Dr Benjamin Miller, who probably has personally experienced more pain than any other commentator on the euthanasia scene, observes:

Anyone who has been severely ill knows how distorted his judgment became during the worst moments of the illness. Pain and the toxic effect of disease, or the violent reaction to certain surgical procedures may change our capacity for rational and courageous thought.[27]

Undoubtedly, some euthanasia candidates will have their lucid moments. How they are to be distinguished from fellow-sufferers who do not, or how these instances are to be distinguished from others when the patient is exercising an irrational judgment, is not an easy matter. Particularly is this so under Williams's proposal, where no specially qualified persons, psychiatrically trained or otherwise, are to assist in the process.

Assuming, for purposes of argument, that the occasion when a euthanasia candidate possesses a sufficiently clear mind can be ascertained and that a request for euthanasia is then made, there remain other problems. The mind of the pain-racked may occasionally be clear, but is it not also likely to be uncertain and variable? This point was pressed hard by the great physician, Lord Horder, in the House of Lords debates:

During the morning depression he [the patient] will be found to favour the application under this Bill, later in the day he will think quite differently, or will have forgotten all about it. The mental clarity with which noble Lords who present this Bill are able to think and to speak must not be thought to have any counterpart in the alternating moods and confused judgments of the sick man.[28]

The concept of 'voluntary' in voluntary euthanasia would have a great deal more substance to it if, as is the case with voluntary admission statutes for the mentally ill, the patient retained the right to reverse the process within a specified number of days after he gives written notice of his desire to do so—but unfortunately this cannot be. The choice here, of course, is an irrevocable one.

The likelihood of confusion, distortion or vacillation would appear to be serious drawbacks to any voluntary plan. Moreover, Williams's proposal is particularly vulnerable in this regard, since as he admits, by eliminating the fairly elaborate procedure of the American and British Societies' plans, he also eliminates a time period which would furnish substantial evidence of the patient's settled intention to avail himself of euthanasia.[29] But if Williams does not always choose to slug it out, he can box neatly and parry gingerly:

[T]he problem can be exaggerated. Every law has to face difficulties in application, and these difficulties are not a conclusive argument against a law if it has a beneficial operation. The measure here proposed is designed to meet the situation where the patient's consent to euthanasia is clear and incontrovertible. The physician, conscious of the need to protect himself against malicious accusations, can devise his own safeguards appropriate to the circumstances; he would normally be well advised to get the patient's consent in writing, just as is now the practice before operations. Sometimes the patient's consent will be particularly clear because he will have expressed a desire for ultimate euthanasia while he is still clear-headed and before he comes to be racked by pain; if the expression of desire is never revoked, but rather is reaffirmed under the pain, there is the best possible proof of full consent. If, on the other hand, there is no such settled frame of

mind, and if the physician chooses to administer euthanasia when the patient's mind is in a variable state, he will be walking in the margin of the law and may find himself unprotected.[30]

If consent is given at a time when the patient's condition has so degenerated that he has become a fit candidate for euthanasia, when, if ever, will it be 'clear and incontrovertible'? Is the suggested alternative of consent in advance a satisfactory solution? Can such a consent be deemed an informed one? Is this much different from holding a man to a prior statement of intent that if such and such an employment opportunity would present itself he would accept it, or if such and such a young woman were to come along he would marry her? Need one marshal authority for the proposition that many an 'iffy' inclination is disregarded when the actual facts are at hand?

Professor Williams states that where a pre-pain desire for 'ultimate euthanasia' is 'reaffirmed' under pain, 'there is the best possible proof of full consent.' Perhaps. But what if it is alternately renounced and reaffirmed under pain? What if it is neither affirmed or renounced? What if it is only renounced? Will a physician be free to go ahead on the ground that the prior desire was 'rational,' but the present desire 'irrational'? Under Williams's plan, will not the physician frequently 'be walking in the margin of the law' —just as he is now? Do we really accomplish much more under this proposal than to put the euthanasia principle on the books?

Even if the patient's choice could be said to be 'clear and incontrovertible,' do not other difficulties remain? Is this the kind of choice, assuming that it can be made in a fixed and rational manner, that we want to offer a gravely ill person? Will we not sweep up, in the process, some who are not really tired of life, but think others are tired of them; some who do not really want to die, but who feel they should not live on, because to do so when there looms the legal alternative of euthanasia is to do a selfish or a cowardly act? Will not some feel an obligation to have themselves 'eliminated' in order that funds allocated for their terminal care might be better used by their families or, financial worries aside, in order to relieve their families of the emotional strain involved?

It would not be surprising for the gravely ill person to seek to inquire of those close to him whether he should avail himself of the legal alternative of euthanasia. Certainly, he is likely to wonder about their attitude in the matter. It is quite possible, is it not, that he will not exactly be gratified by any inclination on their part —however noble their motives may be in fact— that he resort to the new procedure? At this stage, the patient-family relationship may well be a good deal less than it ought to be.

And what of the relatives? If their views will not always influence the patient, will they not at least influence the attending physician? Will a physician assume the risks to his reputation, if not his pocketbook, by administering the *coup de grâce* over the objection—however irrational—of a close relative. Do not the relatives, then, also have a 'choice'? Is not the decision on their part to do nothing and say nothing *itself* a 'choice'? In many families there will be some, will there not, who will consider a stand against euthanasia the only proof of love, devotion and gratitude for past events? What of the stress and strife if close relatives differ over the desirability of euthanatizing the patient?

At such a time, members of the family are not likely to be in the best state of mind, either, to make this kind of decision. Financial stress and conscious or unconscious competition for the family's estate aside,

The chronic illness and persistent pain in terminal carcinoma may place strong and excessive stresses upon the family's emotional ties with the patient. The family members who have strong emotional attachment to start with are most likely to take the patient's fears, pains and fate personally. Panic often strikes them. Whatever guilt feelings they may have toward the patient emerge to plague them.

If the patient is maintained at home, many frustrations and physical demands may be imposed on the family by the advanced illness. There may develop extreme weakness, incontinence and bad odors. The pressure of caring for the individual under these circumstances is likely to arouse a resentment and, in turn, guilt feelings on the part of those who have to do the nursing.[31]

Nor should it be overlooked that while Professor Williams would remove the various procedural steps and personnel contemplated in the British and American Bills and bank his all on the 'good sense' of the general practitioner, no man is immune to the fear, anxieties and frustrations engendered by the apparently helpless, hopeless patient. Not even the general practitioner:

Working with a patient suffering from a malignancy causes special problems for the physician. First of all, the patient with a malignancy is most likely to engender anxiety concerning death, even in the doctor. And at the same time, this type of patient constitutes a serious threat or frustration to medical ambition. As a result, a doctor may react more emotionally and less objectively than in any other area of medical practice. . . . His deep concern may make him more pessimistic than is necessary. As a result of the feeling of frustration in his wish to help, the doctor may have moments of annoyance with the patient. He may even feel almost inclined to want to avoid this type of patient.[32]

Putting aside the problem of whether the good sense of the general practitioner warrants dispensing with other personnel, there still remain the problems posed by *any* voluntary euthanasia programme: the aforementioned considerable pressures on the patient and his family. Are these the kind of pressures we want to inflict on any person, let alone a very sick person? Are these the kind of pressures we want to impose on any family, let alone an emotionally shattered family? And if so, why are they not also proper considerations for the crippled, the paralyzed, the quadruple amputee, the iron-lung occupant and their families?

Might it not be said of the existing ban on euthanasia, as Professor Herbert Wechsler has said of the criminal law in another connection:

It also operates, and perhaps more significantly, at anterior stages in the patterns of conduct, the dark shadow of organized disapproval eliminating from the ambit of consideration alternatives that might otherwise present themselves in the final competition of choice.[33]

C. THE 'HOPELESSLY INCURABLE' PATIENT AND THE FALLIBLE DOCTOR

Professor Williams notes as 'standard argument' the plea that 'no sufferer from an apparently fatal illness should be deprived of his life because there is always the possibility that the diagnosis is wrong, or else that some remarkable cure will be discovered in time.'[34] But he does not reach the issue until he has already dismissed it with this prefatory remark:

It has been noticed before in this work that writers who object to a practice for theological reasons frequently try to support their condemnation on medical grounds. With euthanasia this is difficult, but the effort is made.[35]

Does not Williams, while he pleads that euthanasia be not theologically prejudged, at the same time invite the inference that nontheological objections to euthanasia are simply camouflage?

It is no doubt true that many theological opponents employ medical arguments as well, but it is also true that the doctor who has probably most forcefully advanced medical objections to euthanasia of the so-called incurables, Cornell University's world-renowned Foster Kennedy, a former President of the Euthanasia Society of America, *advocates* euthanasia in other areas where error in diagnosis and prospect of new relief or cures are much reduced—that is, for the 'congenitally unfit.'[36] In large part for the same reasons, Great Britain's Dr A. Leslie Banks, then Principal Medical Officer of the Ministry of Health, maintained that a better case could be made for the destruction of congenital idiots and those in the final stages of dementia, particularly senile dementia, than could be made for the doing away of the pain-stricken incurable.[37] Surely, such opponents of voluntary euthanasia cannot be accused of wrapping theological objections in medical dressing!

Until the Euthanasia Societies of Great Britain and America had been organized and a party decision reached, shall we say, to advocate euthanasia only for incurables on their request, Dr Abraham L. Wolbarst, one of the most ardent supporters of the movement, was less troubled about putting away 'insane or defective people [who] have suffered mental incapacity and tortures of the mind for many years' than he was about the 'incurables'.[38] He recognized the 'difficulty involved in the decision as to incurability' as one of the 'doubtful aspects of euthanasia': 'Doctors are only human beings, with few if any supermen among them. They make honest mistakes, like other men, because of the limitations of the human mind.'[39]

He noted further that 'it goes without saying that, in recently developed cases with a possibility of cure, euthanasia should not even be considered,' that 'the law might establish a limit of, say, ten years in which there is a chance of the patient's recovery.'[40]

Dr Benjamin Miller is another who is unlikely to harbour an ulterior theological motive. His interest is more personal. He himself was left to die the death of a 'hopeless' tuberculosis victim, only to discover that he was suffering from a rare malady which affects the lungs in much the same manner but seldom kills. Five years and sixteen hospitalizations later, Dr Miller dramatized his point by recalling the last diagnostic clinic of the brilliant Richard Cabot, on the occasion of his official retirement:

He was given the case records [complete medical histories and results of careful examinations] of two patients and asked to diagnose their illnesses. . . . The patients had died and only the hospital pathologist knew the exact diagnosis beyond doubt, for he had seen the descriptions of the postmortem findings. Dr Cabot, usually very accurate in his diagnosis, that day missed both.

The chief pathologist who had selected the cases was a wise person. He had purposely chosen two of the most deceptive to remind the medical students and young physicians that even at the end of a long and rich experience one of the greatest diagnosticians of our time was still not infallible.[41]

Richard Cabot was the John W. Davis, the John Lord O'Brian, of his profession. When one reads the account of his last clinic, one cannot help but think of how fallible the *average* general practitioner must be, how fallible the *young doctor just starting practice* must be—and this, of course, is all that some small communities have in the way of medical care—how fallible the *worst* practitioner, young or old, must be. If the range of skill and judgment among licensed physicians approaches the wide gap between the very best and the very worst members of the bar—and I have no reason to think it does not—then the minimally competent physician is hardly the man to be given the responsibility for ending another's life.[42] Yet, under Williams's proposal at least, the marginal physician, as well as his more distinguished brethren, would have legal authorization to make just such decisions. Under Williams's proposal, euthanatizing a patient or two would all be part of the routine day's work.

Perhaps it is not amiss to add as a final note, that no less a euthanasiast than Dr C. Killick

Millard [43] had such little faith in the averge general practitioner that as regards, the *mere administering* of the *coup de grâce,* he observed:

In order to prevent any likelihood of bungling, it would be very necessary that only medical practitioners who had been specially licensed to euthanize (after acquiring special knowledge and skill) should be allowed to administer euthanasia. Quite possibly, the work would largely be left in the hands of the official euthanizors who would have to be appointed specially for each area.[44]

True, the percentage of correct diagnosis is particularly high in cancer.[45] The short answer, however, is that euthanasiasts most emphatically do not propose to restrict mercy-killing to cancer cases. Dr Millard has maintained that 'there are very many diseases besides cancer which tend to kill "by inches," and where death, when it does at last come to the rescue, is brought about by pain and exhaustion.' [46] Furthermore, even if mercy-killings were to be limited to cancer, however relatively accurate the diagnosis in these cases, here, too, 'incurability of a disease is never more than an estimate based upon experience, and how fallacious experience may be in medicine only those who have had a great deal of experience fully realize.' [47]

Dr Daniel Laszlo, Chief of Division of Neoplastic Diseases, Montefiore Hospital, New York City, and three other physicians have observed:

The mass crowding of a group of patients labeled 'terminal' in institutions designated for that kind of care carries a grave danger. The experience gathered from this group makes it seem reasonable to conclude that a fresh evaluation of any large group in mental institutions, in institutions for chronic care, or in homes for the incurably sick, would unearth a rewarding number of salvageable patients who can be returned to their normal place in society.... For purposes of this study we were especially interested in those with a diagnosis of advanced cancer. In a number of these patients, major errors in diagnosis or management were encountered.[48]

Faulty diagnosis is only one ground for error. Even if the diagnosis is correct, a second ground for error lies in the possibility that some measure of relief, if not a full cure, may come to the fore within the life expectancy of the patient. Since Glanville Williams does not deign this objection to euthanasia worth more than a passing reference,[49] it is necessary to turn elsewhere to ascer-

tain how it has been met. One answer is: 'It must be little comfort to a man slowly coming apart from multiple sclerosis to think that fifteen years from now, death might not be his only hope.' [50]

To state the problem this way is of course, to avoid it entirely. How do we know that fifteen *days* or fifteen *hours* from now, 'death might not be [the incurable's] only hope'?

A second answer is: '[N]o cure for cancer which might be found "tomorrow" would be of any value to a man or woman "so far advanced in cancerous toxemia as to be an applicant for euthanasia."' [51]

As I shall endeavour to show, this approach is a good deal easier to formulate than it is to apply. For one thing, it presumes that we know today *what* cures will be found tomorrow. For another, it overlooks that if such cases can be said to exist, the patient is likely to be *so far* advanced in cancerous toxemia as to be no longer capable of understanding the step he is taking and hence *beyond* the stage when euthanasia ought to be administered.[52]

Thirty-six years ago, Dr Haven Emerson, then President of the American Public Health Association, made the point that 'no one can say today what will be incurable tomorrow. No one can predict what disease will be fatal or permanently incurable until medicine becomes stationary and sterile.' Dr Emerson went so far as to say that 'to be at all accurate we must drop altogether the term "incurables" and substitute for it some such term as "chronic illness."' [53]

At that time Dr Emerson did not have to go back more than a decade to document his contention. Before Banting and Best's insulin discovery, many a diabetic had been doomed. Before the Whipple-Minot-Murphy liver treatment made it a relatively minor malady, many a pernicious anaemia sufferer had been branded 'hopeless.' Before the uses of sulphanilomide were disclosed, a patient with widespread streptococcal blood-poisoning was a condemned man.[54]

Today, we may take even that most resolute disease, cancer, and we need look back no further than the last two decades of research in this field to document the same contention.[55] True, many types of cancer still run their course virtually unhampered by man's arduous efforts to inhibit them. But the number of cancers coming under some control is ever increasing. With medicine attacking on so many fronts with so many weapons, who would bet a man's life on when and how the next type of cancer will yield, if only just a bit? Of course, we would not be betting much of a life. For even in those areas where gains have been registered, the life is not 'saved,' death is only postponed. In a sense this is the case with every 'cure' for every ailment. But it may be urged that, after all, there is a great deal of difference between the typical 'cure' which achieves an indefinite postponement, more or less, and the cancer respite which results in only a brief intermission, so to speak, of rarely more than six months or a year. Is this really long enough to warrant all the bother?

Well, how long *is* long enough? In many recent cases of cancer respite, the patient, though experiencing only temporary relief, underwent sufficient improvement to retake his place in society. Six or twelve or eighteen months is long enough to do most of the things which socially justify our existence, is it not? Long enough for a nurse to care for more patients, a teacher to impart learning to more classes, a judge to write a great opinion, a novelist to write a stimulating book, a scientist to make an important discovery and, after all, for a factory-hand to put the wheels on another year's Cadillac.

D. 'MISTAKES ARE ALWAYS POSSIBLE'

Under Professor Williams's 'legislative suggestion' a doctor could 'refrain from taking steps to prolong the patient's life by medical means' solely on his own authority. Only when disposition by affirmative 'mercy-killing' is a considered alternative, need he do so much as, and only so much as, consult another general practitioner.[56] There are no other safeguards: no 'euthanasia referee' no requirement that death be administered in the presence of an official witness, as in the British Society's bill; no court to petition, no committee to investigate and report back to the court, as in the American Society's bill. Professor Williams's view is:

It may be allowed that mistakes are always possible, but this is so in any of the affairs of life. And it is just as possible to make a mistake by doing nothing as by acting. All that can be expected of any moral agent is that he should do his best on the facts as they appear to him.[57]

That mistakes are always possible, that mistakes are always made, does not, it is true, deter society from pursuing a particular line of conduct —if the line of conduct is *compelled* by needs which override the risk of mistake. A thousand *Convicting the Innocent's*[58] or *Not Guilty's*[59] may stir us, may spur us to improve the administration of the criminal law, but they cannot and should not bring the business of deterring and incapacitating dangerous criminals or would-be dangerous criminals to an abrupt and complete halt.

A relevant question, then, is what is the need for euthanasia which leads us to tolerate the mistakes, the very fatal mistakes, which will inevitably occur? What is the compelling force which requires us to tinker with deeply entrenched and almost universal precepts of criminal law?

Let us first examine the qualitative need for euthanasia.

Proponents of euthanasia like to present for consideration the case of the surgical operation, particularly a highly dangerous one: risk of death is substantial, perhaps even more probable than not; in addition, there is always the risk that the doctors have misjudged the situation and that no operation was needed at all. Yet it is not unlawful to perform the operation.

The short answer is the witticism that whatever the incidence of death in connection with different types of operations, 'no doubt, it is in all cases below 100 per cent, which is the incidence rate for euthanasia.'[60] But this may not be the full answer. There are occasions where the law permits action involving about a 100 per cent incidence of death—for example, self-defence. There may well be other instances where the law should condone such action—for example, the 'necessity' cases illustrated by the overcrowded lifeboat,[61] the starving survivors of a shipwreck [62] and—perhaps best of all—by Professor Lon Fuller's penetrating and fascinating tale of the trapped cave explorers.[63]

In all these situations, death for some may well be excused, if not justified, yet the prospect that some deaths will be unnecessary is a real one. He who kills in self-defence may have misjudged the facts. They who throw passengers overboard to lighten the load may no sooner do so than see 'masts and sails of rescue . . . emerge out of the fog.'[64] But no human being will ever find himself in a situation where he knows for an absolute certainty that one or several must die that he or others may live. 'Modern legal systems . . . do not require divine knowledge of human beings.' [65]

Reasonable mistakes, then, may be tolerated if, as in the above circumstances and as in the case of the surgical operation, these mistakes are the inevitable by-products of efforts to save one or more human lives.[66]

The need the euthanasiast advances, however, is a good deal less compelling. It is only to ease pain.

Let us next examine the quantitative need for euthanasia.

No figures are available, so far as I can determine, as to the number of, say, cancer victims, who undergo intolerable or overwhelming pain. That an appreciable number do suffer such pain, I have no doubt. But that anything approaching this number whatever it is, need suffer such pain, I have—viewing the many sundry palliative measures now available—considerable doubt. The whole field of severe pain and its management in the terminal stage of cancer is, according to an eminent physician, 'a subject neglected far too much by the medical profession.' [67] Other well-qualified commentators have recently noted the 'obvious lack of interest in the literature about the problem of cancer pain' [68] and have scored 'the deplorable attitude of defeatism and therapeutic inactivity found in some quarters.' [69]

The picture of the advanced cancer victim beyond the relief of morphine and like drugs is a poignant one, but apparently no small number of these situations may have been brought about by premature or excessive application of these drugs. Psychotherapy 'unfortunately . . . has barely been explored' [70] in this area, although a survey conducted on approximately three hundred patients with advanced cancer disclosed that 'over 50 per cent of patients who had received analgesics for long periods of time could be adequately controlled by placebo medication.' [71] Nor should it be overlooked that nowadays drugs are only one of many ways—and by no means always the most effective way—of attacking the pain problem. Radiation, Röntgen and X-ray therapy; the administration of various endocrine substances; intrathecal alcohol injections and other types of nerve blocking; and various neuro-

surgical operations such as spinothalmic chordotomy and spinothalmic tractomy, have all furnished striking relief in many cases. These various formidable non-narcotic measures, it should be added, are conspicuously absent from the prolific writings of the euthanasiasts.

That of those who do suffer and must necessarily suffer the requisite pain, many *really* desire death, I have considerable doubt.[72] Further, that of those who may desire death at a given moment, many have a fixed and rational desire for death, I likewise have considerable doubt. Finally, taking those who may have such a desire, again I must register a strong note of scepticism that many cannot do the job themselves.[73] It is not that I condone suicide. It is simply that I find it easier to prefer a *laissez-faire* approach in such matters over an approach aided and sanctioned by the state.

The need is only one variable. The incidence of mistake is another. Can it not be said that although the need is not very great it is great enough to outweigh the few mistakes which are likely to occur? I think not. The incidence of error may be small in euthanasia, but as I have endeavoured to show, and as Professor Williams has not taken pains to deny, under our present state of knowledge appreciable error is inevitable.

Even if the need for voluntary euthanasia could be said to outweigh the risk of mistake, this is not the end of the matter. That 'all that can be expected of any moral agent is that he should do his best on the facts as they appear to him' [74] may be true as far as it goes, but it would seem that where the consequence of error is so irreparable it is not too much to expect of society that there be *a good deal more than one moral agent* 'to do his best on the facts as they appear to him.'

2. A LONG-RANGE VIEW OF EUTHANASIA

A. VOLUNTARY VERSUS INVOLUNTARY EUTHANASIA

Ever since the 1870s, when what was probably the first euthanasia debate of the modern era took place,[75] most proponents of the movement—at least when they are pressed—have taken considerable pains to restrict the question to the plight of the unbearably suffering incurable who *voluntarily seeks* death, while most of their opponents have striven equally hard to frame the issue in terms which would encompass certain involuntary situations as well, e.g. the 'congenital idiots,' the 'permanently insane,' and the senile.

Glanville Williams reflects the outward mood of many euthanasiasts when he scores those who insist on considering the question from a broader angle:

The [British Society's] bill [debated in the House of Lords in 1936 and 1950] excluded any question of compulsory euthanasia, even for hopelessly defective infants. Unfortunately, a legislative proposal is not assured of success merely because it is worded in a studiously moderate and restrictive form. The method of attack, by those who dislike the proposal, is to use the 'thin end of the wedge' argument. . . . There is no proposal for reform on any topic, however conciliatory and moderate, that cannot be opposed by this dialectic.[76]

Why was the bill 'worded in a studiously moderate and restrictive form'? If it were done as a matter of principle, if it were done in recognition of the ethico-moral-legal 'wall of separation' which stands between voluntary and compulsory 'mercy-killings,' much can be said for the euthanasiasts' lament about the methods employed by the opposition. But if it were done as a matter of political expediency—with great hopes and expectations of pushing through a second and somewhat less restrictive bill as soon as the first one had sufficiently 'educated' public opinion and next a third, still less restrictive bill—what standing do the euthanasiasts then have to attack the methods of the opposition? No cry of righteous indignation could ring more hollow, I would think, than the protest from those utilizing the 'wedge' principle themselves that their opponents are making the wedge objection.

In this regard the words and action of the euthanasiasts are not insignificant.

In the 1936 debate in the House of Lords, Lord Ponsonby of Shulbrede, who moved the second reading of the Voluntary Euthanasia Bill, described two appealing actual cases, one where a man drowned his four-year-old daughter 'who had contracted tuberculosis and had developed gangrene in the face,'[77] and another where a woman killed her mother who was suffering from 'general paralysis of the insane.'[78] Both cases of course were of the compulsory variety of euthanasia. True, Lord Ponsonby readily admitted

that these cases were not covered by the proposed bill, but the fact remains that they were the *only* specific cases he chose to describe.

In 1950, Lord Chorley once again called the Voluntary Euthanasia Bill to the attention of the House of Lords. He was most articulate, if not too discreet, on excluding compulsory euthanasia cases from coverage:

. . . Another objection is that the Bill does not go far enough, because it applies only to adults and does not apply to children who come into the world deaf, dumb and crippled, and who have a much better cause than those for whom the Bill provides. That may be so, but we must go step by step.[79]

In 1938, two years after the British Society was organized and its bill had been introduced into the House of Lords, the Euthanasia Society of America was formed.[80] At its first annual meeting the following year, it offered proposed euthanasia legislation:

Infant imbeciles, hopelessly insane persons . . . and any person not requesting his own death would not come within the scope of the proposed act. Charles E. Nixdorff, New York lawyer and treasurer of the society, who offered the bill for consideration, explained to some of the members who desired to broaden the scope of the proposed law, that it was *limited purposely to voluntary euthanasia because public opinion is not ready to accept the broader principle*. He said, however, that *the society hoped eventually to legalize the putting to death of nonvolunteers* beyond the help of medical science.[81]

At a meeting of the Society of Medical Jurisprudence held several weeks after the American Society's Voluntary Euthanasia Bill had been drafted, Dr Foster Kennedy, newly elected President of the Society, urged 'the legalizing of euthanasia primarily in cases of born defectives who are doomed to remain defective, rather than for normal persons who have become miserable through incurable illness' and scored the 'absurd and misplaced sentimental kindness' that seeks to preserve the life of a 'person who is not a person.' 'If the law sought to restrict euthanasia to those who could speak out for it, and thus overlooked these creatures who cannot speak, then, I say as Dickens did, "The law's an ass." '[82] As pointed out elsewhere, *while President* of the Society, Dr Kennedy not only eloquently advocated involuntary euthanasia but strenuously *opposed* the voluntary variety.[83] Is it any wonder that opponents of the movement do not always respect the voluntary-involuntary dichotomy?

In 1950, the 'mercy-killings' perpetrated by Dr Herman N. Sander on his cancer-stricken patient and by Miss Carol Ann Paight on her cancer-stricken father put the euthanasia question on page one.[84] In the midst of the fervour over these cases, Dr Clarence Cook Little, one of the leaders in the movement and a former President of the American Society, suggested specific safeguards for a law legalizing 'mercy-killings' for the 'incurably ill but mentally fit' *and* for 'mental defectives.' [85] The Reverend Charles Francis Potter, the founder and first president of the American Society, hailed Dr Sander's action as 'morally right' and hence that which 'should be legally right.' [86] Shortly thereafter, at its annual meeting, the American Society 'voted to continue support' of both Dr Sander and Miss Paight.[87]

Now, one of the interesting, albeit underplayed, features of these cases—and this was evident all along—was that both were *involuntary* 'mercy-killings.' There was considerable conflict in the testimony at the Sander Trial as to whether or not the victim's *husband* had pleaded with the doctor to end her suffering,[88] but nobody claimed that the victim herself had done such pleading. There was considerable evidence in the *Paight* case to the effect that the victim's *daughter* had a 'cancer phobia,' the cancer deaths of two aunts having left a deep mark on her,[89] but nobody suggested that the victim had a 'cancer phobia.'

It is true that Mother Paight said approvingly of her mercy-killing daughter that 'she had the old Paight guts,' [90] but it is no less true that Father Paight had no opportunity to pass judgment on the question. He was asleep, still under the anaesthetic of the exploratory operation which revealed the cancer in his stomach when his daughter, after having taken one practice shot in the woods, fired into his left temple.[91] Is it not just possible that Father Paight would have preferred to have had the vaunted Paight intestinal fortitude channelled in other directions, e.g. by his daughter bearing to see him suffer? [92]

The *Sander* and *Paight* cases amply demonstrate that to the press, the public, and many euthanasiasts, the killing of one who does not or cannot speak is no less a 'mercy-killing' than the killing of one who asks for death. Indeed, the overwhelming majority of known or alleged 'mercy-killings' have occurred without the consent of the victim. If the *Sander* and *Paight* cases are typical at all, they are so only in that the victims were not ill or retarded children, as in the *Simpson,*[93] *Brownhill*[94] and *Long*[95] English cases, and the *Greenfield, Repouille, Noxon* and *Braunsdorf* American cases.[96]

These situations are all quite moving. So much so that two of the strongest presentations of the need for *voluntary* euthanasia, free copies of which may be obtained from the American Society, lead off with sympathetic discussions of the *Brownhill* and *Greenfield* cases.[97] This, it need hardly be said, is not the way to honour the voluntary-involuntary boundary; not the way to ease the pressure to legalize at least this type of involuntary euthanasia as well, if any changes in the broad area are to be made at all.

Nor, it should be noted, is Williams free from criticism in this regard. In his discussion of 'the present law,' apparently a discussion of voluntary euthanasia, he cites only one case, *Simpson,* an involuntary situation.[98] In his section on 'the administration of the law' he describes only the *Sander* case and the 'compassionate acquittal' of a man who drowned his four-year-old daughter, a sufferer of tuberculosis and gangrene of the face.[99] Again, both are involuntary cases. For 'some other' American mercy-killing cases, Williams refers generally to an article by Helen Silving,[100] but two of the three cases he seems to have in mind are likewise cases of involuntary euthanasia.[101]

That the press and general public are not alone in viewing an act as a 'mercy-killing,' lack of consent on the part of the victim notwithstanding, is well evidenced by the deliberations of the Royal Commission on Capital Punishment.[102] The report itself described 'mercy-killings' as 'for example, where a mother has killed her child or a husband has killed his wife from merciful motives of pity and humanity.' [103] The only specific proposal to exclude 'mercy-killings' from the category of murder discussed in the report is a suggestion by the Society of Labour Lawyers which disregards the voluntary-involuntary distinction:

If a person who has killed another person proves that he killed that person with the compassionate intention of saving him physical or mental suffering, he shall not be guilty of murder.[104]

Another proposal, one by Hector Hughes, M.P., to the effect that only those who 'maliciously' cause the death of another shall be guilty of murder,[105] likewise treated the voluntary and involuntary 'mercy-killer' as one and the same.

Testimony before the Commission underscored the great appeal of the *involuntary* 'mercy-killings.' Thus, Lord Goddard, the Lord Chief Justice, referred to the famous *Brownhill* case, which he himself had tried some fifteen years earlier, as 'a dreadfully pathetic case.' [106] 'The son,' he pointed out, 'was a hopeless imbecile, more than imbecile, a mindless idiot.' [107]

Mr Justice Humphreys recalled 'one case that was the most pathetic sight I ever saw,' [108] a case which literally had the trial judge, Mr Justice Hawkins, in tears. It involved a young father who smothered his infant child to death when he learned the child had contracted syphilis from the mother (whose morals turned out to be something less than represented) and would be blind for life. 'That,' Mr Justice Humphreys told the Commission, 'was a real "mercy-killing." ' [109]

The boldness and daring which characterize most of Glanville Williams's book dim perceptibly when he comes to involuntary euthanasia proposals. As to the senile, he states:

At present the problem has certainly not reached the degree of seriousness that would warrant an effort being made to change traditional attitudes towards the sanctity of life of the aged. Only the grimmest necessity could bring about a change that, however cautious in its approach, would probably cause apprehension and deep distress to many people, and inflict a traumatic injury upon the accepted code of behaviour built up by two thousand years of the Christian religion. It may be, however, that as the problem becomes more acute it will itself cause a reversal of generally accepted values.[110]

To me, this passage is the most startling one in the book. On page 310 Williams invokes 'traditional attitudes towards the sanctity of life' and 'the accepted code of behaviour built up by two thousand years of the Christian religion' to check the extension of euthanasia to the senile, but for 309 pages he had been merrily rolling along debunking both. Substitute 'cancer victim' for 'the aged' and Williams's passage is essentially the argument of many of his *opponents* on the voluntary euthanasia question.

The unsupported comment that 'the problem [of senility] has certainly not reached the degree of seriousness' to warrant euthanasia is also rather puzzling, particularly coming as it does after an observation by Williams on the immediately preceding page that 'it is increasingly common for men and women to reach an age of "second childishness and mere oblivion," with a loss of almost all adult faculties except that of digestion.' [111]

How 'serious' does a problem have to be to warrant a change in these 'traditional attitudes'? If, as the statement seems to indicate, 'seriousness' of the problem is to be determined numerically, the problem of the cancer victim does not appear to be as substantial as the problem of the senile. For example, taking just the 95,837 first admissions to 'public prolonged-care hospitals' for mental diseases in the United States in 1955, 23,561—or one-fourth—were cerebral arteriosclerosis or senile brain disease cases. I am not at all sure that there are twenty thousand cancer victims per year who die *unbearably painful* deaths. Even if there were, I cannot believe that among their ranks are some twenty thousand per year who, when still in a rational state, so long for a quick and easy death that they would avail themselves of legal machinery for euthanasia.

If the problem of the incurable cancer victim has reached 'the degree of seriousness that would warrant an effort being made to change traditional attitudes towards the sanctity of life,' as Williams obviously thinks it has, then so has the problem of senility. In any event, the senility problem will undoubtedly soon reach even Williams's requisite degree of seriousness:

A decision concerning the senile may have to be taken within the next twenty years. The number of old people are increasing by leaps and bounds. Pneumonia, 'the old man's friend,' is now checked by antibiotics. The effects of hardship, exposure, starvation and accident are now minimized. Where is this leading us? . . . What of the drooling, helpless, disorientated old man or the doubly incontinent old woman lying log-like in bed? Is it here that the real need for euthanasia exists? [112]

If, as Williams indicates, 'seriousness' of the problem is a major criterion for euthanatizing a category of unfortunates, the sum total of mentally deficient persons would appear to warrant high priority, indeed.[113]

When Williams turns to the plight of the 'hopelessly defective infants,' his characteristic vim and vigour are, as in the senility discussion, conspicuously absent:

While the Euthanasia Society of England has never advocated this, the Euthanasia Society of America did include it in its original programme. The proposal certainly escapes the chief objection to the similar proposal for senile dementia: it does not create a sense of insecurity in society, because infants cannot, like adults, feel anticipatory dread of being done to death if their condition should worsen. Moreover, the proposal receives some support on eugenic grounds, and more importantly on humanitarian grounds—both on account of the parents, to whom the child will be a burden all their lives, and on account of the handicapped child itself. (It is not, however, proposed that any child should be destroyed against the wishes of its parents.) Finally, the legalization of euthanasia for handicapped children would bring the law into closer relation to its practical administration, because juries do not regard parental mercy-killing as murder. For these various reasons the proposal to legalize humanitarian infanticide is put forward from time to time by individuals. They remain in a very small minority, and the proposal may at present be dismissed as politically insignificant.[114]

It is understandable for a reformer to limit his present proposals for change to those with a real prospect of success. But it is hardly reassuring for Williams to cite the fact that only 'a very small minority' has urged euthanasia for 'hopelessly defective infants' as the *only* reason for not pressing for such legislation now. If, as Williams sees it, the only advantage voluntary euthanasia has over the involuntary variety lies in the organized movements on its behalf, that advantage can readily be wiped out.

In any event, I do not think that such 'a very small minority' has advocated 'humanitarian infanticide.' Until the organization of the British and American societies led to a concentration on the voluntary type, and until the by-products of the Nazi euthanasia programme somewhat embarrassed, if only temporarily, most proponents of involuntary euthanasia, about as many writers urged one type as another.[115] Indeed, some euthanasiasts have taken considerable pains to demonstrate the superiority of defective infant euthanasia over incurably ill euthanasia.[116]

As for dismissing euthanasia of defective infants as 'politically insignificant,' the only poll that I know of which measured the public response to both types of euthanasia revealed that *45 per cent favoured euthanasia for defective infants under certain conditions while only 37.3 per cent approved euthanasia for the incurably and painfully ill under any conditions.*[117] Furthermore, of those who favoured the mercy-killing cure for incurable adults, some 40 per cent would require only family permission or medical board approval, but not the patient's permission.[118]

Nor do I think it irrelevant that while public resistance caused Hitler to yield on the adult euthanasia front, the killing of malformed and idiot children continued unhindered to the end of the war, the definition of 'children' expanding all the while.[119] Is it the embarrassing experience of the Nazi euthanasia programme which has rendered destruction of defective infants presently 'politically insignificant'? If so, is it any more of a jump for the incurably and painfully ill to the unorthodox political thinker than it is from the hopelessly defective infant to the same 'unsavoury character'? Or is it not so much that the euthanasiasts are troubled by the Nazi experience as it is that they are troubled that the public is troubled by the Nazi experience?

I read Williams's comments on defective infants for the proposition that there are some very good reasons for euthanatizing defective infants, but the time is not yet ripe. When will it be? When will the proposal become politically significant? After a voluntary euthanasia law is on the books and public opinion is sufficiently 'educated'?

Williams's reasons for not extending euthanasia—once we legalize it in the narrow 'voluntary' area—to the senile and the defective are much less forceful and much less persuasive than his arguments for legalizing voluntary euthanasia in the first place. I regard this as another reason for not legalizing voluntary euthanasia in the first place.

B. THE PARADE OF HORRORS

'Look, when the messenger cometh, shut the door, and hold him fast at the door: *is* not the sound of his master's feet behind him?'[120]

This is the 'wedge principle,' the 'parade of horrors' objection, if you will, to voluntary euthanasia. Glanville Williams's peremptory retort is:

This use of the 'wedge' objection evidently involves a particular determination as to the meaning of words, namely the words 'if raised to a general line of conduct.' The author supposes, for the sake of argument, that the merciful extinction of life in a suffering patient is not in itself immoral. Still it is immoral, because if it were permitted this would admit 'a most dangerous wedge that might eventually put all life in a precarious condition.' It seems a sufficient reply to say that this type of reasoning could be used to condemn any act whatever, because there is no human conduct from which evil cannot be imagined to follow if it is persisted in when some of the circumstances are changed. All moral questions involve the drawing of a line, but the 'wedge principle' would make it impossible to draw a line, because the line would have to be pushed farther and farther back until all action became vetoed.[121]

I agree with Williams that if a first step is 'moral' it is moral wherever a second step may take us. The real point, however, the point that Williams sloughs, is that whether or not the first step is precarious, is perilous, is worth taking, rests in part on what the second step is likely to be.

It is true that the 'wedge' objection can always be advanced, the horrors can always be paraded. But it is no less true that on some occasions the objection is much more valid than it is on others. One reason why the 'parade of horrors' cannot be too lightly dismissed in this particular instance is that Miss Voluntary Euthanasia is not likely to be going it alone for very long. Many of her admirers, as I have endeavoured to show in the preceding section, would be neither surprised nor distressed to see her joined by Miss Euthanatize the Congenital Idiots and Miss Euthanatize the Permanently Insane and Miss Euthanatize the Senile Dementia. And these lasses—whether or not they themselves constitute a 'parade of horrors'—certainly make excellent majorettes for such a parade:

Some are proposing what is called euthanasia; at present only a proposal for killing those who are a nuisance to themselves; but soon to be applied to those who are a nuisance to other people.[122]

Another reason why the 'parade of horrors' argument cannot be too lightly dismissed in this particular instance, it seems to me, *is* that the parade *has* taken place in our time and the order of procession has been headed by the killing of the 'incurables' and the 'useless':

Even before the Nazis took open charge in Germany, a propaganda barrage was directed against the traditional compassionate nineteenth-century attitudes toward the chronically ill, and for the adoption of a utilitarian, Hegelian point of view. . . . Lay opinion was not neglected in this campaign. Adults were propagandized by motion pictures, one of which, entitled 'I Accuse,' deals entirely with euthanasia. This film depicts the life history of a woman suffering from multiple sclerosis; in it her husband, a doctor, finally kills her to the accompaniment of soft piano music rendered by a sympathetic colleague in an adjoining room. Acceptance of this ideology was implanted even in the children. A widely used high-school mathematics text . . . included problems stated in distorted terms of the cost of caring for and rehabilitating the chronically sick and crippled. One of the problems asked, for instance, how many new housing units could be built and how many marriage-allowance loans could be given to newly wedded couples for the amount of money it cost the state to care for 'the crippled, the criminal and the insane. . . .' The beginnings at first were merely a subtle shift in emphasis in the basic attitude of the physicians. *It started with the acceptance of the attitude, basic in the euthanasia movement, that there is such a thing as life not worthy to be lived.* This attitude in its early stages concerned itself merely with the severely and chronically sick. Gradually the sphere of those to be included in this category was enlarged to encompass the socially unproductive, the ideologically unwanted, the racially unwanted and finally all non-Germans. But it is important to realize that the infinitely small wedged-in lever from which this entire trend of mind received its impetus was the attitude toward the non-rehabilitatable sick.[123]

The apparent innocuousness of Germany's 'small beginnings' is perhaps best shown by the fact that German Jews were at first excluded from the programme. For it was originally conceived that 'the blessing of euthanasia should be granted only to [true] Germans.'[124]

Relatively early in the German programme, Pastor Braune, Chairman of the Executive Committee of the Domestic Welfare Council of the German Protestant Church, called for a halt to euthanasia measures 'since they strike sharply at the moral foundations of the nation as a whole. The inviolability of human life is a pillar of any social order.'[125] And the pastor raised the same question which euthanasia opponents ask today, as well they might, considering the disinclination of many in the movement to stop at voluntary 'mercy-killings': Where do we, how do we, draw the line? The good pastor asked:

How far is the destruction of socially unfit life to go? The mass-methods used so far have quite evidently taken in many people who are to a considerable degree of sound mind. . . . Is it intended to strike only at the utterly hopeless cases—the idiots and imbeciles? The instruction sheet, as already mentioned, also lists senile diseases. The latest decree by the same authorities requires that children with serious congenital disease and malformation of every kind be registered, to be collected and processed in special institutions. This necessarily gives rise to grave apprehensions. Will a line be drawn at the tubercular? In the case of persons in custody by court order, euthanasia measures have evidently already been initiated. Are other abnormal or anti-social persons likewise to be included? Where is the borderline? Who is abnormal, anti-social, hopelessly sick? [126]

Williams makes no attempt to distinguish or minimize the Nazi Germany experience. Apparently he does not consider it worthy of mention in a euthanasia discussion.

A FINAL REFLECTION

There have been and there will continue to be compelling circumstances when a doctor or relative or friend will violate The Law on the Books and, more often than not, receive protection from The Law in Action. But this is not to deny that there are other occasions when The Law on the Books operates to stay the hand of all concerned, among them situations where the patient is in fact (1) presently incurable, (2) beyond the aid of any respite which may come along in his life expectancy, suffering (3) intolerable and (4) unmitigable pain and of a (5) fixed and (6) rational desire to die. That any euthanasia programme may only be the opening wedge for far more objectionable practices, and that even within the bounds of a 'voluntary' plan such as Williams's the incidence of mistake or abuse is likely to be substantial, are not much solace to one in the above plight.

It may be conceded that in a narrow sense it is an 'evil' for such a patient to have to continue to suffer—if only for a little while. But in a narrow sense, long-term sentences and capital punishment are 'evils,' too.[127] If we can justify the infliction of imprisonment and death by the state 'on the ground of the social interests to be protected,' then surely we can similarly justify the postponement of death by the state. The objection that the individual is thereby treated not as an 'end' in himself but only as a 'means' to further

the common good was, I think, aptly disposed of by Holmes long ago: 'If a man lives in society, he is likely to find himself so treated.' [128]

NOTES

1. First published in the U.S. in 1957, by arrangement with the Columbia Law School. Page references in the notes following relate to the British edition (Faber & Faber, 1958).

2. Joseph Fletcher, *Morals and Medicine* (1954; Gollancz, 1955). Subsequent page references (*n*. 19, 20) relate to the U.S. edition.

3. In a number of countries, e.g. Germany, Norway, Switzerland, a compassionate motive and/or 'homicide upon request' operates to reduce the penalty. See generally Silving, 'Euthanasia: A Study in Comparative Criminal Law,' *Univ. of Pennsylvania Law Review*, 103 (1954), 350. However, apparently only Uruguayan law completely immunizes a homicide characterized by both of the above factors. The Silving article also contains an interesting and fairly extensive comparative study of assisted suicide and the degree to which it is treated differently from a direct 'mercy-killing.' In this regard see also Friedman, 'Suicide, Euthanasia and the Law,' *Medical Times*, 85 (1957), 681.

4. Williams, p. 293.

5. Id., p. 278. This seems to be the position taken by Bertrand Russell in reviewing Williams's book: 'The central theme of the book is the conflict in the criminal law between the two divergent systems of ethics which may be called respectively utilitarian and taboo morality. . . . Utilitarian morality in the wide sense in which I am using the word, judges actions by their effects. . . . In taboo morality . . . forbidden actions are sin, and they do not cease to be so when their consequences are such as we should all welcome.' (*Stanford Law Review*, 10 [1958], 382) I trust Russell would agree, should he read this article, that the issue is not quite so simple. At any rate, I trust he would agree that I stay within the system of utilitarian ethics.

6. Wechsler and Michael, 'A Rationale of the Law of Homicide,' *Columbia Law Review*, 37 (1937).

7. Williams, p. 302.

8. Cf. G. K. Chesterton, 'Euthanasia and Murder,' *American Law Review*, 8 (1937), 486, 490.

9. Williams, pp. 304, 309.

10. Section 2 (1) of the British Bill. The full text is set forth in H. Roberts, *Euthanasia and Other Aspects of Life and Death* (1936), pp. 21–6. For the Bill now favoured by the Society, see Appendix to the present volume.

11. Section 301 of the American Bill. The full text is set forth in Sullivan, *The Morality of Mercy Killing* (1950), pp. 25–8.

12. *Royal Commission on Capital Punishment*, Report (1953), Cmd No. 8932, para. 179. Cf. Bentham, *The Theory of Legislation* (Ogden edn, 1931), p. 256: 'Let us recollect that there is no room for considering the motive except when it is manifest and palpable. It would often be very difficult to discover the true or dominant motive, when the action might be equally produced by different motives, or where motives of several sorts might have co-operated in its production. In the interpretation of these doubtful cases it is necessary to distrust the malignity of the human heart, and that general disposition to exhibit a brilliant sagacity at the expense of good nature. We involuntarily deceive even ourselves as to what puts us into action. In relation even to our own motives we are wilfully blind, and are always ready to break into a passion against the occulist who desires to remove the cataract of ignorance and prejudice.' Cf. Roberts, op. cit., pp.

10–11: 'Self-deception as to one's motives, what the psychologists call "rationalization," is one of the most powerful of man's self-protective mechanisms. It is an old observation of criminal psychologists that the day-dreamers and the rationalizers account for a very large proportion of the criminal population; whilst, in murderers, this habit of self-deception is often carried to incredible lengths.' It should be noted, however, that the likelihood of faked mercy-killings would seem to be substantially reduced when such acts are not completely immunized but only categorized as a lesser degree of criminal homicide. If mercy-killings were simply taken out of the category of murder, a second line of defence might well be the appearance of a mercy-killing, but in planned murders generally the primary concern of the murderer must surely be to escape all punishment whatever, not to give a serious, but not the most serious, appearance to his act, not to substitute a long period of imprisonment for execution. Cf. the discussion of faked suicide pacts in the Royal Commission findings, op. cit., Minutes of Evidence, paras 804–7. This paper deals with proposals to legalize 'mercy-killing' completely, not with the advisability of removing it from the category of murder.

13. *House of Lords Debates,* 103, 5th series (1936), cols 484–5.

14. Banks, 'Euthanasia,' *General Practitioner,* 161 (1948), 101, 104.

15. Frohman, 'Vexing Problems in Forensic Medicine: A Physician's View' *New York Univ. Law Review,* 31 (1956), 1215, 1222.

16. Roberts, op. cit. (*n.* 10 above), pp. 14–15.

17. Earengey, 'Voluntary Euthanasia,' *Medico-Legal and Criminal Review,* 8 (1940), 91, 106 (discussion following the reading of Judge Earengey's paper).

18. 'The promoters of the bill hoped that they might be able to mollify the opposition by providing stringent safeguards. Now, they were right in thinking that if they had put in no safeguards—if they had merely said that a doctor could kill his patient whenever he thought it right—they would have been passionately opposed on this ground. So they put in the safeguards. . . . Did the opposition like these elaborate safeguards? On the contrary, they made them a matter of complaint. The safeguards would, it was said, bring too much formality into the sick-room, and destroy the relationship between doctor and patient. So the safeguards were wrong, but not one of the opposition speakers said that he would have voted for the bill without the safeguards.' (Williams, p. 298)

19. Id., pp. 302 ff. The desire to give doctors a free hand is expressed *passim* numerous times, e.g.: '[T]here should be no formalities and . . . everything should be left to the discretion of the doctor.' (p. 303) '. . . the bill would merely leave this question to the discretion and conscience of the individual medical practitioner.' (p. 304) 'It would be the purpose of the proposed legislation to set doctors free from the fear of the law so that they can think only of the relief of their patients.' (p. 305) 'It would bring the whole subject within ordinary medical practice.' (Ibid.) Williams suggests that the pertinent provisions might be worded as follows:

'1. For the avoidance of doubt, it is hereby declared that it shall be lawful for a physician whose patient is seriously ill . . . 'b. to refrain from taking steps to prolong the patient's life by medical means; . . . unless it is proved that . . . the omission was not made, in good faith for the purpose of saving the patient from severe pain in an illness believed to be of an incurable and fatal character.

'2. It shall be lawful for a physician, after consultation with another physician, to accelerate by any merciful means the death of a patient who is seriously ill, unless it is proved that the act was not done in good faith with the consent of the patient and for the purpose of saving him from severe pain in an illness believed to be of an incurable and fatal character.' (p. 308)

The completely unrestricted authorization to kill by omission may well be based on Williams's belief that, under existing law, ' "mercy-killing" by omission to prolong life is probably lawful' since the physician is 'probably exempted' from the duty to use reasonable care to conserve his patient's life 'if life has become a burden.' (p. 291) And he adds—as if this settles the legal question—that 'the morality of an omission in these circumstances is conceded by Catholics.' (Ibid.) If Williams means, as he seems to, *that once a doctor has undertaken treatment and the patient is entrusted solely to his care* he may sit by the bedside of the patient whose life has 'become a burden' and let him die—e.g. by not replacing the oxygen bottle—I submit that he is quite mistaken.

The outer limits of criminal liability for inaction are hardly free from doubt, but it seems fairly clear under existing law that the special and traditional relationship of physician and patient imposes a 'legal duty to act,' particularly where the patient is helpless and completely dependent on the physician, and that the physician who withholds life-preserving medical means of the type described above commits criminal homicide by omission. In this regard, see Burdick, *Crimes,* 2 (1946), § 466c; Hall, *Principles of Criminal Law* (1947), pp. 272–8; Kenny, *Outlines of Criminal Law* (16th edn: Turner, 1952), pp. 14–15, 107–9; Perkins, *Criminal Law* (1957), pp. 513–27; Russell, *Crime,* 1 (10th edn: Turner, 1950), pp. 449–66; Hughes, 'Criminal Omissions,' *Yale Law Journal,* 67 (1958), 590, 599–600, 621–6, 630 *n.* 142; Kirchheimer, 'Criminal Omissions,' *Harvard Law Review,* 55 (1942), 615, 625–8; Wechsler and Michael, op. cit. (*n.* 6 above), 724–5. Nor am I at all certain that the Catholics do 'concede' this point. Williams's reference is to Sullivan, op. cit. (*n.* 11 above), p. 64. But Sullivan considers therein what might be viewed as relatively remote and indirect omissions, e.g. whether to call in a very expensive specialist, whether to undergo a very painful or very drastic operation.

The Catholic approach raises nice questions and draws fine lines, e.g. how many limbs must be amputated before an operation is to be regarded as non-obligatory 'extraordinary,' as opposed to 'ordinary,' means; but they will not be dwelt upon herein. Suffice to say that apparently there has never been an indictment, let alone a conviction, for a 'mercy-killing' by omission, not even one which directly and immediately produces death. This, of course, is not to say that no such negative 'mercy-killings' have ever occurred. There is reason to think that not too infrequently this is the fate of the defective newborn infant. Williams simply asserts that the 'beneficient tendency of nature [in that 'monsters' usually die quickly after birth] is assisted, in Britain at any rate, by the practice of doctors and nurses, who, when an infant is born seriously malformed, do not "strive officiously to keep alive." ' (p. 32) Fletcher makes a similar and likewise undocumented observation that 'it has always been a quite common practice of midwives and, in modern times doctors, simply to fail to respirate monstrous babies at birth.' (op. cit [*n.* 2 above], p. 207 *n.* 54) A supposition to the same effect was made twenty years earlier in Gregg, 'The Right to Kill,' *N. American Review,* 237 (1934), 239, 242. A noted obstetrician and gynaecologist, Dr Frederick Loomis, has told of occasions where expectant fathers have, in effect, asked him to destroy the child, if born abnormal. (Loomis, *Consultation Room* [1946], p. 53) For an eloquent presentation of the problem raised by the defective infant, see id., pp. 53–64.

It is difficult to discuss the consultation feature of Williams's proposal for affirmative 'mercy-killing,' because Williams himself never discusses it. This fact, plus the fact that Williams's recurrent theme is to give the general practitioner a free hand, indicates that he himself does not regard consultation as a significant feature of his plan. The attending physician need only consult another general practitioner and there is no requirement that there be any concurrence in his diagnosis. There is no requirement of a written report. There is no indication as to what point in time there need be consultation. Probably consultation would be thought necessary only in regard to diagnosis of the disease and from that point in respect of the extent and mitigatory nature of the pain, the firmness and rationality of the desire to die to be judged solely by the attending physician. For the view that even under rather elaborate consultation requirements, in many thinly staffed communities the consultant doctor would merely reflect the view of the attending physician, see 'Life and Death,' *Time Magazine* (March 13, 1950), p. 50. After reviewing eleven case-histories of patients wrongly diagnosed as having advanced cancer—diagnoses that stood uncorrected over long periods of time and after several admissions at leading hospitals—Drs Laszlo, Colmer, Silver and Standard conclude: '[I]t became increasingly clear that the original error was one easily made, but that the continuation of that error was due to an acceptance of the original data without exploring their verity and completeness.' ('Errors in Diagnosis and Management of Cancer,' *Annals of Internal Medicine,* 33 [1950], 670)

20. In 1950 the General Assembly of the World Medical Association approved a resolution recommending to all national associations that they 'condemn the practice of euthanasia under any circumstances.' (*New York Times* [Oct. 18, 1950], p. 22) Earlier that year the Medical Society of the State of New York went on record as being 'unalterably opposed to euthanasia and to any legislation which will legalize euthanasia.' (Ibid. [May 10, 1950], p. 29).

On the other hand, euthanasiasts claim their movement finds great support in the medical profession. The most impressive and most frequently cited piece of evidence is the formation, in 1946, of a committee of 1,776 physicians for the legalization of voluntary euthanasia in New York. (See Williams, p. 296; Fletcher, op. cit. [*n.* 2 above], p. 187) Williams states that of 3,272 physicians who replied to a questionnaire in New York State in 1946, 80 per cent approved voluntary euthanasia and the Committee of 1,776 came from among this favourable group. I have been unable to find any authority for the 80 per cent figure, and Williams cites none. Some years ago, Gertrude Anne Edwards, then editor of the *Euthanasia Society Bulletin,* claimed 3,272 physicians—apparently *all* who replied—favoured legalizing voluntary euthanasia. (Edwards, 'Mercy Death for Incurables Should Be Made Legal,' *Daily Compass* [Aug. 24, 1949], p. 8) Presumably, as in the case of the recent New Jersey questionnaire discussed below, *every* physician in New York was sent a questionnaire. If so, then the figure cited, whether Williams's or Edwards's, would mean a great deal more (and support the euthanasiasts a great deal less) if it were added that 88 or 89 per cent of the physicians in the state did not reply at all. In 1940, there were over 26,000 physicians in the State of New York (U.S. Dept of Commerce, Bureau of the Census: *The Labor Force,* Pt 4, p. 366); and in 1950 there were over 30,000 (id.: *Characteristics of the Population,* Pt 32, p. 260).

In 1957 a petition for legalized euthanasia was signed by 166 New Jersey physicians, urging in effect the adoption of the American Society's Bill. (See Anderson, 'Who Signed for Euthanasia?', *America,* 96 [1957], 573) About 98 per cent of the state medical profession *declined* to sign such a petition. The Medical Society of New Jersey immediately issued a statement that 'euthanasia has been and continues to be in conflict with accepted principles of morality and sound medi-

cal practice.' When their names were published in a state newspaper, many of the 166 claimed they had not signed the petition or that they had misunderstood its purpose or that, unknown to them, it had been handled by a secretary as a routine matter.

21. It should be noted that under what might be termed the 'family plan' feature of Williams's proposal, minors might be euthanatized too. Their fate is to be 'left to the good sense of the doctor, taking into account, as he always does, the wishes of parents as well as those of the child.' (Williams, p. 303 *n.* 1) The dubious quality of the 'voluntariness' of euthanasia in these circumstances need not be laboured.

22. Frohman, loc. cit (*n.* 15 above).

23. The disturbing mental effects of morphine, 'the classic opiate for the relief of severe pain' (Schiffrin and Gross, 'Systematic Analgetics,' *Management of Pain in Cancer* [Schiffrin edn, 1956], p. 22), and 'still the most commonly used potent narcotic analgesic in treatment of cancer pain' (Bonica, 'The Management of Cancer Pain,' *General Practitioner* [Nov. 1954], pp. 35, 39), have been described in considerable detail by Drs Wolff, Hardy and Goodell in 'Studies on Pain: Measurement of the Effect of Morphine, Codeine and Other Opiates on the Pain Threshold and an Analysis of Their Relation to the Pain Experience,' *Journal of Clinical Investigation,* 19 (1940), 659, 664. The increasing use of ACTH or cortisone therapy in cancer palliation presents further problems. Such therapy 'frequently' leads to a 'severe degree of disturbance in capacity for rational, sequential thought.' (Lindemann and Clark, 'Modifications in Ego Structure and Personality Reactions under the Influence of the Effects of Drugs,' *American Journal of Psychiatry,* 108 [1952], 561, 566)

24. Goodman and Gilman, *The Pharmacological Basis of Therapeutics* (2nd edn, 1955), p. 235. To the same effect is Seevers and Pfeiffer, 'A Study of the Analgesia, Subjective Depression and Euphoria Produced by Morphine, Heroin, Dilaudid and Codeine in the Normal Human Subject,' *Journal of Pharmacological and Experimental Therapy,* 56 (1936), 166, 182, 187.

25. Sharpe, 'Medication as a Threat to Testamentary Capacity,' *N. Carolina Law Review,* 35 (1957), 380, 392, and medical authorities cited therein. In the case of ACTH or cortisone therapy, the situation is complicated by the fact that 'a frequent pattern of recovery' from psychoses induced by such therapy is 'by the occurrence of lucid intervals of increasing frequency and duration, punctuated by relapses in psychotic behavior.' (Clark *et al.,* 'Further Observations on Mental Disturbances Associated with Cortisone and ACTH Therapy,' *New England Journal of Medicine,* 249 [1953], 178, 183)

26. Sharpe, op. cit., 384. Goodman and Gilman observe that while 'different individuals require varying periods of time before the repeated administration of morphine results in tolerance . . . as a rule . . . after about two to three weeks of continued use of the same dose of alkaloid the usual depressant effects fail to appear,' whereupon 'phenomenally large doses may be taken.' (Op. cit. [*n.* 24 above], p. 234) For a discussion of 'the nature of addiction,' see Maurer and Vogel, *Narcotics and Narcotic Addiction* (1954), pp. 20–31.

27. 'Why I Oppose Mercy Killings,' *Woman's Home Companion* (June 1950), pp. 38, 103.

28. *House of Lords Debates,* 103, 5th series (1936), cols 466, 492–3. To the same effect is Lord Horder's speech in the 1950 debates (op. cit., 169, 5th series [1950], cols 551, 569). See also Gumpert, 'A False Mercy,' *The Nation,* 170 (1950), 80: 'Even the incapacitated, agonized patient in despair most of the time, may still get some joy from existence. His mood will change between longing for death and fear of death. Who would want to decide what should be done on such unsafe ground?'

29. Williams, pp. 306–7.

30. Id., p. 307.

31. Zarling, 'Psychological Aspects of Pain in Terminal Malignancies,' *Management of Pain in Cancer* (Schiffrin edn, 1956), pp. 211–12.

32. Id., pp. 213–14. See also Dr Benjamin Miller to the effect that cancer 'can be a "horrible experience" for the doctor too' and that 'a long, difficult illness may emotionally exhaust the relatives and physician even more than the patient' (op. cit. [*n.* 27 above], p. 103); and Stephen, commenting on the disclosure by a Dr Thwing that he had practised euthanasia: 'The boldness of this avowal is made particularly conspicuous by Dr Thwing's express admission that the only person for whom the lady's death, if she had been allowed to die naturally, would have been in any degree painful was not the lady herself, but Dr Thwing.' ('Murder from the Best of Motives,' *Law Quarterly Review,* 5 [1889], 188)

33. Wechsler, 'The Issues of the Nuremburg Trial,' *Political Science Quarterly,* 62 (1947), 11, 16. Cf. Cardozo, 'What Medicine Can Do for Law,' *Law and Literature* (1931), pp. 88–9: 'Punishment is necessary, indeed, not only to deter the man who is a criminal at heart, who has felt the criminal impulse, who is on the brink of indecision, but also to deter others who in our existing social organization have never felt the criminal impulse and shrink from crime in horror. Most of us have such a scorn and loathing of robbery or forgery that the temptation to rob or forge is never within the range of choice; it is never a real alternative. There can be little doubt, however, that some of this repugnance is due to the ignominy that has been attached to these and like offenses through the sanctions of the criminal law. If the ignominy were withdrawn, the horror might be dimmed.'

34. Williams, p. 283.

35. Ibid.

36. 'What to do with the hopelessly unfit? I had thought at a younger time of my life that the legalizing of euthanasia—a soft gentle-sounding word—was a thing to be encouraged; but as I pondered, and as my experience in medicine grew, I became less sure. Now my face is set against the legalization of euthanasia for any person, who, having been well, has at last become ill, for however ill they be, many get well and help the world for years after. But I *am* in favor of euthanasia for those hopeless ones who should never have been born—Nature's mistakes. In this category it is, with care and knowledge, impossible to be mistaken in either diagnosis or prognosis.' (Kennedy, 'The Problem of Social Control of the Congenital Defective,' *American Journal of Psychiatry,* 99 [1942], 13, 14)

'We doctors do not always know when a disease in a previously healthy person has become entirely incurable. But there are thousands and tens of thousands of the congenitally unfit, about whom no diagnostic error would be possible . . . with nature's mistakes . . . there can be, after five years . . . of life, no error in diagnosis, nor any hope of betterment.' (Kennedy, 'Euthanasia: To be or Not to Be,' *Colliers* [May 20, 1939], pp. 15, 58; reprinted in *Colliers* [Apr. 22, 1950], pp. 13, 51)

37. Banks, op. cit. (*n.* 14 above), 101, 106. According to him, neither 'pain' nor 'incurability' 'is capable of precise and final definition, and indeed if each case had to be argued in open court there would be conflict of medical opinion in practically every instance.' (Id., 104)

38. Wolbarst, 'Legalize Euthanasia!', *The Forum,* 94 (1935), 330, 332. But see Wolbarst, 'The Doctor Looks at Euthanasia,' *Medical Record,* 149 (1939), 354.

39. Wolbarst, 'Legalize Euthanasia!', loc. cit.

40. Ibid., 332.

41. Op. cit. (*n.* 27 above), p. 39.

42. As to how bad the bad physician can be, see generally,

even with a grain of salt, Belli, *Modern Trials,* 3 (1954), §§ 327–53. See also Regan, *Doctor and Patient and the Law* (3rd edn, 1956), pp. 17–40.

43. As Williams points out (p. 295), Dr Millard introduced the topic of euthanasia into public debate in 1932 when, in his presidential address to the Society of Medical Officers of Health, he advocated that 'mercy-killing' should be legalized. In moving the second reading of the Voluntary Euthanasia Bill, Lord Ponsonby stated that 'the movement in favour of drafting a Bill' had 'originated' with Dr Millard. (*House of Lords Debates,* 103, 5th series [1936], cols 466–7)

44. 'The Case for Euthanasia,' *Fortnightly Review,* 136 (1931), 701, 717. Under his proposed safeguards (two independent doctors, followed by a 'medical referee') Dr Millard viewed error in diagnosis as a non-deterrable 'remote possibility.' (Ibid.)

45. Euthanasia opponents readily admit this. See e.g. Miller, op. cit. (*n.* 27 above), p. 38.

46. Op. cit., 702.

47. Frohman, op. cit. (*n.* 15 above), 1215, 1216. Dr Frohman added: 'We practice our art with the tools and information yielded by laboratory and research scientists, but an ill patient is not subject to experimental control, nor are his reactions always predictable. A good physician employs his scientific tools whenever they are useful, but many are the times when intuition, chance, and faith are his most successful techniques.'

48. Laszlo *et al.,* loc. cit. (*n.* 19 above). For more detailed references, see my article as it originally appeared, *Minnesota Law Review,* 42 (1958), 997–8.

49. See Williams, p. 283.

50. 'Pro & Con: Shall We Legalize "Mercy Killing"?', *Reader's Digest* (Nov. 1938), pp. 94, 96.

51. James, 'Euthanasia—Right or Wrong?', *Survey Graphic* (May 1948), pp. 241, 243; Wolbarst, 'The Doctor Looks at Euthanasia,' *Medical Record,* 149 (1939), 354, 355.

52. Thus Dr Millard in his leading article, op. cit. (*n.* 44 above), 710, states: 'A patient who is too ill to understand the significance of the step he is taking has got beyond the stage when euthanasia ought to be administered. In any case his sufferings are probably nearly over.' Glanville Williams similarly observes (pp. 342–4): 'Under the bill as I have proposed to word it, the consent of the patient would be required, whereas it seems that some doctors are now accustomed to give fatal doses without consulting the patient. I take it to be clear that no legislative sanction can be accorded to this practice, in so far as the course of the disease is deliberately anticipated. The essence of the measures proposed by the two societies is that euthanasia should be voluntarily accepted by the patient. . . . The measure here proposed is designed to meet the situation where the patient's consent to euthanasia is clear and incontrovertible.'

53. Emerson, 'Who Is Incurable? A Query and a Reply,' *New York Times* (Oct. 22, 1933), § 8, p. 5 col. 1.

54. Miller, op. cit. (*n.* 27 above), p. 39.

55. For advances in the treatment of cancer, see the fuller version of the present article, op. cit. 1000–3.

56. For a discussion of the legal significance of 'mercy-killing' by omission and Williams's consultation feature for affirmative 'mercy-killing,' see *n.* 19 above.

57. Williams, p. 283.

58. Borchard, *Convicting the Innocent* (1932).

59. Frank and Frank, *Not Guilty* (1957).

60. Rudd, 'Euthanasia,' *Journal of Clinical & Experimental Psychopathology,* 14 (1953), 1, 4.

61. See United States v. Holmes, *Federal Cases,* 26, No. 15, 383 (C.C.E.D. Pa. 1842).

62. See Regina v. Dudley and Stephens, *Queen's Bench Division,* 14 (1884), 273.

63. Fuller, 'The Case of the Speluncean Explorers,' *Harvard Law Review*, 62 (1949), 616.

64. Cardozo, op. cit. (*n.* 33 above), p. 113.

65. Hall, *General Principles of Criminal Law* (1947), p. 399. Cardozo, on the other hand, seems to say that without such certainty it is wrong for those in a 'necessity' situation to escape their plight by sacrificing any life. (Loc. cit. [*n.* 64 above]) On this point, as on the whole question of 'necessity,' his reasoning, it is submitted, is paled by the careful, intensive analyses found in Hall, op. cit., pp. 377–426, and Williams, *Criminal Law: The General Part* (Wm Stevens, 1953; 2nd edn, 1961), pp. 737–44. See also Cahn, *The Moral Decision* (1955). Although he takes the position that in the Holmes' situation, 'if none sacrifice themselves of free will to spare the others—they must all wait and die together,' Cahn rejects Cardozo's view as one which 'seems to deny that we can ever reach enough certainty as to our factual beliefs to be morally justified in the action we take.' (Ibid., pp. 70–71)

Section 3.02 of the *Model Penal Code* (Tent. Draft No. 8, 1958) provides (unless the legislature has otherwise spoken) that certain 'necessity' killings shall be deemed justifiable so long as the actor was not 'reckless or negligent in bringing about the situation requiring a choice of evils or in appraising the necessity for his conduct.' The section only applies to a situation where 'the evil sought to be avoided by such conduct is greater than that sought to be prevented by the law,' e.g. killing one that several may live. The defence would not be available, e.g. 'to one who acted to save himself at the expense of another, as by seizing a raft when men are shipwrecked.' (Ibid., *Comment* to Section 3.02, p. 8) For 'in all ordinary circumstances lives in being must be assumed . . . to be of equal value, equally deserving of the law.' (Ibid.)

66. Cf. Macaulay, *Notes on the Indian Penal Code* (1851). Note B, p. 131, reprinted in *The Miscellaneous Works of Lord Macaulay*, 7 (Bibliophile edn), p. 252: 'It is often the wisest thing that a man can do to expose his life to great hazard. It is often the greatest service that can be rendered to him to do what may very probably cause his death. He may labour under a cruel and wasting malady which is certain to shorten his life, and which renders his life, while it lasts, useless to others and a torment to himself. Suppose that under these circumstances he, undeceived, gives his free and intelligent consent to take the risk of an operation which in a large proportion of cases has proved fatal, but which is the only method by which his disease can possibly be cured, and which, if it succeeds, will restore him to health and vigour. We do not conceive that it would be expedient to punish the surgeon who should perform the operation, though by performing it he might cause death, not intending to cause death, but knowing himself to be likely to cause it.'

67. Foreword by Dr Warren H. Cole in *Management of Pain in Cancer* (Schiffrin edn, 1956).

68. Bonica and Backup, 'Control of Cancer Pain,' *New Medicine*, 54 (1955), 22; Bonica, op. cit. (*n.* 23 above), 35.

69. Ibid.

70. 'The opinion appears to prevail in the medical profession that severe pain requiring potent analgesics and narcotics frequently occurs in advanced cancer. Fortunately, this does not appear to be the case. Fear and anxiety, the patient's need for more attention from the family or from the physician, are frequently mistaken for expressions of pain. Reassurance and an unhesitating approach in presenting a plan of management to the patient are well known patient "remedies," and probably the clue to success of many medical quackeries. Since superficial psychotherapy as practiced by physicians without psychiatric training is often helpful, actual psychiatric treatment is expected to be of more value. Unfortunately, the potential therapeutic usefulness of this tool has barely been explored.' (Laszlo and Spencer, 'Medical Problems in the Management of Cancer,' *Medical Clinics of N. America*, 57 [1953], 869, 875)

71. Ibid. 'Placebo' medication is medication having no pharmacologic effect given for the purpose of pleasing or humouring the patient. The survey was conducted on patients in Montefiore Hospital, New York City. One clear implication is that 'analgesics should be prescribed only after an adequate trial of placebos.'

72. The one thing agreed upon by the eminent physicians Abraham L. Wolbarst, later an officer of the Euthanasia Society of America, and James J. Walsh in their debate on 'The Right to Die' was that very, very few people ever really want to die.

Dr Walsh reported that in all the time he worked at Mother Alphonsa's Home for Incurable Cancer he never heard one patient express the wish that he 'would be better off dead' and 'I know, too, that Mother Alphonsa had very rarely heard it.' 'On the other hand,' adds Walsh, 'I have often heard neurotic patients wish that they might be taken out of existence because they could no longer bear up under the pain they were suffering. . . . They were overcome mainly by self-pity. Above all, they were sympathy seekers . . . of physical pain there was almost no trace, but they were hysterically ready, so they claimed to welcome death.' (Walsh, 'Life Is Sacred,' *The Forum*, 94 [1935], 333) Walsh's opponent, Dr Wolbarst, conceded at the outset that 'very few incurables have or express the wish to die. However great their physical suffering may be, the will to live, the desire for life, is such an overwhelming force that pain and suffering become bearable and they prefer to live.' (Wolbarst, 'Legalize Euthanasia!', loc. cit. [*n.* 38 above]) The first 'lesson' the noted British physician A. Leslie Banks learned as Resident Officer to cancer wards at the Middlesex Hospital, London, was that 'the patients, however ill they were and however much they suffered, never asked for death.' (Banks, 'Euthanasia,' *Bulletin of the New York Academy of Medicine*, 26 [1950], 297, 301)

73. On p. 241 of 'Euthanasia—Right or Wrong,' op. cit. (*n.* 51 above), Selwyn James makes considerably hay of the Euthanasia Society of America's claim that numerous cancer patients telephone the Society and beg for a doctor who will administer euthanasia. If a person retains sufficient physical and mental ability to look up a number, get to a telephone and dial, does he really have to ask *others* to deal him death? That is, if it is death he really desires and not, say, attention or pity.

74. Williams, p. 283.

75. L. A. Tollemache—and not since has there been a more persuasive euthanasiast—made an eloquent plea for voluntary euthanasia ('The New Cure for Incurables,' *Fortnightly Review*, 19 [1873], 218) in support of a similar proposal the previous year (S. D. Williams, *Euthanasia* [1872]). Tollemache's article was bitterly criticized by *The Spectator*, which stated: '[I]t appears to be quite evident, though we do not think it is expressly stated in Mr. Tollemache's article, that much the strongest arguments to be alleged for putting an end to human sufferings apply to cases where you cannot by any possibility have the consent of the sufferer to that course.' ('Mr Tollemache on the Right to Die,' *The Spectator*, 46 [1873], 206) In a letter to the editor, Mr Tollemache retorted: 'I tried to make it clear that I disapproved of such relief ever being given without the dying man's express consent. . . . But it is said that all my reasoning would apply to cases like lingering paralysis, where the sufferer might be speechless. I think not . . . where these safeguards cannot be obtained, the sufferer must be allowed to linger on. Half a loaf, says the

proverb, is better than no bread; one may be anxious to relieve what suffering one can, even though the conditions necessary for the relief of other (and perhaps worse) suffering may not exist. . . . . I have stated my meaning thus fully, because I believe it is a common misunderstanding of Euthanasia, that it must needs involve some such proceedings as the late Mr Charles Buxton advocated (not perhaps quite seriously)—namely, the summary extinction of idiots and of persons in their dotage.' ('The Limits of Euthanasia,' *The Spectator,* 46 [1873], 240) I give this round to the voluntary euthanasiasts.

76. Williams, pp. 297–8.

77. *House of Lords Debates,* 103, 5th series (1936), cols 466, 471.

78. Ibid.

79. Ibid., 169 (1950), cols 551, 559.

80. *New York Times* (Jan. 17, 1938), p. 21 col. 8.

81. Ibid. (Jan. 27, 1939), p. 21 col. 7 (my italics). That the report was accurate in this regard is underscored by Mr Nixdorff's letter to the editor, wherein he complained only that 'the patient who petitions the court for euthanasia should not be described as a "voluntary"' and that 'the best definition of euthanasia is "merciful release"' rather than 'mercy "killing"' or even mercy "death"' because "being killed is associated with fear, injury and the desire to escape' and 'many people dislike even to talk about death.' (Ibid. [Jan. 30, 1939], p. 12 col. 7).

82. Ibid. (Feb. 14, 1939), p. 2 col. 6.

83. See *n.* 36 and accompanying text.

84. See *n.* 88–92 below. More than a hundred reporters, photographers and broadcasters attended the Sander trial. In ten days of court sessions, the press corps filed 1,600,000 words. ('Not Since Scopes?', *Time Magazine* [March 13, 1950], p. 43)

85. *New York Times* (Jan. 12, 1950), p. 54 col. 1.

86. Ibid. (Jan. 9, 1950), p. 40 col. 2.

87. Ibid. (Jan. 18, 1950), p. 33 col. 5.

88. Ibid. (Feb. 24, 1950), p. 1 col. 6; ibid. (Feb. 28, 1950), p. 1 col. 2; 'Similar to Murder,' *Time Magazine* (March 6, 1950), p. 20. Although Dr Sander's own notation was to the effect that he had given the patient 'ten cc of air intravenously repeated four times' and that the patient 'expired within ten minutes after this was started' (*New York Times* [Feb. 24, 1950], p. 15 col. 5; 'Similar to Murder,' loc. cit.), and the attending nurse testified that the patient was still 'gasping' when the doctor injected the air (*New York Times* [Feb. 28, 1950], p. 1 col. 2), the defendant's position at the trial was that the patient was dead before he injected the air (ibid. [March 7, 1950], p. 1 col. 1; 'The Obsessed,' *Time Magazine* [March 13, 1950], p. 23); his notes were not meant to be taken literally, 'it's a casual dictation . . . merely a way of closing out the chart' (*New York Times* [March 7, 1950], p. 19 col. 2). Dr Sander was acquitted. (Ibid. [March 10, 1950], p. 1 col. 6) The alleged 'mercy-killing' split the patient's family: the husband and one brother sided with the doctor; another brother felt that the patient's fate 'should have been left to the will of God.' ('40 cc of Air,' *Time Magazine* [Jan. 9, 1950], p. 13) Shortly afterwards, Dr Sander's licence to practise medicine in New Hampshire was revoked, but was soon restored. (*New York Times* [June 29, 1950], p. 31 col. 6) He was also ousted from his county medical society, but after four years' struggle gained admission to one. (Ibid. [Dec. 2, 1954], p. 25 col. 6)

89. Ibid. (Jan. 28, 1950), p. 30 col. 1; ibid. (Feb. 1, 1950), p. 54 col. 3; ibid. (Feb. 2, 1950), p. 22 col. 5; 'For Love or Pity,' *Time Magazine* (Feb. 6, 1950), p. 15; 'The Father Killer,' *Newsweek* (Feb. 13, 1950), p. 21. Miss Paight was acquitted on the ground of 'temporary insanity.' (*New York Times* [Feb. 8, 1950], p. 1 col. 2)

90. 'The Father Killer,' *Newsweek* (Feb. 13, 1950), p. 21.

91. See *n.* 89 above. Miss Paight was obsessed with the idea that 'Daddy must never know he had cancer.' (*New York Times* [Jan. 28, 1950], p. 30 col. 1)

92. ' "I had to do it. I couldn't bear to see him suffering." . . . Once, when she woke up from a strong sedative, she said: "Is Daddy dead yet? I can't ever sleep until he is dead." ' ('The Father Killer,' loc. cit.)

93. Rex v. Simpson (*Criminal Appeals Reports,* 11, p. 218; *Law Journal King's Bench,* 84 [1915], 1893) dealt with a young soldier on leave, who, while watching his severely ill child and waiting for his unfaithful wife to return home, cut the child's throat with a razor. His statement was as follows: 'The reason why I done it was I could not see it suffer any more than what it really had done. She was not looking after the child, and it was lying there from morning to night, and no one to look after it, and I could not see it suffer any longer and have to go away and leave it.' Simpson was convicted of murder and his application for leave to appeal dismissed. The trial judge was held to have properly directed the jury that they were not at liberty to find a verdict of manslaughter, though the prisoner killed the child 'with the best and kindest motives.'

94. Told to undergo a serious operation, and worried about the fate of her thirty-one-year-old imbecile son if she were to succumb, sixty-two-year-old Mrs May Brownhill took his life by giving him about a hundred aspirins and then placing a gas-tube in his mouth. (*The Times,* London [Oct. 2, 1934], p. 11 col. 2; *New York Times* [Dec. 2, 1934], p. 25 col. 1; ibid. [Dec. 4, 1934], p. 15 col. 3) Her family doctor testified that the boy's life had been 'a veritable living death.' (*The Times,* London [Dec. 3, 1934], p. 11 col. 4) She was sentenced to death, with a strong recommendation for mercy (ibid.; also *New York Times* [Dec. 2, 1934], p. 25 col. 1), then reprieved two days later (*The Times,* London [Dec. 4, 1934], p. 14 col. 2), and finally pardoned and set free three months later (ibid. [March 4, 1935], p. 11, col. 3; 'Mother May's Holiday,' *Time Magazine* [March 11, 1935], p. 21). According to one report, the Home Office acted 'in response to nation-wide sentiment.' (*New York Times* [March 3, 1935], p. 3 col. 2) The *Chicago Tribune* report of the case is reprinted in Harno, *Criminal Law and Procedure* (4th edn. 1957), p. 36 *n.* 2. Incidentally, Mrs Brownhill's own operation was quite successful. (*The Times,* London [Dec. 3, 1934], p. 11 col. 4)

95. Gordon Long gassed his deformed and imbecile seven-year-old daughter to death, stating he loved her 'more so than if she had been normal.' ('Goodbye,' *Time Magazine* [Dec. 2, 1946], p. 32) He pleaded guilty and was sentenced to death, but within a week the sentence was commuted to life imprisonment. (*The Times,* London [Nov. 23, 1946], p. 2 col. 7; ibid. [Nov. 29, 1946], p. 2 col. 7)

96. For the American cases referred to here, see *Minnesota Law Review,* 42 (1958), 1021.

97. In 'The Doctor Looks at Euthanasia,' loc. cit. (*n.* 38 above), Dr Wolbarst describes the Brownhill case as an 'act of mercy, based on pure mother-love' for which, thanks to the growth of the euthanasia movement in England, 'it is doubtful that this poor woman even would be put on trial at the present day.'

In 'Taking Life Legally,' *Magazine Digest* (1947), Louis Greenfield's testimony that what he did 'was against the law of man, but not against the law of God' is cited with apparent approval. The article continues: 'The acquittal of Mr Greenfield is indicative of a growing attitude towards euthanasia, or "mercy-killing," as the popular press phrases it. Years ago, a similar act would have drawn the death sentence; today, the mercy-killer can usually count on the sympathy and under-standing of the court—and his freedom.'

98. Williams, p. 283 n. 1. For a discussion of the Simpson case, see n. 93 above.

99. Williams, p. 293. For a discussion of the Sander case, see n. 88 above. The other case as Williams notes (p. 293 n. 2), is the same as that described by Lord Ponsonby in 1936 in the House of Lords debate (see p. 107).

100. Williams, p. 293. Williams does not cite any particular part of the 39-page Silving article, 'Euthanasia: A Study in Comparative Criminal Law,' op. cit. (n. 3 above), but in context he appears to allude to pp. 353–4 of that article.

101. In addition to the Sander case, the cases to which Williams seems to refer are: the Paight case (see n. 89–92 above and accompanying text); the Braunsdorf case (see n. 96 above); and the Mohr case. Only in the Mohr case was there apparently euthanasia by request.

102. According to the Royal Warrant, the Commission was appointed in May 1949 'to consider and report whether liability under the criminal law in Great Britain to suffer capital punishment for murder should be limited or modified,' but was precluded from considering whether capital punishment should be abolished. (*Royal Commission on Capital Punishment*, Report [1953], Cmd No. 8932, p. iii) For an account of the circumstances which led to the appointment of the Commission, see Prevezer, 'The English Homicide Act: A New Attempt to Revise the Law of Murder,' *Columbia Law Review*, 57 (1957), 624, 629.

103. 'It was agreed by almost all witnesses' that it would 'often prove extremely difficult to distinguish killings where the motive was merciful from those where it was not.' (Report, para. 179) Thus the Commission 'reluctantly' concluded that 'it would not be possible' to frame and apply a definition which would satisfactorily cover these cases. (Ibid., para. 180)

104. Ibid.

105. Minutes of Evidence (Dec. 1, 1949), pp. 219–20. Mr Hughes, however, would try the apparent 'mercy-killer' for murder rather than manslaughter, 'because the evidence should be considered not in *camera* but in open court, when it may turn out that it was not manslaughter.' (Ibid., para. 2825) '[T]he onus should rest upon the person so charged to prove that it was not a malicious, but a merciful killing.' (Ibid., para. 2826)

106. Minutes of Evidence (Jan. 5, 1950), para. 3120. The Lord Chief Justice did not refer to the case by name, but his reference to Brownhill is unmistakable. For an account of this case, see n. 94 above.

107. Ibid.

108. Ibid., para. 3315.

109. Ibid.

110. Williams, p. 310.

111. Ibid.

112. Banks, 'Euthanasia,' op. cit. (n. 72 above), 297, 305.

313. 'Mental diseases are said to be responsible for as much time lost in hospitals as all other diseases combined.' (Boudreau, 'Mental Health: The New Public Health Frontier,' *Annals of the American Academy of Political & Social Science*, 286 [1953], 1) Some twenty years ago, there were 'over 900,-000 patients under the care and supervision of mental hospitals'. (Felix and Kramer, 'Extent of the Problem of Mental Disorders,' op. cit. this n., 5, 10) Taking only the figures of persons sufficiently ill to warrant admission into a hospital for long-term care of psychiatric disorders, 'at the end of 1950 there were 577,000 patients . . . in all long-term mental hospitals.' (Ibid., 9) This figure represents 3.8 per thousand population, and a 'fourfold increase in number of patients and a twofold increase in ratio of patients to general population since 1903.' (Ibid.) 'During 1950, the state, county and city

mental hospitals spent \$390,000,000 for care and maintenance of their patients.' (Ibid., 13)

114. Williams, pp. 311–12.

115. See *Minnesota Law Review*, 42 (1958), 1027–8.

116. Dr Foster Kennedy believes euthanasia of congenital idiots has two major advantages over voluntary euthanasia: (1) error in diagnosis and possibility of betterment by unforeseen discoveries are greatly reduced, and (2) there is not mind enough to hold any dream or hope which is likely to be crushed by the forthright statement that one is doomed, a necessary communication under a voluntary euthanasia programme. Kennedy's views are contained in 'Euthanasia: To Be or Not to Be,' op. cit. (n. 36 above), 15; reprinted, with the notation that his views remained unchanged, op. cit. (n. 36), 13; 'The Problem of Social Control of the Congenital Defective,' op. cit. (n. 36), 13. See also text quoted n. 36 above.

117. The Fortune Quarterly Survey: IX, *Fortune Magazine* (July 1937), pp. 96, 106. Actually, a slight *majority* of those who took a position on the defective infants favoured euthanasia under certain circumstances since 45 per cent approved under certain circumstances, 40.5 per cent were unconditionally opposed, and 14.5 per cent were undecided. In the case of the incurably ill, only 37.3 per cent were in favour of euthanasia under any set of safeguards, 47.5 per cent were flatly opposed, and 15.2 per cent took no position.

Every major poll taken in the United States on the question has shown popular opposition to voluntary euthanasia. In 1937 and 1939 the American Institute of Public Opinion polls found 46 per cent in favour, 54 per cent opposed. A 1947 poll by the same group found only 37 per cent in favour, 54 per cent opposed and 9 per cent of no opinion. For a discussion of these and other polls by various newspapers and a breakdown of the public attitude on the question in terms of age, sex, economic and educational levels, see note, 'Judicial Determination of Moral Conduct in Citizenship Hearings,' *Univ. of Chicago Law Review*, 16 (1948), 138, 141–2 and n. 11. As Williams notes, however (p. 296), a 1939 British Institute of Public Opinion poll found 68 per cent of the British in favour of some form of legal euthanasia.

118. The Fortune Quarterly Survey, op. cit. (n. 117 above), p. 106.

119. Mitscherlich and Meilke, *Doctors of Infamy* (1949), p. 114. The Reich Committee for Research on Hereditary Diseases and Constitutional Susceptibility to Severe Diseases originally dealt only with child patients up to the age of three; but the age limit was later raised to eight, twelve and apparently even sixteen or seventeen. (Ibid., p. 116)

120. II Kings, 6: 32, quoted and applied in Sperry, 'The Case against Mercy Killing,' *American Mercury*, 70 (1950), 271, 276.

121. Williams, pp. 280–1. At this point Williams is quoting from Sullivan, *Catholic Teaching on the Morality of Euthanasia* (1949), pp. 54–5. This thorough exposition of the Catholic Church's attitude to euthanasia was originally published by the Catholic Univ. of America Press, then republished in 1950 by the Newman Press under the title *The Morality of Mercy Killing* (cf. n. 11 above).

122. Chesterton, 'Euthanasia and Murder,' loc. cit. (n. 8 above).

123. Alexander, 'Medical Science under Dictatorship,' *New England Journal of Medicine*, 241 (1949), 39, 40, 44 (my italics). To the same effect is Ivy, 'Nazi War Crimes of a Medical Nature,' *Journal of the American Medical Association*, 139 (1949), 131, 132, concluding that the practice of euthanasia was a factor which led to 'mass killing of the aged, the chronically ill, "useless eaters" and the politically undesirable,' and Ivy, 'Nazi War Crimes of a Medical Nature,' *Federation Bulletin*, 33 (1947), 133, 142, noting that one of the

arguments the Nazis employed to condone their criminal medical experiments was that 'if it is right to take the life of useless and incurable persons, which as they point out has been suggested in England and the United States, then it is right to take the lives of persons who are destined to die for political reasons, (Drs Leo Alexander and I. C. Ivy were both expert medical advisers to the prosecution at the Nuremberg Trials.)

See also the entry for Nov. 25, 1940, in Shirer, *Berlin Diary* (1941), pp. 454, 458–9: 'I have at last got to the bottom of these "mercy killings." It's an evil tale. The Gestapo, with the knowledge and approval of the German government, is systematically putting to death the mentally deficient population of the Reich. . . . X, a German, told me yesterday that relatives are rushing to get their kin out of private asylums and out of the clutches of the authorities. He says the Gestapo is doing to death persons who are merely suffering temporary derangement or just plain nervous breakdown. What is still unclear to me is the motive for these murders. Germans themselves advance three: . . . [3] That they are simply the result of the extreme Nazis deciding to carry out their eugenic and sociological ideas. . . . The third motive seems most likely to me. For years a group of radical Nazi sociologists who were instrumental in putting through the Reich's sterilization laws have pressed for a national policy of eliminating the mentally unfit. They say they have disciples among many sociologists in other lands, and perhaps they have. Paragraph two of the form letter sent to the relatives plainly bears the stamp of the sociological thinking: "In view of the nature of his serious, incurable ailment, his death, which saved him from a lifelong institutional sojourn, is to be regarded merely as a release." '

This contemporaneous report is supported by evidence uncovered at the Nuremberg Medical Trial. Thus, an August 1940 form letter to the relatives of a deceased mental patient states in part: 'Because of her grave mental illness life was a torment for the deceased. You must therefore look on her death as a release.' This form letter is reproduced in Mitscherlich and Mielke, op. cit. (*n.* 119 above), p. 103. Dr Alexander Mitscherlich and Mr Fred Mielke attended the trial as delegates chosen by a group of German medical societies and universities.

According to the testimony of the chief defendant at the Nuremberg Medical Trial, Karl Brandt, Reich Commissioner for Health and Sanitation and personal physician to Hitler, the Führer had indicated in 1935 that if war came he would effectuate the policy of euthanasia, since in the general upheaval of war the open resistance to be anticipated on the part of the Church would not be the potent force it might otherwise be. (Ibid., p. 91) Certain petitions to Hitler by parents of malformed children requesting authority for 'mercy deaths' seem to have played a part in definitely making up his mind. (Ibid.)

124. Defendant Viktor Brack, Chief Administrative Officer in Hitler's private chancellery, so testified at the Nuremberg Medical Trial. (*Trials of War Criminals before the Nuremberg Military Tribunal under Control Council Law No. 10,* 1 [1950], 877–80 ['The Medical Case'])

125. Mitscherlich and Mielke, op. cit., p. 107.

126. Ibid. According to testimony at the Nuremberg Medical Trial, although they were told that 'only incurable patients, suffering severely, were involved,' even the medical consultants to the programme were 'not quite clear on where the line was to be drawn.' (Ibid., p. 94)

127. Perhaps this would not be true if the only purpose of punishment was to reform the criminal. But whatever *ought to be* the case, this obviously *is not.* 'If it were, every prisoner should be released as soon as it appears clear that he will never repeat his offence, and if he is incurable he should not be punished at all.' (Holmes, *The Common Law* [1881], p. 42)

128. Ibid., p. 44.

Natural Death Act*

7185. This act shall be known and may be cited as the Natural Death Act.

7186. The Legislature finds that adult persons have the fundamental right to control the decisions relating to the rendering of their own medical care, including the decision to have life-sustaining procedures withheld or withdrawn in instances of a terminal condition.

The Legislature further finds that modern medical technology has made possible the artificial prolongation of human life beyond natural limits.

The Legislature further finds that, *in the interest of protecting individual autonomy,* such prolongation of life for persons with a terminal condition may cause loss of patient dignity, *and* unnecessary pain and suffering, [and an unreasonable emotional and financial hardship on the patient's family,] [1] while providing nothing medically necessary or beneficial to the patient.

The Legislature further finds that there exists considerable uncertainty in the medical and legal professions as to the legality of terminating the

* Passed by the California state legislature and signed into law by Governor Edmund G. Brown, Jr. in 1976.

use or application of life-sustaining procedures where the patient has voluntarily and in sound mind evidenced a desire that such procedures be withheld or withdrawn.

In recognition of the dignity and privacy which patients have a right to expect, the Legislature hereby declares that the laws of the State of California shall recognize the right of an adult person to make a written directive instructing his physician to withhold or withdraw life-sustaining procedures in the event of a terminal condition.

7187. The following definitions shall govern the construction of this chapter:

(a) "Attending physician" means the physician selected by, or assigned to, the patient who has primary responsibility for the treatment and care of the patient.

(b) "Directive" means a written document voluntarily executed by the declarant in accordance with the requirements of Section 7188. The directive, or a copy of the directive, shall be made part of the patient's medical records.

(c) "Life-sustaining procedure" means any medical procedure or intervention which utilizes mechanical or other artificial means to sustain, restore, or supplant a vital function, which, when applied to a qualified patient, would serve only to artificially prolong the moment of death and where, in the judgment of the attending physician, death is imminent whether or not such procedures are utilized. "Life-sustaining procedure" shall not include the administration of medication or the performance of any medical procedure deemed necessary to alleviate pain.

(d) "Physician" means a physician and surgeon licensed by the Board of Medical Quality Assurance or the Board of Osteopathic Examiners.

(e) "Qualified patient" means a patient diagnosed and certified in writing to be afflicted with a terminal condition by two physicians, one of whom shall be the attending physician, who have personally examined the patient.

(f) "Terminal condition" means an incurable condition caused by injury, disease, or illness, which, regardless of the application of life-sustaining procedures, would, within reasonable medical judgment, produce death, and where the application of life-sustaining procedures serve only to postpone the moment of death of the patient.

7188. Any adult person may execute a directive directing the withholding or withdrawal of life-sustaining procedures in a terminal condition. The directive shall be signed by the declarant in the presence of two witnesses not related to the declarant by blood or marriage and who would not be entitled to any portion of the estate of the declarant upon his decease under any will of the declarant or codicil thereto then existing or, at the time of the directive, by operation of law then existing. In addition, a witness to a directive shall not be the attending physician, an employee of the attending physician or a health facility in which the declarant is a patient, or any person who has a claim against any portion of the estate of the declarant upon his decease at the time of the execution of the directive. The directive shall be in the following form:

DIRECTIVE TO PHYSICIANS

Directive made this _____ day of _____ (month, year).

I _____, being of sound mind, willfully, and voluntarily make known my desire that my life shall not be artificially prolonged under the circumstances set forth below, do hereby declare:

1. If at any time I should have an incurable injury, disease, or illness certified to be a terminal condition by two physicians, and where the application of life-sustaining procedures would serve only to artifically prolong the moment of my death and where my physician determines that my death is imminent whether or not life-sustaining procedures are utilized, I direct that such procedures be withheld or withdrawn, and that I be permitted to die naturally.

2. In the absence of my ability to give directions regarding the use of such life-sustaining procedures, it is my intention that this directive shall be honored by my family and physician(s) as the final expression of my legal right to refuse medical or surgical treatment and accept the consequences from such refusal.

3. If I have been diagnosed as pregnant and that diagnosis is known to my physician, this directive shall have no force or effect during the course of my pregnancy.

4. I have been diagnosed and notified at least 14 days ago as having a terminal condition by _____, M.D., whose address is _____, and whose telephone number is _____. I understand

that if I have not filled in the physician's name and address, it shall be presumed that I did not have a terminal condition when I made out this directive.

5. This directive shall have no force or effect five years from the date filled in above.

6. I understand the full import of this directive and I am emotionally and mentally competent to make this directive.

Signed _____

City, County and State of Residence _____

The declarant has been personally known to me and I believe him or her to be of sound mind.

Witness _____

Witness _____

7188.5. A directive shall have no force or effect if the declarant is *a* patient in a skilled nursing facility as defined in subdivision (c) of Section 1250 at the time the directive is executed unless one of the two witnesses to the directive is a patient advocate or ombudsman as may be designated by the State Department of Aging for this purpose pursuant to any other applicable provision of law. The patient advocate or ombudsman shall have the same qualifications as a witness under Section 7188.

The intent of this section is to recognize that some patients in skilled nursing facilities may be so insulated from a voluntary decisionmaking role, by virtue of the custodial nature of their care, as to require special assurance that they are capable of willfully and voluntarily executing a directive.

7189. (a) A directive may be revoked at any time by the declarant, without regard to his mental state or competency, by any of the following methods:

(1) By being canceled, defaced, obliterated, or burnt, torn, or otherwise destroyed by the declarant or by some person in his presence and by his direction.

(2) By a written revocation of the declarant expressing his intent to revoke, signed and dated by the declarant. Such revocation shall become effective only upon communication to the attending physician by the declarant or by a person acting on behalf of the declarant. The attending physician shall record in the patient's medical record the time and date when he received notification of the written revocation.

(3) By a verbal expression by the declarant of his intent to revoke the directive. Such revocation shall become effective only upon communication to the attending physician by the declarant or by a person acting on behalf of the declarant. The attending physician shall record in the patient's medical record the time, date, and place of the revocation and the time, date, and place, if different, of when he received notification of the revocation.

(b) There shall be no criminal or civil liability on the part of any person for failure to act upon a revocation made pursuant to this section unless that person has actual knowledge of the revocation.

7189.5. A directive shall be effective for five years from the date of execution thereof unless sooner revoked in a manner prescribed in Section 7189. Nothing in this chapter shall be construed to prevent a declarant from reexecuting a directive at any time in accordance with the formalities of Section 7188, including reexecution subsequent to a diagnosis of a terminal condition. If the declarant has executed more than one directive, such time shall be determined from the date of execution of the last directive known to the attending physician. If the declarant becomes comatose or is rendered incapable of communicating with the attending physician, the directive shall remain in effect for the duration of the comatose condition or until such time as the declarant's condition renders him or her able to communicate with the attending physician.

7190. No physician or health facility which, acting in accordance with the requirements of this chapter, causes the withholding or withdrawal of life-sustaining procedures from a qualified patient, shall be subject to civil liability therefrom. No licensed health professional, acting under the direction of a physician, who participates in the withholding or withdrawal of life-sustaining procedures in accordance with the provisions of this chapter shall be subject to any civil liability. No physician, or licensed health professional acting under the direction of a physician, who participates in the withholding or withdrawal of life-sustaining procedures in accordance with the provisions of this chapter shall be guilty of any criminal act or of unprofessional conduct.

7191. (a) Prior to effecting a withholding or

withdrawal of life-sustaining procedures from a qualified patient pursuant to the directive, the attending physician shall determine that the directive complies with Section 7188, and, if the patient is mentally competent, that the directive and all steps proposed by the attending physician to be undertaken are in accord with the desires of the qualified patient.

(b) If the declarant was a qualified patient at least 14 days prior to executing or reexecuting the directive, the directive shall be conclusively presumed, unless revoked, to be the directions of the patient regarding the withholding or withdrawal of life-sustaining procedures. No physician, and no licensed health professional acting under the direction of a physician, shall be criminally or civilly liable for failing to effectuate the directive of the qualified patient pursuant to this subdivision. A failure by a physician to effectuate the directive of a qualified patient pursuant to this division shall constitute unprofessional conduct if the physician refuses to make the necessary arrangements, or fails to take the necessary steps, to effect the transfer of the qualifed patient to another physician who will effectuate the directive of the qualified patient.

(c) If the declarant becomes a qualified patient subsequent to executing the directive, and has not subsequently reexecuted the directive, the attending physician may give weight to the directive as evidence of the patient's directions regarding the withholding or withdrawal of life-sustaining procedures and may consider other factors, such as information from the affected family or the nature of the patient's illness, injury, or disease, in determining whether the totality of circumstances known to the attending physician justify effectuating the directive. No physician, and no licensed health professional acting under the direction of a physician, shall be criminally or civilly liable for failing to effectuate the directive of the qualified patient pursuant to this subdivision.

7192. (a) The withholding or withdrawal of life-sustaining procedures from a qualified patient in accordance with the provisions of this chapter shall not, for any purpose, constitute a suicide.

(b) The making of a directive pursuant to Section 7188 shall not restrict, inhibit, or impair in any manner the sale, procurement, or issuance of any policy of life insurance, nor shall it be deemed to modify the terms of an existing policy of life insurance. No policy of life insurance shall be legally impaired or invalidated in any manner by the withholding or withdrawal of life-sustaining procedures from an insured qualifed patient, notwithstanding any term of the policy to the contrary.

(c) No physician, health facility, or other health provider, and no health care service plan, insurer issuing disability insurance, self-insured employee welfare benefit plan, or nonprofit hospital service plan, shall require any person to execute a directive as a condition for being insured for, or receiving, health care services.

7193. Nothing in this chapter shall impair or supersede any legal right or legal responsibility which any person may have to effect the withholding or withdrawal of life-sustaining procedures in any lawful manner. In such respect the provisions of this chapter are cumulative.

7194. Any person who willfully conceals, cancels, defaces, obliterates, or damages the directive of another without such declarant's consent shall be guilty of a misdemeanor. Any person who, except where justified or excused by law, falsifies or forges the directive of another, or willfully conceals or withholds personal knowledge of a revocation as provided in Section 7189, with the intent to cause a withholding or withdrawal of life-sustaining procedures contrary to the wishes of the declarant, and thereby, because of any such act, directly causes life-sustaining procedures to be withheld or withdrawn and death to thereby be hastened, shall be subject to prosecution for unlawful homicide as provided in Chapter 1 (commencing with Section 187) of Title 8 of Part 1 of the Penal Code.

7195. Nothing in this chapter shall be construed to condone, authorize, or approve mercy killing, or to permit any affirmative or deliberate act or omission to end life other than to permit the natural process of dying as provided in this chapter.

SEC. 2. If any provision of this act or the application thereof to any person or circumstances is held invalid, such invalidity shall not affect other provisions or applications of the act which can be given effect without the invalid provision or application, and to this end the provisions of this act are severable.

SEC. 3. Notwithstanding Section 2231 of the

Revenue and Taxation Code, there shall be no reimbursement pursuant to this section nor shall there be any appropriation made by this act because the Legislature recognizes that during any legislative session a variety of changes to laws relating to crimes and infractions may cause both increased and decreased costs to local government entities and school districts which, in the aggregate, do not result in significant identifiable cost changes.

NOTE

1. This clause was stricken from the final version of the bill as enacted. [Ed.]

RONALD M. DWORKIN

On Not Prosecuting Civil Disobedience*

How should the government deal with those who disobey the draft laws out of conscience? Many people think the answer is obvious: the government must prosecute the dissenters, and if they are convicted it must punish them. Some people reach this conclusion easily, because they hold the mindless view that conscientious disobedience is the same as lawlessness. They think that the dissenters are anarchists who must be punished before their corruption spreads. Many lawyers and intellectuals come to the same conclusion, however, on what looks like a more sophisticated argument. They recognize that disobedience to law may be *morally* justified, but they insist that it cannot be *legally* justified, and they think that it follows from this truism that the law must be enforced. Erwin Griswold, the Solicitor General of the United States, and the former dean of the Harvard Law School, appears to have adopted this view in a recent statement. "[It] is of the essence of law," he said, "that it is equally applied to all, that it binds all alike, irrespective of personal motive. For this reason, one who contemplates civil disobedience out of moral conviction should not be surprised and must not be bitter if a criminal conviction ensues. And he must accept the fact that organized society cannot endure on any other basis."

The New York Times applauded that statement. A thousand faculty members of several universities had signed a *Times* advertisement calling on the Justice Department to quash the indictments of the Rev. William Sloane Coffin, Dr. Benjamin Spock, Marcus Raskin, Mitchell Goodman, and Michael Ferber, for conspiring to counsel various draft offenses. The *Times* said that the request to quash the indictments "confused moral rights with legal responsibilities."

But the argument that, because the government believes a man has committed a crime, it must prosecute him is much weaker than it seems. Society "cannot endure" if it tolerates all disobedience; it does not follow, however, nor is there evidence, that it will collapse if it tolerates some. In the United States prosecutors have discretion whether to enforce criminal laws in particular cases. A prosecutor may properly decide not to press charges if the lawbreaker is young, or inexperienced, or the sole support of a family, or is repentant, or turns state's evidence, or if the law is unpopular or unworkable or generally disobeyed, or if the courts are clogged with more important cases, or for dozens of other reasons. This discretion is not license—we expect prosecutors to have good reasons for exercising it—but there are, at least *prima facie,* some good reasons for not prosecuting those who disobey the draft laws out of conscience. One is the obvious reason that they act out of better motives than those who break the law out of greed or a desire to subvert government. Another is the practical reason that our society suffers a loss if it punishes a group that includes—as a group of draft dissenters does—some of its most thoughtful and loyal citizens. Jailing such men solidifies their alienation from society, and alienates many like them who are deterred by the threat.

Those who think that conscientious draft offenders should always be punished must show that these are not good reasons for exercising discretion, or they must find contrary reasons that outweigh them. What arguments might they produce? There are practical reasons for enforcing the draft laws, and I shall consider some of these later. But Dean Griswold and those who agree with him seem to rely on a fundamental moral argument that it would be unfair, not merely impractical, to let the dissenters go unpunished. They think it would be unfair, I gather,

* Reprinted from *The New York Review of Books,* June 6, 1968. Copyright © 1968–76, NYREV, Inc. Reprinted by permission of the author and the publisher.

because society could not function if everyone disobeyed laws he disapproved of or found disadvantageous. If the government tolerates those few who will not "play the game," it allows them to secure the benefits of everyone else's deference to law, without shouldering the burdens, such as the burden of the draft.

This argument is a serious one. It cannot be answered simply by saying that the dissenters would allow everyone else the privilege of disobeying a law he believed immoral. In fact, few draft dissenters would accept a changed society in which sincere segregationists were free to break civil rights laws they hated. The majority want no such change, in any event, because they think that society would be worse off for it; until they are shown this is wrong, they will expect their officials to punish anyone who assumes a privilege which they, for the general benefit, do not assume.

There is, however, a flaw in the argument. The reasoning contains a hidden assumption that makes it almost entirely irrelevant to the draft cases, and indeed to any serious case of civil disobedience in the United States. The argument assumes that the dissenters know that they are breaking a valid law, and that the privilege they assert is the privilege to do that. Of course, almost everyone who discusses civil disobedience recognizes that in America a law may be invalid because it is unconstitutional. But the critics handle this complexity by arguing on separate hypotheses: If the law is invalid, then no crime is committed, and society may not punish. If the law is valid, then a crime has been committed, and society must punish. This reasoning hides the crucial fact that the validity of the law may be doubtful. The officials and judges may believe that the law is valid, the dissenters may disagree, and both sides may have plausible arguments for their positions. If so, then the issues are different from what they would be if the law were clearly valid or clearly invalid, and the argument of fairness, designed for these alternatives, is irrelevant.

Doubtful law is by no means special or exotic in cases of civil disobedience. On the contrary. In the United States, at least, almost any law which a significant number of people would be tempted to disobey on moral grounds would be doubtful —if not clearly invalid—on constitutional grounds as well. The Constitution makes our conventional political morality relevant to the question of validity; any statute that appears to compromise that morality raises constitutional questions, and if the compromise is serious, the constitutional doubts are serious also.

The connection between moral and legal issues is especially clear in the current draft cases. Dissent has largely been based on the following moral objections: (a) The United States is using immoral weapons and tactics in Vietnam. (b) The war has never been endorsed by deliberate, considered, and open vote of the peoples' representatives. (c) The United States has no interest at stake in Vietnam remotely strong enough to justify forcing a segment of its citizens to risk death there. (d) If an army is to be raised to fight that war, it is immoral to raise it by a draft that defers or exempts college students, and thus discriminates against the economically underprivileged. (e) The draft exempts those who object to all wars on religious grounds, but not those who object to particular wars on moral grounds; there is no relevant difference between these positions, and so the draft, by making the distinction, implies that the second group is less worthy of the nation's respect than the first. (f) The law that makes it a crime to counsel draft resistance stifles those who oppose the war, because it is morally impossible to argue that the war is profoundly immoral, without encouraging and assisting those who refuse to fight it.

Lawyers will recognize that these moral positions, if we accept them, provide the basis for the following constitutional arguments: (a) The Constitution makes treaties part of the law of the land, and the United States is a party to international conventions and covenants that make illegal the acts of war the dissenters charge the nation with committing. (b) The Constitution provides that Congress must declare war; the legal issue of whether our action in Vietnam is a "war" and whether the Tonkin Bay Resolution was a "declaration" is the heart of the moral issue of whether the government has made a deliberate and open decision. (c) Both the due process clause of the Fifth and Fourteenth Amendments and the equal protection clause of the Fourteenth Amendment condemn special burdens placed on a selected class of citizens when the burden or the classification is not reasonable; the burden is unreasonable when it patently does not serve the public interest, or when it is vastly disproportionate to the interest served. If our military action in Vietnam is frivolous or perverse, as the dissenters claim, then the burden we place on men of draft age is unreasonable and unconstitutional. (d) In any event, the discrimination in favor of college students denies to the poor the equal protection of the law that is guaranteed by the Constitution. (e) If there is no pertinent difference between religious objection to all wars, and moral objection to some wars, then the classification the draft makes is arbitrary and unreasonable, and unconstitutional on that ground. The "establishment of religion" clause of the First Amendment forbids governmental pressure in favor of organized religion; if the draft's distinction coerces men in this direction, it is invalid on that count also. (f) The First Amendment also condemns invasions of freedom of speech. If the draft law's prohibition on counseling does inhibit expression of a range of views on the war, it abridges free speech.

The principal counterargument, supporting the view that the courts ought not to hold the draft unconstitutional, also involves moral issues. Under the so-called "political question" doctrine, the courts deny their own jurisdiction to pass on matters—such as foreign or military policy—whose resolution is best assigned to other branches of the government. The Boston court trying the Coffin, Spock case has already declared, on the basis of this doctrine, that it will not hear arguments about the legality of the war. But the Supreme Court has shown itself (in the reapportionment cases, for example) reluctant to refuse jurisdiction when it believed that the gravest issues of political morality were at stake and that no remedy was available through the political process. If the dissenters are right, and the war and the draft are state crimes of profound injustice to a group of citizens, then the argument that the courts must refuse jurisdiction is considerably weakened.

We cannot conclude from these arguments that the draft (or any part of it) is unconstitutional. If the Supreme Court is called upon to rule on the question, it will probably reject some of them, and refuse to consider the others on grounds that they are political. The majority of lawyers would probably agree with this result. But the arguments of unconstitutionality are at least plausible, and a reasonable and competent

lawyer might well think that they present a stronger case, on balance, than the counterarguments. If he does, he will consider that the draft is not constitutional, and there will be no way of proving that he is wrong.

Therefore we cannot assume, in judging what to do with the draft dissenters, that they are asserting a privilege to disobey valid laws. We cannot decide that fairness demands their punishment until we try to answer the further question: What should a citizen do when the law is unclear, and when he thinks it allows what others think it does not? I do not mean to ask, of course, what it is *legally* proper for him to do, or what his *legal* rights are—that would be begging the question, because it depends upon whether he is right or they are right. I mean to ask what his proper course is as a citizen, what in other words, we would consider to be "playing the game." That is a crucial question, because it cannot be wrong not to punish him if he is acting as, given his opinions, we think he should.[1]

There is no obvious answer on which most citizens would readily agree, and that is itself significant. If we examine our legal institutions and practices, however, we shall discover some relevant underlying principles and policies. I shall set out three possible answers to the question, and then try to show which of these best fits our practices and expectations. The three possibilities I want to consider are these:

(1) If the law is doubtful, and it is therefore unclear whether it permits someone to do what he wants, he should assume the worst, and act on the assumption that it does not. He should obey the executive authorities who command him, even though he thinks they are wrong, while using the political process, if he can, to change the law.

(2) If the law is doubtful, he may follow his own judgment, that is, he may do what he wants if he believes that the case that the law permits this is stronger than the case that it does not. But he may follow his own judgment only until an authoritative institution, like a court, decides the other way in a case involving him or someone else. Once an institutional decision has been reached, he must abide by that decision, even though he thinks that it was wrong. (There are, in theory, many subdivisions of this second possibility. We may say that the individual's choice is

foreclosed by the contrary decision of any court, including the lowest court in the system if the case is not appealed. Or we may require a decision of some particular court or institution. I shall discuss this second possibility in its most liberal form, namely that the individual may properly follow his own judgment until a contrary decision of the highest court competent to pass on the issue, which, in the case of the draft, is the United States Supreme Court.)

(3) If the law is doubtful, he may follow his own judgment, even after a contrary decision by the highest competent court. Of course, he must take the contrary decision of any court into account in making his judgment of what the law requires. Otherwise the judgment would not be an honest or reasonable one, because the doctrine of precedent, which is an established part of our legal system, has the effect of allowing the decision of the courts to *change* the law. Suppose, for example, that a taxpayer believes that he is not required to pay tax on certain forms of income. If the Supreme Court decides to the contrary, he should, taking into account the practice of according great weight to the decisions of the Supreme Court on tax matters, decide that the Court's decision has itself tipped the balance, and that the law now requires him to pay the tax.

Someone might think that this qualification erases the difference between the third and the second models, but it does not. The doctrine of precedent gives different weights to the decisions of different courts, and greatest weight to the decisions of the Supreme Court, but it does not make the decision of any court conclusive. Sometimes, even after a contrary Supreme Court decision, an individual may still reasonably believe that the law is on his side; such cases are rare, but they are most likely in disputes over constitutional law when civil disobedience is involved. The Court has shown itself more likely to overrule its past decisions if these have limited important personal or political rights, and it is just these decisions that a dissenter might want to challenge.

We cannot assume, in other words, that the Constitution is always what the Supreme Court says it is. Oliver Wendell Holmes, for example, did not follow such a rule in his famous dissent in the *Gitlow* case. A few years before, in *Abrams,* he had lost his battle to persuade the court that

the First Amendment protected an anarchist who had been urging general strikes against the government. A similar issue was presented in *Gitlow,* and Holmes once again dissented. "It is true," he said, "that in my opinion this criterion was departed from in [Abrams] but the convictions that I expressed in that case are too deep for it to be possible for me as yet to believe that it . . . settled the law." Holmes voted for acquitting Gitlow, on the ground that what Gitlow had done was no crime, even though the Supreme Court had recently held that it was.

Here then are three possible models for the behavior of dissenters who disagree with the executive authorities when the law is doubtful. Which of them best fits our legal and social practices?

I think it plain that we do not follow the first of these models, that is, that we do not expect citizens to assume the worst. If no court has decided the issue, and a man thinks, on balance, that the law is on his side, most of our lawyers and critics think it perfectly proper for him to follow his own judgment. Even when many disapprove of what he does—such as peddling pornography—they do not think he must desist just because its legality is subject to doubt.

It is worth pausing a moment to consider what society would lose if it did follow the first model or, to put the matter the other way, what society gains when people follow their own judgment in cases like this. When the law is uncertain, in the sense that lawyers can reasonably disagree on what a court ought to decide, the reason usually is that different legal principles and policies have collided, and it is unclear how best to accommodate these conflicting principles and policies.

Our practice, in which different parties are encouraged to pursue their own understanding, provides a means of testing relevant hypotheses. If the question is whether a particular rule would have certain undesirable consequences, or whether these consequences would have limited or broad ramifications, then, before the issue is decided, it is useful to know what does in fact take place when some people proceed on that rule. (Much anti-trust and business regulation law has developed through this kind of testing.) If the question is whether and to what degree a particular solution would offend principles of justice or fair play deeply respected by the community, it is useful, again, to experiment by testing the community's response. The extent of community in-difference to anticontraception laws, for example, would never have become established had not some organizations deliberately flouted those laws in Connecticut.

If the first model were followed, we would lose the advantages of these tests. The law would suffer, particularly if this model were applied to constitutional issues. When the validity of a crim-inal statute is in doubt, the statute will almost always strike some people as being unfair or un-just, because it will infringe some principle of liberty or justice or fairness which they take to be built into the Constitution. If our practice were that whenever a law is doubtful on these grounds, one must act as if it were valid, then the chief vehicle we have for challenging the law on moral grounds would be lost, and over time the law we obeyed would certainly become less fair and just, and the liberty of our citizens would certainly be diminished.

We would lose almost as much if we used a variation of the first model, that a citizen must assume the worst unless he can anticipate that the courts will agree with his view of the law. If everyone deferred to his guess of what the courts would do, society and its law would be poorer. Our assumption in rejecting the first model was that the record a citizen makes in following his own judgment, together with the arguments he makes supporting that judgment when he has the opportunity, are helpful in creating the best judi-cial decision possible. This remains true even when, at the time the citizen acts, the odds are against his success in court. We must remember, too, that the value of the citizen's example is not exhausted once the decision has been made. Our practices require that the decision be criticized, by the legal profession and the law schools, and the record of dissent may be invaluable here.

Of course a man must consider what the courts will do when he decides whether it would be *pru-dent* to follow his own judgment. He may have to face jail, bankruptcy, or opprobrium if he does. But it is essential that we separate the calculation of prudence from the question of what, as a good citizen, he may properly do. We are investigating how society ought to treat him when its courts believe that he judged wrong; therefore we must ask what he is justified in doing when his judg-ment differs from others. We beg the question if

we assume that what he may properly do depends on his guess as to how society will treat him.

We must also reject the second model, that if the law is unclear a citizen may properly follow his own judgment until the highest court has ruled that he is wrong. This fails to take into account the fact that any court, including the Supreme Court, may overrule itself. In 1940 the Court decided that a West Virginia law requiring students to salute the Flag was constitutional. In 1943 it reversed itself, and decided that such a statute was unconstitutional after all. What was the duty, as citizens, of those people who in 1941 and 1942 objected to saluting the Flag on grounds of conscience, and thought that the Court's 1940 decision was wrong? We can hardly say that their duty was to follow the first decision. They be-lieved that saluting the Flag was unconscionable, and they believed, reasonably, that no valid law required them to do so. The Supreme Court later decided that in this they were right. The Court did not simply hold that after the second decision failing to salute would not be a crime; it held (as in a case like this it almost always would) that it was no crime after the first decision either.

Some will say that the flag-salute dissenters should have obeyed the Court's first decision, while they worked in the legislatures to have the law repealed, and tried in the courts to find some way to challenge the law again without actually violating it. That would be, perhaps, a plausible recommendation if conscience were not involved, because it would then be arguable that the gain in orderly procedure was worth the personal sac-rifice of patience. But conscience was involved, and if the dissenters had obeyed the law while biding their time, they would have suffered the irreparable injury of having done what their con-science forbade them to do. It is one thing to say that an individual must sometimes violate his conscience when he knows that the law com-mands him to do it. It is quite another to say that he must violate his conscience even when he rea-sonably believes that the law does not require it, because it would inconvenience his fellow citizens if he took the most direct, and perhaps the only, method of attempting to show that he is right and they are wrong.

Since a court may overrule itself, the same rea-sons we listed for rejecting the first model count against the second as well. If we did not have the pressure of dissent, we would not have a dramatic statement of the degree to which a court decision against the dissenter is felt to be wrong, a demonstration that is surely pertinent to the question of whether it was right. We would increase the chance of being governed by rules that offend the principles we claim to serve.

These considerations force us, I think, from the second model, but some will want to substitute a variation of it. They will argue that once the Supreme Court has decided that a criminal law is valid, then citizens have a duty to abide by that decision until they have a reasonable belief, not merely that the decision is bad law, but that the Supreme Court is likely to overrule it. Under this view the West Virginia dissenters who refused to salute the flag in 1942 were acting properly, because they might reasonably have anticipated that the Court would change its mind. But if the Court were to hold the draft laws constitutional, it would be improper to continue to challenge these laws, because there would be no great likelihood that the Court would soon change its mind. This suggestion must also be rejected, however. For once we say that a citizen may properly follow his own judgment of the law, in spite of his judgment that the courts will probably find against him, there is no plausible reason why he should act differently because a contrary decision is already on the books.

Thus the third model, or something close to it, seems to be the fairest statement of a man's social duty in our community. A citizen's allegiance is to the law, not to any particular person's view of what the law is, and he does not behave improperly or unfairly so long as he proceeds on his own considered and reasonable view of what the law requires. Let me repeat (because it is crucial) that this is not the same as saying that an individual may disregard what the courts have said. The doctrine of precedent lies near the core of our legal system, and no one can make a reasonable effort to follow the law unless he grants the courts the general power to alter it by their decisions. But if the issue is one touching fundamental personal or political rights, and it is arguable that the Supreme Court has made a mistake, a man is within his social rights in refusing to accept that decision as conclusive.

One large question remains before we can apply these observations to the problem of draft resistance. I have been talking about the case of a man who believes that the law is not what other people think, or what the courts have held. This description may fit some of those who disobey the draft laws out of conscience, but it does not fit most of them. Most of the dissenters are not lawyers or political philosophers; they believe that the laws on the books are immoral, and inconsistent with their country's legal ideals, but they have not considered the question of whether they may be invalid as well. Of what relevance to their situation, then, is the proposition that one may properly follow one's own view of the law?

To answer this, I shall have to return to the point I made earlier. The Constitution, through the due process clause, the equal protection clause, the First Amendment, and the other provisions I mentioned, injects an extraordinary amount of our political morality into the issue of whether a law is valid. The statement that most draft dissenters are unaware that the law is invalid therefore needs qualification. They hold beliefs that, if true, strongly support the view that the law is on their side; the fact that they have not reached that further conclusion can be traced, in at least most cases, to their lack of legal sophistication. If we believe that when the law is doubtful people who follow their own judgment of the law may be acting properly, it would seem wrong not to extend that view to those dissenters whose judgments come to the same thing. No part of the case that I made for the third model would entitle us to distinguish them from their more knowledgeable colleagues.

We can draw several tentative conclusions from the argument so far: When the law is uncertain, in the sense that a plausible case can be made on both sides, then a citizen who follows his own judgment is not behaving unfairly. Our practices permit and encourage him to follow his own judgment in such cases. For that reason, our government has a special responsibility to try to protect him, and soften his predicament, whenever it can do so without great damage to other policies. It does not follow that the government can guarantee him immunity—it cannot adopt the rule that it will prosecute no one who acts out of conscience, or convict no one who reasonably disagrees with the courts. That would paralyze the government's ability to carry out its policies; it would, moreover, throw away the most important benefit of following the third model. If the state never prosecuted, then the courts could not act on the experience and the arguments the dissent has generated. But it does follow from the government's responsibility that when the practical reasons for prosecuting are relatively weak in a particular case, or can be met in other ways, the path of fairness may lie in tolerance. The popular view that the law is the law and must always be enforced refuses to distinguish the man who acts on his own judgment of a doubtful law, and thus behaves as our practices provide, from the common criminal. I know of no reason, short of moral blindness, for not drawing a distinction in principle between the two cases.

I anticipate a philosophical objection to these conclusions: that I am treating law as a "brooding omnipresence in the sky." I have spoken of people making judgments about what the law requires, even in cases in which the law is unclear and undemonstrable. I have spoken of cases in which a man might think that the law requires one thing, even though the Supreme Court has said that it requires another, and even when it was not likely that the Supreme Court would soon change its mind. It will therefore be charged with the view that there is always a "right answer" to a legal problem to be found in natural law or locked up in some transcendental strongbox.

The strongbox theory of law is, of course, nonsense. When I say that people hold views on the law when the law is doubtful, and that these views are not merely predictions of what the courts will hold, I intend no such metaphysics. I mean only to summarize as accurately as I can many of the practices that are part of our legal process.

Lawyers and judges make statements of legal right and duty, even when they know these are not demonstrable, and support them with arguments even when they know that these arguments will not appeal to everyone. They make these arguments to one another in the professional journals, in the classroom, and in the courts. They respond to these arguments, when others make them, by judging them good or bad or mediocre. In so doing they assume that some arguments for a given doubtful position are better than others. They also assume that the case on one side of a doubtful proposition may be stronger than the case on the other, which is what

I take a claim of law in a doubtful case to mean. They distinguish, without too much difficulty, these arguments from predictions of what the courts will decide.

These practices are poorly represented by the theory that judgments of law on doubtful issues are nonsense, or are merely predictions of what the courts will do. Those who hold such theories cannot deny the fact of these practices; perhaps these theorists mean that the practices are not sensible, because they are based on suppositions that do not hold, or for some other reason. But this makes their objection mysterious, because they never specify what they take the purposes underlying these practices to be; and unless these goals are specified, one cannot decide whether the practices are sensible. I understand these underlying purposes to be those I described earlier: the development and testing of the law through experimentation by citizens and through the adversary process.

Our legal system pursues these goals by inviting citizens to decide the strengths and weaknesses of legal arguments for themselves, or through their own counsel, and to act on these judgments, although that permission is qualified by the limited threat that they may suffer if the courts do not agree. Success in this strategy depends on whether there is sufficient agreement within the community on what counts as a good or bad argument, so that, although different people will reach different judgments, these differences will be neither so profound nor so frequent as to make the system unworkable, or dangerous for those who act by their own lights. I believe there is sufficient agreement on the criteria of the argument to avoid these traps, although one of the main tasks of legal philosophy is to exhibit and clarify these criteria. In any event, the practices I have described have not yet been shown to be misguided; they therefore must count in determining whether it is just and fair to be lenient to those who break what others think is the law.

I have said that the government has a special responsibility to those who act on a reasonable judgment that a law is invalid. It should make accommodation for them as far as possible, when this is consistent with other policies. It may be difficult to decide what the government ought to do, in the name of that responsibility, in particular cases. The decision will be a matter of balance, and flat rules will not help. Still, some principles can be set out.

I shall start with the prosecutor's decision whether to press charges. He must balance both his responsibility to be lenient and the risk that convictions will rend the society, against the damage to the law's policy that may follow if he leaves the dissenters alone. In making his calculation he must consider not only the extent to which others will be harmed, but also how the law evaluates that harm; and he must therefore make the following distinction. Every rule of law is supported, and presumably justified, by a set of policies it is supposed to advance and principles it is supposed to respect. Some rules (the laws prohibiting murder and theft, for example) are supported by the proposition that the individuals protected have a moral right to be free from the harm proscribed. Other rules (the more technical anti-trust rules, for example) are not supported by any supposition of an underlying right; their support comes chiefly from the alleged utility of the economic and social policies they promote. These may be supplemented with moral principles (like the view that it is a harsh business practice to undercut a weak competitor's prices) but these fall short of recognizing a moral right against the harm in question.

The point of the distinction here is this: The judgment that someone has a moral right to be free from certain injuries is a very strong form of moral judgment, because a moral right, once acknowledged, outweighs competing claims of utility or virtue. When a law rests on such a judgment, that is a powerful argument against tolerating violations which inflict those injuries— for example, violations that involve personal injury or the destruction of property. The prosecutor may respect the dissenter's view that the law is invalid, but unless he agrees, he must honor the law's judgment that others have an overriding claim of right.

It may be controversial, of course, whether a law rests on the assumption of a right. One must study the background and administration of the law, and reflect on whether any social practices of right and obligation support it. We may take one example in which the judgment is relatively easy. There are many sincere and ardent segregationists who believe that the civil rights laws and decisions are unconstitutional, because they com-promise principles of local government and of freedom of association. This is an arguable, though not a persuasive, view. But the constitutional provisions that support these laws clearly embody the view that Negroes, as individuals, have a right not to be segregated. They do not rest simply on the judgment that national policies are best pursued by preventing their segregation. If we take no action against the man who blocks the school house door, therefore, we violate the rights, confirmed by law, of the schoolgirl he blocks. The responsibility of leniency cannot go this far.

The schoolgirl's position is different, however, from that of the draftee who may be called up sooner or given a more dangerous post if draft offenders are not punished. The draft laws do not reflect a judgment that a man has a social or moral right to be drafted only after certain other men or groups have been called. The draft classifications, and the order-of-call according to age within classifications, are arranged for social and administrative convenience. They also reflect considerations of fairness, like the proposition that a mother who has lost one of two sons in war ought not to be made to risk losing the other. But they presuppose no fixed rights. The draft boards are given considerable discretion in the classification process, and the army, of course, has almost complete discretion in assigning dangerous posts. If the prosecutor tolerates draft offenders, he makes small shifts in the law's calculations of fairness and utility. These may cause disadvantage to others in the pool of draftees but that is a different matter from contradicting their social or moral rights.

It is wrong therefore to analyze draft cases and segregation cases in the same way, as many critics do when considering whether tolerance is justified. I do not mean that fairness to others is irrelevant in draft cases; it must be taken into account, and balanced against fairness to dissenters and the long-term benefit to society. But it does not play the commanding role here that it does in segregation cases, and in other cases when rights are at stake.

Where, then, does the balance of fairness and utility lie in the case of those who counsel draft resistance? If these men had encouraged violence or otherwise trespassed on the rights of others, then there would be a strong case for prosecution.

But in the absence of such actions, the balance of fairness and utility seems to me to lie the other way, and I therefore think that the decision to prosecute Coffin, Spock, Raskin, Goodman, and Ferber was wrong. It may be argued that if those who counsel draft resistance are free from prosecution, the number who resist induction will increase; but it will not, I think, increase much beyond the number of those who would resist on any event.

If I am wrong, and there is much greater resistance, then a sense of this residual discontent is of importance to policy makers, and it ought not to be hidden under a ban on speech. Conscience is deeply involved—it is hard to believe that many who counsel resistance do so on any other grounds. The case is strong that the laws making counseling a crime are unconstitutional; even those who do not find the case persuasive will admit that its arguments have substance. The harm to potential draftees, both those who may be persuaded to resist and those who maybe called earlier because others have been persuaded, is remote and speculative.

The cases of men who refuse induction when drafted are more complicated. The crucial question is whether a failure to prosecute will lead to wholesale refusals to serve. It may not—there are social pressures, including the threat of career disadvantages, that would force many young Americans to serve if drafted, even if they knew they would not go to jail if they refused. If the number would not much increase, then the state should leave the dissenters alone, and I see no great harm in delaying any prosecution until the effect of that policy becomes clearer. If the number of those who refuse induction turns out to be large, this would argue for prosecution. But it would also make the problem academic, because if there were sufficient dissent to bring us to that pass, it would be most difficult to pursue the war in any event, except under a near-totalitarian regime.

There may seem to be a paradox in these conclusions. I argued earlier that when the law is unclear citizens have the right to follow their own judgment, partly on the grounds that this practice helps to shape issues for adjudication; now I propose a course that eliminates or postpones adjudication. But the contradiction is only apparent. It does not follow from the fact that our practice

facilitates adjudication, and renders it more useful in developing the law, that a trial should follow whenever citizens do act by their own lights. The question arises in each case whether the issues are ripe for adjudication, and whether adjudication would settle these issues in a manner that would decrease the chance of, or remove the grounds for, further dissent.

In the draft cases, the answer to both these questions is negative: There is much ambivalence about the war just now, and uncertainty and ignorance about the scope of the moral issues involved in the draft. It is far from the best time for a court to pass on these issues, and tolerating dissent for a time is one way of allowing the debate to continue until it has produced something clearer. Moreover, it is plain that an adjudication of the constitutional issues now will not settle the law. Those who have doubts whether the draft is constitutional will have the same doubts even if the Supreme Court says that it is. This is one of those cases, touching fundamental rights, in which our practices of precedent will encourage these doubts. Certainly this will be so if, as seems likely, the Supreme Court appeals to the political question doctrine, and refuses to pass on the more serious constitutional issues.

Even if the prosecutor does not act, however, the underlying problem will be only temporarily relieved. So long as the law appears to make acts of dissent criminal, a man of conscience will face danger. What can Congress, which shares the responsibility of leniency, do to lessen this danger?

Congress can review the laws in question to see how much accommodation can be given the dissenters. Every program a legislature adopts is a mixture of policies and restraining principles. We accept loss of efficiency in crime detection and urban renewal, for example, so that we can respect the rights of accused criminals and compensate property owners for their damages. Congress may properly defer to its responsibility toward the dissenters by adjusting or compromising other policies. The relevant questions are these: What means can be found for allowing the greatest possible tolerance of conscientious dissent while minimizing its impact on policy? How strong is the government's responsibility for leniency in this case—how deeply is conscience involved, and how strong is the case that the law is invalid after all? How important is the policy in question—is interference with that policy too great a price to pay? These questions are no doubt too simple, but they suggest the heart of the choices that must be made.

For the same reasons that those who counsel resistance should not be prosecuted, I think that the law that makes this a crime should be repealed. The case is strong that this law abridges free speech. It certainly coerces conscience, and it probably serves no beneficial effect. If counseling would persuade only a few to resist who otherwise would not, the value of the restraint is small; if counseling would persuade many, that should be known.

The issues are more complex, again, in the case of draft resistance itself. Those who believe that the war in Vietnam is itself a grotesque blunder will favor any change in the law that makes peace more likely. But if we take the position of those who think the war is necessary, then we must admit that a policy that continues the draft but wholly exempts dissenters would be unwise. Two less drastic alternatives might be considered, however: a volunteer army, and an expanded conscientious objector category that includes those who find this war immoral. There is much to be said against both proposals, but once the requirement of respect for dissent is recognized, the balance of principle may be tipped in their favor.

So the case for not prosecuting conscientious draft offenders, and for changing the laws in their favor, is a strong one. It would be unrealistic to expect this policy to prevail, however, for political pressures now oppose it. Relatively few of those who have refused induction have been indicted so far, but the pace of prosecution is quickening, and many more indictments are expected if the resistance many college seniors have pledged does in fact develop. The Coffin, Spock trial continues, although when the present steps toward peace negotiation were announced, many lawyers had hoped it would be dropped or delayed. There is no sign of any movement to amend the draft laws in the way I have suggested.

We must consider, therefore, what the courts can and should now do. A court might, of course, uphold the arguments that the draft laws are in some way unconstitutional, in general or as applied to the defendants in the case at hand. Or it may acquit the defendants because the facts necessary for conviction are not proved. I shall not argue the constitutional issues, or the facts of any particular case. I want instead to suggest that a court ought not to convict, at least in some circumstances, even if it sustains the statutes and finds the facts as charged. The Supreme Court has not ruled on the chief arguments that the present draft is unconstitutional, nor has it held that these arguments raise political questions that are not relevant to its jurisdiction. If the alleged violations take place before the Supreme Court has decided these issues, and the case reaches that Court, there are strong reasons why the Court should acquit even if it does then sustain the draft. It ought to acquit on the ground that before its decision the validity of the draft was doubtful, and it is unfair to punish men for disobeying a doubtful law.

There would be precedent for a decision along these lines. The Court has several times reversed criminal convictions, on due process grounds, because the law in question was too vague. (It has overturned convictions, for example, under laws that made it a crime to charge "unreasonable prices" or to be a member of a "gang.") Conviction under a vague criminal law offends the moral and political ideals of due process in two ways. First, it places a citizen in the unfair position of either acting at his peril or accepting a more stringent restriction on his life than the legislature may have authorized: As I argued earlier, it is not acceptable, as a model of social behavior, that in such cases he ought to assume the worst. Second, it gives power to the prosecutor and the courts to make criminal law, by opting for one or the other possible interpretations after the event. This would be a delegation of authority by the legislature that is inconsistent with our scheme of separation of powers.

Conviction under a criminal law whose terms are not vague, but whose constitutional validity is doubtful, offends due process in the first of these ways. It forces a citizen to assume the worst, or act at his peril. It offends due process in something like the second way as well. Most citizens would be deterred by a doubtful statute if they were to risk jail by violating it. Congress, and not the courts, would then be the effective voice in deciding the constitutionality of criminal enactments, and this also violates the separation of powers.

If acts of dissent continue to occur after the Supreme Court has ruled that the laws are valid, or that the political question doctrine applies, then acquittal on the grounds I have described is no longer appropriate. The Court's decision will not have finally settled the law, for the reasons given earlier, but the Court will have done all that can be done to settle it. The courts may still exercise their sentencing discretion, however, and impose minimal or suspended sentences as a mark of respect for the dissenters' position.

Some lawyers will be shocked by my general conclusion that we have a responsibility toward those who disobey the draft laws out of conscience, and that we may be required not to prosecute them, but rather to change our laws or adjust our sentencing procedures to accommodate them. The simple Draconian propositions, that crime must be punished, and that he who misjudges the law must take the consequences, have an extraordinary hold on the professional as well as the popular imagination. But the rule of law is more complex and more intelligent than that and it is important that it survive.

NOTE

1. I do not mean to imply that the government should always punish a man who deliberately breaks a law he knows is valid. There may be reasons of fairness or practicality, like those I listed in the third paragraph, for not prosecuting such men. But cases like the draft cases present special arguments for tolerance; I want to concentrate on these arguments and therefore have isolated these cases.

Suggestions for Further Reading

American Law Institute, *Model Penal Code,* Part II, Proposed Official Draft and Comments (1962).

Amsterdam, Anthony, "Federal Constitutional Restrictions on the Punishment of Crimes of Status, Crimes of General Obnoxiousness, Crimes of Displeasing Police Officers and the Like," 3 *Crim. L. Bull.* 205 (1967).

Bayles, Michael, "Comments: Offensive Conduct and the Law," in *Issues in Law and Morality,* eds. N. Care and T. Trelogan. (1973), pp. 111–26.

Becker, L. C., "Human Being: The Boundaries of the Concept," *Philosophy and Public Affairs,* Vol. 4 (1975).

Bedau, Hugo ed., *Civil Disobedience: Theory and Practice* (1969).

Benn, S. I. and R. S. Peters, *Social Principles and the Democratic State* (1959).

Berlin, Isaiah, *Four Essays on Liberty* (1969).

Bok, Sissela, "Ethical Problems of Abortion," *The Hastings Center Studies,* Vol. 2 (1974), pp. 32–52.

———, "Personal Directions for Care at the End of Life," *The New England Journal of Medicine,* Vol. 295, (1976) pp. 367–369.

——— (ed.), *The Dilemma of Euthanasia* (1975).

Brecher, Edward M., *Licit and Illicit Drugs* (1972).

Callahan, Daniel, *Abortion: Law, Choice, and Morality* (1970).

Camenisch, Paul F., "Abortion: For the Fetus's Sake?", *Hastings Center Report* (1976).

Chafee, Zechariah, Jr., *Free Speech in the United States* (1941).

———, *Three Human Rights in the Constitution* (1956).

Cohen, Carl, *Conscience, Tactics, and the Law* (1971).

Cohen, Marshall, "Liberalism and Disobedience," *Philosophy and Public Affairs,* Vol. 1 (1972).

Cohen, M., Nagel, T., and Scanlon, T. G. (eds.), *The Rights and Wrongs of Abortion* (1974). Contains articles from the journal *Philosophy and Public Affairs.*

Commission on Obscenity and Pornography, *Report* (1970).

Delgado, R., "Euthanasia Reconsidered—The Choice of Death as an Aspect of the Right of Privacy," 17 *Arizona Law Rev.* 474 (1975).

Devlin, Patrick, "Encounter with Lord Devlin," *Listener,* Vol. 71 (1964), pp. 980 ff.

———, *The Enforcement of Morals* (1965).

Dorsen, Norman, ed., *The Rights of Americans,* Sections II and III (1970).

Downing, A. B. (ed.), *Euthanasia and the Right to Die* (1970).

Dworkin, G., "Autonomy and Behavioral Control," *Hastings Center Report.* Vol. 6 (1976), pp. 23–28.

Dworkin, Ronald, "Lord Devlin and the Enforcement

of Morals," 75 *Yale L.J.* 986 (1966).

Dyck, Arthur, "An Alternative to the Ethic of Euthanasia," in Williams, R. H. (ed.), *To Live and to Die* (1973), pp. 98–112.

Emerson, Thomas I., *The System of Freedom of Expression* (1970).

Englehardt, H. T., Jr., "The Ontology of Abortion," *Ethics*, Vol. 84, (1967), pp. 217–34.

English, Jane, "Abortion and the Concept of a Person," *Canadian Journal of Philosophy*, Vol. 5 (1975).

Feinberg, Joel, " 'Harmless Immoralities' and Offensive Nuisances," in *Issues in Law and Morality*, eds. N. Care and T. Trelogan. (1973), pp. 85–109.

———, "Is there a Right to Be Born?" in Rachels, James (ed.), *Moral Philosophy: Problems of Theory and Practice* (1976).

———, "Legal Paternalism," *Canadian Journal of Philosophy*, Vol. 1 (1971), pp. 105–24.

——— (ed.), *The Problem of Abortion* (1973).

———, *Social Philosophy* (1973), Chaps. 2, 3.

Foot, Philippa (Commenting on Jeffcoate, T.N.A.), "Abortion," in Clow, A. (ed.), *Morals and Medicine* (1970).

Fortas, Abe, *Concerning Dissent and Civil Disobedience* (1968).

Frantz, Laurent B., "The First Amendment in the Balance," 71 *Yale L.J.* 1424 (1962).

Fried, C., "Terminating Life Support," *The New England Journal of Medicine*, Vol. 295, (1976), pp. 390–391.

Fried, Charles, "Privacy," 77 *Yale L.J.* 475 (1968).

Friedman, Milton, *Capitalism and Freedom* (1962).

Friedrich, C. J., ed., *Nomos IV: Liberty* (1962).

Ginsberg, Morris, "Law and Morals," *The British Journal of Criminology* (1964).

Goodhart, Arthur L., *English Law and the Moral Law* (1953).

Gorovitz, Samuel, *et al* (eds.), *Moral Problems in Medicine* (1976).

Green, Ronald, "Conferred Rights and the Fetus," *Journal of Religious Ethics* (1974).

Greenawalt, K., "All or Nothing at All: The Defeat of Selective Conscientious Objection," 1971 *Supreme Court Review* 31.

Grisez, Germain C., *Abortion: The Myths, The Realities, and the Arguments* (1970).

Gross, Hyman, "The Concept of Privacy," 42 *N.Y.U. L. Rev.* 34 (1967).

Gussfield, J., "On Legislating Morals: The Symbolic Process of Designating Deviancy," 56 *Cal. L. Rev.* 54–59 (1968).

Hall, Robert, *The Morality of Civil Disobedience* (1971).

Harnett, B. and J. Thornton, "The Truth Hurts: A Critique of a Defense to Defamation," 35 *Va. L. Rev.* 425 (1949).

Hart, Harold H., ed., *Censorship, For and Against* (1971).

Hart, H. L. A., "Immorality and Treason," *Listener*, Vol. 62 (1959), pp. 162 ff.

———, *Law, Liberty, and Morality* (1963).

———, "Social Solidarity and the Enforcement of Morality," 35 *U. Chi. L. Rev.* 1 (1967).

Henkin, L., "Morals and the Constitution: The Sin of Obscenity," 63 *Col. L. Rev.* 391 (1963).

Hobhouse, L. T., *The Elements of Social Justice* (1922), Chap. 4.

Home Office Scottish Home Department, *Report of the Committee on Homosexual Offenses and Prostitution (Wolfenden Report)* (1963).

Hook, Sydney, ed., *Law and Philosophy*, Part I (1964).

Hoover, James F., "An Adult's Right to Resist Blood Transfusions: A View through John F. Kennedy Memorial Hospital v. Heston," 47 *Notre Dame Lawyer* 571 (1972).

Hughes, Graham, "Civil Disobedience and the Political Question Doctrine," 43 *N.Y.U.L. Rev.* 1 (1968).

———, "Morals and the Criminal Law," 71 *Yale L.J.* 662 (1962).

Jeffcoate, T. N. A., "Abortion" in A. Clow (ed.), *Morals and Medicine* (London, 1970).

Kadish, S. H., "The Crisis of Overcriminalization," 374 *Annals* 157 (1957).

Kadish, M. R. and S. H. Kadish, *Discretion to Disobey* (1973).

Kalven, Harry, Jr., "The Metaphysics of the Law of Obscenity," in *The Supreme Court Review*, ed. P. B. Kurland, (1960).

Kaufman, Arnold S. and Felix E. Oppenheim, "Democracy and Disorder, A Symposium," in *Society, Revolution and Reform*, eds. R. H. Grimm and A. F. MacKay. (1971).

Kelly, G., *Medico-Moral Problems* (1958), Chap. 9—"Destruction or Risk of Life."

Kohl, Marvin, *The Morality of Killing: Euthanasia, Abortion, and Transplants* (1974).

——— (ed.), *Beneficent Euthanasia* (1975).

Kronhausen, E. and P., *Pornography and the Law*, rev. ed., (1964).

Livermore, J. M., C. P. Malmquist, and P. E. Meehl, "On the Justification for Civil Commitment," 117 *U. Pa. L. Rev.*, 75 (1968).

Louch, A. R., "Sins and Crimes," *Philosophy*, Vol. 43 (1968), pp. 163 ff.

McCloskey, H. J., "Mill's Liberalism," *Philosophical Quarterly*, Vol. XIII (1963).

Maguire, Daniel C., *Death by Choice* (1974).

Malament, D., "Selective Conscientious Objections and the *Gillette* Decision," *Philosophy and Public Affairs*, Vol. 1 (1972) 363–386.

Margolis, Joseph, *Negativities* (1975), Chap. 3.

Mewett, A., "Morality and the Criminal Law," 14

University of Toronto L.J. 213 (1962).

Miller, Arthur R., *The Assault on Privacy* (1971).

Morris, Norval and Gordon Hawkins, *The Honest Politician's Guide to Crime Control,* (1969), Chapters 1 and 2.

Noonan, John T., Jr. (ed.), *The Morality of Abortion: Legal and Historical Perspectives* (1970).

————, *How to Argue About Abortion* (1974).

————, "Why a Constitutional Amendment?", *Human Life Review* (1975).

Note, "Civil Commitment of Narcotic Addicts," 76 *Yale L.J.* 1160 (1967).

Note, "Criminal Law—The Principle of Harm and its Application to Laws Criminalizing Prostitution," 51 *Denver Law Journal* 235 (1974).

Note, "Informed Consent and the Dying Patient," 83 *Yale Law Journal* 1632 (1974).

Packer, Herbert, *The Limits of the Criminal Sanction* (1968).

Parker, R. B., "A Definition of Privacy," 27 *Rutgers Law Review* 275 (1974).

Parliamentary Debates on the Voluntary Euthanasia Bill. House of Lords Official Report, Vol. 300, No. 50 (1969).

Pennock, J. R. and J. W. Chapman, eds., Nomos XII: *Political and Legal Obligation* (1970).

————, eds., Nomos XIII: *Privacy* (1971).

————, eds., *Nomos XV: Limits of Law* (1974).

Perkins, Robert L. (ed.), *Abortion* (1974).

Pope Pius XII, "The Prolongation of Life," (excerpts), *The Pope Speaks,* Vol. 3–4 (1956–58), pp. 393–95.

Powers, W. C., Jr., "Autonomy and the Legal Control of Self-Regarding Conduct," 51 *Washington Law Review* 33 (1975).

Rabkin, M. T., Gillerman, G., Rice, N. R., "Orders not to Resuscitate," *The New England Journal of Medicine,* Vol. 295 (1976), pp. 364–66.

Rachels, James, "Active and Passive Euthanasia," *New England Journal of Medicine,* Vol. 292 (1975), pp. 78–80.

————, "Why Privacy Is Important," *Philosophy and Public Affairs,* Vol. 4 (1975), pp. 323–333.

Ramsey, Paul, "The Morality of Abortion," in D. H. Labby (ed.), *Life or Death: Ethics and Options* (1968).

————, "Abortion, A Review Article," *The Thomist,* Vol. 73 (1973).

Report of the Critical Care Committee of the Massachusetts General Hospital, "Optimum Care for Hopelessly Ill Patients," *The New England Journal of Medicine,* Vol. 295 (1976) 362–364.

Riesman, David, "Democracy and Defamation: Control of Group Libel," 42 *Col. L. Rev.* 751 (1942).

Richards, D. A. J., "Free Speech and Obscenity Law: Toward a Moral Theory of the First Amendment," 123 *Univ. of Pa. Law Rev.* 45 (1974).

Rostow, Eugene, The Sovereign Prerogative (1962), Chap. 2.

Russell, O. Ruth, *Freedom to Die* (1975).

Ryan, Alan, *The Philosophy of John Stuart Mill* (1970), Chap. XIII.

Sartorius, Rolf, "The Enforcement of Morality," 81 *Yale L. J.* 891 (1972).

————, *Individual Conduct and Social Norms* (1975).

Scanlon, T., "Thomson on Privacy," *Philosophy and Public Affairs,* Vol. 4 (1975), pp. 315–322.

Scanlon, Thomas, "A Theory of Freedom of Expression," *Philosophy and Public Affairs,* Vol. I (1972), pp. 204–26.

Schur, E. M. and Bedau, H. A., *Victimless Crimes: Two Sides of a Controversy* (1974).

Silberman, Barry D., "The Right of a Patient to Refuse Blood Transfusions: A Dilemma of Conscience and Law for Patient, Physician, and Hospital," 3 *Univ. of San Fernando Valley Law Rev.* 91 (1974).

Singer, Peter, *Democracy and Disobedience* (1974).

Skolnick, Jerome, "Coercion to Virtue," 41 *S. Cal. L. Rev.* 588 (1968).

Stephen, James F., *Liberty, Equality, Fraternity* (1873).

Summer, L. W., "Towards a Credible View of Abortion," *Canadian Journal of Philosophy,* Vol. 4 (1974).

Thomson, J. J., "The Right to Privacy," *Philosophy and Public Affairs,* Vol. 4 (1975), pp. 295–314.

Tribe, Laurence H., *Channeling Technology through Law* (1973).

Van de Veer, Donald, "Justifying "Wholesale Slaughter,'" *Canadian Journal of Philosophy,* Vol. 5 (1975).

Wasserstrom, R. A. (ed.), *Morality and the Law* (1971).

————, "The Obligation to Obey the Law," 10 *U.C.L.A.L. Rev.* 780 (1963).

Williams, G., "Authoritarian Morals and the Criminal Law," [1966] *Crim. L. Rev.* 132.

————, *The Sanctity of Life and the Criminal Law,* (1957) Chapters 7 and 8.

Wollheim, Richard, "Crime, Sin and Mr. Justice Devlin," *Encounter* (1959), pp. 34 ff.

Woozley, A. D., "Civil Disobedience and Punishment," *Ethics,* Vol. 86 (1976), pp. 323–32.

————, "Socrates on Disobeying the Law," in *The Philosophy of Socrates,* ed. Gregory Vlastos, (1971).

Zinn, Howard, *Disobedience and Democracy* (1968).